EDIFIED!

EDIFIED!

365 Devotions to Stimulate Personal Worship and Spark Inner Transformation

S. M. Wibberley

Illustrations by
Nat and Josh Wibberley

Edifying Services Press
www.edifyingservices.com

Other books by S. M. Wibberley

EQUIPPED! 12 Empowering Truths and How to Use Them. Be Ready for Everyday Spiritual Warfare (2012)
(formerly *Knowing Jesus is Enough for Joy, Period!*)

In preparation:

EFFECTIVE: Learning to Lead Yourself Well

From Connecticut to the Ends of the Earth and Back: The Memoirs of a Connecticut Yankee's Spiritual Journey

Available at www.edifyingservices.com and at Amazon.com

Copyright © 2013 S. M. Wibberley

Unless otherwise indicated, artwork copyright © Nathanael Wibberley. Used by permission.

Printed in United States of America

ISBN 9780983207733

All rights reserved solely by the author. The author guarantees that, to his knowledge, all contents are original and do not infringe upon the legal rights of any other person or work. No part of this book may be reproduced in any form without the permission of the author.

Unless otherwise marked, Scripture quotations are taken from the Holy Bible, New International Version®. Copyright © 1973, 1978, 1984 by International Bible Society. Used by permission of the International Bible Society.

"NIV" and "New International Version" are trademarks registered in the United States Patent and Trademark Office by International Bible Society.

www.edifyingservices.com

Dedicated to

Bea Seavey,

who for years has encouraged me to write this book,

and to

Pastor Harold Burchett,

who helped equip me to live life in the power of the Spirit.

www.edifyingserives.com

TABLE OF CONTENTS

Introduction 1

JANUARY 5

FEBRUARY 37

MARCH 68

APRIL 102

MAY 135

JUNE 174

JULY 212

AUGUST 249

SEPTEMBER 286

OCTOBER 323

NOVEMBER 360

DECEMBER 403

Introduction

This book flows out of forty-two years of life with Jesus, with more than thirty of those years involved in church planting in the Middle East. The deep work of God and the revelation of truth through His Word, combined with the challenging experiences of ministry brought many insights and much growth.

I regularly wrote about these lessons in our family's monthly prayer letters and these letters are one source for this book. A second source is my worship journal where I daily spend time exalting the Lord with what His Word has to say about Him.

As you read these devotions, one day you will get an excerpt from a prayer letter, the next day an entry from my worship journal. Each track is approximately chronological in order, so you can trace the growth in my spiritual life. Hopefully this will spark similar growth in yours.

You will notice that I write a lot about the gospel, especially from the perspective of how it applies to us as believers. This is because that we are transformed through a growing understanding of God's holiness, of our depravity and how much God loves and forgives us.

So bear with me when you start a devotional and think, "Not again!" Press on, for the perspective is a bit different in each one. [1]

The foundational wellspring for all these writings is meditation on God's Word. That is, first memorizing significant passages, which transformed my thinking. Then personalizing the passage, which brought transformation of my emotions. And finally, praying that the details of the passage would be true in my life, which brought the transformation of my will. [2]

---

[1] Repetition is not viewed positively by our culture because if we hear something once, we think we've grasped it—but if so, only in a superficial way. Successive hearings of God's Truth will bring new insights.

The Apostle Peter pointed this out in 2 Peter 1:13-14. Watch how many times he talks about reminding us: "For this reason I will not be negligent to *remind you always* of these things, though you know and are established in the present truth. Yes, I think it is right, as long as I am in this tent, to stir you up *by reminding you*, knowing that shortly I must put off my tent, just as our Lord Jesus Christ showed me. Moreover I will be careful to ensure that you always have *a reminder* of these things after my decease." Three times in three verses! God thinks repetition is important. So should we.

[2] I learned about this from Bill Gothard. See the Appendix for more information on such meditation.

This discipline opened the sluice gates of God's grace, bringing a continual flow of spiritual water to my spirit and soul. As a result of practicing this type of meditation, the difficulties, setbacks, failures, and persecutions that came our way were all transformed from burdens and roadblocks into "steps up" in life.

I cannot recommend this practice of meditation too highly.[3] Most will not partake because it requires too much self-denial and discipline, but maybe you will be one of those who want to be "like a tree planted by the river which bears its fruit in its season, whose leaf never withers and whatever he does will prosper" (Ps. 1:3). That's the result of meditation, for it is one effective way of cooperating with God in His desire to transform our lives. In this book you will be continually sampling the fruit that the Spirit brought into my life through meditation.

A note on the worship journal entries: worship has two parts, thanksgiving and praise. Praise focuses more on God's character, while thanksgiving tends to focus more on what He has given and done. Some entries are almost pure praise, others mostly thanksgiving. As the book moves along you will see an intertwining of the two more and more, with thanksgiving being elevated by praise so that thanks flows more from God's character than from what He's given us. This is the kind of worship that gives Him glory and transforms us as we bask in the light of His character. My prayer is that your participating in the worship in this book will bring transformation to your soul and growth to your spirit.

I also pray that your using this one year devotional will move you onward and upward in your walk with Jesus as you see Him more in His Greatness, Glory, Grace and Goodness. May you be transformed by gazing on Him each day.

---

[3] See the Appendix for a more complete explanation of this type of meditation.

JANUARY

January 1

"The Mighty One, God, the LORD, speaks and summons the earth from the rising of the sun to the place where it sets.... 'Gather to me my consecrated ones, who made a covenant with me by sacrifice.'"

Psalm 50:1,5

The Christian life is like a spiral staircase winding upward to Heaven. The central support, the column of Truth, is made of pure gold, while the steps of obedience are of translucent crystal.

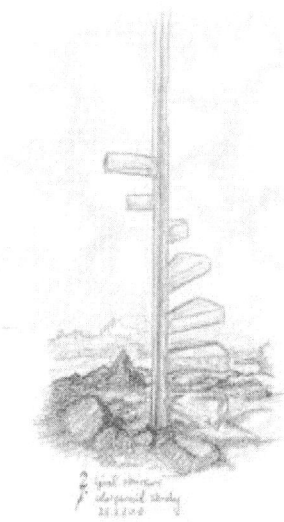

When we first become followers of Jesus, there are seven steps in place, taking us up one full turn of the stairway. Each step is a major lesson the Lord has for us, teaching us the basics in dealing with our personal sinful tendencies and practices, such as impatience, selfishness, pride, jealousy, greed or lust.

Depending on how teachable we are, going up these first steps may go quite quickly, or may take us a long, long time. Some who are unwilling to learn and repent may never make it up these seven steps at all; their refusal to listen to the Spirit strands them on the lower rungs of the spiritual life.

When we come to the seventh step, we have to stop. The golden central support goes on up, but with nothing more to step up on, we are stymied.

"OK, Lord, I need another step to go higher!" we pray. No step is given, but in time a big black burden, some type of problem, appears on our shoulder. "What's this, Lord?" We exclaim. "I need a step up, not something to weigh me down!"

Then as we struggle to balance this burden, we realize it looks familiar. It is a variation of one of those sins we learned to deal with on the way up. If we respond in repentance, we can lower this burden before the Lord, confessing our sin to Him, thanking Him for revealing this to us again and praising Him for His goodness and wisdom. As we do this, the black, ugly burden is miraculously transformed into translucent crystal, becoming the next step up!

So it goes: each problem that comes to us has the potential to be a burden or to be the next step up to move us onward in our walk with Jesus. The key is our response to it. As Psalm 50:23 says, "He who offers the sacrifice of thanksgiving [giving thanks by faith when we don't feel like it] honors me, and opens the way that I may show him the salvation of the Lord." Praise and thanksgiving given out of faith as acts of the will, not the emotions, are powerful transformers of problems and sins into the next step up.

As we spiral up the staircase, we will have to deal with the same weaknesses of our character over and over. Satan will say, "Look, you aren't making any progress; you might as well just give in and surrender to this temptation. Enjoy this sin!" The truth is, however, that we *are* making progress, for each time we encounter the same sins we are on a higher level; and the answer is the same as before: praise God for the revelation, apply truth in obedience and repentance, step up.

As you read through these devotionals, which are presented in the approximate order in which they were originally written in my journal or prayer letters, you will see the upward spiral. Themes will be repeated, each time from a little different perspective. You will sense growth, movement, maturing. Hopefully this will help you, too, to move upward in your journey with Jesus, making each problem, each difficulty, each suffering and each hardship the next step up.

Prayer: "Lord, help me to cooperate with you as you desire to lead me on to higher levels. Help me to think as you think, to become a person of praise, turning problems into progress. Amen."

January 2

"I love you, O LORD, my strength. The LORD is my rock, my fortress and my deliverer; my God is my rock, in whom I take refuge."

Psalm 18:1,2a

Thank you, Lord God, that you are the Protector, the Refuge, the Shelter we need in a storm. Truly, Lord Jesus, you are the unshakable Rock: eternal, immutable, almighty. You are pure and positive, holy and righteous, good and absolutely trust-worthy. In you there is no evil, no sin, no darkness, no negative. You are powerful beyond conception, you are forever faithful, you are eternally good.

Praise be to you, Lord God: the Creator, Sustainer, Architect and Ender of history. You are moving the world to a conclusion and taking us with you. What a future you have in store for us! I praise you for your graceful and good working in our lives. In all that comes our way, we can rest in your wisdom, your power, your love, your faithfulness and your grace.

I praise you for the perfection of your character: you are always righteous, always loving, always true and forever good. I am deeply, firmly, continually thankful that you are real, that you are there, that you are actively, intimately involved in my world.

Without you, what is life but an empty pursuit of selfishness, ending in meaninglessness and death? We were made for you: by you we are loved, with you we are complete, in you we have protection, purpose in life, power in troubles and provision for all our needs. You, the God of hope, desire to give us all joy and peace as we trust in you, so that our lives can overflow with hope by the power of the Holy Spirit (Rom. 15:13).

You constantly and consistently pour beauty and grace into our lives. To know you is to have all that the human heart could desire: belonging, worth and competence. And, in addition to all this, you are ever at work in us to make us more and more into the image of Christ.

You are the center of my life, you are the meaning of my existence, you are the love of my heart. I want to praise you, glorify you and exalt you in word, thought and deed. You are worthy of worship and glory and honor no matter what, and I will seek to give these to you today!

Prayer: "Lord, bring a continual revival in my life, revealing to me more of your holiness, more of my depravity and more of your great love and forgiveness. Undo me, so that I may be redone in the image of Christ. Amen."

January 3

"For the message of the cross is foolishness to those who are perishing, but to us who are being saved it is the power of God."

1 Corinthians 1:18

This verse was just what I needed to hear. In the Middle East, where we lived for many years, as well as back in America, I have found myself trying to make the gospel more acceptable, more respectable, more comfortable for people to accept—but to no avail.

To those who do not believe, the pure gospel can never be attractive or easy to accept, for it is foreign, unnatural and repulsive. To think of themselves as so sinful that they need a Savior, to think of God Himself dying on a cross in their place, to think of surrender to Him and having a total change of life as a result—this is more than they want to hear!

Facing this truth of man's natural rejection of the gospel throws me back to dependence on God, on the Holy Spirit's work, thereby saving me from dependence on myself—I cannot convince anyone to believe, only God can do that. It also frees me to go ahead and share without being controlled by fear of rejection.

As the King's heralds, we will be rejected by many listeners, but that must not stop our proclamation of Truth, unpalatable as it may be to unbelievers. "God has chosen the foolish things…the weak things…the base…the despised…the things which are counted as nothing…that no flesh should glory in His presence" (1Cor. 1:27-29).

So we are sharing, sowing seed and looking for those whom God has prepared for the next step in their spiritual journey. What freedom there is in knowing that we are joining Him in His reaching out to the world. To be committed to the Lord of the universe, seeking to cooperate with Him in what He is doing, knowing that He will guide and lead us to those He's already working in—these are wonderful privileges and fear-killing truths. We can trust the One who said His Spirit is at work convicting all of sin, righteousness and judgment. He will bring forth fruit at the right time as we faithfully follow Him.

Prayer: "Lord Jesus, I confess to you my fear of man, which keeps me from being an effective witness. Help me to fear you instead, to stand in awe of you, to love Truth and to share it with all who will listen. Amen."

January 4

"The Lord is my shepherd, I shall not want. He makes me to lie down in green pastures."

Psalm 23:1,2

Praise be to you, O Heavenly Father, Lord Jesus, Holy Spirit, for you are the great Triune One who does all things right and righteously. You are Wise and Pure, Just and Merciful, Perfect and Holy: in you there is no flaw, no lack, no darkness, no error, no imperfection. You have done all things well, for you are excellent all the time.

You, Lord Jesus, are the good and great Shepherd who tenderly leads your flock, your rebellious sheep, although we don't deserve it. We often don't cooperate with you and thereby grieve your heart, but you press on in your faithfulness despite our rebellion.

I praise and thank you, Lord Jesus, that you are *my* Shepherd--that I belong to *you*, the Creator and Sustainer of all--because you have chosen me. I am thankful that you, in your wisdom and power, love and goodness, make sure that I lack nothing necessary. Thank you that in my present painful circumstances with my failures and mistakes, you are making this situation into a green pasture for me. You command me to lie down in it because here I can grow and mature and be more useful for you.

Thank you for Psalm 23 which tells me that while I am in these difficulties you lead me to the refreshing water of your Word, that you are at work transforming my soul, and that you will lead me in paths of righteousness. These truths are certain and sure, for you always do what will bring glory to your name, you will never lead me into anything that will disgrace you.

It is so good to know how trustable you are, Lord Jesus. Your wisdom is wonderful, your faithfulness is fabulous, your love is lavish, and your might is marvelous. Praise be to you continually, O God, for you are worthy!

Prayer: "Lord Jesus, help me to live in the truth that you are my Shepherd, that I lack nothing, no matter how it appears to me. Help me to trust you and stay where you put me, painful as it may be. Help me to be thankful for all you've given and to reject the tendency to complain about not having all I desire. Amen."

January 5

"He who is full loathes honey, but to the hungry even what is bitter tastes sweet."

Proverbs 27:7

To read through the Bible continually and consistently is a powerful practice. This gives the Lord opportunity to impress me with a verse, insight or conviction in each morning's reading. For instance, recently the verse listed above struck me: "He who is full loathes honey, but to the hungry even what is bitter tastes sweet."

As I thought on this, the Lord said to me, "What are you full of?" I had to answer, "Plans, schedules, projects, worries and fears." The Spirit then helped me to see that I need to empty myself of these and allow Him to fill me instead with wisdom, submission, obedience and the fruit of the Spirit.

One way of emptying myself is to list in my journal all my plans, schedules, projects, worries and fears, then put them into the Lord's hands by confession, prayer and surrender. I must let Him carry these; they are beyond my control anyway!

When I have done that, I can be ready for what the Lord has for me today. Every "bitter" happening can become sweet as we trust the Lord to work it out for good rather than getting upset because "my plans" were disturbed.

As with every other aspect of our walk with Jesus, the practice of putting all in the Lord's powerful and proficient hands is a growing one. To help the process, I am putting a sign up on our refrigerator:

"What are you full of?" This reminds me to put things in the Lord's hands and be filled with His Spirit instead.

Prayer: "Lord, help me to pour out to you all that occupies my mind, my heart, my soul; then I pray that you will fill me with your Spirit so I can serve you well today, bringing joy to your heart."

January 6

"He who dwells in the shelter of the Most High will rest in the shadow of the Almighty."

Psalm 91:1

I exalt you, O Lord Jesus Christ, for you are the Most High, the Final Authority, the Absolute Measure of right and wrong, the Perfect Standard of what is correct and what is error. You are the Almighty One, full of power, endued with strength, undefeatable, never threatened, never in danger, always in control. We can rest in your great strength, your mighty wisdom and in your marvelous character.

You are pure, holy and righteous; you are the antithesis of evil, sin and wickedness. We rejoice in your purity and give to you the honor due your name for your rich goodness and powerful greatness.

You, Lord Jesus, are the Author of life, the Redeemer of rebels, the Savior of the world, the Lord of those who believe. I praise you for your desire to redeem us, your foes. You were willing to limit yourself to a human body, to suffer at the hands of sinners, to expose yourself to attacks by Satan and to suffer physically, mentally, emotionally and spiritually on the cross to save stubborn sinners.

Beyond that you were willing to endure the greater anguish of actually becoming sin for us and as a result, having your Father turn away from you. As the Father poured out His wrath on you, the fabric of the Trinity was rent and your eternal relationship with the Father and the Spirit was broken. This, I believe, was the most painful part of your great sacrifice.

Then you were willing to endure time in death and the lower earthly regions (Eph. 4:9) while patiently awaiting the right moment to rise up and conquer death—and all this you did for your enemies!

You, Lord Jesus, are completely, entirely, incredibly good and we glorify you for it. Your marvelous mercy and glorious grace are at the heart of your eternal, rich and powerful love for your foes.

We praise you and honor you for your multiplied grace, your munificent kindness, your magnificent faithfulness and your majestic holiness. We exalt you in all, we praise you in all, we thank you in all, for you are worthy.

Prayer: "Lord, help me to grasp more and more your mighty love, long and high, to understand how deep and wide your forgiveness is, and to live in continual worship of you, honoring your marvelous grace by obeying you, especially in the small things of life. Amen."

January 7

"Rejoice in the Lord always…do not be anxious about anything but in everything by prayer, supplication and thanksgiving present your requests to God…whatsoever things are true…honest…just…pure… lovely… admirable… excellent and praiseworthy think about such things."

Philippians 4:4-8

This familiar passage has opened my eyes again to how often I think in human terms rather than in biblical ones. Sometimes I am so overwhelmed by the negatives pressing in on me that it is a struggle to be positive about anything!

In the midst of this daily fight, God's Word is such a wonderful help. It is the Touchstone of Truth, the Window on the Wonderful and the Revelation of our Riches. If we obey it, thinking on the positives listed above, our thoughts will be lifted to the Lord Jesus, for He is certainly all of these: He is true, honest, just, pure, lovely, admirable, excellent and praiseworthy.

When all is going well and there isn't a great deal of pressure, it's easy to be positive—but, when things get difficult, thinking on the Lord Jesus and all He is becomes both a struggle and significant.

As I read the other day, if we faint in the day of adversity, our strength is small (Pro. 24:10). So before adversity comes, we need to strengthen our spiritual lives by willfully thinking on what is positively true, both in big things and small. When I lose my keys, I can think on the truth that God knows where they are and will help me find them, if that's best. When tragedy comes, I can remember that God has a plan and is going to work it out. Through this way of thinking truth, we can nurture our soul, grow strong, deepen our trust in God and will move to praising Him in all. That will make us ready for the day of adversity.

These weeks past have given us a testing ground for our strength (which often proves to be too small). Taking classes in the local language here every day plus teaching English classes every night, along with the preparation for both, plus my work with the foundation, and other activities have all allowed us to see just how much we must rely on the Lord for strength. There is certainly always room for growth!

One area where we are really encouraged is health: we are all remaining healthy and strong in spite of the pressures and the cold temperatures in our house. Although it is mid October and the temperatures are in the 30s and 40s F outside, by law the central heating won't be turned on until Nov 15. So we just dress more warmly and heat up one room with an electric heater--when the electricity is on; it's off more than on here. God is our provider and we will praise Him for whatever He allows.

Prayer: "Father, forgive me for my tendency to complain; help me to reject the natural, negative thoughts that rise up from my selfishness, and to think instead of you in all your excellence and perfection, and of all the good things you provide. Make praise the keynote of my life. Amen."

January 8

"God is our refuge and strength, an ever-present help in trouble…The Lord Almighty is with us, the God of Jacob is our fortress."
Psalm 46:1,7

Praise be to you, Lord God: I awoke and found you there, waiting for me. I give you glory and honor and praise for your good and powerful presence, your lingering, long-lasting love, your wonderfully wise ways and your unending, unrelenting undergirding of life.

Truly you are glorious, you are great, you are good through and through. You are mighty in love, in justice, in wisdom, in mercy, in grace. You are worthy of worship and wonder.

Praise be to you for your working in your children to bring change: giving us knowledge, revelation and guidance in your Word; bringing us conviction leading to repentance; giving goodness every day so that we might walk with you.

It is wonderful that you know, understand and think far beyond our tiny capabilities. Before the foundation of the world you knew each of us, long before we came to pass, you knew what would transpire in our lives, what our decisions would be, what each person's response to you would be. You knew that many would reject your offer of grace, pardon and adoption--yet you chose to pay for the purchase of forgiveness for all human beings at great personal expense.

You see into the future, weaving the innumerable strands of human decisions and events into the fabric of your will, bringing about your overall desired end, as well as the just outcome of our choices. You give people power to make real and valid decisions, though these decisions may bring people to the conclusion you abhor: spending eternity without you.

Your thoughts are deep and mysterious, high and holy, yet are sufficiently revealed in your Word for us to search out and we praise you for it, Lord God. Your depth of wisdom, of insight, of knowledge, of goodness, of holiness, of righteousness, of grace flows from the spring of your perfect being. You are flawless, you are trustable, you are worthy of worship. May praise ever be yours—may you be glorified in my life today.

Prayer: "Lord God, help me to praise you throughout this day, to focus on the truth of your presence, your goodness, your constant care for your children. Help me to lift my eyes by faith from the nagging negatives in life to the transcendent truth of your wonderful working out all things for your glory and my good. Amen."

January 9

"The Lord is my shepherd…He leads me beside quiet waters, he restores my soul."

Psalm 23:1-3a

"What are you doing now?" asked John as I took a clean sheet of paper from my brief case.

"I'm going to make a list of the new words I learned today," I replied without looking up. "You said that we may be here a long time and I don't want to waste the hours!"

John smiled and continued his conversation with the policemen who were holding us under arrest.

This was typical of the need to utilize every opportunity for learning the language of our new country. Since there are only four of us in our group, many tasks fall to us that wouldn't normally be given to language students. Our goal of 6 hours of study a day is rarely met—personally I felt that 3 hours of book study was enough—but the exposure we got through ministry more than made up for the lack of formal study, for we got to learn new words from the myriad of interesting experiences that came each week.

On this particular day, certain grammatical forms and vocabulary were lodged permanently in my mind. For instance, the passive form of the verb "to apprehend or arrest," was graphically illustrated as the police led us away. We had come to this remote village in the north of the country to give help to poor families. However, since there are rarely any foreigners in the area, the police assumed we must be doing something wrong and arrested us.

We spent several hours in the police station, drinking lots of tea while they investigated our activities. But finding no evidence of wrongdoing, in the end we were released. At that juncture I learned another word meaning "they were embarrassed," for the police were forced to admit their mistake.

God has a way of guiding and providing for us that is beyond normal human thought. This was language learning at its best, disguised as trouble, which was uncomfortable and disquieting--and would later to lead to bigger difficulties--but was very effective for both language learning and spiritual growth.

The question we always need to ask ourselves is: "Am I willing to look at things from God's perfect perspective so I can thank Him and take advantage of the opportunity that is offered in my present problem?" Such times are the opportunity to live the truth that "The Lord is my shepherd, I shall not want."

Prayer: "Lord, help me to live today in the light of your presence, seeing your gracious working in all that happens. Help me to have a heart that praises without knowing how you are going to work things out. Amen."

January 10

"...I have this against you, that you have abandoned the love you had at first."

Revelation 2:4

Barbara says it's easy to tell when I am "in cahoots" with God, because then I am in tune with her. What she is referring to is the condition of my first love for Christ. I can perform all the spiritual disciplines correctly (quiet time, prayer, attendance, giving, being nice) but Barbara can tell when the connection with God is missing, when I have no passion for Him.

As you may remember, when Jesus spoke to the Ephesians in the opening chapters of Revelation, He had a lot of positives to say about them, but ended with rebuking them for losing their first love. They had all the mechanics right, but their hearts had grown cold.

His command to them was, "Remember therefore from where you have fallen. Repent and do the things you did at first. If you do not repent, I will come to you and remove your lampstand from its place" (Rev. 2:5).

So it is with us: we get busy, we give our heart and passion to something else, like our work/ministry/hobby/sport. As a result, our relationship with God grows cold, so slowly that we don't notice it. But our spouse often does because our marriage relationship reflects the warmth or coolness of our walk with God.

What can we do to nurture, strengthen and deepen our first love for Christ? Here's what I've found effective in rekindling that love.

First, <u>repent</u>: acknowledge that our relationship is not what it should be.

Second, <u>remember</u>: take the time to think about the early days of our walk with Him, the delicious sense of freedom from condemnation, the giddy wonder of having a new start, the soothing warmth of being fully accepted by God.

Third, <u>reveal</u>: practice lifting our souls to God, regularly telling Him honestly what we are thinking (mind), wanting (will) and feeling (emotions), then evaluate these by the Word, surrendering each to Him.

Fourth, <u>rejoice</u>: spend time daily in personal worship, extolling Him for who He is without thinking about how that benefits us. This kind of worship is standing in the light of God, seeing more and more of Him, having sin exposed, being transformed (2 Cor. 3:18), reveling in His love and grace. As I do this, usually by writing my worship thoughts in my journal, there is continual renewing of my first love, there is a growing passion for Christ—and Barbara can see the difference!

Here's an example of personal worship, using Psalm 84, meditating on the name "Lord Almighty" or "Lord of Hosts".

"Praise be to you, Lord God Almighty, Commander of the hosts of Heaven. To you we give glory and honor and praise, for you, Lord God, King Jesus, Gracious Father, Holy Spirit, are the most High, the most Wise, the most Powerful, the most Good and the most Holy of all. You are without beginning or end. You are the junction point of seeming opposites: justice and mercy, truth and grace, holiness and redemption. Only you could be so, only you are worthy of honor and praise. It is right to bow down in worship before you. It is right to surrender all to you. It is right to rise up in obedience. Praise be to you, Lord God Almighty."

I encourage us all to make a fresh beginning for our first love for Christ, and intentionally nurture it. With time, those around us will be amazed at the difference!

Prayer: "Lord, I confess my failure to intentionally nurture my first love for you. Forgive me and help me to do this every day in worship, in your Word, in praise and in obedience to what I know to be right. Amen."

January 11

"Praise be to the God and Father of our Lord Jesus Christ, the Father of compassion and the God of all comfort, who comforts us in all our troubles, so that we can comfort those in any trouble with the comfort we ourselves have received from God."

2 Corinthians 1:3,4

This week we have been operating under the "lay aside" plan. That is, the Lord has seen fit to lay us aside so He can have some undistracted time with us. We all have gotten some kind of powerful flu bug, which seems to run 5 to 7 days with fever and great weakness.

As in all things, the Lord is working out several purposes in this. For one thing, our team leader took the two little local girls living with us, which gives us a break. Then, we were able to relax some in the midst of being sick because we can't possibly be involved in anything outside of surviving.

A more significant reason is that I've been too busy with work and have neglected undergirding everything by prayer. Now I've been able to spend some good hours in intercession and prayed about some things that have been gnawing at me, but I hadn't taken to the Lord. What a relief to lift my soul to Him concerning these burdens, getting out the jumble of thoughts and feelings so I could process them in the light of Scripture..

I praise God for His patience and persistence with us. He knows exactly what to do to get our attention and bring correction. And if we don't pay attention, He will turn up the volume until we do hear. "For the Lord disciplines the one he loves, and chastises every son whom he receives" (Heb. 12:6).

I see how I subtly began to place more emphasis on doing and less on praying. Even though my prayer life was still there, it was not of the over-riding importance that it should always be. Now we have some more days of prayer ahead of us, as we will probably be down for a while longer. But we know, "…this happened that we might not rely on ourselves but on God who raises the dead" (2 Cor. 1:9).

Prayer: "Lord, help me to always have your perspective on the happenings in life, to praise you in and for all and to cooperate with what you are seeking to accomplish in me. Amen."

January 12

"Whom have I in heaven but you, and earth has nothing I desire besides you."

Psalm 73:25

Praise your name, Lord Jesus, for you are the most High: you are the Almighty, powerful beyond conception, mighty beyond imagination; you are the Victor, undefeated and undefeatable; you are the Creator, wise and good; You are the Savior, gracious and kind. I praise you for your perfect and powerful character, persistently and providentially guiding all in the lives of your children.

Thank you that as my Shepherd you are loving and leading me, protecting and providing, teaching and revealing. Thank you that during the night as I was attacked again by fear in my dreams and thoughts, as I awoke and turned to the truths of Psalm 23, you defeated the enemy. As I spoke out loud these truths from your Word, the fear and distress lessened and dissolved away. I was able to sleep again and my dreams were positive.

You, dear God, are the One and only Savior. You are the only constant Lover of my soul: no matter what I do, you love me, consistently, completely, creatively.

You describe this in Psalm 73:21-25. In your love you rebuke and discipline, revealing to us our sin: "When my heart was grieved, and my soul embittered, I was senseless and ignorant, I was a brute beast before you."

You consistently draw us on to repentance: "Yet, I am always with you."

You guide, direct and protect: "You hold me by my right hand. You guide me with your counsel, and afterwards you will take me into glory."

And your great love creates in me an ever-deepening responsive love for you: "Whom have I in heaven but you, and earth has nothing I desire besides you". Praise be to you, Lord Jesus for your great, unquenchable, ever flowing love!

Prayer: "Lord Jesus, develop in me that intense first love for you which the author of Psalm 73 had, so that my passion for you will eclipse all the world has to offer. Amen."

January 13

"A righteous man's….heart is secure, he will have no fear; in the end he will look in triumph on his foes."

Psalm 112:8

A notice finally arrived from the police to come and get the reply to our application for new residence permits. We had expected a "yes," since we knew of no reason for any other answer. To our surprise and amazment, however, we not only got a "no," but were told that we had to leave the country within 24 hours!

The reason for expulsion, the police said, was "top secret" so they could not tell us why we were being deported just 18 months after we had arrived. Following some intense "discussion" we were granted 10 days to finish our business and get out.

To say the least it was a shock. After years of planning and preparation to come here, after raising support and leaving all that was familiar and safe for what was different and dangerous, after all the effort of language learning and cultural adjustment, we are now to be suddenly thrust out of this new land that we had adopted.

Had we make a mistake in coming here? No, God's Word stands strong. Psalm 112 was my touchstone with reality: "The man who fears God...has no fear of bad news; his heart is steadfast, trusting in God" (Ps. 112:6). So, our expulsion was not really bad news and the Lord would give new direction.

In the next few days our plans changed often, for we did not know where to go from here. Again the Word gave wisdom; Psalm 86 says "In the day of my trouble I will call upon you for you will answer me." The Lord knew this exit was coming and had prepared the way.

First He had sent a single German woman, Renate, to work with us, so while we are gone, she could stay with the little local boy living with us. Second, a couple who is exploring the possibility of working with us will stay in our apartment and help Renate. Third, a new couple on our team is willing to watch the two little local girls living with us. God has it in hand.

We were able to pack up, knowing that He would bring us back or send us elsewhere, whichever was better. We had no way to know which would happen. To hold what we value with an open hand means that the Lord can truly be our God and choose what He deems best, while we can rest in His wisdom and goodness. God always goes before, prepares, protects and guides. Our part is to trust and praise.

Prayer: "Lord, help me to hold all that you've given me with an open hand, trusting you to give and take as you deem best. May my primary affection be for you, not for what you've given. Amen."

January 14

"Great is the LORD and most worthy of praise; his greatness no one can fathom."

Psalm 145:3

Yes, praise be to you, Lord God, the Triune One, Breather of the stars, Lighter of the sun, Spinner of the earth, Bringer of the dawn. We glorify your name, for you are the Holy One, sparkling in purity, shining truth into our lives, spreading light with every act.

We exalt you, the totally good One, pouring grace upon your creation, watering the garden of our souls with your love, planting seeds of good desire in our hearts. You are the mighty One, towering far above all creation, powerful in every good work, filling the universe with your majestic, gracious Presence.

You, Triune God, O heavenly Father, O heavenly Son, O heavenly Spirit are worthy of all honor, all worship, all glory. All creation points to you, all will bow down to you, all will proclaim you to be Lord, for you are the only holy and pure One, eternal, unchanging and perfect, deserving of full adoration, exaltation and magnification.

You, Lord God, are the Most High: the Wise Creator, the Mighty and Kind King, the Successful Savior, the Righteous Redeemer, the Faithful Father, the Perfect Planner, the Powerful Protector, the Beginner and Ender of time. Therefore, it is right to submit to you in joy, it is right to rise up in obedience, it is right to live in the light of your presence, it is right to exalt you in all we do. Yes, praise belongs to you forever and ever!

Prayer: "May I walk in the light of your presence through this day, Lord, aware of your mighty grace, your powerful wisdom, your majestic goodness. May I give you praise in each event, whether it be pleasant or painful, for you are always worthy of worship. Amen."

January 15

"My help comes from the LORD, the Maker of heaven and earth. He will not let your foot slip—he who watches over you will not slumber;"

Psalm 121:2,3

As we prepared for our "expulsion journey," I was worried about the dangerous, three day, arduous drive from our Middle Eastern country to Germany—we had come that way before and knew how difficult it was—and I had to constantly give it over to God.

While struggling with the situation, Psalm 121 came up in my daily reading. The last verse promises, "the LORD will watch over your going out and coming in both now and forevermore." He has declared that He will guide us through all circumstances, and this is exactly what I needed to hear at this point.

Looking back on it now, the whole trip was one long demonstration of God's faithfulness. Most of the road we traveled to Germany was just one lane each way and, being the main route between Europe and the Middle East, was crowded with large trucks. It was a constant game of "catch up and pass:" coming up behind a long line of trucks, then finding opportunity to pass them, often one at a time. Along the sides of the road were wrecks of cars and trucks whose drivers had miscalculated in their attempts to pass, a reminder to be careful.

Since many of the truckers stopped for the night, we decided to continue driving right through until the next day, and made it to Munich by the morning. There we went by the Word of Life castle where Barbara had worked years before and found a reunion of students from her Bible school going on! What a wonderful God sighting, a pleasant gift from the Lord!

Our time in Germany helped us to see more clearly the strain that we are constantly under in our country of work: having to be careful in what we say, write and do, while having so little fellowship. It is a gift to be again with more believers who share our vision. And it confirmed that God was watching over our going out and coming in. His Word is true, His character is pure, His protection is sure. "The LORD will keep you from all harm—he will watch over your life…" (Ps. 121:7). We will trust Him for the return trip also.

Prayer: "Praise you, Heavenly Father, for your faithful, constant love. Forgive me for often forgetting your unseen protection. Help me to walk in the certainty that you are my great and powerful Shepherd, protecting, providing and proceeding before us through the day. Thank you for what you will do today. Amen."

January 16

"The LORD watches over you—the LORD is your shade at your right hand; the sun will not harm you by day, nor the moon by night."

Psalm 121:5,6

Praise be to you, Lord, for your faithfulness: you are the God of goodness, the Lord of love, the Almighty One who gives your word and keeps it. I praise you for your being Elohim, the strong and faithful One. Whatever promises you give, you have the power to fulfill them and the faithfulness to do so. I give you praise and honor and exaltation for you are the King of Glory.

You, Lord Jesus, are absolutely faithful—faithful to your righteousness, to your holiness and justice, to the right judgment of evil while causing mercy to triumph over justice. You will always follow through on who you are--the perfect, pure and powerful King, the Lord of all, Ruler of righteousness and Redeemer of your enemies.

You, Heavenly Father, being both perfectly righteous and love itself, are faithful in your hatred of sin, of evil, of anything contrary to your character. In such love, you provide the solution to the problem of evil. In your righteousness, you judge sin, rebellion, and anything contrary to good; if you didn't judge, you would not be righteously loving, for righteous, pure and perfect love cannot abide with anything that is tainted by unlove, by selfishness, pride and evil.

I praise you, O Lord God, for you, in your greatness, rise far above our ability to comprehend. How could One who hates sin so profoundly, provide, against all human logic, a pardon for your creatures who are so thoroughly evil, rebellious and contrary to you?

Yet, in your wonderful, rich grace you made the way, providing reconciliation, crushing your Son without mercy that mercy might flow to your enemies. You did this because you are faithful to your character: you are Light, you are Life, you are Love and you are lovely.

Praise you for the truth that as I move into this new day, I go with you. You know every single detail of what will come and you have already made provision to protect me from what is evil, for you are all-knowing and all-wise; you are strong and faithful, trustable and good. I praise you now, ahead of time, for what you will bring into my life today, both in challenges and in the grace to meet them.

Prayer: "Help me, Lord, to hate evil as you do, to walk in awe of your love, in fear of your greatness and in the joy of obedience to you. Amen."

January 17

"He who dwells in the shelter of the Most High will rest in the shadow of the Almighty."

Psalm 91:1

Someone told me that we seldom learn anything once for all in the spiritual realm. Coming from the Middle East to Germany has been a shock culturally, and I have forgotten at times two important principles.

First, that our "struggle is not against flesh and blood, but against the rulers, against the authorities, against the powers of this dark world..." (Ephesians 6:12). It is easy to see the people behind the slow bureaucracy here as the problem, instead of the spiritual forces using them!

Second, "...in all things God works for the good of those who love him, who have been called according to his purpose" (Rom. 8:28). This means seeing that delays are things God uses for good. When I forgot these and fell into the swamp of impatience and self-pity, the Lord Jesus, in His magnificent patience and splendorous grace, set me back on the right thought paths.

The main reason we came to Germany was to reregister our car and then try to reenter our Middle Eastern country, not knowing whether we'd be allowed in or not. Having lost our residence permit in our country of work, we also lost the privilege of having a car registered there. However, here in Germany we were hampered initially by two holidays in the first week, then by three big blunders made by the repair shop. This forced us to put off our return date by a week—but the Lord had reasons for the delay, and these reasons unfolded one at a time.

First, the delay meant we had time to visit Barbara's Bible school where we had three important interactions. One with a future worker, the second with the director of the Bible school who is very interested in our work, and the third with an organization that is collecting gifts for us—and they had just enough money to cover the repairs of our car! It also gave us more time with Barbara's parents and the ability to help them. Plus we were able to make more preparations that otherwise would have been impossible.

Looking back it is easy to see God's hand and praise Him for what He has done; I pray that in the future when such challenges come I will remember His provision and praise Him ahead of time in belief, giving Him more glory. As God says in Psalm 50:23, "He who offers the sacrifice of thanksgiving honors me...." for that is an exercise of faith.

Prayer: "Thank you, Lord, for the opportunities to trust you before we see things work out. Help me to be a person of praise first and sight second. Amen."

January 18

"The angel of the LORD encamps around those who fear him, and he delivers them."

Psalm 34:7

I praise you, Lord God, for your care and protection, your guidance and direction. It is so very good to know you, the great and mighty One--and truly, knowing you is enough for joy. I praise you that you are freeing me from the fear of men and are helping me to grasp that you, Lord God, are the only One to be feared.

It is wonderful that you give us a clear description in Psalm 34:13,14 of what it means to fear you. These points are such ordinary, everyday things; yet as I obey you in them, it means I am fearing you, not people, or my own ideas. It means I care what you think more than what others or I think.

"Keep your tongue from evil...." Help me to be aware when I'm about to speak any evil, like gossip, negative, judgmental statements, cutting remarks or humor that makes fun of others. Convict me so I can repent and instead speak what is good, helpful, healing and kind.

"And [keep] your lips from speaking lies." Alert me to when I am formulating lies in my thinking, like "poor me" or "this is terrible" when the truth is, "This is difficult, but I praise you that you will help me through" or "This is uncomfortable, but I thank you for what you are going to do with it, Lord."

"Turn from evil and do good;" Make me aware of whenever I am contemplating something evil, like selfishness, lustful thoughts, impatience or resentment. Help me to repent immediately and choose good instead.

"Seek peace and pursue it." Help me to have the courage and determination to actively work for peace with all those around me rather than avoiding those who clash with me or refusing to forgive or not wanting to ask forgiveness.

In response to these truths, Lord, I must resolve to be deeply concerned for what you think. I want to live for you a life worthy of your great Name, with a love growing in knowledge and depth of insight so that I may be able to "discern what is best, and be pure and blameless until the day of Christ, filled with the fruit of righteousness, which comes through Jesus Christ, to the glory and praise of God" (Phil. 1:9-11).

And thank you, LORD, that we can obey you because you are Yahweh, whose glory is in your holiness; because you are Elohim, whose great power is seen in creation and whose full faithfulness is seen in your promised provision of salvation; because you are Adonai, who is worthy to be obeyed fully and promises to provide completely so we can obey.

Prayer: "I bow before you, O Triune God, Creator and Lord of the universe. I surrender my all to you. Help me to fear you in each decision I make so that you can be glorified in my life today. Amen."

January 19

"The LORD himself goes before you and will be with you; he will never leave you nor forsake you."

Deuteronomy 31:8

Leaving Germany to return to our country we got caught in a traffic jam—another chance to practice praising God before seeing His reasons! This delay necessitated our staying overnight again at the Word of Life castle in the Munich area, giving us a good night's rest. Leaving there the next morning we drove all day, all night and until 3 pm the next day when we arrived in the last town before the border of our work country.

On the drive through Yugoslavia we had two "God sightings." First, expecting to find plenty of gas stations around a major city we saw a sign that said, "Next gas 50 kilometers," but I knew from experience that there were only about 40 kilometers of gas left in my tank! Praising and pressing on we came to a new gas station 42 kilometers later! Just in time!

Then as evening came, I was hoping, not really praying, for someone to follow on the dark, winding, narrow roads through the mountains. There were no lights, no guardrails and often fog, making it a difficult drive in the night. As I drove along at dusk, a car waiting beside the road pulled out in front of me and then led us for the next 500 kilometers through the night!

Just think about the wonders God worked to get us there at just the right moment to join our "escort," who was an excellent driver and obviously knew the road well. Following him saved us much time and stress as we didn't have to creep slowly along not sure where the next sharp curve would be!

The following day we reentered our country, not sure what would happen, but there were no problems with customs: no one knew that we had been expelled. We then made the 13-hour drive to our city, where we received a very warm welcome from the little team we'd left behind. God's goodness was clear to us all and we praised Him for it. I needed to remember this demonstration of His goodness and power in the events that would soon come.

Prayer: Father, remind me of how you have helped me in the past so that I will immediately come to you in prayer for each fresh crisis and give you honor with trust and praise before any answer comes. Amen."

January 20

"Blessed are those who have learned to acclaim you, who walk in the light of your presence, O Lord."

Psalm 89:15

Praise be to you, Lord God, for your goodness and grace, for your fineness and faithfulness: I wake up each morning and there you are, watching over me with a new day ready for me to live in your presence.

Praise be to you, Elohim, the triune God, powerful beyond imagination, faithful beyond conception, always good, always wise, always at work.

As it says in Psalm 89:15,16, "Blessed are those who have learned to acclaim you..." They praise you in every circumstance, recognize you in every detail, are constantly aware of "God sightings" as you protect and provide.

"who walk in the light of your presence." They are aware by faith of your being with them, of your watching over them, leading them, lighting the way.

"They rejoice in your name all day long, they exalt in your righteousness..." you are their focus; their knowledge of your qualities guides their thoughts, and therefore their actions and reactions.

"...for you are their glory and strength." They are constantly drawing their significance from you, aware that belonging to you is a great privilege bringing joy, that you are the meaning of life, the importance of existence, the greatness of being. And you are their security, for you are strong and with your strength you protect them, give them power spiritually, mentally, volitionally emotionally, physically and in many other ways.

They recognize you as the source of all, the goal of all, the God of all, the glory of all, the end of all. They live in the light of your goodness, they rest in the shadow of the Almighty, they rejoice in knowing intimately the Lord Jesus, Creator of all.

Praise you, Lord Jesus, that in your wisdom you always do the right thing, allowing us to make choices for good or bad, allowing us to live out the consequences of our decisions, whether wise or foolish. Then you take all this and weave it into your plan for bringing about the end of history and the beginning of eternity.

In this great plan you are working towards the salvation of as many as possible and towards the end of evil, which you will lock up in the lake of fire. Praise you for your unlimited power to bring all this to pass, your unwavering faithfulness to follow through and your high and wide wisdom in doing it all in rightness and righteousness. You are worthy of all praise and honor, worship and obedience.

Prayer: "Praise you that in light of all this truth, it is certain that you have the wisdom and power to guide me in this day before me. Help me to walk in faith, in the light of your presence, acclaiming you in all so that I may bring glory to your name. Amen."

January 21

"…we also rejoice in our sufferings, because we know that suffering produces perseverance; perseverance, character; and character, hope."

Romans 5:3,4

As we sat beside the road looking at our broken down car, I was finding it hard to thank God. Here we were, stranded out in the wild Eastern part of the country, literally a hundred miles from the nearest city and many miles from the nearest village, with no help in sight and certainly no sign of any goodness in the situation.

A verse I'd memorized came to mind, "I remembered the days of long ago; I meditate on all your works and consider what your hands have done" (Ps. 143:5). Then some thoughts came to mind of how God had recently worked in our lives to get us into this predicament.

While we were gone in Germany, the mother of the three "orphans" we'd been taking care of had turned up with a court order giving the father custody of the children. After consulting a lawyer, it was obvious that we had to take them to their father who lived far out in the East.

So we had loaded ten of us (the three children, our local ministry partner, "Charles," and his daughter, our German helper, and us four) into our little Volkswagen station wagon—not a van, but one of those little rear engine station wagons--and headed off. About 400 kilometers into the trip, a large stone in the road put a crack in our transmission case, causing an unseen oil leak, which eventually resulted in us being stranded beside the road.

The Lord had many reasons for allowing this to happen, the primary one being to teach us (and especially me) to praise Him in and for all things. I had the theory of praise, but needed the practice!

Psalm 34 came to my mind, "I will bless the Lord at all times…" especially when it isn't pleasant! And Psalm 23, "The Lord is my shepherd, I shall not want." I had to bow my head and thank Him for this discouraging and distressing situation, knowing that He is good and wise and loving. This gave Him far more glory than when I thanked Him after the whole event had come to a good conclusion.

Prayer: "Lord, help me to be a disciple of praise, giving you thanks while in the midst of difficulty, before I see your reasons or answers, thereby honoring you with faith. Amen."

January 22

"Praise, O servants of the LORD, praise the name of the LORD."

Psalm 113:1

This morning I came to Psalm 113 in my reading. I was tired, had a busy schedule before me and was unhappy with some things that had occurred. The day looked bleak from a human perspective. So, it is very good to look up and away to the Lord, to get His perspective, to remember what He is like and what He does.

Verse seven of Psalm 113 especially spoke to me: "He raises up the poor out of the dust, and lifts the needy out of the ash heap…." That perspective turned my day into a much better one.

You reminded me, Lord, that although I am poor and needy, stranded in the dust and dirt of this world, you are going to do some "lifting up" today. This immediately encouraged my spirit and gave me a tangible hope for a positive day with you.

In you, Lord, we have a powerful God. I just marvel at the way you used your Word to empower me with the kind of encouragement and uplift I needed. Our part is to take the time to look and listen, and you certainly will meet us with what we need to hear.

Praise be to you, Lord God, Creator of heaven and earth, the sea and all that is in them. Glory be to you for your goodness, greatness and grandeur. We are your children and as such are not to view life as being only a series of small, everyday events. We are to fulfill our responsibilities as a part of being involved in your great and grand scheme to redeem, release and re-form the universe. Keep this grand vision ever before us to give us perspective for the day.

You, Lord God, are wise and loving, patient and perfect, powerful and persistent. We can trust you as you strongly sweep us up in your arms, your family, your plans, your purpose. You are moving history to a conclusion and taking us with you and we praise you for it!

Prayer: "Help us today to see the unseen, to live in the invisible, to think by faith, praising you, Lord God, in and for all things, for you are worthy of such praise. May we listen, grasp and respond to what your Word tells us. Amen."

January 23

"But I will sing of your strength, in the morning I will sing of your love; for you are my fortress, my refuge in times of trouble'.

Psalm 59:16

As we waited beside our broken-down car, Charles, the local with us, was able to hitchhike to the next village. He returned with a mechanic who patched the hole in the transmission, pumped new oil in and got it going. We were then able to limp some 100 kilometers to the nearest city, creeping over several mountain passes.

There we found a mechanic who took the transmission apart and pronounced it "terminally wounded." We would have to order a new one from Germany. So, Charles took the three "orphans" along with his daughter and continued his journey to the East by bus. We got on another bus and rode in the opposite direction, 12 hours back to the capital city, where I called Germany and ordered a rebuilt transmission.

When it came a week later, I had to go to the airport customs hall with the old transmission to get it. Since our car was an imported foreign one, in order to get any new parts shipped in, I had to surrender the old parts to customs. Well, the customs man didn't want to take the old transmission and instead wrote it into my passport, telling me that the next time we left the country by car I should take it with me. I wasn't very happy with having to drag two transmissions with me to the bus stop and then home. But I wasn't yet aware of what the Lord was doing with this.

We took the new transmission, got on the night bus, rode 12 uncomfortable hours to the East, arriving in the morning tired and disheveled. We got a taxi and arrived at the mechanic's place just as he was opening. There we were given two disturbing pieces of news.

First, after not hearing from us for a week, he thought we didn't want the car anymore so had begun to sell parts off of it! Second, after looking at the new transmission, he asked, "Where's the old one?" Well, I'd left it in at home. "Ah," he said, "that's too bad because I need several parts from it for the new one to work. You won't find them here. You'll have to go back to your city and get the old transmission."

Trying to apply what God had been teaching us, we thanked the Lord for this unexpected happening, and asked Him for direction. The mechanic's widow neighbor, who had befriended us on our first visit, came over and invited Barbara, our German friend, Renate, and the boys to stay with her while I went back to the capital. This gave Barbara and Renate a wonderful chance to see more culture and make lots of new friends. Being the only foreigners that many there had ever seen, they were quite the attraction! The Lord had His reasons for our difficulties, and I would see another one on my trip to and from the capital.

Prayer: "When things all seem to go wrong, when I can see no solution, help me to praise you for what you are going to do in it all, Lord, giving you honor before men and angels. Amen."

January 24

"The Mighty One, God, the Lord, speaks and summons the earth from the rising of the sun to the place where it sets."

Psalm 50:1

You are the Mighty One who spoke the universe into existence, who knows the name of every star, who holds together the nucleus of every atom. Your might is without margin, your strength is without stricture and your power is without perimeter. There is no good that you cannot do, there is no evil you cannot overcome, there is no plan that can stand against you. You are mighty in virtue, powerful in wisdom, strong in love and vigorous in justice. To you belongs all honor and worship!

You are Elohim, the God who is powerful and faithful. You have shown your power in being the Creator of all and the Sustainer of all. You have shown your faithfulness in providing salvation for all at just the right time: you make a promise, you follow through no matter how long it takes, no matter what it costs. You are worthy of worship.

In Hebrew "Elohim" is plural for three or more, giving us a clue of your Triune Nature. I glorify you for being a Trinity—Father, Son and

Holy Spirit—among whom there is perfect harmony, rich community, lavish love and gracious interdependence from long before creation. Praise be to you for your love of unity and diversity, for your joyful submitting to one another, for your demonstration of rich, healthy relationships.

You, O God, have the right and power to call the whole earth to judgment. And I praise you that you will judge all according to what each has done and that you will do this righteously, correctly, perfectly. All whose names are written in the Lamb's book of life will be declared righteous because of Christ's work. And those who have refused the heavenly way of salvation, who have rejected your path of righteousness and insisted on their own evil, destructive, condemning plans, will be consigned, by their own choice, to an eternity without God, to eternal separation from all that is good, all that is right, all that is beautiful, holy and perfect. This is not what you want for them, Lord, but it is your perfect and righteous judgment to remove all evil from the future.

I praise you, Lord, for right now you judge and chasten your children, pointing out to us where we need to repent, change, grow and deepen. In your complete knowledge, deep wisdom and gracious kindness, you always do this correctly, in love, in faithfulness, in power.

Praise be to you Lord, for your greatness that goes beyond the grasp of the human mind. You know what is coming, you prepare us for it, you help us through it, you transform us in it, you witness through us in it. Only you could do such great things. You are worthy of exaltation.

Prayer: "I worship you, O Triune God, I adore you, exalt you, bow before you and rise up to obey you. Help me today to live this out in moment-by-moment reality. Amen."

January 25

"My loving God will go before me...."

Psalm 59:10

To get the missing parts from the old transmission, that evening I got on another night bus and headed back to the capital, 12 hours away. I arrived on Sunday morning and while taking a taxi home, I saw my local mechanic drive by--I had never before seen him anywhere but in his shop! An amazing God sighting! I had the taxi driver follow and stop him. The mechanic graciously came to my house, took the necessary parts from the old transmission and put them on the new one for me.

So, that night I again got on a bus and for the third night in a row spent an uncomfortable, mostly sleepless 12 hours traveling. I noticed that the bus driver was the same one I'd had the previous night. He also recognized me (not too many foreigners ride buses in that direction) and greeted me warmly. At 3 am when the bus stopped for a break, the driver invited me to have "breakfast" with him and we had a good time chatting.

When I got to the mechanic's the next morning, I was relieved and thankful that everything needed for the transmission was there, and he set to work putting it in the car. During the days we had to wait for the repairs to be done there were many opportunities to practice language, share spiritual truth and experience the local culture as never before.

At the end of the week, with all the parts sold from our car recovered and reinstalled, it was finally ready. We set off for home, stopping in the first good-sized town to buy some food for lunch. There were about 20 little stores on the main street, all of which sold the things we were looking for. I randomly picked one and when I walked in, there was my bus driver friend sitting there! He was just as surprised as I was and told me that he is home only one day a month, and that was the day we came by! And I could have gone into any of the other 20 little stores rather than this one and missed him! God guides! What an amazing God sighting.

He took us to his home for tea and that began a long-term friendship that opened opportunities to share the gospel with him, a person who never would have heard otherwise. God had more than one positive reason for our "accident," bringing much good out of it! Truly, without telling us why beforehand, or asking us our opinion, "He [made us] lie down in green pastures" (Ps. 23:2). We just have to trust Him to have control of the big picture and to praise Him in faith.

Prayer: "Lord, your knowledge of what is happening is so far beyond mine. Help me to trust you, to rest in you when all looks confusing to me. Help me to be a 'glory giver' by praising you before I understand. Amen."

January 26

"The Maker of heaven and earth, the sea, and everything in them—the LORD, who remains faithful forever."

Psalm 146:6

Praise be to you, O triune Elohim, that when I am not faithful, not open to you, not obedient, you remain faithful, you remain wise and good, patient and forgiving. You work powerfully and persistently to bring me back to surrender. Praise you for your strong, rock-like character, never changing, never shifting, never moving from perfection.

Thank you, Lord, for a new fresh today to live for you. I praise you for your watching over me all night, for arranging things for this new day, preparing grace for the challenges to come, providing enough wisdom for me (and do I need it!), and for sending your angels before to protect me. Praise be to you, O Lord God for your goodness and grace.

"...the LORD is righteous; he has cut me free from the cords of the wicked" (Ps. 129:4). When I look back and compare my life today with what it was like at age 18, or 26, or 33, or 46, what a difference I see! There is so much more light, so much more freedom, so much more joy because you, Lord Jesus, are ever cutting me free from my own wickedness, from the work of Satan and from the warped thinking of the world. Thank you for revealing these cords one at a time and leading me in repentance so you can cut those cords and I can withdraw any ground I'd given the enemy.

You, Jesus, have given us light from your Wisdom, conviction and guidance from your Spirit, transformation and insight through your Word and worship, as well as help from other believers. In you is life, in you is Light, in you is Love and in you I am free and fulfilled, forever.

Lord Jesus, to know you is such a wonder, to give you worship is such a privilege, to love you is such an honor. You are the Creator, you are the Guide, the Protector, the Beginner and Ender of all. We can trust you fully. To you alone belongs worship and power, glory and exaltation.

Prayer: "Lord, forgive me for how I forget that you are there and tend to operate on my own. Help me to live in the truth of your Love and Power, in the light of your Goodness and Grace today so that you may be honored before all. Amen."

January 27

"Submit yourselves, then, to God. Resist the devil, and he will flee from you."

James 4:7

The Lord has been giving us a lot of direction these last few weeks—direction on the need to praise Him more, to praise Him in and for all things. To me it is both amazing and wonderful how He can bring a thing to our attention and then give us needed information on it, "coincidentally" bringing it to us at the right time.

For instance, on a day when I was suffering from a nice, strong headache, I lay down for a moment and picked up a book on praise I'd been reading. Opening to the page where I left off, the next paragraph started with this sentence, "For years I'd been suffering from migraine headaches...." And the author went on to tell how God taught him to praise him for these and how, when the lessons were learned, the Lord took the headaches away.

Praise is a great privilege, and a great responsibility. To praise for and in all things is expressing faith in a God who controls everything for our good and His glory. Praise is certainly the gateway to surrender and freedom in Christ. As you already know, such praise comes by the working of the Holy Spirit through the Word and flows out as we obey what we know to be true.

James 4:7-10 has taken on a new depth for us as we see the importance of praise: "Submit yourselves, then, to God [by praise]. Resist the devil [by praise], and he will flee from you. Come near to God [by praise] and he will come near to you. Wash your hands, you sinners, and purify your hearts, you double-minded [repent of complaining and griping while we claim to trust God]. Grieve, mourn and wail. Change your laughter to mourning and your joy to gloom [treat grumbling and complaining as the serious sins they are and repent in sadness]. Humble yourselves before the Lord [by praising in faith], and he will lift you up."

This past week we moved to a new apartment. It was not my first choice, but the Lord knew better. Our new apartment is right next to a lot of things: the bus stop (so we don't have to use the car much), a butcher, fruit stand and grocery store. And it is within walking distance of the weekly farmer's market.

We are also near a mosque, so five times a day we get reminded by the call to prayer why we are here. Plus there are lots of children and a big, dirt parking area behind the house where our boys can play with their new friends. This, especially, is a direct answer to prayer, as we had asked that God would provide local friends for the boys—the previous place we lived had very few children in the neighborhood.

Most importantly, in contrast to our old apartment, we are in a neighborhood with almost all locals. This area has a different flavor from those where many foreigners live. We are looking forward to all the new contacts God will give us, and praising Him for them ahead of time!

Prayer: "Lord, help me to humble myself through praise, trusting you with my lips when I don't feel like it in my heart. May you be honored today by my willful praise. Amen."

January 28

"For the LORD God is a sun and shield; the LORD bestows favor and honor; no good thing does he withhold from those whose walk is blameless. O LORD Almighty, blessed is the man who trusts in you."

Psalm 84:11,12

Praise be to you, Lord God Almighty, Commander of the hosts of Heaven. To you we give glory and honor and praise, for you, King Jesus, Mighty Father, Holy Spirit, are the most High, the most Wise, the most Powerful, the most Good and the most Holy One. You are without beginning, without end, without change, without lack, without evil, sin or darkness. You are all that is good, all that is right, all that is positive. You are perfect, you are present, you are powerful.

You are the junction point of opposites; your wisdom is on display as you combine what to us looks like oil and water, or square and circle. You join justice and mercy, truth and grace, holiness and redemption, sovereignty and man's responsibility. You remain just while having mercy triumph over justice. You speak the truth, hurtful and condemning as it may be ("...light has come into the world, but men loved darkness instead of light because their deeds were evil" John 3:19), while using this truth to open us to the grace of your gospel ("But whoever lives by the truth comes into the light, so that it may be seen plainly that what he has done has been done through God" John 3:21). You, Lord Jesus, remained holy while becoming sin for us. Only you in your eternal infiniteness could combine such qualities which to us are so different as to be mutually exclusive.

Truly, only you are worthy of obedience in total surrender. It is right to bow down to you in worship, it is right to rise up before you in obedience. Praise be to you, Lord God, King of Glory and Lord of all.

Prayer: "Lord, I so often rely on my own understanding of things, forgetting that you have a much fuller, deeper, longer, higher view of the situation. Help me to rely on you, not my own weak logic. Help me to submit my intellect to your Word. May I value and obey your Word above all. Amen."

January 29

"I will extol the LORD at all times; his praise will always be on my lips. "

Psalm 34:1

Psalm 23 is very familiar to everyone, but recently the Lord has shown me some new, very interesting points in it from the perspective of praise. Praise in and for all things is really the act of surrendering to the Lord at that moment and in that situation. In addition, it is resisting the devil and his suggestion that "this situation is just awful! Poor me!"

Psalm 23 says, "The Lord is my shepherd." That means He is watching over me all the time, with great care and attention, holding at a distance what is truly bad.

He "makes me lie down in green pastures." That is, He finds for me the situations which are profitable for growth and brings me there. He doesn't ask if I like it, nor does He ask my opinion. He *makes* me lie down there until I've learned what is needed. In this I can cooperate with Him by praising Him for what He is doing whether I like it or not.

"Even though I walk through the valley of the shadow of death...." This refers not just to physical danger and death, but to other aspects, such as dying to self, to ego, to my plans and desires and opinions. This can mean having my plans fail, my vision perish, my hopes dashed.

"I will fear no evil for you are with me…" The difficult happenings in this "valley" are not evil but are allowed by God for my good—being all powerful He could easily prevent them, especially since He is with me all the time, but He allows what He knows is useful for my growth and for my giving Him glory.

Thinking through this Psalm in terms of praise has brought great joy to me and removed some of my natural thought patterns (the tendency to resent what is hard, to complain, to fear being hurt or rejected)--patterns which make it difficult to praise in and for all things. Take a look at the rest of Psalm 23 from this perspective and see what things you can find to encourage you to praise Him in and for all.

Prayer: "Lord, keep opening my eyes to your view of things; speak to me through your Word as I read it daily; move me forward in the discipline of praise. Amen."

January 30

"Through Jesus, therefore, let us continually offer to God a sacrifice of praise—the fruit of lips that confess his name."

Hebrews 13:15

Once upon a time there were two people living in a foreign land who got a package from Germany. When they went to the post office to pick it up, the customs official opened it and took out two packages of tea, the kind of tea that they really liked but wasn't available locally. Smiling, he said, "You can't have these; customs regulations!" And with that he put the tea into his desk drawer.

Now, how should these two people react to such random injustice? There are only two basic possibilities: to complain or to praise, and we all know which is correct. These two people took a moment to pray,

"Lord, thank you for all the times tea did come to us and customs let it through. Thank you that this time you chose to have it otherwise." Then those two left the post office with light hearts and good thoughts and had a really good day.

Praise is a wonderful responsibility that God has given us. It keeps us dwelling in the Truth, and, as you know, Jesus said in John 8:32, "…the truth will set you free." Praise sets us free from the nasty so we can dwell on the nice, as Paul pointed out in Philippians 4:8 (think on whatever is true, noble and right, whatever is pure, lovely and admirable).

Very often we seek God's will in certain matters, but more often we forget God's will for all matters: Praise. "…give thanks in all circumstances, for this is God's will for you in Christ Jesus" (1Thes. 5:18).

Praise is commanded or demonstrated over 250 times in Scripture—that alone is a powerful indication of its importance in our lives. And in Revelation it is indicated that praise will be our primary occupation in the life to come.

Do you know why we can praise God in and for all things? It is because of His Character. He is light itself; He is clothed in light, shining in glory, resplendent in honor, glorious in truth and beautiful in holiness. In the light of His wisdom He sees all, understands all, does all that is best in the long run. The Son shines ultimate goodness into our lives. Praise itself directs our attention to the powerfully beautiful Character of our Lord Jesus Christ and releases into our lives a fragrance that will attract others to Him.

Prayer: "Lord, such praise is so unnatural for me. Help me to gaze upon your Character everyday so I will respond to the events in my life with praise rather than complaining. May I thus give you a continual stream of glory before all those around me and shine your light upon them. Amen."

January 31

"Delight yourself in the Lord and He will give you the desires of your heart."

Psalm 37:4

To delight in you, Lord, in one sense is so easy, for in every aspect you are wonderful beyond conception. You made all, you know all, you hold all together. You know the makeup of every atom, the information in every DNA molecule, the workings of every synapse in the brain, the condition of every artery, the reproduction of every cell—nothing escapes your attention and knowledge.

You have control of all events, balancing perfectly the genuinely responsible choices of billions of people with the specific plans you have for each individual, each moment, each generation, each epoch—and at the right time you will bring about the end of history, of time and of evil. You are perfect in your wisdom, perfect in your love, perfect in your justice, perfect in your mercy, perfect in your timing.

You are the God of grace, the Dispenser of justice, the King of righteousness and mercy, of truth and love, Heaven and Hell, light and mystery, purity and punishment, forgiveness and vengeance—each in its time and place.

You are in every way the delightful God: there is no repugnant, ugly, unjust, impure, evil or wrong aspect to your nature, your character, your thoughts or your actions. All is good, all is pure, loving, just, positive, gracious, righteous, wise and perfect.

You are all that our hearts ever desired, you are beyond what we could conceive, you are the fulfillment of every positive dream, you are "too good to be true" and yet are not only true but Truth itself.

We praise you for the wonder of your persons, the joy of being your child and the privilege of walking with you every day. You have made us to be with you, to find in you alone our meaning, fulfillment, joy, peace, grace, help, direction, safety, wisdom and goodness.

Forgive me, Lord, for seeking these things elsewhere, wanting them now, in my way, for my reasons. Forgive me for making these my idols, the things I demand to be happy. Help me instead to turn my eyes to you, to lift up my thoughts and feelings, desires and fears to you so in the light of your presence Thereby Truth may rule, Reality may reign and my heart may be united in living for you alone. Put your desires in my heart. Then I will praise you, O Lord my God, with all my heart and glorify your name forever more. For you have redeemed my soul from the pit, from the grave, from the lowest hell (Ps. 86:12,13).

Prayer: "You are worthy of trust, of obedience, of worship, of glory. May these overflow from my heart, my thoughts, my lips on all around me as your Spirit rules in my life today. Amen"

FEBRUARY

February 1

"Trust in the LORD with all your heart and lean not on your own understanding;"

Proverbs 3:5

Proverbs 3:7 says, "Do not be wise in your own eyes; fear the LORD and turn away from evil." Sometimes we find ourselves frustrated in all our plans with none of the things we'd like to see happen getting accomplished. In this I have to remind myself that my main purpose as a Christian is not productivity, but knowing and worshiping our Lord Jesus Christ. We are to be ever drawing closer to Him. We may be successful in the eyes of the world because of our accomplishments, but if we aren't close to Him, it's all a mirage.

The Lord has been stressing to us again and again the importance of getting closer to Him by praising, and recently gave me a new insight about this. When we praise God for each thing that comes to us, whether it seems good or bad from our perspective, we are surrendering to God at that particular moment, reaffirming our trust in Him. In such praise we are declaring His goodness and His power to all those around us. We are getting up the shield of faith and quenching the fiery darts of the devil. We are proclaiming God's intent to bring to us only what is for our good and His glory.

Conversely, failure to praise (complaining) is resisting God's working in our lives. It is a form of rebellion. This is declared in Psalm 106:24-26, which tells of the Israelites' response to the report of the spies after they had seen the promised land. "Then they despised the pleasant land; they did not believe his promise. [They failed to praise, to trust, to submit to God's leadership] They grumbled in their tents and did not obey the LORD. [Instead of praising, they complained, rebelling against what the Lord was giving them.] So he swore to them with uplifted hand that he would make them fall in the desert." [So the Lord did not give them the good things He had offered and waited till all those grumblers had died before bringing the Israelites into the land].

In contrast, we should more follow David's example in Psalm 34:1-2. "I will extol the Lord at **all times**; His praise shall **continually** be on my lips." [We can always say, "Thank you, Lord God, that in every happening there is potential growth in my focus on you and a platform upon which I can demonstrate your grace to the world."]

"My soul **will** boast in the Lord." [Thank you, Lord, for the continual reminder that in myself I can do nothing and that the thrust of my life is to give glory to you, not to me!]

"The afflicted hear and rejoice." [How good that we can encourage others by praise, helping them also to praise, as we lead the way in extolling God.]

It is so good to look at all things through the purifying lens of God's Word and to keep up the shield of faith with words of praise. We thank God that He is teaching us to praise, even though we are slow learners!

Prayer: "Lord, help me to remember in each disappointment, difficulty and discomfort, as well as in the positive and pleasant, to respond with praise, surrendering to the Truth of your being God, the final Authority, the all wise One. Help me to affirm my trust in you by praising when I feel like complaining, by giving thanks when I feel like rebelling. May you be exalted in my life today through praise and thanksgiving. Amen."

February 2

"Do you not know? Have you not heard? The LORD is the everlasting God, the Creator of the ends of the earth. He will not grow tired or weary, and his understanding no one can fathom."

Isaiah 40:28

What a wonder you are, O Triune God: the Mighty Ruler, Gracious Savior and Powerful Shepherd. Isaiah wrote of your greatness in chapter 40, starting in verse10, "See, the Sovereign LORD comes with power, and his arm rules for him." You, Lord God, the King of Glory, Almighty Ruler, Powerful Creator and Eternal Sustainer, are faithful to govern rightly with overwhelming power. No one can withstand you, no one can successfully resist your overall glorious plans. You will come at the perfect time to right all wrongs in grace and justice. Glory be to you.

"See, his reward is with him, and his recompense accompanies him." You are a generous and rich God with endless resources, who pours out blessing and grace and goodness on all people, and especially on your children. You gift us with salvation, forgiveness, grace and goodness when we actually deserve punishment, suffering, death and destruction. Glory be to you. You have rewards, crowns and blessings in heavenly places awaiting those who love and follow the Lord Jesus.

"He tends his flock like a shepherd:" You are the Faithful One who protects your sheep at all costs. You watch over us with care, with compassion, with competence, with completeness. In your sight we are not just possessions but your beloved children.

"He gathers the lambs in his arms and carries them close to his heart;" You are tender with us when we are weak. You love us graciously, kindly, gently. You think of each of us continually, aware of our needs, protecting and guiding us through the difficulties and joys of life.

"…he gently leads those that have young." You know our condition, you adjust your leadership according to what we are able to do and take. You are gracious and good, providing and protecting, caring and compassionate.

You, Lord Jesus, are the ever-present Shepherd, the powerful King, the perfect Savior and our pleasant Lord. You are trustable at every moment, always worthy of obedience, of love, of honor, glory and praise. We bow before your majesty, we rise up in awe of your magnificence, we obey in the light of your might.

Prayer: "May you, Lord God, be lifted up in my life today through thoughts of thanksgiving, words of worship, actions of obedience and attitudes of trust, for you, as the Good Shepherd, are worthy of all exaltation and honor. Amen."

February 3

"The LORD Almighty is with us; the God of Jacob is our fortress."

Psalm 46:7

We certainly have been privileged to live here in the Middle East for the last two years. Although it's been difficult at times, we are glad to be here where God wants us. He has given us a much larger vision of what He is like, changing our perspective on problems. Instead of looking at them as hills to climb, bringing discouragement and exhaustion, He has taught us to look at them as rapids in a river through which He guides us. Every moment there is an unexpected turn, and we must perform to our utmost while the Lord is the One who takes our obedience and carries us through. "The Lord is my shepherd" has taken on new and rich meaning for us as He shepherds us through the rapids of life.

His title, "Lord Almighty" ("Lord of Hosts" in the King James) has also been very comforting for us: He has never lost a battle, never been defeated and never will. As our hearts are right and we wait on Him, He fights for us.

When King Hezekiah was unexpectedly faced with a huge army, he called on the Lord of Hosts and the enemy was vanquished. Joshua, before the battle for Jericho, met with the captain of the Lord's hosts and got his instructions for a victory. And we wait for Him now, knowing He will help as we pray Psalm 25:2, "…in you I trust, O my God. Do not let me be put to shame, nor let my enemies triumph over me."

Right now we are facing a minor battle. Friends in the States have sent us good used clothing to be distributed to poor people here, but the customs officials say we must pay very high taxes on them. Our lawyer says this is not what the law says, but the only way to counter the decision of the customs agents is to open a court case. This does not seem the best route, especially as court cases can drag on for years here. Instead we are praying for God to do something about and for the person responsible for imposing the non-legal tax on our package. No answer is in sight, but our Lord is fighting for us. We can praise Him now for whatever answer He chooses to give before it comes.

Prayer: "Lord, today help me to live in the light of your being the Lord of Hosts, trusting you to fight for me where I can't fight for myself. Help me to pray first and work second, recognizing that without you I can do nothing. Glorify yourself in me as I trust in you. Amen."

February 4

"To whom, then, will you compare God? What image will you compare him to?"

Isaiah 40:18

You, O Triune God, are the Great One, living far above the tiny collection of atoms we call home. To grasp how eternally and infinitely huge you are is impossible for our finite minds. As Isaiah wrote: "Surely the nations are like a drop in a bucket, they are regarded as dust on the scales" (Isa. 40:15). The billions of people on earth, to us a mighty throng, are to you a tiny, insignificant speck, one drop, hardly noticeable. You are so much greater than all the people who have ever lived and you are involved in much bigger things, like the birth and death of stars, yet you love and care for each insignificant, tiny person.

"[He] weighs the islands as though they were fine dust." All the islands of the world are microscopic before you, Lord, easily blown away by a breath. You, in contrast, are massive, monumental, majestic, immovable and mighty. You are eternal and everlasting, the opposite of the temporary, tiny and tentative islands of the earth.

"Lebanon is not sufficient for altar fires, nor its animals enough for burnt offerings" (Isa. 40:16). Your greatness, your holiness, your righteousness all deserve lavish, abundant, continual worship, but in the world there is not enough wood or animals to offer up in sufficient sacrifices. Which is why you offered up yourself as Jesus to pay our penalty, to move worship beyond blood sacrifice to Spirit and Truth, to the sacrifice of praise. Praise be to you, the worthy One, the righteous Ruler, the caring King.

"Before him all the nations are as nothing; they are regarded by him as worthless and less than nothing" (Isa 40:17). In the light of your presence, Lord, the nations are like microscopic flecks of dust, unimportant, useless, harmful. All their cultures, wars, cities and achievements are less than nothing, for they flow out of sinful hearts and are on such a tiny scale that they are not worth noting.

But, Lord, in spite of your greatness that fills the whole universe, you not only note the nations, you love each individual, you see what they do each day, you send your Spirit to strive with each one, desiring that every person come to belief and allow you to qualify them to enter the Kingdom of Light (1 Tim. 2:4). You are the Great Lover of your corrupted creatures. You are the Powerful Redeemer of twisted sinners. You are the Tenacious Transformer of our evil actions into impetus to believe. You are amazing, marvelous, majestic and mighty. To you belongs all glory and exaltation.

Prayer: "We praise you and glorify you, Lord Jesus, for your wonderful, complex, inscrutable, holy and gracious nature. You are worthy of honor, exaltation, worship and glory. May I live in such a way today before men and demons, before angels and neighbors so that glory will flow to you from my thoughts, motives, words and actions. Amen."

February 5

"But I tell you, Love your enemies and pray for those who persecute you...."

Matthew 5:44

It never fails to amaze me how the Word can continue to have a keen cutting edge in our lives, even after we've gone over and over a passage and it seems to have gotten dull. But it's our own perception that has become dull, not the Word. God uses difficulties to sharpen both our perception and appetite for the Word.

In confronting the problems God allows into my life, I like to use what I call "God's medicine chest", a set of several chapters dealing with specific topics. Some of these are:
- Psalm 1 --God's road to success.
- Psalm 23 --God's shepherding: provision and protection.
- Psalm 37 –Dealing with difficult people.
- James 1 --Wisdom and dealing with sin.
- James 4 --War and peace.
- John 15 –Growth.

- Romans 12 –Guidance.
- 1 Thessalonians 4 --A Pure Life.
- Hebrews 12:1-17 --Difficulties: why and what to do with them.
- 1 Corinthians 13 --God's Love, my love.
- Colossians 3 --Transforming our thoughts.

I am in the process of rememorizing and meditating on these, spending a week or so on each one. Such wonderful insights come from spending this time of soaking in the Word. Following is an example of how God is using this in my life.

We have been praying very much about a person of authority who has been opposing our work here. My prayer, much like David's in the Psalms has been "Lord, cause this woman to fall from her position, remove her, etc." But God brought to my attention Romans 12:14 "Bless them that persecute you, bless them and curse not!"

Now, how can I bless this woman who seems bound to block any possibility of our doing good? Romans 12 also says in verse 21, "Do not be overcome with evil, but overcome evil with good." How can we do that?

In thinking on this, an idea came: instead of praying for her downfall, I'll pray for her promotion, up and out of the way! Another possibility is to pray for her coming to know Christ. We will see what the Lord will do, as we pray for her--for He will do something. We'll keep you posted. To meditate on the Word in the midst of such problems is certainly profitable and joy-producing.

Prayer: "Lord, help me to pray for those who give me a hard time, to do good to them, to bless them in some practical way. Help me thus to be a light for you in this dark world. Amen."

February 6

"Commit your way to the LORD; trust in him…"

Psalm 37:5a

You, Lord God, are great and strong, wise and firm as you wonderfully guide and direct. Thank you for your careful, precise, powerful and loving ordering of things in our lives. Praise you, Lord God, for your provision for me of illness followed by sleep and healing. Thank you that I feel better after a good night's rest.

This "illness" of tiredness and pain in my chest came at just the right time and in just the right way so I could rest, reflect, relax and be refreshed. Thank you for the quiet times in these days of illness: time for prayer, thought and reflection, planning and creativity.

Praise you, too, Lord for your great work in my life so that last Sunday morning when we missed our exit on our way to speak in a church, my reaction was one of grace: no impatience, no complaining, no grouchiness, just a quiet rest in your grace! This is your doing in my life, for it is exactly the opposite of what is natural for me!

And you showed yourself faithful to orchestrate things for us in this. After driving the 10 miles to the next exit, turning around and coming back, we got to the church at the same time as the church leader who unlocked the door for us! Right on time.

Then I found I'd forgotten the power cord for my computer. However, just before leaving home I'd prayed, "Lord help me to remember anything else I should take." Nothing came to mind, so when I noticed that the cord was missing and thoughts of worry began to come ("Will the battery hold out for both the computer and projector?"), I could reprove myself by saying, "No, the Lord guided and He will provide. It will last as long as is needed." Peace came and in the end, the computer's battery lasted the whole time, no problem. Praise be to you, Lord, for what you gave: the direction, the peace, the power and the good outcome. To remember your goodness and to trust in you is good!

Prayer: "Lord, today things will come which I won't like. Help me to greet them with praise and thanksgiving, to lay down my understanding of things and to embrace the truth of your love and power being at work in the situation, remembering that you have a plan and will work it out well. Amen."

February 7

"Do not be afraid. Stand firm and you will see the deliverance the Lord will bring you…The Lord will fight for you; you need only to be still."

Exodus 14:13,14

When Moses was faced with Pharaoh's great army at the Red Sea, he directed those following him to look to God to fight the powerful enemies pursuing them.

As we face the daunting challenges here of official opposition and bureaucratic labyrinths, folks at home have been praying for God to fight for us. And the Living God, the Lord of Hosts, has been powerfully answering their prayers, giving progress on a number of fronts. It's a fulfillment of Psalm 37:3 "Trust in the Lord and do good, so shall you dwell in the land and truly you will be fed."(KJV)

Here are a few examples, all related to the foundation we've been working to set up. It has been shackled for several months by opposition from various authorities and a lack of competent help. The Lord has used these difficulties to "prune" our plans so they fit what He wants, and then began setting us free to work. He accomplished this by:

- clearing up the police investigation against us.
- giving us an accountant who is well versed in how to handle customs matters for foundations
- giving us an experienced man who could advise us on what to do and what to avoid.
- giving us two new board members and providing a cooperative spirit among all the board members (a nice change from previous infighting).
- Most wonderfully, God is changing the heart of the woman in the government who has opposed us strongly, the woman I mentioned a couple of days ago, the one we'd been praying for God to bless. She wrote a letter asking us to help a man with TB of the bone. We are sure this is a "test" for us (we will definitely help this man), and see it as a breakthrough.

Folks interceded, God answered. Partnership successful. We are thankful for those who "prayed" their part.

Prayer: "Lord, today help me to believe that you are at work when I can see no answers to my prayers, to fear you, not people or events, to stand in awe of your before you answer. Help me to remember the truth of your Word: 'The angel of the LORD encamps around <u>those who fear him,</u> and he delivers them' (Ps. 34:7). Amen."

February 8

"The LORD is faithful to all his promises and loving toward all he has made."

Ps 145:13b

I've been thinking on, basking in, reveling in the wonderful forgiveness, acceptance and love the Lord Jesus has given and continues to give us. Praise be to you, O Lord my God, for you are a God full of love, gracious, long suffering and plenteous in mercy and truth (Ps 86:15). You are completely "other" than human beings: you are great in your thoughts and perspective; you are mighty in your acts; you are faithful to all your promises, you are consistent in doing what is right.

Praise be to you because you are full of compassion, great in grace and caring for your creation. In you there is no selfishness, no negative motive, no evil. You are love itself, a love that flows because it is part of your essence. It is not prompted by any object of love, nor is it affected by anything any of your creatures can do.

You will to love and do so continuously—a rich, warm, wise, firm, powerful ever flowing and transforming love—a love that desires every one of your enemies to be saved and spend eternity with you, a love that strives with rebellious, uncooperative, selfish people, seeking to bring good into their lives, to bring them out of darkness into the light of your presence--when what they all naturally desire is more darkness: "Light has come into the world, but people loved darkness instead of light because their deeds were evil" (John 3:19).

You, O God, are so kind, so gracious, so giving when we deserve the opposite. You are full of mercy and truth—two seemingly contradictive opposites: truth would demand punishment, banishment and total rejection of sinners; mercy, however, at great cost to you, brings forgiveness, reconciliation, transformation, adoption and acceptance, all provided in grace and love. You do not accept us reluctantly, but with warmth, enthusiasm and rejoicing, and we stand in your presence dearly loved, deeply cared for, doted on and delighted in!

You, O Elohim, are the wonderful, Triune God whose love and compassion, grace and patience, mercy and goodness are far beyond what we can comprehend. Glory be to you, honor be to you, exaltation be to you forever and ever.

Prayer: "Lord, help me today to live in the light of your Love, growing in my grasp of who I am in you: a child of the King, a sibling of the Lord Jesus, a partner in your plans. Help me to reject the view of the world, that I am of no importance, and to live in the truth of your Word, that in you I am chosen, holy and dearly loved. Amen."

February 9

"And pray in the Spirit on all occasions with all kinds of prayers and requests. With this in mind, be alert and always keep on praying for all the saints."

Ephesians 6:18

This week I've had the privilege of strolling about in Romans 8, admiring all the treasures found there. How good it is to memorize these verses and let the Truth of them sink deep into my soul.

One point that stood out is the emphasis on prayer: "Likewise the Spirit helps our weaknesses…the Spirit intercedes for us…he intercedes for the saints according to the will of God." And later, speaking of the Lord Jesus, he "is at the right hand of God and is also interceding for us…" (Rom. 8:26,27,34).

With a prayer team like this of Jesus and the Holy Spirit behind us as we seek to obey Him, how can we be failures!!!? Well, if we refuse to obey God, we will fail, but if we want to be a profitable child of God and live according to His Word, we can be effectively useful for Him (2 Pet. 1:8).

What a comfort to know that the Lord Jesus is so involved in all we do and is not just watching us but is doing something about each event, the first being to pray for us. This is a good example for us: He prays before acting—so should we.

Jesus demonstrated His commitment to prayer in his life on earth: "Very early in the morning, while it was still dark, Jesus got up, left the house and went off to a solitary place, where he prayed" (Mar. 1:35).

Even shortly before his final tortures began, he thought of others and prayed for all His future children, saying "My prayer is not that you take them out of the world, but that you protect them from the evil one…My prayer is not for them alone. I pray also for those who will believe in me through their message, that all of them may be one, Father, just as you are in me and I am in you. May they also be in us so that the world may believe that you have sent me" (John 17:15,20-21).

Knowing this gives me confidence in His love, a desire to imitate His prayer life and an impetus to encourage others to intercede for the unreached. May these glimpses of truth move us all forward in our intercessory prayer lives.

Prayer: "Lord, help me to value prayer the way you do. Help me come to you before deciding and acting, to submit myself to you, asking for your wisdom, your power, your working in this world. Glorify yourself in my life first through my submitting through prayer and then in your answers. Amen."

February 10

"…to You, O Lord, I lift up my soul. For You, Lord, are good, and ready to forgive, and abundant in mercy to all those who call upon You."

Psalm 86:4b,5 (NKJV)

Praise be to you, Jesus, my Lord, Adonai, the One who has the right to expect from us complete obedience and gives complete provision empowering us to do so. I give you glory for your merciful and gracious heart.

I thank you that we can lift our souls to you, telling you what we are thinking, wanting and feeling--being completely honest and transparent before you, knowing that in your Omniscience and Love, you desire our full honesty before you. You aren't shocked by what we confess—you already know it all! You don't condemn us for our openness, you are delighted by it, and through it you give us joy in the light of your presence. You pour out your forgiveness on us! You give us mercy! You give us goodness! (Ps. 86:4,5).

You, O Lord Jesus, are wonderful to your rebellious creatures, showing your grace in giving unearned, undeserved mercy. This flows from your character, for you are majestically glorious in your mercy, even though it is uncalled for, undeserved, unexpected—it is the opposite of what even the angels thought would happen. But such goodness flows from you, O Lord Jesus, because you are Love, you are Light, you are Life. You are Holy, totally other than your creation. You are completely good, wholeheartedly giving, and totally gracious.

At the same time you are also purely righteous, fully just and faithfully true. No one will escape your power to judge and you will judge correctly. Praise you for your umbrella of mercy you have provided for all who will believe, to protect them from your coming wrath, which must fall on all sin.

For these great truths I give you praise and honor in my heart, in my thoughts, in my words, and in my obedience. You, Lord Jesus, are the Perfect One, the Trustable One, the Powerful One, the Eternal One. You are worthy of our obedience, our worship, our trust, our submission. To you belongs all praise and I bow before you, desiring to bring you such exaltation today.

Prayer: "May I obey you out of love this day, Lord Jesus, bringing glory to your name. I want to be transparent before you, letting your light shine down into my soul and then out of me to others. Protect me, O Lord, from myself and my tendency to sin. I want to bring you joy today through obedience. Help me to follow you alone and I praise you now for how you will answer. Amen."

February 11

"He who offers the sacrifice of thanksgiving honors me and opens the way that I may show him the salvation of the Lord."

Psalm 50:23

The Syrian border policeman looked up from our passports. "Not only does your wife have the wrong visa, but your children are not mentioned in it! You'll have to go back to the capital and get her visa changed or she won't be able to reenter your country."

We had just driven two difficult days over narrow, crowded roads from the capital city, and now stood in the gathering darkness between the border of our country and of Syria, caught in a no man's land. Since our tourist visas for our country had run out this day, going back was not possible. Plus, without a stamp from the Syrian border in our passports proving we had entered another country, we could not return to our country.

We went outside the border guards' building and stood there wondering what to do. The Lord brought Psalm 23 to mind, "The Lord is my shepherd, I shall not want." We bowed our heads and prayed, "Well, Lord, it isn't easy to thank you for this, but certainly you know what you're doing here. Thank you, heavenly Father, both for the situation and for how you are going to help!"

This tension-filled event of unexpected difficulty was in reality the privilege of living out the truth of Psalm 86:6-8: "Hear my prayer, O LORD; listen to my cry for mercy. In the day of my trouble I will call to you, for you will answer me. Among the gods there is none like you, O Lord; no deeds can compare with yours." We did not know what God would do, but were certain from both this Psalm and past experience that He would help us.

After praying I went back in and talked with the policeman again. In God's providence he spoke English well (my Arabic is lower than zero!) and listened to my plea. He sighed and stood up.

"I will help you," he said, taking our passports, "But you must go to the police station in Aleppo and get the proper visa for your wife." He stamped and signed the passports and waved us off into the night. God answers when we praise Him! In this case the answer was immediate and we were thankful.

Prayer: "Lord, help me to remember who you are, the Lord of power and help, and to praise you in the midst of whatever difficulties that come to me today! Amen."

February 12

"Turn to me and have mercy on me...."

Psalm 86:16

Lord, thank you for your constant presence, for your being my stability and strength. It is wonderful that, unlike me, you have no sin, no wrong motives, no evil interests.

Praise be to you, Lord God, that you are a God of mercy—six times in Psalm 86 the author mentions your monumental mercy, two of them being, "You are good and ready to forgive and <u>abundant in mercy</u> to all who call upon you" (86:5). And, "You are a God full of compassion, gracious, slow to anger and <u>abundant in mercy</u> and truth" (86:15 NKJV).

In this list of qualities we see the complexity of your perfect character, Lord, putting together aspects that, from our perspective, are mutually exclusive: your marvelous mercy and your tough truth. The reality is that we deserve punishment, death and eternal separation from you, that you hate sin and will punish it, that this must and will happen—yet in your marvelous, unwarranted mercy you have opened a door in the hard, unyielding rock wall of Truth, a way through for us to flee from what we deserve to the forgiveness you have offered us.

And this door of mercy, grace and forgiveness was opened at great personal cost to you, a cost that is ongoing, as you allow us to grieve you in our rebellion, sin, indifference and selfishness. As J.I. Packer put it, you have willfully tied your happiness to your relationship with us! Therefore you share with us the sweet and sour experience of waiting for the as-of-yet unfulfilled perfection of Heaven. We have the longing to be with you, yet need to remain here until your time for us is complete.

Yesterday, Lord, you reminded me of this tension of longing to be like you, but falling so short so often. In my talking with a fellow worker I went over the line in being negative about leadership and fed his already critical spirit. That was not good. I wanted to build up, but did the opposite. Forgive me, Lord, have mercy on me, give me wisdom in how to act now in this situation to make it right, and I praise you now for what you will do.

We praise you, O Elohim, the triune God, who has joined us in suffering, who knows from the inside out what we feel and think—and can therefore give us exactly the mercy, grace and help we need.

Praise be to you, O Perfect One, Glorious One, Lovely One, Great One—you are certainly worthy of praise, glory, honor and exaltation. In you there is both Majesty and Meekness, both Strength and Submission, both Truth and Tenderness--what wonderful combinations. In honor to you I bow down to worship and I rise up to praise.

Prayer: "Lord, help me today to remember how easily I can grieve you with my selfishness and complaining. Help me to choose instead to bring you joy in my belief demonstrated in
obedience. Amen."

February 13

"Bow down your ear and hear me, O Lord, for I am poor and needy...." (NKJV)

Psalm 86:1

If there is one thing that we've begun to learn here in living in the Middle East, it's how poor and needy we are—that is, how much we are in need of the Lord in every way. While we are becoming more and more aware of our sinfulness (lack of "natural" goodness), we also see in a greater way how little control we have over our circumstances—and therefore how much we need the Lord's help in every day life.

In the States, if you want to do something that is right and good, you could be reasonably sure it could be accomplished. Here, we must wait on the Lord to work out all things. For example, someone sent us one hundred pacemakers to give to those who can't afford them here. However, they are being held in customs. Some officials say we won't ever be able to get them; others that we will only get them if we pay a large sum. Our part is to praise the Lord, ask for His help and wait on Him to work it out.

There are many other opportunities for God to act into our neediness. We recently returned from our exit trip to Syria, and the next night real winter weather set in with freezing temperatures and snow. We are thankful that He got us home before the bad weather came.

The trip itself was long and arduous with heavy traffic and rough, winding roads making travel slow. Near evening in one place I failed to see a large pothole and when I hit it, the right front rim was bent and the tire began to go flat. But, praise God, it was not totally dark yet and we were able to drive far enough to find a place to get off the narrow, heavily traveled road and change the tire.

Speaking of the car, difficulties that arose over its insurance still have not been fully settled. Three times we thought all was ironed out, but each time a new problem came up. The Lord is using this to make us look to Him, and also to get us involved with new people here. He is using our neediness to make us more effective for Him! And we praise Him for it!

Prayer: "Lord, help me to see my weakness and neediness in myself and in situations of life as positives, as opportunities to see your power at work, as chances to praise you by faith before I see your help. Amen."

February 14

"God is our refuge and strength, an ever-present help in trouble."

Psalm 46:1

Praise you, Lord God, for you bless your children with your continual presence. Today I feel far from you, without much positive emotion and for this I thank you—it is an opportunity to live in faith, to trust your Word, to live by Truth, not sight or sense.

You, O Lord, have proclaimed yourself as the God who saves us—you are there, despite all the negatives. And in the midst of our woes, you are at work, guiding, protecting, carrying and teaching. You are giving faith-opportunities to offer the sacrifice of praise—times when there is no visible reason to trust you, but plenty of reason from your Word to rejoice in you.

Thank you that our feelings are not the measure of truth, that although our view is so limited, yours is high and wide, full and complete, total and eternal. We can trust you to act in power and wisdom out of your understanding.

Lord God, as I grasp more and more of your greatness, goodness and grace, I love you more and more. You have made us as responders to you great love, which the Holy Spirit has poured out into our hearts. We are deeply thankful for your mighty, undeserved, ever-flowing love that comes out of your very essence: you are Love itself.

In the light of this truth, with your grace, Lord, I want to reject the cultural perception (and feeling) that since you are good, you will protect us from all that is uncomfortable. Praise you for the discomfort and difficulties you allow and send. These events give us platforms to practice and demonstrate the response of faith as we give the sacrifice of thanksgiving, opening the way so you can show us the salvation of the Lord! (Ps. 50:23)

Prayer: "Help me, Lord to reject feelings of insecurity and instead to think Truth, that whatever you allow is part of your plan to bring good, growth and glory to yourself. Help me to praise you in and for the difficulties that come. May you be glorified in my life today. Amen."

February 15

" For you are great, and do wondrous things; You alone are God."

Psalm 86:10

I tell you, it is so profitable to spend time "gazing at the treasures" by meditating on the Word of God. After several weeks in Psalm 86, it still continues to yield new insights. Verses 11 and 12 especially spoke to me.

"Teach me your way, O Lord; I will walk in your truth...." That is a dangerous prayer! It is a serious commitment: "Show me what you want, Lord, and I'll do it!" It means a promise to do things His way, to be teachable, to be kind and humble when I feel like being grumpy, doing my own thing and being left alone. It means praising God when everything falls down around me. It means ignoring my feelings and instead acting on what His Word says. It means, in short, walking in His Truth rather than in my own perceptions and desires.

David realizes that even after he knows God's way, he can't obey in his own strength, so he continues his prayer with, "…give me an undivided heart, that I may fear your name." Our hearts are naturally so divided and deceptive. Only as God works to help us focus our affections on Him, helping us see His wonderful greatness can we really fear and obey Him well.

And the results of such surrender and follow through? "I will praise you, O Lord my God, with all my heart; I will glorify your name forever." True obedience always leads to worship, and true worship leads to wholehearted obedience.

I am thankful that the Lord gives spiritual insight to understand things from His point of view, and then the grace to act in accordance with that Truth. To be able to live this way, we must commit ourselves in the same sense that David did ("I will walk in your truth,") for then we will be able to appropriate that grace. Ah, I have so much to learn, so much growing to do! Praise God for His great patience and persistence with me.

Prayer: "Lord, I confess how often I am half-hearted in following you. Unite my heart to fear your name, help me to obey you rather than to obey myself. Amen"

February 16

"He who dwells in the shelter of the Most High will rest in the shadow of the Almighty."

Psalm 91:1

This verse expresses a powerful biblical worldview: that is, he who sees God as the Most High Authority will obey God rather than his own culture or the pressures of society or the people around him or his own desires.

He who has this worldview understands that our God is the Most High in Power, in Wisdom, in Knowledge, in Ability, in Grace and in Love. Therefore he chooses to dwell in the shelter the Most High God has given: the protection of Christ's blood, the commands, guidance and principles of the Word, the direction of the Spirit in line with the Word, and the wise, godly input of mature believers.

When we choose to obey the Most High rather than the god of culture or comfort or convenience, we can rest in the shadow of the Almighty, trusting Him to protect us from what is truly harmful. If we don't dwell in His shelter, we wander off the path of His protection into the attractive fields of the world where Satan is free to attack us.

Our God is able to protect us because He is Almighty in power, there is no one greater than Him--He is undefeated and undefeatable. By His strong right arm He created all. By His strong Son He provided redemption for all who will believe.

If we have such a biblical view of God, we can say, "The Lord is my refuge [from all that the flesh offers to give me and all the grief that comes my way in a sinful world], my fortress [from the attacks of the world, the flesh and the devil], my God [my highest authority, the One I love and obey], in Him will I trust. [rather than in my own cultural understanding; therefore I submit myself, my intellect and my day to His wisdom and Word, praising Him in and for all]" (Ps 91:2).

Prayer: "Lord help me to nurture a biblical worldview of who you are, so I will choose the Creator over the created, choose you over what your creatures have thought up. You, Lord God are the One who deserves my obedience, my praise, my worship. I exalt you, the great I AM, the Most High over all, the Beginner and Ender of time. To you be honor and glory throughout my day today. Amen."

February 17

"And we pray this in order that you may live a life worthy of the Lord and may please him in every way: bearing fruit in every good work...."

Colossians 1:10

In cold weather the transmission in our car doesn't shift very well. Sometimes it doesn't shift at all, especially when I first try to start off. My mechanic said it was partly due to the low quality of oil here. My wife suggested that being less forceful in trying to shift might make it go easier. Having begun to learn that I don't have the last answer to everything, I accepted the mechanic's suggestion to let the transmission warm up for a few minutes in the morning, and took my wife's suggestion to be gentler in changing gears. The combination works quite well.

Then the Lord brought to mind the fact that relations among people are like my car's transmission. When you want to help someone change a bit, it helps to warm things up first with prayer and grace, and then be gentle in helping them "shift." Those who know my forceful, straightforward character can see from this little insight that the Lord Himself is doing some "shifting" in my own approach to life, and I'm thankful for it—as are others!

The real source of this insight came through a prayer that I use each morning for my family: "Lord help us to bear Fruit of the Spirit today, to take up and use the grace that you have given us," and then I'd go on to name each part of the Fruit of the Spirit.

Through this the Lord helped me to see that often we each have an overriding need to bear one particular aspect of the Fruit of the Spirit, so I would pray that each of us would take up what the Spirit was showing us we lacked: for Nat self-control, for Josh kindness, for Barbara peace, and as you may guess, for me gentleness. So God has answered my prayer by using my balky transmission to get my attention and illustrate what I need to do. Praise God that He works so specifically, so individually, so personally to transform us precisely where we need it right now!

Prayer: "Lord, doing things in my own strength and wisdom is so fruitless; work in me to bring out the fruit of the Spirit; help me to cooperate with you in this. Amen."

February 18

"O LORD, the God who saves me, day and night, I cry out before you."

Psalm 88:1

May your name be exalted, Lord Jesus, for your willingness to be the Suffering Servant. You are glorious in your desire to suffer for your enemies. As Psalm 88 prophetically says about you, "You have put me in the lowest pit, in the darkest depths. Your wrath lies heavily on me. You have overwhelmed me with all your waves. I am confined and cannot escape." So you were, Lord Jesus, overwhelmed, struck down, trapped under wrath, totally crushed and hemmed in by death. You placed yourself directly in the path of God's anger and were unescapably confined to it.

"Why do you reject me and hide your face from me?" When you became sin, the Father turned from you, leaving you utterly alone under His wrath. "I was taken from my closest friends; you made me repulsive to them." You took upon yourself the sin of the whole world. You became sin for us: ugly, repulsive and despised . And because of this, the fabric of the Trinity was torn—those eternal, rich, beautiful, warm and perfect relationships were ripped apart as you, Lord Jesus, became sin for us and as you, heavenly Father, crushed the Son to save your enemies.

"Your wrath swept over me, your terrors destroyed me…the darkness is my closest friend." You, Lord Jesus, endured this wrath, moved through it, drinking every last drop of the bitter pain—you not only endured the jeers of the Jews and the goading of the gentiles, but also all the aggressive attacks of the absolutely evil demonic forces. You waited until the right second and then rose up to defeat the devil and death, shattering the strength of the foe who had enslaved all mankind with the fear of death. You triumphed in a dazzling blaze of glory: defeating, dethroning, destroying death and the devil with all his diabolic deceit.

Only you, only you, Lord Jesus, could have done this, and you did it at the right time and in the right way! You accomplished it perfectly! Your work is finished, you have opened a doorway between the dominion of darkness and the Kingdom of Light, calling all the prisoners of the devil to come out into the warmth of your love and forgiveness.

You, Lord Jesus Christ, are worthy of all Praise and Honor, Exaltation and Magnification. You are the Great and Humble Lord, the Mighty and Meek Savior, the Most High and the Most Holy. To you be glory, both now and forever more!

Prayer: "Lord Jesus, help me to grow in grasping the greatness of your sacrifice, the depth of my natural depravity, and the height of the love and forgiveness you offer to all who will come, that I may be more transformed into your likeness and bring you more glory. Amen."

February 19

"…the Spirit helps us in our weakness."

Romans 8:26

It is so good to be weak, to realize that our strength is insufficient so we can say, "O Lord our God…we do not know what to do, but our eyes are upon you" (2 Chron. 20:12b). It is in this weakness that we begin to really see that His ways are far above our ways, and His thoughts much better than ours.

When I see a need, my first inclination is to jump in and meet that need with my own ideas, strength and resources. However, as I am slowly learning, that is not always the best thing, for I can inadvertently remove a pressure the Lord wanted to use in that person's life.

Fortunately, most of the time the problems here have been so big and complex that there is no way my feeble efforts could begin to solve them. The only recourse open to me is prayer, and asking others so pray with us. And now we are seeing some significant answers to big problems through persistent prayers. Here are several examples.

- There have been some drastic reversals in attitudes. In one person, long-standing bitterness is melting away and he is making efforts to reestablish broken relationships.

- Some of the believers who have been blasé in their faith have recently showed interest in important things, beginning to read and apply Truth.
- People we have shared with are now sharing with others, eagerly asking for material to pass on.
- Our son Joshua has had a hard time fitting in at school. He's learning some very needed lessons about how to be a leader (as opposed to a dictator!).
- Our health is improving. The Lord has been spotlighting some areas where we were wasting energy, and with repentance and redirection, things have been steadily improving.

God uses our weaknesses to draw us to Himself and into His way, getting our eyes off ourselves. Our weaknesses are blessings as they teach us not to trust in ourselves but in the One who made the heavens and the earth, the sea and all that is in it. Are we listening to the message of weakness and responding well?

Prayer: "Lord, help me to see my weakness and inabilities as opportunities to pray more and thereby join you in the great things you are doing, rather than complaining and feeling sorry for myself. Amen."

February 20

"I will declare that your love stands firm forever, that you established your faithfulness in heaven itself."

Psalm 89:2

Thank you, Lord Jesus, for your great faithfulness, which you demonstrated in our talk a year ago with a couple with a troubled marriage. We were in a position of weakness, as we didn't know what to say. In the end you gave the idea to simply encourage them to individually nurture their first love for you.

Then we rested in the fact that as we prayed, you, Lord God, the powerful and faithful One would do the work in them, drawing them to yourself, igniting their first love for you and then for each other. We thanked you then for what you were going to do. Now one year later this couple is doing wonderfully: love renewed, working in harmony and growing in the Lord—not because we were good counselors, but because you gave wisdom, you answered prayer, you brought a new first love. As you said in John 15:5, without you we can do nothing.

Praise be to you for your faithfulness, love and might. You are the Lord God, the Almighty Creator who in your power spoke the stars into being and hung the earth on nothing. You, in your vast strength, are the

Great Shepherd who protected your chosen people, beginning with Abraham and going right through to Jesus, keeping your promise to David to have one from his family on the throne forever. You are the totally faithful One.

You, Lord, are also the undefeated One, marvelous in the way you weave into your works all the responses of your rebellious creatures, giving them power to obey or rebel. You work in wooing, disciplining, correcting, guiding and protecting so you have always had a remnant who followed through in belief and obedience. Praise be to you, Lord, that in your greatness, grace and goodness, your overall plans can never be thwarted.

Righteousness and Justice are the foundation of your throne, Lord, love and faithfulness go before you. You, O God, are Elohim, the great I AM, the powerful, faithful and Triune Creator, the majestic Lord, the mighty Leader and the powerful Provider. I praise you and lift up your name, for you are worthy to be honored and glorified in our lives.

Prayer: "Praise you that today is another opportunity to trust you, honor you, obey you, Lord God. May you, in your greatness be exalted in my life today! May my words and actions and attitudes bring honor to your name. May your personal power, your intimate wisdom, your wonderful knowledge and your loving care be ever before me today so that I will remember to praise you through each hour and bring more glory to your name. Amen."

February 21

"Fear of man brings a snare, but he who trusts in the Lord shall be safe." (NKJV)

Proverbs 29:25

If our time here in the Middle East and the things learned could be summarized in one verse, it would be Psalm 118:6, "The LORD is on my side; I will not fear; what can man do to me?" This lesson has been coming at me from a new angle these past weeks.

As a leader I have repeatedly had the responsibility of telling people news which was not pleasant for them to hear—fellow workers, locals and family members. These were unrelated events, but the basic task was the same: relate a truth I didn't want to tell and they didn't want to hear.

With each occurrence, I had a struggle with fear: what would the person say? Would I lose their friendship? Would there be negative repercussions for me personally? Would they become angry and tell me off?

Obedience, however, is not to be predicated on how easy or comfortable the assignment is. God leads us firmly and clearly. He is as gentle with us in His guidance as we let Him be! If I quench the Spirit by refusing to follow His lead, then I force God to use a stronger way to get my attention. He faithfully disciplines those He loves, including those who resist His leadership. But when we obey, fearing Him, not people, He can reward us the right way, taking us to the next step up in growth.

Knowing this, in each case, after much prayer, in fear and trembling I obeyed what I knew to be the Lord's desire. And, in each case, in the end it worked out well.

Obviously obedience is the best path, but when it comes down to the nitty-gritty, it requires faith in God and His ways, denial of self and love for the other. It is so good to obey in spite of the possible problems and pain, for the Lord can always handle those, working them out for good (James 1;2,3). Our job is simply to trust Him and obey. This life with our Lord is tough at times, but so very good!

Prayer: "Lord, today as you will bring me opportunities to trust you, to deny myself and love others, help me to obey you, thereby bringing you glory and providing blessing those around me. Amen."

February 22

"He who dwells in the shelter of the Most High will rest in the shadow of the Almighty."

Psalm 91:1

Praise be to you, O Lord, for your wonderful faithfulness—you never leave your children: you always protect, always guide and always encourage. I praise you that you have given your children a shelter that is both your Word and yourself—you who are the Most High, the Final Authority, the Almighty, the All Wise, All Knowing, All Loving God.

You, in your grace, wisdom and love, have provided us with this needed shelter in a twisted, dangerous and sin-filled world. Your commands, principles and examples show us how to live within your protection from sin, self and Satan. And you yourself spread your wings over us to keep us safe; under your feathers of grace we find protection.

Praise you for your invitation for us to come to your shelter and remain in your refuge. As we obey your Word, think Truth, listen to the Spirit and make prayer the foundation of all we do, we remain in your fortress. There we are protected from unnecessary mistakes and unneeded difficulties. We are spared the troubles of those who reject your shelter: the confusion of the wicked, the fall of the proud, the anguish of the stubborn, the foolish decisions of rebels, the stumbling of the self-confident.

As your Word says, "The path of the righteous is like the first gleam of dawn, shining ever more brightly till the full light of day. But the path of the wicked is like deep darkness; they do not know what makes them stumble" (Pro. 4:18,19).

You are our Refuge, calling us to your arms, to your lap, to your embrace. You are our Fortress, calling us to safety behind your walls of truth and power. You are our Deliverer, calling us to worship and obedience as our God, our final authority. You are the Righteous One who has the right to rule—and who imputes your righteousness to us, protecting us from the wrath to come, sheltering us from the evil around us and in us.

You are thorough, you are wise, you are persistent: protecting us and providing for us even when we protest against your profound and perfect Word. You keep on working, bringing us to repentance, bringing us to your refuge, bringing us to transformation.
From within your protection, we will see the downfall of those who refuse your invitation, who decline to obey you. As we stay in your shelter, true harm, true evil (that which will damage us spiritually) will not come to us, for you, Lord God, will work out all that is needful for our safety: "If you say, 'The LORD is my refuge,' and you make the Most High your dwelling, no harm will overtake you…" (Ps. 91:9,10).

I exalt you today, O Eternal Lord of creation and God of graciousness, who rules forever in complete goodness, out of unending love and with deep wisdom. You are worthy of worship, praise, honor and obedience, Glory be to you!

Prayer: "Lord, help me to dwell in your shelter today, thinking truth, obeying what I know to be true, praising you in and for all. Amen."

February 23

"Let not mercy and truth forsake you…." (NKJV)

Proverbs 3:3

Working with a team is not easy. To do so while starting a fellowship in a difficult country makes it a bigger challenge. First, we did not choose each other. Second, we are so diverse. Third, we don't have much natural affinity for each other: I never would have selected any of my present teammates even as colleagues, to say nothing of friends. However God chose us to work together and that needs to be our perspective.

As a team, we decided to make unity a top priority and selected Proverbs 3:3-4 NKJV to be the guide for our relationships: "Let not *mercy and truth* forsake you; bind them about your neck, write them on the tables of your heart; so shall you find favor and good understanding in the sight of God and men." (Emphasis mine)

Mercy is extending to others the undeserved grace we ourselves have received from Jesus. Mercy is the opposite of being judgmental, critical and negative.

Mercy flows from humility, which can be defined as "seeing myself as God sees me." That is, we are all sinners who are faulty and make mistakes, but are also children of the King, forgiven, accepted, delighted in and deeply loved by God. Thus as we will see ourselves as no better than others, we will be in awe of God's acceptance of us and be more willing to extend to others the grace God has given us.

Truth is the foundational part of our spiritual armor, and is to be spoken in love for the purpose of restoration, not accusation. In John 3:16 we see that: because God is merciful with us, we can bear to hear the truth that we are sinners. And, as we are merciful with others, they will be more willing to hear truth about a blind spot they have—and if they are merciful with us, we will be more willing to have our blind spots pointed out.

The practical aspect of this is that we should take time to learn the truth about others. Many times we jump to conclusions about another's actions or words or motives without bothering to find out, in a non-accusing manner, the intent and background.

We here on our team are committed to each other. Each of us is a miracle of God, redeemed and justified, called and transformed, and sent to this difficult country to work together. And we are committed to living together in Mercy and Truth so that we may be more useful for God.

The last part of Proverbs 3:4 points out that if we do live in mercy and truth, we will be better witnesses for God: "…so shall you find favor and good understanding in the sight of God and men." This is a very good motive to get along well with my family, my teammates and my fellow believers!

Prayer: "Lord, unity is not natural; help me to live in mercy and truth so that in humility I can accept, love, "care-front" and listen to those around me, and thereby be more useful for you. Amen."

February 24

"I will say of the LORD, 'He is my refuge and my fortress, my God, in whom I trust.' Surely he will save you from the fowler's snare and from the deadly pestilence."

Psalm 91:2,3

Praise be to you for your great promises, Lord Jesus, fastened at one end to your plans laid out before the foundation of the earth, then stretched over time as a canopy of protection, and fastened at the other end in the conclusion of history when all evil and sin will be swept away and confined to Hell and the lake of fire.

Your faithfulness is our shield and rampart, throwing back the attacks of the enemy. We live every day under your powerful, pure and persistent protection. And you give us a part in this, equipping us with the ever-present and portable protection in the spiritual armor (Ephesians 6:10-18). I praise you especially for the shield of faith, which we can choose to raise with praise to quench all the fiery arrows of lies and accusations the enemy shoots at us.

At the same time, we live with the ever-present possibility of "escaping" to our own devices, wandering off into the fields of self and sin, exposing ourselves to the sinister attacks of Satan. You have certainly given us great freedom of choice, great power to dwell in your shelter or not—and in giving us this choice-potential, you have exposed yourself to grief and pain as we often choose to disobey, to not forgive, to not get up the shield of faith. Thank you for your willingness to continue to suffer grief as you work in our lives to conform us to Christ.

Praise you for your persistence in moving us towards maturity, bringing diverse difficulties our way so that we can practice procuring your grace, persisting in prayer, acting in wisdom, obeying in joy, and thereby be protected from the "snares of the fowler."

Yours is such love, such kindness, such empowering, such willingness to suffer for the good of your children! There is no other like you! You are the Lord my God, you are the Creator and Savior, King and Shield, Protector and Redeemer, to you be glory and honor and praise forever.

Prayer: "I bow before you, my King, and give myself to you anew with all my heart, mind, soul and strength. May I honor you today in all I say and do. Lead me in what is righteous, good, lovely and graceful. Amen."

February 25

"The LORD is righteous in all his ways and loving toward all he has made."

> Psalm 145:17

Today I read an article on the powerful, devastating earthquake that occurred in Haiti: much suffering and heartbreak, much death and destruction, much stench from the thousands of dead bodies piled up in a warm climate. What a horrendous happening.

Yet you, Lord are there and at work. This is true, and I must thank you for it, even though my heart is pained to see all the devastation and suffering. I cannot imagine what it must be like to be in such a place, to have to deal with such chaos, suffering, trauma and heart wrenching scenes: piles of dead bodies, the wounded with no help, people thirsty and hungry with no supplies, all the buildings just piles of rubble, the streets clogged with debris. Yet I know from your Word that you give grace to your children who are in the midst of that disaster so that they are not just able to cope, but to rise up and help others. I can rest in you.

And You, Lord God, are not just there, you also suffer with them, you hurt with them. And you are active, working out greater things for the good of all: the salvation of many, the repentance of many, the long term, eternal good of many, and for your glory. You know their hearts, their needs, their desires and how open they are to truth. You are working in all of them to bring as many as are willing into the Kingdom.

Yes, you are there, Lord. You are working powerfully for good, to open eyes, to show that the only stability in this world is in you, to bring people to yourself. As it says in Rev. 9:20,21, "The rest of mankind who were not killed by these plagues still did not repent of the work of their hands; they did not stop worshiping demons, and idols of gold, silver, bronze, stone and wood—idols that cannot see or hear or walk. Nor did they repent of their murders, their magic arts, their sexual immorality or their thefts".

You also are working to chasten believers and to give your children opportunity to carry your grace to those in need. You are also exposing the sin of men--shoddy building practices, corruption and lack of maintenance have made the disaster much worse.

Praise you for your greatness, O God, that in the overview of all you know what you are doing, as well as in the details. You are the only One worth trusting, worth following, worth obeying. You are the One who brings meaning in chaos, purpose in suffering, wisdom in disaster.

Epilogue: *Several months later I read a report by a number of Christian agencies working together in Haiti, telling of tens of thousands that have come to Christ in the aftermath of the earthquake, and of many believers who have rededicated their lives to living for Him. God is faithful and good! He uses all that He allows to come to us for our good and His glory.*

Prayer: "Lord, lift my eyes to be able to see and understand the greater picture of what you are doing in the happenings of the world, as you move history to a conclusion and use disasters and difficulties to sweep as many people as are willing into the Kingdom of Light and Eternity. Deepen my trust for you; help me to praise you in and for all things. Amen."

February 26

"Find rest, O my soul, in God alone."

Psalm 62:4

Anxiety, tension and pressure. These are a reality in a fallen world and this week they were very real for me as wave after wave of difficulty rolled over us: broken schedules, dashed hopes, tension-filled relationships, hampering sickness, unreasonable demands of others (at least from my perspective), mistakes, disaster looming in a couple of areas, conflicts of value and potentially dangerous exposure to the authorities. It was enough to make a strong man cringe, and that I am not very strong.

But our Father is faithful. In each case He led me to Scripture which gave perspective: John 8:32, "You will know the truth and the truth will set you free...." And Isaiah 30:15-16, "This is what the Sovereign LORD, the Holy One of Israel, says: 'In repentance and rest is your salvation, in quietness and trust is your strength, but you would have none of it. You said, "No, we will flee on horses." Therefore you will flee!'"

It is very easy, when under pressure, to flee on the horses of our own wisdom, of man's help, of our feeble efforts. But real help and strength come from spending time with our Father, telling Him of our needs and repeating Truth to ourselves.

"He who dwells in the shelter of the Most High will rest in the shadow of the Almighty." (Ps 91:1). The Hebrew word for "Almighty" means the one who satisfies *and* the one who fights for us. We can rest in the midst of anxiety, tension, uncertainty and pressure if our trust is in the Almighty One who has unlimited power, unlimited knowledge as well as unlimited wisdom--and has promised to fight for us.

Our part is to pour out our hearts to Him and to look to His Word, meditating on passages that tell us what ultimate reality is. This allows Him to strengthen us while He works on the problems before us.

It's been a profitable week from the standpoint of spiritual growth! We are happy to be here in the Lord's "precious cooker" and to serve Him.

Prayer: "Lord, as difficulties come today, help me to flee to you in prayer and thanksgiving, to think your truth and to be set free from the worry and stress of this world. Amen."

February 27

"May the God of hope fill you with all joy and peace as you trust in him...."

Romans 15:13a

Praise be to you, Lord Jesus, King of Peace, God of Grace, Giver of Good. You, in your wisdom have brought to us the possibility of peace, but have left to us the practice of taking up, implementing and enjoying it. You invite us to dine with you at the table of peace; if we refuse to sit down and join you by trusting you, we, by our own choice, live in turmoil, worry and fear.

I praise you, Lord Jesus, for what you have done in your great Love, Wisdom and Faithfulness, making peace possible. In your passion you have provided for all people a passage from the kingdom of darkness into the Kingdom of Light. You have made peace available to all by sacrificing yourself.

Without you, Lord Jesus, there can be no peace. Without trusting you there can be no rest. You are a wonder, loving your enemies so much that you provided them peace at great personal cost. And in your wisdom you made us responsible for taking up and enjoying peace through trust and obedience.

So now we can have peace, first with you, Heavenly Father, through the Lord Jesus Christ, by confessing our sins, receiving forgiveness and surrendering to you as our Lord.

Then we can have peace within when we forgive ourselves as you have forgiven us.

After that we can have peace with others by forgiving them as you have forgiven us, and by asking for forgiveness when we commit an offence against them. The outcome is the release of peace from above, bringing peace within and the flow of peace without.

This peace is carried on into our day as we trust in you, lifting up the shield of faith by praise, which is the demonstration of our trust in you, for, "You are good and ready to forgive and plenteous in mercy to all those who call upon you" (Ps. 86:5, KJV).

As we trust in you, your peace continues to fill us, and opens the way for joy and hope: "May the God of hope fill You with all joy and peace *as You trust in Him* so that Your lives may overflow with hope by the power of the Holy Spirit" (Rom. 15:13 – emphasis mine). Without our trusting, none of this will come to pass.

You are wise, O God, you are worthy of praise, you are wonderful in insight, you are a wonderment to all who know you. To you, Lord Jesus, belongs all honor, glory and praise, for you are the Lamb of God, the Savior of the world, the Prince of Peace, the Harbinger of Hope, the Creator of all, the Ender of time, the Lover of our souls, the Bringer of justice, and the Minister of mercy. We exalt you, we lift up your name, we magnify your majesty, we bow down in worship, and we rise up to obey.

Prayer: "Lord God, King of Peace, help me today to have peace with you, confessing all sin and receiving your forgiveness; to have peace with myself, forgiving myself for my failures and sins because your shed blood covers them; and to have peace with others, forgiving them as you have forgiven me. Help me to walk through this day in peace with all because of your great sacrifice, Lord Jesus. Amen."

February 28

"'They will fight against you but will not overcome you, for I am with you to rescue and save you,' declares the LORD."

Jeremiah 15:20

"Yes, we'd like you to work for us; you can probably start next week!" Elapsed time to present: 75 days and work has not started.

"Your telephone will be connected next week." Elapsed time to present: 92 days, still no phone.

Waiting is a major aspect of life here in the Middle East. It isn't that the people making these promises are lying; they believe what they say and may even work hard to get us what they promised, but it's just difficult to get things done here.

God, however, has much use for these delays. In this constant waiting and suspense that fills our lives, the Word has given us great comfort. Psalm 46:7 says, "The Lord of Hosts is with us…." (NKJV)

Who is this, "Lord of Hosts?" He is the commander of the Angelic Armies of Heaven, the only undefeated force in the Universe! His power is unlimited, His knowledge is absolute and His wisdom is unassailable. He wants to fight our battles for us and defeat the enemies who are far more powerful than we are.

In Jeremiah 1:19 God calls to us, "'They will fight against you but will not overcome you, for I am with you and will rescue you,' declares the LORD." All He wants is our admission of our own inadequacy, weakness and need. With that, we can step back to prayer and let the Almighty One do the work in and around us, obeying Him in the part He has for us, rather than carrying the burden of the whole matter.

Instead we tend to fight, push, work and strive against forces we neither understand nor can possibly defeat. All the while our Lord patiently calls to us, "Come, take refuge in me, let me fight this battle for you." Our reply should be, "…the LORD has become my fortress, and my God the rock in whom I take refuge" (Psa. 94:2).

Our part is to pray, praise and trust while we attend to the daily duties that really do belong to us. At the right time and in God's way these desired things will come to pass--as He deems best. In the meantime our Lord is more interested in the development of what we are than in what we get done. As my wife is fond of saying, "Waiting on the Lord is the greatest economy of time."

Prayer: "Lord, help me to bring my problems, frustrations, failures and dreams to you, to leave them with you and to be faithful in obeying you in the mundane duties I know are your will. May you fight for me, may you bring to pass all that you desire. I praise you now for what you will work out. May you be glorified in it all. Amen."

February 29 (For Leap Year)

'Because he loves me,' says the LORD, 'I will rescue him....' "

Psalm 91:14

You, Lord Jesus, are faithful, you are the epitome of follow-through. You speak a promise and it will come to pass. You bind yourself with a Word and always do it. For instance, in Psalm 91:1 you powerfully declare, "He who dwells in the shelter of the Most High *will* rest in the shadow of the Almighty." There is no doubt, no possibility of failure in this rest, if we remain in the protection you have provided.

I praise you, Lord God for your righteousness displayed here: you cannot lie, you always follow through, you promise and act, you continually keep your word. I praise you that your character never changes, your Word never proves false, your faithfulness never ends, your presence never leaves us, and your love endures for eternity.

Psalm 91:14-16 expounds on your faithfulness further: "Because he loves me," says the LORD, "I will rescue him; I will protect him, for he acknowledges my name. He will call upon me, and I will answer him; I will be with him in trouble, I will deliver him and honor him. With long life will I satisfy him and show him my salvation."

You, Lord Jesus, are the Almighty, the all Powerful, all Sustaining and all Providing One. Because of Your unlimited power, you are able to provide whatever is needed in wisdom, direction, protection, help and material things. Your faithfulness guarantees that You will always follow through on your promises to use your Almightiness as the shield and rampart of those who choose to dwell in the shelter of your Word, your salvation, your commands, your guidance. Praise be to you, Lord Jesus, for your great power, your sustaining heart, your rich wisdom, your deep love and your unshakable faithfulness.

Prayer: "You, Lord Jesus, deserve praise and glory both now and forever. I bow down in worship, giving you honor before all, and I rise up to obey you today in all I do. Help me to be a glory-giver by offering the sacrifice of thanksgiving in each event. Amen."

MARCH

March 1

"Blessed are they who maintain justice, who constantly do what is right."

Psalm 106:3

Lord Jesus, you love righteousness and justice. You who are pure and perfect, you call us to your high and holy standards, promising us blessing when we keep them. But sadly, we do not do this, for we are so self-centered, so self-willed, so self-serving. Just like the Israelites, "We have sinned, even as our fathers did; we have done wrong and acted wickedly...they gave no thought to your miracles; they did not remember your many kindnesses, and they rebelled by the sea, the Red Sea" (Ps 106:6,7).

In our crises, large and small, we, like the Israelites, forget your goodness, forget all the ways you have helped us in the past. Instead we get impatient and wallow in disappointment and self-pity. We look only at our own plans and lack of self-fulfillment, forgetting all that you have done in our lives: the protection, the provision, the prayers answered, the many positives.

But, Lord God, even when we don't repent, you are patient and good to us, fulfilling your purpose for us, as you did with the children of Israel: "Yet he saved them for his name's sake, to make his mighty power known" (Ps. 106:8).

You have higher plans, greater purposes, deeper reasons for acting than just dealing with our sins—you save us in spite of what we are, and give us a significant part in your plans. You have mercy because of your great heart of love for all, because of your great and mighty plans for the future.

We however, persist in our rebellious ways: "Then they despised the pleasant land..." (Ps 106:24a). You, Lord, lay before us what you know to be a pleasant possibility, like the country of Canaan; however we see only the problems, with giants in the land, the walled cities and danger—threats to our lust for self-fulfillment, our security, our comfort.

"…. they did not believe his promise" (Ps 106:24b). We look not to you, but to the problems before us; we fail to recognize that each difficulty, each obstacle, each burden is a chance to see your promises come to pass, to see you act, to bring you glory. We fail to flee to your Word, to remind ourselves of your promises and how you have fulfilled them in the past.

"They grumbled in their tents and did not obey the LORD" (Ps 106:25). We fail to praise you for the difficulties you allow in our lives. We choose not to see them as a call to action, to an adventure with you, to a chance to join you in your great redemptive plan for the universe. We see only our own inconvenience.

Therefore we grumble, bringing great dishonor to you—our unbelief, our rebellion against your Word and Character steal glory and praise and honor from you before the unseen hosts of demons and angels, from before the people around us, from our own eyes. We dishonor you for the sake of our own convenience!

Forgive us, Lord God, Heavenly Father. For your name's sake, forgive us, cleanse us, bring us forward in our relationship with you. Help us to remember our sins, our selfish tendencies, our self-absorbed self-serving, self-centered orientation, and to reject them all. Help us to walk instead in the light of your gracious, powerful, wise and loving presence, lifting up your name in praise for all that comes to us: both light and shadow, what is pleasant and distressing, positive and negative, in health and sickness, success and failure, fulfillment and emptiness, fruitfulness and frustration. For then we will be joining you in your great plan of redemption and transformation of all.

Prayer: "Help us, Lord, to see the larger picture of your Greatness, your Glory, your Grace. Help us to view all that comes into our lives from your perspective, knowing that you, the Sovereign Lord, the King of Glory, the Ruler of the Universe have filtered every detail for our good, have given all the grace we need, and in every instance give us opportunity to lift your name on high. This is the purpose of our existence. Help us, O Lord, to continually 'offer the sacrifice of praise that we may honor you, and open the way that you may show us the salvation of the Lord' (Ps 50:23). Amen."

March 2

"Through Jesus, therefore, let us continually offer to God a sacrifice of praise—the fruit of lips that confess his name."

Hebrews 13:15

As I was reading through Psalms in the NIV, a new aspect of an old truth leaped out at me. Ps 50:15 has often been called "God's telephone number:" "…call upon me in the day of trouble; I will deliver you and you will honor me." But, the preceding verse gives two conditions to be fulfilled before we call upon the Lord in our day of trouble. "Sacrifice thank offerings, fulfill your vows in the Most High, and [then] call upon the Lord…."

First we are to give thanks in all. Then we are to obey what we know to be right. And third, we are to call on God as our first resort, not the last.

"Sacrifice thank offerings"—this points to the fact that to give thanks in and for all things is not an easy, inexpensive response; it can require self-denial and sacrifice. In difficult, disappointing situations it requires going against our emotions, sometimes against logic, and usually against the opinion of the crowd. But it opens the way for the Lord's helping us.

The last verse of Psalm 50 reiterates this powerful truth: "He who sacrifices thank offerings honors me, and prepares the way so that I may show him the salvation of God." (NIV) How often have I blocked God's help by a rebellious heart, by an unthankful attitude? When my hands are full of my own concerns, opinions and work, God can't fill my hands with His help, can He?

This truth was demonstrated to me by a friend who was pressed in upon by a number of problematic situations. My advice was to thank God for these, and my friend, totally out of obedience to God's Word, began to offer the sacrifice of thanksgiving. Right after beginning this, God started to open my friend's eyes to powerful promises in His Word which now are giving comfort and strength. The problems remain, but my friend is strengthened in his faith and is therefore able to take some steps to solve his difficulties.

This truth is a vital one for us in this difficult Middle Eastern country as we are continually faced with attacks of all kinds from the enemy. But in giving the "sacrifices of thanksgiving" we open the way so God can turn these seeming defeats into victories, which bring glory to Him instead of us. When we give thanks, we express our faith in God's wisdom in allowing this situation and in His power to straighten it out!

Prayer: "Lord, lift my eyes and thoughts to you when difficulties come. Help to remember to give thanks for what I don't like so I can give you glory and cooperate with you in bringing your desired outcomes. Amen."

March 3

"I will sing of the LORD's great love forever; with my mouth I will make your faithfulness known through all generations. I will declare that your love stands firm forever, that you established your faithfulness in heaven itself."

Psalm 89:1,2

I've been meditating more on Psalm 89:15, "Blessed are those who have learned to acclaim you," meaning those who are learning to recognize you in every detail, to be aware of your constant work in their lives and therefore to praise you in every circumstance. They see frequent "God sightings," as you clearly meet their needs.

These believers, "… walk in the light of your presence.…" They are aware of your faithful attendance to them, of your being with them, shining your wisdom into their lives, lighting the way.

"They rejoice in your name all day long, they exalt in your righteousness.…" You are their focus, your qualities are guiding their thoughts, and therefore their actions and reactions, "for you are their glory and strength." They are constantly looking to you for help, drawing their significance from you, aware that belonging to you is a great joy, that you are the meaning of life, the importance of existence, the greatness of their lives.

And you are their security, for you are strong and with your strength you protect them, give them power in the spiritual, mental, emotional and physical realms.

They recognize you as the source of all, the goal of all, the God of all, the glory of all, the end of all. As they live in the light of your presence, they rest in the shadow of your power, they bask in the warmth of your love, they rejoice in the privilege of knowing you intimately, the Creator of all, the Shepherd of the weak, the King of the needy. They choose to live in the truth that knowing you is enough for joy!

Praise be to You, Lord Jesus, for being the infinite God--you know all things and therefore you can lead us through the maze of mixed, murky motives, confused emotions and tangled thoughts that tend to trip us up.

I praise you that as we come and ask for wisdom and understanding, you help us to see what is going on, shining your light of knowledge and insight into the inner workings of our lives. In this you are gracious, you are patient, you are kind, you are good, you are wonderful, you are wise, and you are firm. You are what we need, for we were made to live with you! Praise be to you forever.

Prayer: "Lord Jesus, I bow before you, exalting you as the Most High, my final authority. I agree to obey you in all I know to be true. Help me to see where I am unthinkingly walking in natural ways instead of your supernatural ones. Help me to think your thoughts, speak your words, do your work. Amen"

March 4

"'For I know the plans I have for you,' declares the LORD, 'plans to prosper you and not to harm you, plans to give you hope and a future.'"

Jeremiah 29:11

Playing games has never been an enjoyable experience for me. In fact, I can very honestly say that I dislike playing almost any kind of game. Part of the reason for this is that life for me is a serious matter, not to be frittered away in pretend things that create unnecessary stress.

A second reason for this intense aversion stems from the fact that I don't like to lose! Well, true, no one likes to lose, but not many like it less than I do.

However, most of our teammates love to play games and I was being called upon to participate with alarming regularity. And in the process was performing very well my function of keeping anyone else from being in last place! But in this God had a purpose: He was very patiently and gently working to show me three great truths from a new angle.

First, about security. Losing is a great a threat when you're already insecure. It just reinforces the negative ideas I already had about myself. However, Ephesians 1 doesn't say we are "accepted in the Beloved" because we are winning at UNO! Losing is a good reminder that we must operate by faith, knowing that we are "more than conquerors in Christ," accepted no matter what. A good dose of meditation in Ephesians 1 helped me here.

Second, about obedience. Psalm 50:12 and 23 in the NIV both point out that when we give thanks, especially for things we don't like, we open the door for God's help. There I was, playing UNO again with a score of minus 25, in last place and feeling very sorry for myself, when those verses popped into my mind. "OK, I'll believe you, Lord and thank you that I'm in last place!" You may not believe it, but I won the next 4 hands and was up to plus 10! I quit at that point while I was no longer in last place, but was very impressed with the faithfulness of the Lord to His Word.

Now, I don't take that to mean that I'll win every game if I give thanks for being in last place, because our Lord is not a Santa Claus, but a God who wants us to live by His Word, even when things don't work out as we'd like.

Third, about God's view of things. In rememorizing Colossians 3, verse 4 leapt out with new meaning: "When Christ, who is your life appears, then shall you also appear with him in glory." That means that we are definitely going to win in the long run. That is an obvious truth which I had grasped intellectually, but not emotionally. For one who is over-familiar with the emotions of losing, this truth about the outcome of my life and the positive emotions associated with it, are a great release from being trapped in the momentary and the unimportant losses in life.

All this points to the words of Christ: "You shall know the Truth and the Truth shall set you free" (John 8:32).

Prayer: "Lord, I praise you that in your love we are all valued, cared for and deeply loved. Help me to live in this truth intellectually, volitionally and emotionally. Amen."

March 5

"I love the LORD, for he heard my voice; he heard my cry for mercy."

Psalm 116:1

O Lord God, You are the great I Am, you are wonderful in your ways, in your mercy, in your goodness, grace and patience. You display your glory in great acts of salvation (Israel from Egypt, David from Saul, us from the kingdom of darkness) and are therefore worthy of worship and wonder, of honor and exaltation, of praise and glory.

You are the One who provides all that your children need. You have poured out upon us worth: created us in your image, redeemed us by the blood of the Lamb, chose us to be your sons and daughters, commissioned and equipped us for meaningful and specific service, and you crown us every day with loving kindness.

You call us to belong to you and in that you become our glory and strength. You give gifts to us out of your glorious riches, calling us to share in your holiness, to share in your righteousness, in your divine nature (2 Pet. 1:4), and in your strength.

You call us to be more than conquerors, to be kings and priests, and to be effective instruments in your hands. In our belonging to you, your glory comes upon us and we participate in it by obeying you, praising in problems, exalting in you, rejoicing in who you are, seeing you more and more through worship and the Word and being transformed into your likeness (2 Cor. 3:18).

You, Lord God, are more than we could have hoped for, more than we could imagine, far more than we can know. We get just a glimpse of your greatness in this verse: "May the God of hope fill you with all joy and peace, as you trust in Him, so that Your lives may overflow with hope by the power of the Holy Spirit" (Rom. 15:13). What more could we ask for in life than overflowing Joy, Peace and Hope from you and with you?

You who are our rock, our strength and our salvation, you are with us in trouble, you will save us through it and out of it. To you be Glory and Honor, Praise and Power, Majesty and Might, Exaltation and Obedience now and forever.

Prayer: "Lord, for your honor I want to walk in the light of who you are today: the Mighty, Majestic, Magnificent and Munificent Creator and Sustainer of all. May I live in the light of your presence, finding my joy, strength, wisdom and help in you. Amen."

March 6

"Be strong in the Lord and the power of his might. Put on the whole armor of God that you might be able to stand against the wiles of the devil."

Ephesians 6:10

My disciple leaned towards me, his face very serious, "You know that lesson on spiritual warfare? Let's do that again next week. It's too important to cover just once!"

It was a joy to hear such a statement from a fellow who had never really been interested in reading or studying the Word. The lessons of Ephesians 6:10-18 have been very useful for my disciples—and for me. Knowing who the enemy is, how God has equipped us and how to use these weapons has clarified a lot for all of us.

We have had plenty of opportunity to apply this knowledge because spiritual warfare is an everyday reality, especially here. When we were expelled from our adopted country twenty-two months ago, I began praying Psalm 86:17, "Give me a sign of your goodness so that my enemies [Satan and his forces] may see it and be put to shame, for you, O Lord have helped me and comforted me."

This week God answered mightily, giving such a sign, showing us His power in a miracle almost as startling as the resurrection of Lazarus from the dead! In fact the authorities had told us after our expulsion that our chances of getting a new residence permit were as good as a dead man coming to life. And yet a couple of days ago, new permits were granted and we have them in our hands! In the history of the work here in this difficult country, only one other expelled worker has ever gotten a new permit and we get to join him! When one of the "old-timers" here saw our new permits, she showed them Middle Eastern respect by kissing them!

Fighting the true enemy with prayer and praise, with truth and trust, with whole-heartedness and obedience is the only way to true victory. This adventure of the last two years with expulsion, return, staying in the midst of uncertainty, applying for a visa knowing it could mean another, perhaps permanent expulsion--all of this has been confirmation of the importance of waiting on God in prayer and faith and not giving up. In the spiritual battle, he who persists in the power of God wins.

Prayer: "Lord, help us to take up and use your spiritual armor every day. Guide us in fighting the true enemy with your truth and praise. Help us to join you in what you desire to accomplish in our lives today. Amen."

March 7

"'Because he loves me,' says the LORD, 'I will rescue him; I will protect him, for he acknowledges my name.' "

Psalm 91:14

You, Lord Jesus, are a wonder, able in your incarnation to combine the unimaginable: you were both God and man, heavenly and earthly, infinite and finite, all-knowing and needing teaching, perfect and learning obedience. No one else could have been these mutually exclusive opposites!

I exalt you for your wisdom, your insight, your ability to put together things that we cannot unite even in our farthest imagination. You are the complete One, the perfect One, the holy One, the worthy One.

You also put together things in our lives that seem opposites. Psalm 91 says, "Because You have made the LORD Your dwelling place—the Most High, who is my refuge— no evil shall be allowed to befall you, no plague come near your tent" (Ps. 91:9-10 ESV). But then I think of Job, a man who made you his refuge, yet he suffered great tragedy, heartache, sickness, pain and problems both with his wife and his "friends."

This is hard for us to understand. We must turn to you, Lord Jesus, as you have a bigger and better view of things. Your understanding of harm or evil is different than ours. Evil or harm is not what makes us uncomfortable or disappointed or gives pain, but evil and harm are what damage us spiritually, what drive us away from you. As we make you our refuge, you are always there to protect us from spiritual harm, "Because he holds fast to me in love, I will deliver him; I will protect him, because he knows my name. When he calls to me, I will answer him; I will be with him in trouble; I will rescue him and honor him" (Ps. 91:14,15 ESV). And so you did for Abraham, Joseph, David, Daniel and Paul.

Praise be to You, Lord Jesus, that you reveal to us wisdom, understanding and knowledge so we may join you in what you are doing by offering the sacrifice of thanksgiving in each happening, no matter how painful or problematical it may be.

Praise you that you have given us the armor to wear so that we may avoid spiritual harm in whatever you bring us through. You are faithful to deal with evil, to protect us, to give needed grace, to carry us along, to deliver us at the right time, to work out your purposes in our lives. Glory be to you. You are worthy of worship, honor, praise and exaltation. I bow before you in amazed worship, I rise up in wholehearted praise to live in joyful obedience to you throughout today.

Prayer: "Lord, help me to think as you do, to view difficulties with your eyes, as opportunites to join you in what you are doing, to honor you, to demonstrate your grace to those around me. Help me to take up your grace, to move into and through suffering and pain with endurance, to learn from it the lessons you have for me. May I honor you in trust demonstrated through praise. Amen."

March 8

"My times are in your hands...."

Psalm 31:15

Nancy sat quietly in the little bus, enjoying the view out the side window as it sped along one of the roads that circle the capital city. Suddenly seeing a movement out of the corner of her eye, she turned and looked out the windshield. Her eyes widened with horror as she saw a big trailer truck pulling out into the road right in front of them. The bus driver slammed on his brakes and all the tires screeched as the bus slid towards the truck. Nancy braced herself for the impact—but it never came. The bus stopped literally one inch from the truck! All the passengers heaved a great sigh of relief and muttered memorized Islamic prayers as the bus driver leaped out and proceeded to ream out the truck driver. Nancy praised God for His obvious protection of her and the others in the bus.

This event brought home to all of us a new realization of how God works through us here. When Joseph was in Egypt, God blessed him, and thereby all those around him also benefited, starting with Potiphar and going out to all in Egypt and the surrounding countries as Joseph provided them with food during the famine. The same was true for Daniel; many in Babylon benefited from his being blessed by God as Daniel ruled with integrity and wisdom.

And here, as our God moves to save us, protect us and bless us as we live for Him, those around us are protected and blessed, too. What a privilege we all have, wherever we are, to be the carriers of God's blessings. We don't know for sure what would have happened if Nancy hadn't been on the bus, but we do know from the Word that we are "immortal" until we complete the work that God has for us here on the earth.

Of course, that doesn't mean we are exempt from accidents and difficulties, suffering and pain, but often the Lord does spare us from many such things, and in doing so also spares those around us. In the years we've worked in this Middle Eastern country, which has one of the highest accident rates in the world, not one worker for the Lord has died in a car accident, despite the many, many miles traveled here.

It is important that we walk in obedience to the Lord, for in so doing we can become the "vehicle" for salvation of others, both physically and spiritually.

Prayer: "Lord today guide me in obeying you in what I know to be true so that I may be a means of blessing and protection to those around me. Amen."

March 9

"… he will command his angels concerning you to guard you in all your ways…."

Psalm 91:11

To you, Lord Jesus, the God of creation, the Guardian of Truth, the Giver of grace and the Guide of believers, to you be glory and honor this day. You are the great One: great in purity, in wisdom, in knowledge, in power, in might, in strength. There is no good you cannot do, there is no evil you can do.

You are Yahweh, the eternal I Am: sharply separate from your creation, utterly other than your creatures, gloriously unique in your holiness, majestically mighty in your strength, astoundingly outstanding in Your awesomeness, beautifully bright in your brilliance. You are all knowing, all seeing, all hearing. You are intensely, intimately aware of what is happening in the lives of each of your children, carefully filtering events, protecting and guiding in each one.

As we make you our dwelling place, "the Most High, who is my refuge….he will command his angels concerning you to guard you in all your ways. On their hands they will bear you up, lest you strike your foot against a stone" (Ps. 91:9,11)

How true this is, Lord Jesus, my Shepherd and Protector. How often while I was driving have you prevented me from changing lanes, when if I had, I would have hit a car in my blind spot. You caused me to hesitate, or to look over my shoulder, or to sense that a car was there when I could not see it. You send your angels to help, guide and protect.

I think of the dark evening when I was about to cross a small street but for no apparent reason hesitated, and suddenly a black car with no lights flew by. If I'd stepped out as I had planned, I would have been run down.

I think of the Sunday evening, lying on the couch, when the thought kept coming, "I must check my credit card online!" and when I did, found that it was the last day to pay that month! You protect and guide in the small as well as the large things of life.

I think of the many times when I was working on some construction project when you narrowly prevented accidents, like when the large rock fell off the stonewall and just nicked the end of my thumb—if my thumb had been ½ inch further in, it would have been cut off! Or when my arm caught in the handle as I jumped off the backhoe and even though I was left dangling, my arm didn't break.

Lord, you have been very active in our lives. You have been with us in the trouble you allowed to come and then saved us out of it each time. You have delivered us from all our fears.

You are wonderful and faithful, powerful and ever present, always true to your Word. You are worthy of praise, of honor, of glory, of adoration, of worship. We bow before you in awe, we rise up to love you in obedience, we go forth to praise you throughout this day for whatever you will bring into our lives in your wisdom, love and grace.

Prayer: "Lord help me to live in the truth of your goodness and the light of your guidance. Help me to see your provision and protection and praise you for them. Help me to obey what I know to be true about you. I thank you now for the answers you will send. Amen."

March 10

"What causes fights and quarrels among you? Don't they come from your desires ["lusts" as KJV says] that battle within you?"

James 4:1

I was unhappy, very unhappy--and didn't know why. I snapped at my wife and was impatient with my boys. I felt very tired. There was no sweet spirit of peace and pleasantness flowing out of my heart; instead there was the acrid stench of bitter selfishness. Situations like this explode out of me periodically and I am taken by surprise when I act so badly. However, our gracious Lord, who knows all and controls all, was simply giving me another lesson in faith.

While this upheaval was going on, 1 Peter 1 came up in my devotions; verses 6 and 7 spoke clearly to this situation: "…for a little while you have had to suffer grief in all kinds of trials, those have come so that your faith…may be proved genuine…"

Aha! One reason for the coming of these inner pressures is the Lord was showing me where my faith is not genuine. I expect myself to be "spiritual" when in actuality I am a desperately wicked sinner in need of God's constant grace.

Turning to James, I read in chapter 1, "Consider it pure joy, brothers, whenever you face trials of many kinds, because you know that the testing of your faith develops perseverance" (Jam. 1:2-3).

Again, here is the truth: God was using this distress to make me grow by giving new revelation of the depravity of my heart. And my responsibility? To give thanks even though I felt the opposite, and then ask forgiveness from God and from those I've trampled on and to repent, being kind to them instead.

Taking a pen and paper, I claimed the promise of Psalm 86 "…Rejoice the soul of your servant, for I lift my soul unto to you," and began telling God all that was in my soul: my worry, fear, anger, frustration, selfishness and impure thoughts that had surfaced under the pressures of my unhappiness. One by one I brought them under the blood, and surrendered them to Christ, asking again for the filling of the Spirit. Then I ripped up the paper.

Along with this, I went to bed early and got a good night's sleep. The result? Today has gone exceedingly well. The outward pressures of today are greater, my responsibilities more, but the Lord is strengthening my faith, leading to trust, praise and rest in the midst of turmoil. As He shows me my weaknesses, I can lift my soul in confession and surrender and He is bringing joy to my soul. What a faithful and wonderful God we have—and what a powerful Word He has given us to bring light and peace.

Prayer: "Today, Lord, help me to remember how weak I am and how great you are. Help me to praise you in the difficulties of the day so your power can work in my life, so I can live in a way that will bring honor to you. Amen."

March 11

"Your faithfulness will be my shield and my rampart…."

Psalm 91:4b

Today, Lord Jesus, I walk in amazement under the canopy of your love, knowing that you look at me, not with tolerance, or thinly disguised disgust because of my stubbornly selfish responses, but you see me clothed in your righteousness! You look on me with delight, with joy, with pleasure, glad to have me as your child, as your brother, in your family, in your Kingdom.

You call me to meet with you each day as you stoop low to gather me to your heart, enjoying our interaction. I praise you that, contrary to all logic, you revel in our relationship, you delight in doing good to me, you rejoice in being my rampart, you savor shielding me from harm.

And all this when I deserve the opposite: there is no earthly reason for your love; no, only heavenly reasons.

I praise you, O Elohim, that in your power and faithfulness you consistently shield my head in the battle of each day, you always stand as the rampart between me and the attack of the enemy; I can rest in you.

You are the Most High, the All-knowing, the All-present One, so you are never caught off guard, are never late, are never out-witted by the enemy. Your defenses are impregnable, your presence is unassailable, your plans are impenetrable: the enemy can never get by you without your permission; you are always the Victor in the end!

You, Lord Jesus, are a wonder, a marvel, majestically awesome, massively powerful. Your great compassion has sowed in me the seed of love for you, the seed of submission, the seed of adoration for you. As I gaze on you in worship with unveiled face, you are moving me towards living those sublime words: "Whom have I in heaven but you, and earth has nothing I desire besides you" (Ps. 73:25).

I adore you, I lift high your name, I revel in you, I exalt you. I offer you praise, glory and worship, O Great and High King, Lord of Glory, Ruler of the Universe, Judge of all, Redeemer of all sinners, Concluder of all history. You only are fully Patient and Profound, Gracious and Good, Pure and Perfect. You only are worthy of worship!

Prayer: "To you, Lord Jesus be joy, power, authority, victory and honor today, now and forever. Guide me in giving you glory this day. Amen."

March 12

"God made him who had no sin to be sin for us, so that in him we might become the righteousness of God."

2 Corinthians 5:21

The death of Jesus on the cross was an event he shrank back from, so horrendous was the prospect. In Gethsemane, "horror and dismay overcame him, and he said…'My heart is ready to break with grief'" (Mark 14:4 NEB). Three things brought on this horror.

First he was to become sin. The ugliness, the stench, the putridness, the repulsiveness of sin, these he would become. Think of being lowered into a pit of liquid cow manure, its surface roiling with maggots, the stench overwhelming; and as you go down into it, it gets into your eyes, nose, mouth, and then lungs, engulfing you in its terribleness. This is nothing compared to Christ's becoming sin for us, the evil of it entering His very being as a human.

Then He was under the righteous wrath of God, which had been stored up from the beginning of time against all the sin ever committed and all that will be committed. This unimaginably immense weight of wrath came down on Jesus, crushing him.

And third, Jesus was torn out of the relationship of the Trinity, the perfect place of peace, the unflawed unity, the beautiful balance, the wonderful warmth that had existed from eternity. As He became sin and had wrath poured upon Him, He could not stay in that intimate relationship. His Father turned away and the fabric was ripped, the essence smashed, the unity destroyed. This brought the greatest suffering of all in His sacrifice, not only to Jesus, but to the Father and the Spirit as well.

The amount of horror for Jesus in this experience was immeasurably great. It is an infinite suffering borne by an infinite heart of love under an infinite wrath. And it brought about an infinite solution for finite beings. Only a God who is Love could do this. Only Jesus could be our Savior, both God and man, willing to go through such suffering, which is beyond the comprehension of even the angels who live in the presence of God. And He did this to save us, who are lower than angels, sin-warped rebels who fight viciously against Him, rejecting His way and serving Satan and self. But now He has given us the possibility of becoming His children. Hallelujah!

Let us stand in ever-growing awe at the amazing, unbelievable, contra-conditional and compassionate sacrifice made by the Living God to save us who are captives of death, of the devil and of destruction. May this awe transform our mind, will and emotions so that we thirst after God and spend time with Him every day.

Prayer: "Lord Jesus, forgive me for trivializing your immense sacrifice to redeem us, your evil enemies. I praise you for your great love, your deep commitment, your incomprehensible grace. Help me to live in the light of your love and to love you back in consistent obedience. May your light shine out of my life today, bringing you ever-increasing glory. Amen."

March 13

"It is good to give thanks to the LORD, to sing praises to your name, O Most High; to declare your steadfast love in the morning, and your faithfulness by night…"

Psalm 92:1,2

Yes, Lord God, it is good to give thanks to you and praise your name, to note the many, many blessings you give us each day: salvation from Satan, self and sin; the gifts of sight, speech and hearing; hands that can do so much; feet that can carry us; hearts that beat thousands of times each day; a brain with millions of connections overseeing the functions of a multitude of organs without us having to give a thought to them. And along with these, you daily give us food, water, warmth, a bed, a home, family, friends, a church family, work, transportation, protection…on and on we could go. You are so gracious to your children, giving us such good gifts when actually in our old selves we deserve the exact opposite.

As we begin each day, we can declare your steadfast love, trusting you to do what is best, to bring to us what is good, to protect us from what is evil. And in the evening we can look back and note God sightings, seeing how you protected, provided and guided, declaring your faithfulness to all around us.

We praise your name, Lord God, the Most High. You are the Source of all, you are the Sustainer of all, you are the Ruler and Ender of all. You are the final Authority, you are the Paragon of Perfection, you are the Righteous Ruler, the Holy Healer, the Powerful Protector.

There is no one like you. "For who in the skies above can compare with the LORD? Who is like the LORD among the heavenly beings? In the council of the holy ones God is greatly feared; he is more awesome than all who surround him" (Ps. 89:6,7). You, O God, are the greatest in power, wisdom and goodness. You are able to create stars by the billions, to hang the earth on nothing, to begin and end history, to defeat any enemy, to protect, guide and lead us in every circumstance. You are worthy of praise and exaltation all day long!

Prayer: "Lord, help me today to look around and see all the wonderful gifts you have given me, to reject complaining and instead rejoice in your rich love, your abundant provision and your loving care. Amen."

March 14

"I pray also for those who will believe in me.…"

John 17:20b

He glanced sideways to make sure no one else in the restaurant was near enough to hear what he was going to say. Then he leaned towards me, his face deadly serious. Only his eyes betrayed the excitement he felt as he spoke.

"Tell me, just where and how I can apply for this eternal life!" My mind went back over the four or five long discussions we had had earlier, and knew that this man, Orin, was serious in his questioning.

God had been preparing him for years for this conversation. He had been born in a remote, primitive village far out in the East where there was no possibility of hearing the gospel. But when he was five years old, while playing in the ruins of a church, he had asked himself this question, "I wonder, is the God of this church the same as the God of our Mosque?" Then he'd spent the next 29 years looking for an answer, and I was the first Christian he had been able to find!

At our first meeting I had given him the Gospel of Mark, which he read extensively, memorizing portions and asking me many questions. He knew he was a sinner ("I can't take one step without sinning"), an unusual insight for a Musl.im, evidencing a genuine work of the Holy Spirit. He somewhat understood the price of persecution he would have to pay for being a Christian: in his excitement of learning about Christ, he had shared with his family and friends and had been strongly opposed. Yet he was eager to put in his application for eternal life, and he did, entering the Kingdom of Christ!

On another day we sat on the hillside, chatting. Below us sprawled the capital city, a wave of red tiled roofs that washed up and over the hills and mountains surrounding the city center. Although sunshine splashed over most of the scene, dark thunderclouds menacingly shouldered their way in from the West, foreshadowing the suffering that would come into his life. But it would be a while before these storm clouds reached us: there was still time to talk.

We watched four children playing in front of their solitary house down below us. The two smaller ones had not a stitch of clothing on. Orin broke the silence. "Yes, I enjoyed reading the book you gave me, but it's more important that we read this," he tapped the New Testament portion lying in his lap. "Tell me," he continued, "what does it mean here…?" And he went on to ask a number of questions.

To have an eager, serious disciple like this who has come out of Isl@m is the dream of every evangelist. This man's coming to Christ is the fruit of many people praying. He is a good reminder to us to be faithful in interceding for the world, for we do not know the distant lives those prayers enter to stir up a desire to know the true and living God.

Prayer: "Lord, help me to be faithful in praying for those who have never heard. Work in them, give them a desire to know Truth. Bring them into contact with your Word. Sweep them into your Kingdom, into your Church, into your protection. Amen."

March 15

"For you, O LORD, have made me glad by your work; at the works of your hands I sing for joy. How great are your works, O LORD! Your thoughts are very deep!"

Psalm 92:4,5 ESV

O Lord God, you are marvelous and we see this in your creation, with the dizzying array of size, shape, variety, color and texture in plants, animals and landscapes. You have shared with us your love of beauty, your graceful shaping, your wisdom in practicality, your intelligence in complexity.

I think about the million optic nerve cells in a developing baby in the womb; at one point, two sets of nerves grow simultaneously, one set from the eye and one set from the brain, joining at the right place, with each individual nerve finding and joining with its corresponding partner. This perfect weaving brings to our brains an exact image of what is before us. And all this is done in the way you designed.

You made our bodies to be so effective, so compact, so efficient, creating some parts to be so multifunctional: mouths for speaking, tasting, eating, breathing, smiling and kissing. Legs for locomotion, lounging, lugging and loving.

You build into our being the ability to enjoy a wide range of experiences. You give us the joy of running, of relaxing, of sleeping, of walking in a snowfall, of feeling the warm sun, the crisp cold air, the tingle of frost, the drumming of rain.

You have given us the delight of flowers with colors vivid and gentle, deep and pastel, having tiny beautiful details within, gorgeous shapes without. I think of the rich red and yellow of a tulip's petals, sheltering the white stem within, like a lady wearing her three pointed crown, surrounded by her deep brown guards—a tiny world of beauty, waiting to be discovered.

You have made joy available everywhere. Think of the joy of a new born colt, staggering to his feet, shaking off the surprise of birth, running at his mother's side. Think of the exuberance of a shooting star, streaking across the night sky. Or the contentment of a crescent moon in winter, cradled low in the West in the bare arms of upstretched winter tree branches. Think of the happy croak of frogs on a warm spring night. Or the joy of a dog, greeting his master in the morning, tail wagging, tongue hanging out, smiling with anticipation of the day.

Your works give us joy, O Lord, they are marvelous, revealing to us your greatness, wisdom and beauty. And this is only a dim reflection of what it will be like with you in heaven, where all will be more of everything: more beautiful, more vivid, more delightful, more tasty, more varied, more vibrant—for there will be no twisting of sin to mar our vision or your creation.

I exalt you, Lord God for your thoughts from which creation flowed, I glorify you for your marvelous and meticulous works. You are worthy, Lord Jesus, of eternal exaltation, of endless adoration, of timeless, whole-hearted worship. To you be glory in my life today and forever.

Prayer: "Lord, I stand in awe of you. May my thoughts, actions and words reflect this awe today. Amen."

March 16

"Since, then, you have been raised with Christ, set your hearts on things above, where Christ is seated at the right hand of God. Set your minds on things above, not on earthly things."

Colossians 3:1,2

The situation here in the Middle East is always interesting—whenever you think it's going to "settle down," to a nice norm, some new problem or emergency arises. Such situations are fertile ground for growing spiritually, and lately there has been such a "growth" in me that I can't begin to describe it. Perhaps "breaking" is a better word than growth. Certainly it is God working as a result of your praying for us and of our meditation on Scripture.

Very simply put, it is an application of Col. 3:1-2 (see these verses at the beginning of this devotional), with God teaching me to set my heart on giving the kind of response Christ would give, instead first of setting my heart on getting things done. This is a commitment to do what God wants instead of what I want: a surrender to obedience. Each disappointment then becomes the opportunity to see where I've set my heart on something here on earth, so I can surrender that to God and praise Him for what He's going to do. This incremental surrender to the inner working of the Spirit brings ever-expanding results.

- Barbara says I am much easier to live with, being more relaxed and less intense.
- More gets done, probably because I have less inner tension and have insight to cut out unnecessary, time-wasting activity.
- I have more energy.
- Things don't get forgotten as much because my mind is clearer and the Spirit can get my attention to remind and guide me.
- The fruit of the Spirit is much more evident.
- And, as a nice side result, I'm a lot happier!

This life with Christ is really something: there seems to be no end to the break-throughs He has for us as we meditate on His Word, deny self and obey Him!

Prayer: "Lord, help me to set my heart on things above, on your values, on obeying you rather than pleasing myself. Help me to think on things above as I memorize and meditate on your Word. Amen." (A good start would be to memorize Colossians 3:1-5).

March 17

"...the wicked spring up like grass and all evildoers flourish, they will be forever destroyed. But you, O LORD, are exalted forever."

Psalm 92:7,8

The world is full of violence, injustice, evil, selfishness, suffering and death. To focus on these is to bring gloom, depression and hopelessness. But we look up to you instead, O Lord Jesus, for you are the Judge, you will bring justice and are doing it even now, in allowing the consequences of our wrong choices to discipline us.

You are on high, you see all from a perfect perspective, understanding the motives as well the meaning of men's actions. You look into our hearts, and weigh all according to truth. You patiently and wisely let us go our way with our tiny view of life, allowing us to bump into walls, fall in to pits and sink into mire so that we can understand the wrongness of our own view and finally surrender to yours so you can lift us up and put us on solid ground.

You work to reveal to us that you have all wisdom, all knowledge, all understanding and insight. You dwell outside of time, see the future and are able to wonderfully guide us in all, if only we will follow you.

You shine your light into our lives, but sadly we naturally prefer darkness, clinging to the ways of the wicked where there is pitch-blackness, where we cannot know what makes us stumble (Pro. 4:19).

In contrast, you Lord Jesus, are light itself, offering illumination to our understanding, light to our path, brightness to our day. With you, "The path of the righteous is like the first gleam of dawn, shining ever more brightly til the full light of day" (Pro. 4:18).

You, Lord Jesus, are to be exalted, to be worshiped, to be lifted up on high and obeyed forever. You are the Almighty One of limitless strength: "Your arm is endued with power, your hand is strong, your right hand exalted" (Ps. 89:13). There is no one able to fight against you and win; you are the Most High King and will bring all of time and history to your desired conclusions. "For surely your enemies, O LORD, surely your enemies will perish; all evildoers will be scattered" (Ps. 92:9). We can trust in you, rest in you, have confidence in your plan when ours fall apart, fail and prove futile. To you belongs all worship and exaltation.

Prayer: "Praise you, O Lord God Almighty. To you we bow down, giving you honor, praise and glory for your invincible might, your impenetrable power and your self-sustaining strength. You are God, you are Lord, you are King—and have made yourself our King, undeserving as we are. We rise up to obey you, for you are worthy. Help us to please you in all we do today. Amen."

March 18

"… set your hearts on things above….set your minds on things above"

Colossians 3:1b, 2

Our God is such a faithful guide. From down here we cannot see much of the future. In fact, we sort of back into it, being very aware of the past and present, but seeing very little of where we should step next. God, however, being outside time, knows what's coming and will guide us if we are willing to listen, as we "seek those things which are above."

Right now God is teaching us that an important part of "seeking things above" is praying through each situation, each event and then waiting for Him to open doors rather than pushing through them in our own strength.

Recently we saw again how God, in His time, answers prayer for guidance. As we have mentioned, the little fellowship we are seeking to start often seems to be on the verge of "taking off" but then gets bogged down on the runway. We have been puzzled by this failure.

This past weekend a man with 25 years of successful church planting experience in the Middle East just "happened" to drop by on his way to other countries. In the discussions with him, a number of areas we have had questions about were illuminated. One sentence he uttered sticks with me: "You can't nail jello to the wall!" That is, you can't start a church with folks who aren't ready for leadership. Such an obvious truth, yet we are so eager to see this church plant "fly" that we had overlooked it, putting leadership responsibilities on those who were not ready. Now we understand the need to back off, do more discipleship and wait until the locals mature enough to step into our shoes.

It is truly an adventure to walk with the Lord Jesus and watch Him unfold for us the terrain where we are to walk. What we need the most is to wait for Him to do so and not run ahead on our own. We need to "Trust in the LORD with all your heart and lean not on your own understanding…" (Pro. 3:5).

Epilogue: *It was ten more years of work before there were men ready for leadership! And then the fellowship took off wonderfully and has done well since then.*

Prayer: "Lord help me today to walk with you, to work with you rather than wanting you to work with me. Help me to go at your pace, with your patience, by your power and in your timing. Amen."

March 19

"The righteous flourish like the palm tree and grow like a cedar in Lebanon. They are planted in the house of the LORD; they flourish in the courts of our God."

Psalm 92:12,13

Praise be to you, Yahweh, the great I AM, the self-existent, eternal, unchanging, holy, perfect One—and paradoxically, the Lover of sinners. While your qualities of righteousness, holiness and justice dictated the necessity of judgment, condemnation and punishment, you chose, through your own suffering, to have mercy triumph over justice, to have grace trump punishment. You called us rebels to yourself, cleansed us, transformed us into new creatures and adopted us into your family, making us righteous in Christ.

You planted us in your courtyard, making us flourish, sprouting lush, green leaves of praise, and succulent, delicious fruit of the Spirit. You make it possible for us to get our roots deep down into the wonderful water of your Word so even in drought we can remain green, bearing our fruit in its season, and being successful in whatever you call us to do (Psalm 1:3).

You are the great Giver of good, supplying what is needed to keep your children growing, maturing, bearing more and more good fruit. You have provided all that is necessary for living a godly life and for overcoming the evil of the world (2 Peter 1:3). Yet in your wisdom and grace, your great patience and kindness, you leave it to us, your children, to draw this living water up through our roots of reading, to remain in your courts, to abide in the vine and to bear your fruit.

To those of your children who keep their roots growing down into the water of the Word, you promise: "They will still bear fruit in old age, they will stay fresh and green…" (Ps. 92:14). As we grow old, lose our physical abilities, have less strength, hear and see less, and may seem to dry up on the outside, we will still bear good, rich, delicious fruit for those around us: the fruit of the Spirit, the fruit of the sacrifice of praise, the fruit of good works, the fruit of people coming to Christ—which is just the opposite of what happens if we live naturally rather than supernaturally. And you cause us to remain fruitful so that we can declare "the LORD is upright; he is my rock, and there is no unrighteousness in him" (Ps. 92:15).

To you, O triune God, be honor and glory and praise. To you be worship, adoration and magnification. To you be power, might and exaltation. You are worthy, you are glorious, You are Elohim.

Prayer: "I bow before you, Heavenly Father in admiration; I rise up in enthusiasm; I go forth to worship you through obedience. May your name be honored today in all I think, say and do, my beloved God. Amen."

March 20

"I will praise you, O LORD, with all my heart, I will tell of all your wonders."

Psalm 9:1

My relationship with the Lord has grown a bit stale of late; I have faithfully met with Him each day, reading the Word, praying and meditating, but it has become quite mechanical. I asked the Lord for a refreshing in our relationship, and He answered with a phrase in a verse that has made a great difference: "seek my face…" (2 Chr. 7:14).

With this phrase came the realization that instead of seeking Him, I had been more seeking His help, His power, and His direction – all gifts He desires to give us – but I had not been seeking Him.

To seek His face, to sit with Him, talk with Him, and to lay in His hands all I have and want, so I can focus on Him, is more important to Him than all that I can accomplish. To seek His face means we have to look away from all that we'd like to be involved in and to look into His eyes. He then, in His love and grace, can pierce us to the soul with the light of His look, helping us to deal with sins we've overlooked or wanted to ignore.

May the Lord ever keep us from "commercializing" our relationship with Him, for always and only "doing business." Instead, may we daily spend time with Him, our Bridegroom, nurturing our first love for Him, gazing upon His loveliness, focusing on His beauty rather than our busyness. Following is an example of focusing on Him.

"I will tell of all your wonders" (Ps. 9:1b). Great and many are your wonders, O Lord, beginning with your character. You are Love, Light and Life. In you there is Purity, Perfection, and Power. You are filled with Greatness, Grace and Goodness. You are Immortal, Invisible and Invincible. In you alone are Righteousness, Riches and Rightness. You are Mighty, Magnificent and Marvelous. You are Holiness, Justice and Mercy. You are God, Lord, and Sovereign. You are without beginning, without end and without time. You are a wonder, you are worthy, you are to be worshiped for you are the One and only God. Glory to be you both now and forever!

Prayer: "Lord, help me to seek your face every day, to bask in the beauty of your character, to fall more in love with you. Then help me to join you in what you have planned for the day, moving in your timing, your power and your wisdom. Amen."

March 21

"The LORD reigns, he is robed in majesty; the LORD is robed in majesty and is armed with strength. The world is firmly established; it cannot be moved. Your throne was established long ago; you are from all eternity".

Psalm 93:1,2

You, O Yahweh, are the Holy One: Pure and Powerful, Sinless and Sincere, Just and Judicious, Rich and Righteous, Glorious and Good. You are majestic, magnificently robed in light, riding on the wings of the wind, commanding the stars, towering over all the heavenly beings in total otherness.

You move in wisdom and grace, you are thorough in your thoughts, powerful in your plans, precise in your actions. You are never shaken, never flustered, never hurried, never late.

In your magnificent being you are awesome in power, overwhelming in scope, fearsome in glory, blinding in beauty, astounding in wisdom, infinite in knowledge. You are the One to be worshiped, the only One to bow before, to surrender to, to live for.

You, O LORD God, are armed with strength. You formed the earth, you shaped the mountains, you created the seas. You hung the earth in space, tilted it at the right angle to provide seasons, spun it at the optimum rate to make each day of perfect length, and sent it off into the proper orbit around the sun, moving it at the best pace, making the year's length just right. You gave it the moon for light at night, for making tides and protecting us from asteroids. You keep all in place until your time is fulfilled and you will end time and history, creating a new heaven and new earth. Your faithfulness is our certainty that the world cannot be moved without your permission.

Truly, we can say with Asaph, "Whom have I in heaven but you, and earth has nothing I desire besides you" (Ps. 73:25). We bow before you, Lord God Almighty, we praise you for your majestic, wise, pure, just and gracious being.

Prayer: "Lord, I give myself to you in offering, bowing in surrender, rising up to obey you in trust, to glorify you in wholehearted application of your Word. To you be glory today in all my motives, attitudes, thoughts, words and actions. Amen."

March 22

"...set your heart on things above..."

Colossians 3:1

I have been somewhat discouraged about how things have been going here. The fellowship is having its ups and downs. Attendance is very erratic and there is a lack of unity and commitment. Most of the people I'm discipling don't have any interest in going to the meetings. Then with university classes starting up and my heavy teaching load, my time and energy have been limited for working with these folks.

Ah, but this discouragement is a very revealing thing: in the light of Colossians 3:1-2, where have I set my heart? Again on results, on success, on my understanding of when and how things should happen. Are these "things above?" No, they are not. When our work and successes become the center of our focus, it is good that we have emptiness and discouragement, for this points us to truth: God wants us to draw our joy, stability and refreshment from our relationship with Him, not our success (Ps. 86:4; 27:4-5; 23:3).

It is a certainty that as people are praying for us to set our hearts on things above, the Lord is using this discouragement to encourage us to do so.

What a wonder-filled thing our relationship with Him is: all that we might naturally consider "bad," such as discouragement, become steps up in our walk with Him as we respond in obedience, rejecting natural understanding and thinking Truth.

In line with all this, in meditating on different passages about God's power such as, "Finally my brothers, be strong in the Lord and the power of his might...." (Eph. 6:10), the question comes to me, "OK, but how can I be strong?" The obvious first answer is prayer. As we ask God to do the things He desires, He will, by His power, accomplish them in His time.

The human tendency, of course, is to push on, try harder and do more; but the higher way is to follow God's plan of action and spend more time in prayer so He will do the work that we can't. "The fear of the Lord tends to life: and he that has it shall abide satisfied..." (Pro. 19:23)

Prayer: "Lord, help me to respond to difficulty with praise, with faith, with a teachable heart. Help me to make prayer the foundation of all I do so you can accomplish what you want in and through my life today and that the credit will go to you. Amen."

March 23

"The LORD [Yahweh] is robed in majesty… Mightier than the thunder of the great waters, mightier than the breakers of the sea—the LORD on high is mighty.'

Psalm 93:1,4,5

Glory and praise be to You, O Yahweh, the Majestic One, the Mighty One, the Magnificent One. Your power is beyond comprehension, far greater than the might of a Tsunami rising out of the ocean, sweeping inland for miles, destroying all in its path. Or the power of the great waves in a storm, pounding at cliffs, wearing them away.

To create the sun you simply spoke. You made it huge, hot, high in the heavens, spewing out tongues of flame millions of miles into space, burning at temperatures beyond our comprehension, emitting heat and light year after year, century after century, millennium after millennium; you control its heat, its light, its life. And the sun is but one of billions of stars in billions of galaxies that you spoke into existence and sustain by your mighty power.

You, O Lord Jesus, also hold together the nucleus of every atom in the universe, keeping positive forces together when they should push apart ("…in him all things hold together" Col. 1:17). Your strength is beyond what the human mind could possibly begin to understand.

In your might you also hold back the forces of evil, you guide the tides of history, you set up and take down leaders, you begin and end empires, you sweep men into eternity when their time comes.

Yet you restrain your might when it comes to salvation. In your love and desire that we love you, you give people the right to choose, enabling them to choose, wooing them into your kingdom rather than forcing them. You are great, you are glorious, you are gracious, you are good.

Your statutes stand firm because you are mighty. You decreed and maintain the force of gravity, the speed of light, the boundaries of the sea, the law of impenetrability—all continue as long as you desire.

And all of this is done in your holiness, meaning that, along with being pure, you are totally independent of your creation. You are absolutely other than your creatures: we are limited, you are infinite; we are bound to time, you are beyond it; we are weak, you are immeasurably powerful; we see so little, you know all; we are foolish, you are complete in wisdom; we are selfish, you are agape love itself.

Like Job, we can only bow before you and say, "You, Lord, are worthy, for you are wise, and have the right to do whatever you desire." You rule, teach, guide, control, direct, decide, decree, act and no one can oppose you. You, Lord Jesus, are the One to be obeyed, for you are perfect and unchanging, powerful and good, wise and all loving.

Prayer: "Lord, we lift your name on high, we magnify you in your majesty, we rejoice in your might, we exult in your perfection, we fall to our faces in awe. You are God alone, you are worthy alone, you are King alone. We worship you in reverence, we bow before you in joy, we rise up with commitment to abide in you in peace and power. Praise be to your name. Amen."

March 24

"Blessed is the man…whose delight is in the law of the Lord, and on his law he meditates day and night."

Psalm 1:1a,2

It never ceases to amaze me how our Lord Jesus works in our lives through meditation. The last few weeks I've been so tired that Barbara has had to urge me out of bed in the morning. I felt sometimes like a 90-year-old cripple. The logical thing would be to get some rest, wouldn't it? However, this is more easily said than done with having to teach 4 hours of English classes every day, plus preparation, responsibility for 12 fellow workers, a number of disciples and the national fellowship plus a family. On top of this there is a stream of visitors in a culture where you can never say, "No." The visitors often stay until late with the average visit being a minimum of 3 hours.

There has so far been no real break where we could get a prolonged rest, so the Lord saw fit to strengthen us in other ways. Each morning as I stood in the bus line on the way to work, I'd run the 23rd Psalm through my mind, quoting it, personalizing it, praying it. Thinking those truths was like turning on the "power faucet."

"'The Lord is my shepherd, I shall not want….' I sure feel like I'm wanting, Lord, but you promise that my needs are being met, so I praise you for this tiredness which makes me depend more on you. Thank you that this situation is a 'green pasture' designed to make me grow."

The Lord wants us to think His thoughts and learn the depths of His truths, to see they are sufficient in every situation. And during this time the Lord kept us going, protected us from getting sick, and enabled us to more than fulfill the responsibilities He has given us. In fact, He taught us how to serve Him better: since I didn't have the strength to do all I wanted, He forced me to spend more time in prayer, and to carefully select what to do, thereby making us more effective.

One day when I was discouraged about the believers and workers as well as my inability to solve the problems, we sang a song in the fellowship "When I am weak, then I am strong…." Again I was encouraged to spend more time praising and praying and the results of this are being seen in those around me. What a great, wise God we have who is faithful to keep us in the Word and to remind us to praise Him!

Prayer: "Lord, I confess my lack of meditation on your Word. Help me to delight in it, to persistently memorize it, to personalize and pray it, getting it down into my soul so I may think your thoughts, will your will and enjoy my emotions without being controlled by them. Amen."

March 25

"O LORD, the God who avenges, O God who avenges, shine forth."

Psalm 94:1

Lord Jesus, you are the conquering One: "El," the God of might; Yahweh ("LORD"), the Holy One who hates sin; Adonai, the powerful ruler who provides all. You are righteous, you are pure, you are clothed in light and robed in majesty. You look down on all mankind and perceive the heart conditions, the motives, the schemes of everyone. "The LORD knows the thoughts of man; he knows that they are futile" (Ps. 94:11).

You are the mighty Judge who in righteousness will ride forth in power to bring perfect justice on earth. You will avenge those who have been mistreated, harmed and exploited. You are the perfect One who knows the exact time to display your righteous anger, bringing judgment, punishment and a proper sentence on those who refuse Your Word, who reject your Truth. You wait in love and grace, showing patience and kindness, continuing to pour out your goodness on all, working to give all the opportunity for repentance.

In the end, however, the time will come for judgment and you will not be late. In perfect knowledge, perfect justice, perfect perception you will mete out the perfect punishment to each and every one who refuses your offer to enter the shelter of the Most High. To those who reject you as Savior, you will come as Judge.

There is so much evil in the world today, seemingly unrestrained, yet we know that you have set a limit, holding back evil from its full extent. Lord, we praise you that you are at work bringing judgment in ways we cannot see: bringing consequences, striking down, removing, preventing and punishing. As evil plays out its role, while evil people "band together against the righteous and condemn the innocent to death," we can rest assured that you, LORD "will repay them for their sins and destroy them for their wickedness; the LORD our God will destroy them" (Ps. 94:21,23).

You are moving now, answering the cries of your people, rescuing them from the fowler's snare, protecting them from the arrow that flies by day and the pestilence that stalks in the darkness. You are our great shield, our fortress, our refuge, our avenger.

Your righteous judgment gives us much comfort, O Lord, for in this world system there is little justice. You hate evil and you will deal with it in truth and wisdom. There is an answer to evil! There is an end coming to turmoil. You, Lord Jesus, are the answer!

To you, Lord Jesus, be honor and glory and strength and wisdom and power and goodness. We lift up your perfect and pure name, we exalt you for your truth, your justice and righteousness.

Prayer: "We bow before your power and love and mercy, we rise up in your goodness, grace and greatness to walk in obedience before you today. Help us to bring you joy in our whole hearted submission. Amen."

March 26

"Trust in the Lord and do good...commit your way to the Lord, trust in Him and He will bring it to pass."

Psalm 37:2

There are so many things that can lead me to anger and reveal the selfishness and impatience within me. This is especially true when living in another culture where questions and responses are very different from what we expect. When taken advantage of, it is easy to feel 'the victim'. This is the result of operating in my own ethical system rather than the local, cultural one.

The Lord has some advice for me about this: "Fret not yourself because of wicked men, and don't envy those who work iniquity, for they will wither like a green herb and be cut down like the grass...." In contrast he tells me, "delight yourself in the Lord..." (Ps. 37:1-3).

When I find myself getting frustrated and angry, it is a sure sign I've been delighting in something other than the Lord, such as setting my heart on a fair deal, or being treated nicely. Then it's time for some confession, surrender and meditation.

I want to praise God for allowing these frustrations in my life as He is leading me to rely on Him rather than my own efforts. Recently several situations have come up where I became angry and frustrated with people; I wanted to collar them and "straighten them out." But, PTL, He didn't allow this, and instead brought me to prayer. Now He is giving opportunities to graciously deal with each situation and individual effectively, one at a time.

For example, for three years I've been working with an older believer who has not wanted to come to the fellowship. He has had lots of excuses. During these three years, the Lord has given opportunities to graciously teach on this point and this man is really convicted now, from the Word to obey God and has begun attending the meetings. This is so much better than going because I wanted him to.

God's work is much deeper and more effective than our little solutions. What a wise God we have, and what a privilege to spend the time preparing the ground with prayer first. When we appeal to the "God of Glory" who "thunders over the mighty waters…whose voice breaks the cedars…and shakes the desert…" (Ps. 29:3), He works powerfully to resolve things in ways far better than ours.

Prayer: "Lord, help me to recognize my anger, frustration and impatience for what they are: selfishness, wanting things my way and idol worship. Help me to do things your way, with prayer, with patience, with wisdom and with grace. May you be honored in my life today. Amen."

March 27

"Blessed is the man you discipline, O LORD, the man you teach from your law…."

Psalm 94:12

How true this is, Lord: there is much joy in learning from your Word— the rich, deep, powerful, transforming, enlightening, convicting, guiding Word of God applied to our lives by your wise and persistent Holy Spirit.

We praise you, Lord God, Father in Heaven, for your great love in disciplining us: your stubborn, rebellious, lazy and self-centered children. You are so patient, so kind, so firm, so persistent in teaching us over and over again the same lessons. Praise you that you never tire of this, that you continue to the end.

Praise be to you for giving us your Word: powerful, perfect, revealing your marvelous character, instructing us in your ways. Praise you that you preserved it down through the years, had it translated and made it available to us. Praise you that your Spirit uses it to transform us as we read, study and meditate on it. As Colossians 3:10 says, we "have put on the new self, *which is being renewed in knowledge* in the image of its Creator."

What joy there is for you and for us as we learn from your Word to trust, to praise in all, to obey without seeing or understanding all. What power there is to rejoice in you when all seems dark, to learn and live in the truth that knowing Jesus is enough for joy, period. That is truly walking in the freedom you have bought for us.

We thank you, we praise you, we lift up your name: the mighty Creator God who is good and gracious, glorious and great, gripping and grand, deserving praise and pomp, worship and wonder, our submission and surrender through all eternity.

Prayer: " We give you glory and praise, Lord Jesus, for all that will come today. We commit ourselves to lift up your name on high by doing what we know is right. We want to praise you in all and make prayer the foundation of all we do. Help us in your power to do so. Amen"

March 28

"Therefore put on the full armor of God, so that when the day of evil comes, you may be able to stand your ground, and after you have done everything, to stand."

Ephesians 6:13

Our days continue to be very interesting and full. Barbara is carrying her multiple responsibilities well: wife, mother, hostess to a continual stream of guests, correspondent to many, witness, counselor, team member and leader. Both she and I have to work at guarding our time and strength, but as long as we consistently spend time with the Lord, things go well.

To give you a taste of the variety of my life here, I will take you through a typical day. Up at 7:15 (overslept because of a late night with visitors). After breakfast took the boys to school and caught the service bus to work at the University at 8:05. During the ride had a very good prayer time covering the different workers and nationals here. 8:40 to 12:30 taught 4 English classes. 12:30-1:30 had a Turkish lesson. 1:30 to 2:00 quiet time and prayer. 2 to 2:45 did editing of an English article. Tried to catch the bus home but it was full. 3 to 3:45 corrected some papers and had some profitable prayer. Was able to get on the 3:50 bus and even got a seat and had a good meditation and prayer time on the way home, arriving at 4;30 PM. Spent time with the boys and had devotions with them. 5:30 a disciple came and we began a Bible study. Interrupted by several phone calls. Then a guest came so we included him in the study. Another disciple came and he joined in too. When another couple dropped by at 8, we ended the study, had supper, and visited until almost 11. Into bed at 11:30 pm.

Although my days are full and challenging, it is my prayer time and meditation on the Word that the Lord uses to keep me going. Thinking the truth keeps me from wasting energy on worry and peripheral items. Keeping on the armor helps in concentrating on the important points and sifting out the unnecessary. As it says in Ephesians 6:13, "Therefore put on the full armor of God, so that when the day of evil comes, you may be able to stand your ground, and after you have done everything [according to God's list, not mine], to stand." Eph 6:13).

We have a good and powerful God who gives us all we need. The problem is that it's so easy to unwisely use what He provides!

Prayer: "Lord, help me to guard my time with you, soaking in your Word, praying for the day, praying through the day. Help me to filter out the trivial, energy draining responses, and to rest in the truth of who you are. Amen."

March 29

"Come, let us sing for joy to the LORD;"

Psalm 95:1

You, O LORD, are the great I AM: holy, utterly other, completely contained in yourself. You need no one, are dependent on no one, stand alone.

You are the triune One, completed and complimented in each person of the Trinity. Within your triuneness all is perfectly shared: all love, all communion, all relationship, all balance, all plans, all honor, all glory.

You never lack anything. From eternity to eternity you have always had perfect peace within, with no sin, no conflict, no strife, no negativeness. Among the Father, Son and Holy Spirit is everlasting harmony, trust, goodness and joy.

And this is the joy you desire to share with all who believe, your former enemies, by coming to them, making yourself known and offering to rescue them from the dominion of darkness, from slavery to sin, self and Satan. You offer us joy, sharing it with us, pouring it out upon us, filling us with it and completing us in it. "I have told you this so that my joy may be in you and your joy may be complete" (John 15:11).

"...let us shout aloud to the Rock of our salvation" (Ps. 95:1b). You have made yourself our Rock, the unchanging, unshakable, undefeatable, strong, great and powerful One. You are faithful, gracious, patient, wise, persistent and firm--the all-good God.

We exalt you, O Triune Lord, Creator of all good and Sustainer of the sin-twisted and injured universe.

You are the Redeemer, Rescuer, Restorer of your rebellious creatures. What a wonder it is to be taken from darkness into the light, from prison to pardon, from slavery to sonship, from despair to the dawn of hope, from evil to eternity, from blindness to beauty, from a stunted life to superlative growth with You!

"Let us come before him with thanksgiving and extol him with music and song" (Ps. 95:2). You, Lord Jesus, are worthy of worship, you who, in providing salvation for your enemies, suffered so deeply in agape love, denying self, enduring the ripping of your soul, the rending of your heavenly relationships, the wrenchingly repulsive role of becoming sin. Through all this agony you continued on and conquered: you rose resoundingly out of death, ascending far above all and have returned to your rightful reign from the throne of the Heaven.

You are glorious in your goodness, wondrous in your wisdom, magnificent in your majesty, powerful in Your pristine supremacy, lovely in light, pure in personality, and exalted in excellence. In you there is no fault, no twistedness, no darkness. You, Lord Jesus, deserve all worship, you are worthy of all exaltation, all adoration, all praise.

Prayer: "We bow down before you, Lord Jesus, in worship and wonder; we rise up to love you in obedience today, for you, Lord Jesus, are worthy. Guide us in exalting your name. Amen"

March 30

"I will bless the Lord at all times."

Psalm 34:1

I had it all planned out as a Valentine's treat for Barb: a relaxed Sunday followed by supper at a pleasant Middle Eastern restaurant and then a Brahms concert by the local Symphony Orchestra.

However, in mid-afternoon came a miscommunication with someone—actually it was not too serious as I was able to adjust things to meet another's expectations—but I was bothered by it, and as time went on my dissatisfaction grew.

So, before going out for the evening, I took some time alone with the Lord, putting down on paper how I was feeling; that was helpful in regaining enough balance for moving positively into our date. And we had a good, enjoyable evening with pleasant memories to tuck away for further savoring in the future. However, there was still a heaviness, a negativeness that clung to my spirit like a cobweb of lead.

The next morning it came to me just as I waking up: in the midst of the disappointment I had not given praise. Yes, that was it! I had failed to praise God in and for the miscommunication and the discomfort it brought. Since praise is how we lift the shield of faith to extinguish the fiery darts of Satan, I had left myself without defense and had been hit again by the dart of self-pity: "Poor me, no one understands! I can't do anything right!"

The next thought was: "How could I have forgotten that? I even wrote about getting up the shield of faith in one of our recent prayer letters and here I am making the same mistake again!" Well, that was another thing to praise God for. My failure illustrates our dependency on Him—we never learn anything once for all in the spiritual realm and we need the Holy Spirit to give us constant guidance. In fact, my failure to praise was not just a single event, but the result of a downward slide in being unthankful.

As I thought more on the whole incident, there was much positive to be thankful for: I hadn't blown up at the other person, we did have a nice evening, and this time it only took a few hours for the Holy Spirit to get through to me instead of the several days it had taken the last time!

This led me back into Psalm 34:1 with its wonderful emphasis on praise: "I will bless the Lord at all times." Bless you God for allowing me to fail and thereby reminding me of my helplessness without you, my constant need to walk in your strength, wisdom and insight. Thank you that you are always there!

Prayer: "Lord, help me today to be a person of praise, raising the shield of faith against every negative happening. May I be alert to the guidance of your Spirit and give you honor through a thanking will and a thankful heart. Amen."

March 31

"The mouth of the righteous man utters wisdom, and his tongue speaks what is just. The law of his God is in his heart; his feet do not slip."

Psalm 37:30,31

Praise be to you this morning, Lord God, for your wonderful Word: living, powerful, deep, transforming and encouraging. It is life-giving, guiding, convicting, protecting.

Ps 94:18,19 says, "When I said, 'My foot is slipping,' your love, O Lord, supported me." This is so true; when I have felt abandoned, a failure, useless, unloved or attacked, in love you used your Word to support me. Your Spirit brought to mind passages of power, towers of Truth to flee to for help and protection.

When attacked by others, Psalm 37 is my favorite fortress, providing powerful protection: "Fret not yourself because of evildoers...for they shall be cut down like the grass and wither as the green herb" (verse 1). This Psalm is a beacon of Truth, giving perspective and guidance: "Trust in the Lord and do good, so shall you dwell in the land and be fed" (verse 3). It is the high and protecting wall of Hope: "Delight yourself in the Lord and he shall give you the desires of your heart" (verse 4).

I praise and thank you, Lord Jesus for sending the Holy Spirit to open my eyes to your love in your Word. I praise you for keeping my foot from slipping—and how often, how faithfully you have done that. "When anxiety was great within me, your consolation brought joy to my soul" (Ps. 94:19). Praise you that with your Word you combat the worry in my soul and its debilitating cousin, anxiety. You not only defeat them, you replace them with that joy of jubilation in worship of you.

Again, Psalm 37 is often the light shining in the darkness of my worry, as conflict, false accusations and others' displaced anger batter my soul: "Commit Your way to the Lord, trust also in Him, and He shall bring it to pass, He shall bring forth your righteousness as the light and your judgment as the noon day sun" (Ps. 37:5,6). And how often did you, in the end, resolve those conflicts, bringing good out of them. This happened because you are faithful and your Word is right; it is powerful, it is effective, it is True and as we obey it--and you--we see you work all out for good, growth and your glory.

Prayer: "Praise you, Lord God, for giving us the living Word, for sending Your good Holy Spirit to open our eyes to the comfort, perspective and truth we need at the moment. Help me to always and immediately flee to your Word in my difficulties. Help me to think Truth, to respond with grace, praise and prayer so you will be glorified. Amen."

APRIL

April 1

"...set your hearts on things above, where Christ is seated at the right hand of God."

Colossians 3:1b

Ever since first memorizing Colossians 3, I have been thinking about the phrase "...set your affections [or heart] on things above...." Just what are those things? Lately the Lord has granted a bit of insight on this question.

All my life I've set my heart on schedules, outcomes, completion of projects and reaching of goals. Most of these are necessary and good things: getting to work on time, doing my homework and praying regularly for people. However, there are only two possible outcomes from such a focus. You reach the goal and experience a fleeting sense of accomplishment followed by a new emptiness that needs to be filled. Or you don't reach your goal and are frustrated!

Certainly this is not the abundant life Christ spoke of. Now slowly it has become clear that I have set these good things ahead of the "things above." And what are those? Simply put: obedience to Christ. Setting my heart on responding like Christ, no matter what the outcome of the particular situation may be, this is setting my heart on things above. Responding with praise for whatever outcome He allows or sends. Responding to those around me with Love, Joy, Peace, Patience, Kindness, Goodness, Faithfulness, Gentleness and Self-control.

Whether some goal is reached or not in a temporal sense, our response is what makes us useful for God—and, as a side benefit, brings the fulfillment that success can't. As Jesus said, "If you obey my commands, you will remain in my love, just as I have obeyed my Father's commands and remain in his love. *I have told you this so that my joy may be in you and that your joy may be full"* (John 15:10,11).

Of course I must still set goals and strive for them, but I also will try not to set my heart on the goals. Instead I will set my heart upon responding as Christ wants.

Jesus was not an intense, goal-oriented person in the modern sense of always being busy—yet when he died, He said, "I have finished the work you gave me to do." This is because He did what He was supposed to and avoided side involvements. He set His heart on pleasing the Father. May I, may we, do the same.

Prayer: "Father, help me today to set my heart on things above, on pleasing you, and help me to use the tasks before me as a vehicle to do so, rather than making them an end in themselves. Help me to rest in you, work well and wisely, according to your Word. Amen."

April 2

Praise be to you, O Lord, for "you are the Great God, the Great King above all gods...."

Psalm 95:3

There is no one above you, Lord God, no one greater than you, no one more powerful than you. We see your greatness and power in creation: in your "hands are the depths of the earth and the mountain peaks belong to you" (all quotes are from Ps. 95:3-7). You are there in these places, so difficult to reach, so far from where people dwell; you shaped them, you own them. "The sea is yours, for you made it and your hands formed the dry land." By your power and design they exist. You are the Great Creator, the Wonderful Owner of the heaven and earth, the sea and all that is in them.

To know about you, to see your works, to discern a bit of your complex and creative character, to see what you have imagined and made, to learn of you in your Word, and then to know you personally-- the Breather of stars, the Spinner of the earth, the Bringer of dawn— this is a wonder beyond anything we could imagine!

We exalt you for your greatness, your marvelous imagination, your love of beauty, your amazing provision (storing up for your creatures coal, oil and gas for energy, metals for molding, minerals for mining).

You are a marvel, a wonder and a mystery. Who would think that the Creator of all good would stoop to draw His enemies to His side and, at great personal cost, offer to cleanse, transform and adopt them.

How could it be possible that we awake each morning and find the Great King above all gods waiting for us to spend time with Him, delighting in us, ready to go with us through the day He has prepared for us, providing all we need to join Him in His great work?

What a privilege that we can say "...you are our God, and we are the people of your pasture, the flock under your care." Therefore we "bow down in worship, we kneel before the Lord our Maker."

Ah, Lord, you are truly the God beyond our wildest dreams. You are gloriously unimaginable, marvelously magnificent, grandly good and wholly here with us each day. With you there is meaning, with you there is order, with you there is security, with you there is hope. We praise you for your rich, sustaining grace, poured out each day on your undeserving creation.

Prayer: "May you be glorified in our lives today, may we go through this day on our spiritual knees, ever bowed before you in our hearts so that our motives, attitudes, thoughts, words and actions will bring glory and honor to your worthy Name! Amen."

April 3

"Enter his gates with thanksgiving and his courts with praise; give thanks to him and praise his name. For the LORD is good and his love endures forever; his faithfulness continues through all generations."

Psalm 100:4,5

There are so many reasons to come into your gates with thanksgiving and praise, Lord God. We were rebellious, hateful, destructive, condemned criminals, worthy of worse than crucifixion. In spite of this we were sought out by you, bought at a great price, cleansed, transformed and adopted. We stand now as your dearly loved children, highly favored, delighted in, rejoiced in.

You in your greatness, your immense, immeasurable love, your superb self-control, your forever faithfulness to your character and Word, your endless working in time, your limitless love, have poured out grace on this rebellious, foretaste-of-hell planet to make your enemies your sons and daughters, to make us heirs of your unimaginably great riches.

We praise you that we can come into your courts with praise, that we who deserve banishment, have been given unlimited access to walk right in and speak directly with you. You have made it possible for us to come and worship at your footstool without any formality, further sacrifice or ceremony. You are the God of accessibility; you are the God of availability; you are the Lord of accumulated grace, always giving, always good, always gracious, your gates always wide open.

Lord, in spite of your great grace towards us, we get tired, we waver, we are inconsistent. But you are entirely different, for your faithfulness continues through all generations. From eternity you, Lord God, have remained unchanged, faithful to your character, your Word and your purposes. You never tire, you never waver, you never are inconsistent.

You are worthy of love and obedience, of exaltation and worship, of praise and honor, for you are beyond human conception, beyond understanding and logic, beyond imagination in your goodness, your greatness, your grace and your glory.

Prayer: "May I bring honor to you today, Lord, in my motives, attitudes, words and actions. Guide me in thinking and living as a child of the King so those around me may be blessed in the reflected glow of your greatness. Amen."

April 4

"How great is the love the Father has lavished on us, that we should be called children of God! And that is what we are!"

1 John 3:1

Heavenly Father, I share John's wonder at this astounding truth: that you, the Holy God, the Righteous One, the Just Judge, the Good Creator King, would take your enemies--evil, depraved, ugly, stubborn, rebellious and destructive as they are—and transform them into new creatures, adopting them as your children! What a turn-around: to bring your adversary into the palace and place him into your family, making him your heir!

Your astounding act of justification is the great gem of Truth in the New Testament—you, the Just Judge, by the propitiation of Christ's shed blood, satisfied the law and bought for us, your enemies, complete forgiveness. By your work, Lord Jesus, we stand justified before the court of heaven.

Adoption, however, is another matter all together. Justification is a forensic idea, meeting the demands of the law, coldly correct, handed down in court. In contrast, adoption is a family idea: warm, welcoming, accepting, being exalted to a new position of privilege and grace.

This Agape love of yours is astounding. In one way it is a brutal love, brutal to you the Lover, who gives and gives, unswayed by the lack of positive response from the rebellious, self-centered, unbelieving, negative objects of your love--us. This love, so painful to you as you are grieved daily by our rebellion, is so gracious to us: caring, kind, forgiving, correcting, guiding, rebuking, nurturing, providing, directing, cherishing

As J.I. Packer puts it in his powerful book, *Knowing God*, the Judge becomes, "our perfect parent—faithful in love and care, generous and thoughtful, interested in all we do, respecting our individuality, skillful in training us, wise in guidance, always available, helping us to find ourselves in maturity, integrity and uprightness...."

In making us your children, Heavenly Father, you have invited us into the deep, intimate relationship you have with the Lord Jesus, giving us what you gave Him in His time on earth: affection, fellowship, honor, and authority. As you loved your only begotten Son, so you love your only adopted children. "Our fellowship is with the Father and with his Son Jesus Christ"!!! (1 John 1:3).

We must stand in awe, in wonder, in thankfulness, Lord God, at your ability and willingness to love us so. You have made us those in whom you delight and rejoice. You are gloriously great in your patience and goodness as you faithfully work in us, suffering grief every day at our hands. We, in our laziness, selfishness, pride, rebellion and unbelief, choose to disobey you and do our own deadly deeds according to our own puny plans instead of responding to your invitation to join you in your glorious and great scheme for restoring the universe to its pristine pre-fall condition. But you forgive us and continue to work lovingly in our lives.

Praise be to you for the greatness of your gift to make me part of your family, your child who is desired, treasured and deeply, dearly loved.

However, the real point of these monumental truths is not my acceptance, fulfillment or joy—and these are certainly some of the gifts you pour out on your children—no, actually the point of all this is that you, Father, Son and Holy Spirit, are worthy of praise and exaltation, worship and honor.

You are a wonder—no, you are THE Wonder of the world, of the universe and I praise you, Eternal Ruler, Lord God, my Father; I praise you, Lord Jesus, my brother, my fellow heir, my Savior and God; I praise you Holy Spirit, the indwelling, transforming One. I give you glory and honor, exaltation and praise, for that is what you deserve.

Prayer: "Forgive us for failing to marvel at, revel in, exalt in and glorify you for this great and uplifting privilege of being your children. I thank you, praise you, rejoice in you, lift you up and honor you. I commit myself to obey you, Father, just as my elder brother, the Lord Jesus, loved you in obedience. May glory be to you forever and ever. Amen."

April 5

"Delight yourself also in the Lord and he shall give you the desire of you heart."

Psalm 37:4 NKJV

Every "decadal birthday" brings a big shift in life, and this one is no exception. My adjustment to being 50 has continued longer than I expected. It has been like doing a slow motion swan dive into a pool. The slow, relaxed fall, which was a move from my normal high adrenaline, high activity state to a greater calmness and inner quiet, has been nice. However, as I was "decelerating", I went beyond where I wanted to be, like going beneath the surface of the water in my dive. I became too relaxed which resulted in a lower work output and missing some important details!

Now, however, I seem to have "bobbed to the surface" of this new stage of life and have a reasonable balance between calmness and activity. I'm sure that the Lord will teach me more about this as time goes on.

In the midst of this adjustment, the Lord gave a little review of how to handle personal conflict. In a discussion with several colleagues, some inaccurate things were said about one of my projects, and this bothered me (understatement!).

That night I woke up chewing on the comments, thinking of how I could "tactfully" defend myself. As I prayed about it, the Lord declined to help me with my plans and instead brought Psalm 37 to mind: "Do not fret because of evil men or be envious of those who do wrong; for like the grass they will soon wither…Trust in the Lord and do good…"

I was certainly fretting about an "unjust" statement. The real issue, however, was to trust God and do good—which is very different from defending myself! As I surrendered my desire and asked Him to help me to know how to do good in this situation, the next verse came to mind: "delight yourself in the Lord and he will give you the desire of you heart." This reminded me that the real issue in life is to bring glory to God, not make myself look good.

The next day, without my doing anything, the Lord brought about a change. The person who had reported the inaccurate and "unjust" statement, came and told me how glad she was that we are working on the same team. There was a clear shift of attitude, worked by God in the other person—and at the same time in me. What freedom there is when we give up our "rights" and follow God's way. I continually need to be reminded of this and God is faithful to do so.

Prayer: "Praise you, Lord, for the truth of your Word. Help me to think your truth, to not view people as the enemy, to delight in you, trust in you and to do good. Amen."

April 6

"Bow down and hear me O Lord, for I am poor and needy."

Psalm 86:1

Yes, Lord, I in myself and we in ourselves are poor and weak. Without you we are powerless, directionless, in the dark. Our tendencies are all in the wrong direction: we are naturally proud, judgmental, divisive, lazy, selfish and unbelieving, fighting each other, wanting control. We are hopeless without you, Lord; alone we can do nothing right. This is one side of the picture. Help us in the church to recognize this.

"Preserve my soul, for I am holy…" (verses from Ps. 86:1-3). The other side is that you have made us holy: you called, cleansed and transformed us; you claimed us as your children; you commissioned and equipped us for special service to you. Now we stand before you dearly loved, decisively accepted, delighted in, deeply cared for, doted on, and doubly blessed in being your children, when what we actually deserve is Hell. We are given over and dedicated to you, Lord. We praise you for the great grace, the immense grace, the unfathomable grace you show us in this. You are the God who deserves worship, praise, love and obedience.

"O my God, save your servant that trusts in you." When faced with these two sides of Truth--my weakness and your gift of holiness--the choice is obvious: don't trust in myself; trust in you. I must throw myself upon your mercy.

You, Lord God, King of Glory, Judge of the Ages, could rightly condemn me immediately to Hell, but instead continually pour out your goodness upon me and all your enemies. How can we not trust you? In the turmoil of life, only you can help us, save us, bring us through. We cannot do it.

"Be merciful to me, for I cry unto you daily, ... all day long." Praise you that we can continually appeal to your wonderful, full-orbed character, oiled with mercy, motivated by love, moved with grace. Heavenly Father, I praise you that we can come to you any time, all the time, and that you delight in our praying. Praise you that your heart is ever open to the cry of your children and that we can be certain that you will answer at just the right time.

Prayer: "Father, in your mercy, in your love, help us in this time of difficulty. Reach into the situation, into the hearts of each of us, convicting of sin, revealing our motives, bringing us to our knees, to confession, to forgiving each other. Break us, transform us, redo us so that we may become useful instruments in your hands and see us and your church become a shining light of grace, truth and love to all around. Amen."

April 7

"Rejoice the soul of your servant, O Lord, for to you do I lift up my soul, for you are good and ready to forgive and plenteous in mercy to all who call upon you."

Psalm 86:4,5 KJV

When I pray for things, I usually have a pretty clear idea of how I want God to answer my prayer. Although God often has the same goal in mind, He usually has a much better idea of how to reach it—and rarely does His idea line up exactly with mine!

In praying for a friend of ours, I've been asking God to help her find her rest in God alone (Ps. 62:1). His answer was to first show her where she wasn't seeking rest in Him—I asked for rest, but God first gave her more turmoil so that He could, in the end, give a much deeper and longer lasting rest.

In my own life I've been asking God to give me growth; His answer has been to reveal sin. For instance, when I recently read an article praising the ministry of a worker I know, I was dismayed that my first reaction was a powerful surge of jealousy. That was certainly my natural self: competing, seeking significance in success, and finding security in being better than others. God brought me back to the Truth of the sinfulness of my old nature and to the very mixed motives I have, giving opportunity to repent of and reject my wrong motives—those which are negative and neutral—and affirm my positive motives. Through this God refocused me on the need to constantly be transparent before Him so He can help me deal with the negative motives before they become action!

I need to consistently practice lifting my soul to Him: telling Him what I am really thinking (mind), wanting (will) and feeling (emotions)—no editing allowed, no making things look good, just raw truth—and then comparing these to what His Word has to say. With this stark picture I can discard the negative and neutral motives and desires so I can affirm what is biblical. He will then "show me the way in which I should go" (Ps. 143:8b) so I can join Him in what He is doing.

Praise God that He doesn't take my ideas of how He should answer prayer but does what is best instead!

Prayer: "Father, I praise you that you are my Heavenly Father: wise, all knowing and good. Praise you that you answer prayer as you know best. Help me to be transparent before you so you can point out my wrong motives and help me to choose right motives to speak, act and live from. Amen."

April 8

"Bring joy to your servant, for to you, O Lord, I lift up my soul."

Psalm 86:4

All around me are difficult situations, problems, barriers and stubborn, hurting people. I do not have the wisdom, the power, the ability to solve their problems, to alter their attitudes or change their perceptions-- I cannot trust in myself to help them.

But you, O Lord God, you are the Most High, the Almighty, the great Transformer who can reach into situations and hearts to bring the change necessary. Only you can open eyes, give conviction, alter circumstances and bring surrender.

Therefore, "In the day of my trouble I will call to you, for you will answer me" (Ps. 86:7). Your faithfulness is my comfort; your wisdom is my joy. "Teach me your way O Lord and I will walk in your truth." (Ps. 86:11).

Praise you, Lord Jesus, that you are our Way, you are the Truth, you are our Life.

Praise you, Holy Spirit, for your continual work in our lives with convicting, rebuking, guiding, teaching, transforming, persuading, protecting.

Praise you, dear Heavenly Father, for your calling us to join you in your work, inviting us to play important roles in bringing change, asking us to tap into your power through the privilege of prayer, and opening the way for us to cooperate with you in seeing your will come to pass.

I praise you now for how you will answer my prayers, doing the work needed in me as well as with all of those around me who are needy, struggling, disappointed, confused and hurting.

I praise you that my trust is in you, O Lord my God, not in my feeble self. "Have mercy on me, grant your strength to your servant…give me a sign of your goodness that my enemies may see it and be put to shame for you, O Lord, have helped me and comforted me" (Ps. 86:17). May those around me see your power in my life and know it is from you.

And I know you will answer these requests, for "you, O Lord, are a compassionate and gracious God, slow to anger, abounding in love and faithfulness" (Ps. 86:15).

Prayer: "For your name's sake, Lord, for your glory and honor, work amongst us to bring revival. Reveal your holiness in such a way as to bring us to our knees; show us our sinfulness sufficiently to strike us to the ground; and then pour out the healing knowledge of how much you love and forgive us. Stand us again on our feet, transformed as Job was: humbled and broken, not trusting in himself, but trusting only in you, the great and mighty King, the Creator of everything. I praise you now for what you are going to do. Amen."

April 9

"…I have learned to be content whatever the circumstances."

Philippians 4:11b

The Monday before I was to speak at church, an inspiration for the sermon came upon me. I sat down at my computer and began to write; the sermon flowed out full and complete, leaving me with a sense of assurance that the Lord had me well prepared.

Then Thursday night when it was time to review the sermon, I turned on the computer and called up what I had written. After reading through the first screen I tried to scroll on down the page, but there was no response. Instantly I recognized what had happened: I had forgotten to save the complete document.

My response was one of discontent, "Oh no! All that work down the drain—and I can't possibly recreate the inspiration that produced it!" But this was quickly followed by another thought: "Maybe the Lord actually has something better for me to say and is using this to direct me!" I didn't really like that thought because now the work of rewriting the sermon was still before me. However, this clearly was a time to lift the shield of faith by thanking God for the situation and praising Him for what He was going to do through it.

I did write another sermon; it did not feel as inspired as the first one, but was more focused. The theme stayed the same, but much of the rest changed, including the passage used. And when I gave the sermon it certainly seemed to speak to the little congregation. God knew what He was doing, and I am glad He got through to me to cooperate with Him, rather than being focusing on my loss and complaining!

This incident reminded me of how discontent is so prevalent in us and our society. What God has for us is contentment, which, as J.I. Packer explains, "is a matter of accepting from God's hand what He sends because we know He is good and therefore it is good." [4]

Simple. Profound. Life-changing--if we utilize it: know God, deny self, rejoice in what He brings. Quite different from what we are pressured to do by the world, the flesh and the devil: know what's available; indulge yourself; want more. The danger with this is that what I desire becomes what owns me.

In reality only God is the true source of our contentment: "Find rest, O my soul, in God alone; my hope comes from him" (Ps. 62:5).

Prayer: "Lord, may we, like Paul, 'learn to be content whatever the circumstances,' knowing that whatever you allow is good because you are good. Amen."

April 10

""My grace is sufficient for you, for my power is made perfect in weakness."

2 Corinthians 12:9a

Lord, today I have meetings with some potentially difficult discussions—we cannot move ahead without your help. I praise you now for the help you will give in your faithfulness, your constant

---

[4] "Secret of Contentment" address given at Wheaton College, February 27, 1984

presence and your grace. The most important is your grace: it is sufficient for us, for your power is made perfect in our weakness. "Therefore I will boast all the more gladly in my weakness so that the power of Christ might rest on me" (2 Cor. 12:9b).

I praise, you, Lord God for my inability in these meetings to bring about the changes in perspective, heart and action that are needed to get these people to work together. I praise you that you are our only hope: if you do not break through, nothing will happen. Praise you for the futility of this effort, humanly speaking, and for the wonderful potential, heavenly speaking.

I praise you now for what you will do, for how you are going to move and lead us. Protect us from our own selfishness and stubbornness, our pride and preferences. You are our God, save us because we trust in you. We cry out to you: have mercy on us—and I praise you that you will.

I love you, Lord Jesus, my God, my King, my Bridegroom, my Brother; there is certainly tension in keeping these last two aspects of you in view (bridegroom and brother), but that tension testifies to your greatness, your being the Almighty I AM, far beyond what I can comprehend. You are the infinite, immeasurable, eternal, all-present God, worthy of praise, honor, glory and obedience. You are the One who can take our weakness and make it into a conduit for your power.

Prayer: "Grant us your strength, O Lord, grant us tokens of your presence and work amongst us, open our eyes so we may see from your perspective. You alone are able to do these things, so you alone are worthy of worship. May we lift you up today in our thoughts, our attitudes, our words, our decisions that you may be glorified. In all. Amen"

April 11

"If a man remains in me and I in him, he will bear much fruit; apart from me you can do nothing."

John 15: 5b

This past month John 15 and Psalm 34 have been my places of meditation, yielding rich, refreshing and transforming truths. It never ceases to amaze me how powerful a channel of grace meditation on Scripture is, not only giving insights into God, but touching and transforming my soul as well. The hard work of memorizing and then meditating (praying and personalizing the passage) pays deep dividends, allowing us glimpses into God's greatness, magnifying our awareness of His majesty.

Meditation opens our eyes to all kinds of new things. On Labor Day weekend I took morning walks in the large park near us, leaving the path and striking out across dew-drenched grass. My meditation on Scripture helped me to see another dimension to the beauty as I wandered along. What stood out was the creativity of God, His love for variety and variation, His building beauty into the common things of life. I saw in a new way the myriad of shapes and textures in leaves, branches, grasses and tree bark; I noticed the thousand shades of green, the sparkling drops of dew at the tip of each leaf and the perky bodies of squirrels as they leaped across the grass and up trees. It is so clear that our God loves beauty; our God is beautiful and His creation reflects it.

"I will extol the LORD at all times; his praise will always be on my lips. My soul will boast in the LORD…" (Ps. 34:1,2). The more we meditate on His Word, the more we can appreciate the rich, majestic character of our God, making us more aware of His lovely fingerprints on all around us, giving us sight beyond today into eternity. Such a God must be worshipped and meditation draws us into this eternal occupation with our Lord!

Prayer: "Lord God, praise you for your Word which reveals your wonderful, pristine, perfect character. Help me to be so committed to learning your Word that I will memorize and meditate on it regularly. Help me to thus internalize your truth and deepen my relationship with you. Amen."

April 12

"He guides me in paths of righteousness for his name's sake."

Psalm 23:3

Praise be to you Lord God, our heavenly Father, Jesus our heavenly Brother, Holy Spirit our heavenly, indwelling Teacher and Guide. In your triune perfection you are marvelous, you are gracious, you are faithful, leading us in what is righteous. You are the wise prayer-answering God who is ever attentive to your children's cries and will answer in wisdom, power and goodness.

I praise you for how you worked yesterday in our meeting, bringing things out into the open, helping all to speak honestly and carefully about sensitive issues, about doubts and hesitancies. Praise you that you brought things to a good conclusion, with all agreeing to move forward, in being willing to do what is right in spite of fears and reservations.

Praise be to you, Lord Jesus, for your giving guidance in how to begin, in talking about changing our world view, about truly making you our focus, our Lord and our God.

What a wonderful privilege to call all to surrender to you in your majesty and glory and wisdom and love! Thank you that we can join you in the great work you are doing in our hearts.

You, Lord God, are mighty and you are tender: you work on the great level of galaxies and on the delicate and difficult level of the heart. Only you can open understanding, reveal motives, expose sin, shine your light of understanding within and bring repentance and change. You, Lord, are marvelous.

You are the Master Surgeon, cutting through layer after layer of thinly disguised sin, getting down to the root of things, helping us to pull it out and be cleansed, to renounce all that stands against you. Without you we are lost, we haven't a clue of how to proceed, not a hint of wisdom, not an ounce of power to change.

All glory goes to you, Lord Jesus, for you are the Creator, the Savior, the Sustainer, the Beginner and Ender of time. You are the Weaver of the tapestry of history and the Transformer of the tumultuous and troubling events flowing from man's flawed reasoning, using them for good. What patience you have, what care you take, what wisdom you show, what power you exercise in the delicate control of what men and the devil are allowed to do—only so far and then they must stop; only so much and then judgment.

The Lord reigns, let all the earth rejoice. In Him our hope is great: joy flows, justice is stirring, glory shines, His Name is lifted up.

Prayer: "May all that be true in my life today, O Father of all, King of Glory, Ruler of my life. May I continually lift up your worthy name, glorify you with all my heart, magnify your honor and bow before your majesty. I love you, Lord Jesus, I praise you and exalt you. Help me to obey you for your honor today, O Lord. Amen"

April 13

"My command is this: love each other as I have loved you."

John 15:12

The Lord has a way of answering our prayers at unexpected times with unusual means. Recently for me the answer began with a discussion about how to hang up clothes in the closet.

Barb hangs them so the opening of the garment faces right; I have always hung them the opposite way. One evening as Barb was putting freshly ironed shirts in the closet, she asked if I would start hanging my clothes the opposite way, the way she did.

I had had a day filled with details and pressures. I was not ready for a request that would add another detail to my already full plate, and that demanded reversing a habit (and a harmless habit at that) which had been 50 years in the making.

"What difference does it make?" I asked.

"To me it makes a difference," Barb replied. As I pushed her for a reason, she continued, "The shirts won't hang into each other if you put them in like this!"

Well, that didn't make any sense to me, so I began to let her know that.

"Fine," Barb said quietly, "Do it as you want."

That gentle reply cut through my resistance like a hot knife through fat, as the Lord brought to mind a prayer I'd offered earlier in the week: "Lord, help me to serve Barb with joy, to do things which will reduce her stress and help her to be more effective for you." What Barb had asked for was very small, something that would make her life easier, and here I was resisting. How foolish!

Verses from John 15 flooded my thoughts, "I am the true vine; my father is the husbandman…every branch that bears fruit, he prunes it so that it might bring forth more fruit." That knife I felt cutting through my resistance was the Holy Spirit pruning off the useless, harmful growth in my life: selfishness, impatience, laziness and pride, to name a few. I want to bring forth more fruit, but often don't want the pruning that is the prerequisite.

I am thankful that God is patient and faithful to keep working on me, that my dear wife is a patient and gracious soul and that I could repent, apologize to her and hang those shirts in a way that made her life easier.

In this process of growth, God is pleased with us when we submit to Him and to each other in love, and He also gives us wonderful, undeserved benefits. In John 15:11 Jesus says, "These things have I said unto you so that my joy might remain in you and your joy might be full."

And what did He say right before that? "Let me prune you; abide in me; do whatever I command you." These are not things that we humans naturally want, but it is obedience that brings what everyone does want: joy.

Prayer: "Lord, help me this day to willingly submit to your pruning so that I may better love others as you have loved me and that your joy may be complete in me. Amen."

.

April 14

"Come, let us sing for joy to the LORD; let us shout aloud to the Rock of our salvation. Let us come before him with thanksgiving and extol him with music and song."

Psalm 95:1,2

Yes, O Yahweh, you are worthy of honor and praise, you are worthy of fearing and obeying, "For the LORD is the great God, the great King above all gods" (Ps. 95:3).

You are the One who is in charge; you are Ruler, Director, Limiter, Controller and King. Nothing happens without your permission. You allow only what contributes to your plans, to bring glory to your name by sweeping all willing into your Dominion, and to protect, equip, mature, break and deepen those who are in your Kingdom of Light. You have evil on a short leash, able to do only what you will use to bring your plans to pass.

You cannot be defeated: there is no wisdom, no insight, no plan that can succeed against you (Ps. 33:10,11). Your power is unimaginable: your grasp of detail goes from the miniscule to the mighty, from subatomic to super-galactic, from counting hairs and watching sparrows, to moving the universe and history to your desired conclusion.

I praise you, heavenly Father, that in your compassion and grace, your patience and wisdom, your power and love, you are able and eager to transform, train and teach each of your saints.

You are the Mighty King, the Gracious God who is:
- great in power (speaking all into existence),
- great in strength (having armed yourself with strength, you made the mountains),
- great in wisdom (in understanding you laid the foundations of the earth),
- great in knowledge (you can look into the future and know what is going to happen),
- great in Love (your astounding compassion cares for your bitter enemies),
- great in faithfulness (you kept your word and at great cost gave salvation to your rebellious creatures).

There is no one and nothing that can compare with you in greatness. You tower over all creation. You are outside of, over, surrounding and filling the entire universe. You are the only true God.

We bow down before your greatness, we exalt your divinity, we lift up your beautiful name, we praise your unending faithfulness: you are great, you are good, you are God.

I praise you that you are in control of my day right now, that you are working things out, bringing power into my weakness, holding back the tide of evil, limiting what Satan can do in my life, arranging the details of timing, providing and protecting. In you I can rest.

Prayer: "Lord, I willfully enter your rest, trusting you, the Great I AM, to guide me today. Help me to stay in your shelter, O God, so I can give you further glory before the unseen hosts. May the words of my mouth and the meditations of my heart be pleasing in your sight, O Lord, my Rock and my Redeemer. Amen."

April 15

"Show me the way I should go, for to you I lift up my soul."

Psalm 143:8b

We came in the door just before midnight following a long and stimulating visit with some local friends. There had been several opportunities to share spiritual truth. The wife of one friend showed a real interest, asked a lot of questions and listened carefully to a full presentation of the gospel.

In spite of this wonderfully encouraging time, my heart was as heavy as my eyelids, and I longed to just drop into bed and forget 'til the morning the things that weighed on my heart. However, the Lord reminded me of the importance of "lifting my soul" to Him, getting out my troubled thoughts and "processing" them. So I sat down with my journal and began to write about the email I'd gotten that day.

"Lord, after getting that negative email from Charlie I am angry, disappointed, discouraged and hurt – I feel sorry for myself! I feel like reacting in a similar way, writing back and fully, exquisitely expressing my anger—but that is not your way, Lord. I know the key is to not give in to a negative response flowing out of self-pity and a sense of failure, but to praise you, Lord, for the unseen good you are working in this situation both in Charlie and in me, and to press on in truth. Thank you, Lord, for reminding me of Psalm 50:23, 'He who offers the sacrifice of thanksgiving honors me and opens the way that I may show him the salvation of the Lord.' Thank you for helping me to ever lift up your name, to praise you and move on."

There was a release of the burden as I thanked God for the situation and praised Him for what He was doing. It was fulfillment of David's prayer, "Rejoice the soul of your servant, O Lord, for to you I lift up my soul" (Ps. 86:4, NKJV). That night I slept wonderfully and deeply, waking refreshed in spite of the late night.

During my quiet time the next morning, new thoughts came to mind of what to share with Charlie and a positive letter poured out of my head and into an email–it was truly a letter from the Lord. Charlie responded by asking forgiveness for his incorrect interaction, and later another email came expressing further remorse at his angry words.

The Lord worked; I am deeply thankful that He got me to listen, and to write out my thoughts in the evening, not the morning, so that He could give me both a good night's sleep and His positive perspective. The key was lifting my soul to God by writing out my thoughts and then comparing them to Scripture–to just express them verbally does not bring for me the insight that comes with writing. It brings clarity on what is actually happening so the Lord can give perspective and direction. It is truly good to "pour out our hearts to Him, for God is our refuge" (Ps. 62:8).

Prayer: "Lord, praise you that you call us to lift our souls to you. Help me to be consistent in honestly telling you what I am thinking, feeling, wanting, and to process these in the light of your Word. Restore my soul so that you may rule me wholly. Amen."

April 16

"Teach me your way, O Lord; I will walk in your truth;"

Psalm 86:11

Praise be to you, Lord Jesus, that you came to be the Way, to teach the way, to be the Truth, to reveal truth. It is wonderful that in you we can now know truth, see what is right and wrong, be aware of what is hurtful before we act, of what is good before choosing.

"Unite my heart to fear your name…" (Ps. 86:11b). You are the only One who can heal and unite our hearts, making us single-minded, whole-hearted, completely committed. You are the only One who is worthy of that commitment, for you are the great God, the obedient Son, the willing Sacrifice, the Healer of broken creation, and the Bridegroom dying for your bride. You bind up our wounded hearts and masterfully, tenderly to unite them to yourself.

"I will praise you, O Lord my God, with all my heart, And I will glorify your name forevermore" (Ps. 86:12). Yes, I WILL praise you, for you are my Lord, my God—my final Authority, my King, the real Ruler, the Mighty I AM, the Great Lord and Savior, Jesus Christ. Yes, I WILL glorify your name, Lamb of God, King of Glory, Redeemer of all, Everlasting Father, Son of Man, Son of God, the Most High, the Almighty One, the Gracious One, the Compassionate One, the Patient One, the Holy One.

You are worthy of exaltation, magnification, glory and praise forever and ever and ever. There will be no end to the revelation of new facets of your beautiful person, your rich personality, your infinite graciousness. And I thank you that we will be with you to praise you forever and ever and ever.

You are our All in all. You are glorious in goodness. You are majestic in mercy. You are wonderful in your works. To you be glory and honor, joy and worship in my life today. I love you.

Prayer: "Praise you that you give us the ability to choose to walk in your way, Lord Jesus. Help me to deny self and sin and to walk in your words. I bow before you in worship, in surrender and commitment, agreeing to do your will, to walk in your Truth, for you, Lord Jesus, are worthy of obedience. Amen."

April 17

"If you belonged to the world, it would love you as its own. As it is, you do not belong to the world, but I have chosen you out of the world. That is why the world hates you."

John 15:19

Both God's Word and history tell us that the cause of Christ is usually advanced at a cost. We are in a battle. People get hurt and sometimes killed. At times it's easy to be lulled into the lie that if we follow Christ, He will give us a "good" life, meaning one of comfort, material possessions, and quick solutions to all problems. However, recently we were reminded again that such a view is not at all in line with Scripture, and that the truly "good life" consists of a close, obedient walk with Christ through all circumstances.

Starting early one morning last month the police began to arrest the local believers in our city, one-by-one. The incident actually began with the apprehension of a car thief whom one believer had witnessed to.

In order to get the attention off himself, the thief told all he knew about the believers here. To the police, with their mistaken ideas about Christianity, it sounded like an illegal group of political activists, so they began to round them up. By Sunday they had five believers and some people who had shown interest in the Gospel. They visited the home of one worker to "invite" him, too, but he was away at the time.

We had to piece the story together from the newspaper articles and from what scant information we could get from distraught relatives. Much of what was in the papers was quite distorted and made those arrested look like a group of terrorists.

We knew that it was very possible for me to be taken in next, so I got everything ready. Although I was very willing to go, I asked the Lord if I might just finish out the week of teaching, since it was the end of the semester, and He graciously granted that desire.

Then on Thursday evening we got a call from a joyous believer, saying that all but one had been released and all charges had been dropped. The one person left in police custody was not a believer, but had been witnessed to. However, he had earlier actually been involved in a terrorist group and was in possession of a gun. Praise the Lord that the authorities were able to see him as separate from the rest.

God is in control; we are sure He will use this difficult event for good, so we can praise Him now for what further difficulties will come in the future. Our God is trustable!

Prayer: "Lord, praise you that you have rescued us from the dominion of darkness and brought us into the Kingdom of Light. Help me to live in your light, obeying you no matter what the cost. Help me to boldly obey you today. Amen."

April 18

"For great is the LORD and most worthy of praise; he is to be feared above all gods."

Psalm 96:4

You, O Yahweh, are great beyond comprehension: great in wisdom, great in power, great in patience, great in creativity, great in knowledge, great in holiness, great in love, great in mercy, great in justice, great in strength, great in kindness, great in faithfulness.

You are truly most worthy of praise and honor and glory and exaltation, "For all the gods of the nations are idols, but the LORD made the heavens" (Ps. 96:5).

You stretched out the tent of the skies, driving in its pegs firmly, tying its ropes securely, making it strong and sure: it cannot be changed without your desire. You spoke and the stars became, you shepherded them into galaxies, assigning them their places and names, and at your command they settled there. You spread the galaxies across the vast empty stretches, forming immense patterns, beyond the perception and comprehension of man. You, O Lord, are immense in power, wonderful in wisdom, awesome in creativity.

We exalt you in your greatness and your goodness; we submit before you in amazed submission, leading us to whole-hearted obedience. We proclaim among the nations, "The LORD reigns!" You are truly God and I bow before you in awe, in smallness, in humility that flows from a vision of your holiness. You are God, you do what pleases you and it is always good. We tremble before you, the Holy One, the great I AM, the righteous Judge, the faithful Father. You alone are worthy of obedience, of submission, of trust and praise.

Prayer: "You reign rightly, O Lord. Reign in me today. Convict me of where I am following my own whims and desires instead of your great goodness; bring me up short, bring me to submission. Amen."

April 19

"So I will always remind you of these things, even though you know them and are firmly established in the truth you now have. I think it is right to refresh your memory as long as I live in the tent of this body...."

2 Peter 1:12,13

Lately the Lord has been reminding me of two familiar and important truths. The first is stated in Psalm 62:1, "My soul finds rest in God alone." It is so easy to try and find my rest in other things, especially in seeking situations without tension.

On a strictly human level I actually have about the most ideal situation a man could want: a beautiful and intelligent wife, two fine sons, all of us healthy; an interesting, challenging and significant job; and enough income to live comfortably. But these can't give me the fulfillment which each of us seeks. Such completion of our being can only come from our Lord, and we need to be constantly reminded of this, lest we slack off in our seeking to find our rest in Him, and begin drawing on the world's methods for our "rest."

The second truth is stated in 1 Thessalonians 5:18, "Give thanks in all circumstances...." I often forget that the thrust of my life should be to glorify God by thanking Him in and for all things. He is using whatever circumstances surround me both for my good, and to bring about His will in the universe. Praising and thanking the Lord Jesus is such a freeing and enabling activity: "let us continually offer to God a sacrifice of praise–the fruit of lips that confess his name" (Heb. 13:15). Praise is the one practical way of taking "up the shield of faith, with which you can extinguish all the flaming arrows of the evil one" (Eph. 6:16).

So I want to continually live in the rest that only God can give and to honor Him by giving thanks in all circumstances. These are what God calls us to. Are we joining Him in His great plan, fulfilling our part in the restoration of the universe?

Prayer: "Father, help me to remember these basic truths and to live them each day, resting in who you are and thanking you in and for all things. Amen."

April 20

"Worship the Lord in the splendor of his holiness, tremble before him, all the earth."

Psalm 96:9

You, Lord Jesus, are a majestic wonder, rising far above all others, reigning with power, reining in evil, raining down good on all. No detail escapes your attention, no event occurs without your allowing it. "The world is firmly established, it cannot be moved" (Ps. 96:10). Our confidence is in you. We praise you for your great strength and wisdom displayed in your ruling both the universe and our lives.

"…he will judge the peoples with equity" (Ps. 96:10). Praise be to you that you are the just Judge making your decisions with full knowledge and wisdom: "he comes to judge the earth. He will judge the world in righteousness, and the peoples in his truth" (Ps. 96:13).

In the midst of the evil, suffering and the turmoil of life on earth, it is wonderful to know that justice is coming for sure and in power. Praise you, Lord Jesus that you will judge in equity, in righteousness and in truth. Your decisions will be the same for all, there will be no favoritism, no extra harshness to the weak, or leniency for the powerful; all will be judged on an equal basis in your wisdom, knowledge and justice.

Your standard will be righteousness, both for yourself, and for those judged. There can be no arguing against your measurements of glorious goodness. And that is what you are in yourself, Lord Jesus: pure, powerful, perfect rightness and righteousness.

You will judge in truth: no one can deny that your decisions, your sentences will be based on what actually happened, for you know not only the facts, but also the thoughts of men before they speak, you know the intents of their hearts, you know their motives. You discern it all, and you will evaluate it all properly. That is powerfully impressive, it is seriously scary, even to those who are saved, who will not be judged on the basis of their works, but on your work.

You will judge and end evil in your universe. This is a wonderful outflow of your beautiful character, Lord Jesus, the desire for justice that you have had from the beginning and your faithfulness to the promise made in the garden. We long for that: a life without sin in self, without the constant struggle with the world, the flesh and the devil, without the attacks of the enemy, without the ugliness of evil in us as well as around us.

You have given us a foretaste of this now in your walking with us. To be in your shelter of forgiveness and love, to live in your goodness and grace, to experience your teaching and transformation--this is a foretaste of Heaven. It is a great privilege, especially when we realize how much we deserve the opposite.

In your shelter of love, under the wings of your mercy we can be confident that when your wrath rains down in judgment, we will be protected and defended, safe in your arms.

"Let the heavens rejoice, let the earth be glad;
let the sea resound, and all that is in it;
let the fields be jubilant, and everything in them.
Then all the trees of the forest will sing for joy;
they will sing before the LORD, *for he comes*" (Ps. 96:11-13a).

Prayer: "Yes, come, Lord Jesus! Reign in my heart today. May I live before you in obedience to what I know to be right, that you may be exalted before men and angels. Amen."

April 21

"Let a righteous man strike me—it is a kindness; let him rebuke me—it is oil on my head. My head will not refuse it."

Psalm 141:5

Suffering hardship is such a positive thing when accepted in the right spirit. As we've been "pulled through the knothole" in the last weeks, the Lord has driven us into the Word, taught us more of the sufficiency of His Grace, and made us more sensitive to others' difficulties.

He has also been "refining" our lives. That means, in everyday terms, He's gently showed us what we really are. I was able to rejoice through the arrests of this year, the accusations in the newspaper, the death of Barb's father, being fired unjustly from my job, and being brought to trial, but when it came to being kicked out of our apartment, I balked.

This event had nothing to do with our arrests or other troubles, but was arranged by Satan, using our new landlord, to encourage us to give up. It came because our original landlord was in debt; the bank foreclosed and sold the apartment to an investor who wanted us out so he could resell it.

It is not all that hard to stand up against outside pressure, but when your home is snatched out from under you, that is much more difficult, at least for me. I did praise God with my mouth, but at the same time was angry with Him for allowing this. The line between the mechanics of praising God and doing so from the heart is very fine.

The Lord firmly and gently pointed out to me that the actual problem was not losing our home, but my holding on to this place, and my anger about losing it. Of course I was angry at the landlord, but the

Lord reminded me that when I resist what He allows, I'm also angry at Him.

Repentance brought relief, but I had already done a good deal of damage to my body by being so stressed, so it was touch and go with sinusitis again, but the Lord graciously kept me from getting sick.

How weak I am. How great He is. I am thankful that Barb did better than I did in it all. We still don't know what will happen, but are now resting in Him and praising Him for what He's going to do.

Suffering also opens other people to us. As we shared some of what had happened with one of our neighbors, Erdem, he poured out the story of how his son had died tragically ten years before. We would never have guessed there was any such thing in Erdem's life, as he always seemed so happy. If we hadn't suffered, he would not have shared about the "cracks in his soul." Now we will be better able to share some of the Solution with him.

Prayer: "Lord help me to rejoice in every difficulty, to find my security in you, to remember that the purpose of my life is to glorify you and the best opportunities for this is when things are not going the way I like. Amen."

Epilogue: the new landlord sent a realtor to expel us from our apartment, but after talking with us, the realtor became our advocate and convinced the landlord to give us several more months there. That facilitated our being able to find a new and better apartment. The Lord is powerful to fight for us when we are willing to submit to His hand.

April 22

"The Lord reigns, let the earth be glad, let the distant shores rejoice."

Psalm 97:1

Yes, Lord, we rejoice, for you are the sovereign One, the King over all, the Ruler of the universe. No detail escapes your attention, no attitude, no motive, no thought goes unnoticed. You guide the flow of events in each person's life to draw him or her to yourself and then to mature in Christ those who do come.

You are powerful; no one can get around you, no one can thwart you in your great plans—just the opposite is true, you thwart the plans of the nations and topple the purposes of the people (Ps. 33:10,11). You are God alone! "For you, O LORD, are the Most High over all the earth; you are exalted far above all gods" (Ps. 97:9).

Praise be to you for your wisdom, as you have given your human creatures a sphere of responsibility where we are to make decisions. You control what comes to us, each event designed to give us opportunity to move in the right direction, but we have to make the choice.

It would have been much easier if you had just made us puppets or robots—but that would have eliminated the possibility of love. To have genuine love there has to be the chance to choose, to respond to your love with willing decisions to do what pleases you. Praise you that we are made in your image (albeit, now cracked and marred as it is by sin), and therefore able to make moral and ethical decisions with eternal consequences.

There is no event, no happening, no act, no detail or desire that you do not know, evaluate, give permission for, limit or prevent You, Lord God, are in charge, you allow men and devils to go their own ways within certain boundaries. You allow our selfish acts and works to create limited hardships, suffering and difficulties designed to bring us to ourselves, so that we might, on one side, acknowledge our sin and smallness, and on the other, embrace your grace and greatness. Your desire in all is to prepare and call, then to claim and cleanse all who come. "The heavens proclaim his righteousness, and all the peoples see his glory" (Ps. 97:6).

Prayer: "I praise you, Lord God, that in your grace, wisdom and kindness, you have created us with the right and responsibility of choosing to obey in love. Help me today to take up your grace, to obey what I know from your Word and to fulfill the purpose you have given me of living for your glory. To you be praise and honor forever and ever. Amen."

April 23

"If you obey my commands, you will remain in my love, just as I have obeyed my Father's commands and remain in his love. I have told you this so that my joy may be in you and that your joy may be complete."

John 15:10,11

As we learn more and more about worship (giving God the glory and honor due His name for what He is, without reference to how it benefits me), God has been teaching us about the source of joy.

My natural concept of joy is much more related to the warmth of comfort, good relationships and a full belly than to truth.

Biblical joy, however, is independent of the everyday events that surround us. True, godly joy is much more vibrant and vigorous than my natural, feeble, human conception of joy: it is a strong and fierce joy which, with God's power, fights through difficult circumstances to rise above them with the Son from whom it comes.

Biblical joy is rooted in the Truth that we are God's chosen, adopted and dearly loved children (Col. 3:12). That one fact is enough to produce all the joy we need: we have received the opposite of what we deserve; we are rescued from the dominion of darkness and brought into the Kingdom of Light; we have hope of a certain future in Heaven; we have more than enough grace for every circumstance; we are called to partner with God in His great plan for the universe. We are chosen, holy and dearly loved (Col. 3:12) and that is more than enough for joy!

All the other things that God may give us here on earth are just "add ons" to this foundational source of biblical joy. These other things can be taken away, but joy can still remain because it flows from God and our relationship with Him.

Psalm 100:1,3 says it clearly: "Shout for joy to the Lord, all the earth.... Know that the Lord is God. It is he who made us, and we are his...." This is true whether we are sick or well, rich or poor, in a life of ease or under great pressure. As Paul wrote to the Thessalonians, "...in spite of severe suffering, you welcomed the message with the joy given by the Holy Spirit" (1Thes. 1:6b). To know Him, to be His, that is enough for real joy.

Worship is what helps us to focus on that truth; we need to gaze at God's character as revealed in Scripture (especially the Psalms), to give Him praise and glory for what He is, thinking as little of ourselves as possible, and much about Him. The times I "feel" no result from worship can be the best times, for then worship is done out of pure faith, in obedience to the ultimate Truth, bringing God much honor, for without faith we cannot please Him.

Prayer: "Lord, help us remember that real joy is available all day long. Help us to look to you daily and be reminded that being your child for eternity is enough reason for joy. Help me to live out that joy through praising you by faith in all. Amen."

April 24

"The Lord reigns let the earth be glad."

Psalm 97:1

This one statement, Lord—short, clear, to the point—expresses powerfully why knowing you is enough for joy. You are in charge! You are good! You are powerful! You are wise! You are righteous! You are loving! You are faithful! What more could we want?

Well, humanly speaking, we do want more. We want comfortable, painless, suffering-free, self-centered, non-stop-pleasure living. That's us ruling, not you. Such an existence is like living in a Tupperware box. It doesn't take long before oxygen depletion begins to set in, followed by decay and death on every front: spiritually, intellectually, emotionally and finally physically.

In contrast, life with you is out in the open, in the fresh air of freedom with wonderful views and endless possibilities. You we can trust, for you reign with wisdom and purpose, power and grace, firmness and gentleness. You have the big picture. You know where history is going and are taking us with you. You know the outcome of every decision we make, not because you determine it, but because you live outside of time.

You are the One to be obeyed because you are wise and good, and also because you are righteous and just—you will deal with sin, you are awesome in your power and wrath against evil:

"Fire goes before him
    and consumes his foes on every side,
His lightning lights up the world;
    the earth sees and trembles.
The mountains melt like wax before the LORD,
    before the Lord of all the earth.
The heavens proclaim his righteousness,
    and all the peoples see his glory" (Ps. 97:4-6).

Such a God is to be obeyed for fear of consequences as well as for His great love. Your hatred of sin is a comfort to those who believe: there will be an end to evil, there will be justice, there will be an elimination of suffering. And there will be the shelter from your wrath into which you invite all your enemies.

The more we know you, the more reason there is to worship you, O God, for you are fear-inspiring, comfort-giving, sin-revealing, grace-providing, heart-healing, attitude-correcting, soul-transforming, love-infusing, life-giving and eternally-existing—what more could we want?

Knowing you means that daily we can turn more and more to you, more and more away from the tinsel and trinkets the world has to offer. Every day we can move further into your Kingdom, reveling in your Being, obeying the Truth we know, joining you in your work. We can, in your power and goodness, leave behind the burdens of self-centeredness and pleasure-oriented living to plunge into the river of your goodness and grace, to be swept along in the current of your love. Truly "The Lord reigns," and we are glad!

Prayer: "Lord, today in the light of your lovely character, help me to deny self, take up my cross and follow you. Help me to turn away from the call of comfort and self-protection, and instead wholeheartedly follow you in praise and obedience to what I know to be true, for you are worthy! Amen."

April 25

"Therefore, I urge you, brothers, in view of God's mercy, to offer your bodies as living sacrifices, holy and pleasing to God—this is your spiritual act of worship."

Romans 12:1

We stepped off the bus to find our friend, Chris, waiting for us. As we chatted, waiting for the luggage to be unloaded, my wife looked at him more closely and said, "Chris, you look happier. What happened to you?"

He looked a bit startled, then replied, "Well, yes I am happier. Let's get your bags and I'll tell you about it on the way home."

As he steered the car out into the evening traffic, Chris told us that while his wife was away for a few days, he had spent some extra time alone with the Lord and had read a book called, "They Found the Secret." The common thread that ran through each story in the book had to do with an "exchanged life," a deeper surrender to God.

"The story that really spoke to me was of a doctor who, through hearing a sermon on Romans 12:1-2, realized that he had been doing everything in his own strength and wisdom. He saw the need to 'present his body a living sacrifice' and surrendered himself to God, saying something like, 'Lord up until now I have treated you as my servant, calling you when I needed help, asking you to make my plans come to pass. No more. I now give myself to you. I give you my lips to speak your words, my hands to do your work, my feet to take me where you want me to go. This body is yours. Fill it with cancer if you desire. Send it to the Eskimos. Cause it to be paralyzed if that is your will. I am yours to be used in any way you see fit. Amen.'"

We looked at Chris, "So that's what you've done, isn't it?" I asked.

He nodded, smiling. "Yes. This means I am God's to use as He sees fit. This whole concept of the exchanged life is not new to me, but the depth of surrender He has brought me to is new. And this surrender will require some changes of me in the way I interact with the team here."

Barbara and I were deeply happy to hear this, both for Chris, as he shone with the joy of his deepening surrender, and for the team here, as this personal break-through showed God's working in answer to prayer. The change had begun, totally apart from anything we had done–the glory goes to God.

My mind went back to when the Lord brought my own stubborn heart to take a first step in entering "the exchanged life," giving God full rule. It was a cold arctic night in Alaska in December of 1968, where, after miserably failing to adequately handle life on my own, in desperation I'd prayed, "Lord, I give you my will and take yours in its place."

The change the Lord brought was dramatic: from despair to hope, from self-effort to self-denial, from the dryness of legalism to the fresh spring of God's grace. The dry, dusty words of scripture were transformed, bursting with life; it seemed that flowers were growing out of every line!

It was the beginning of a wonderful and ongoing transformation which continues with periodic deepening in my being as the Spirit breaks through one twisted barrier after another. To God be the glory for His patient work within us. We are useful to Him not for what we are, but in spite of what we are!

Prayer: "Lord, help me to surrender to you more deeply each day so that you may be glorified by the joy you pour into my life. I give you my will today and take yours in its place. Amen."

April 26

You "…O LORD, are the Most High over all the earth; you are exalted far above all gods."

Psalm 97:9

You, Lord Jesus, are the exalted One, the highest One, towering far above all creatures, all creation, all time, all eternity. You are the final Authority, the Almighty King, the Measure of all good, the Determiner of what is right.

You see all, you judge all, you will end all. Your righteousness shines out from your being; in your purity you bring light; in your holiness you illuminate the world. You are truly the Most High.

To bow before you in worship is the response of those who know you, see you, love you. You are the One to be praised, adored, exalted and lifted up.

In worship our eyes are opened, our understanding is enhanced, our knowledge is deepened, our souls transformed. As a result we will say: "Let those who love the LORD hate evil" (Ps. 97:10a). Yes, Lord, to love you is to hate evil, for you are purely good.

In your goodness you "guard the lives of your faithful ones and deliver them from the hand of the wicked" (Ps. 97:10b). As we worship you, obey you, walk with you, we can rest in the power of your goodness: "He who dwells in the shelter of the Most High will rest in the shadow of the All Mighty" (Ps. 91:1).

In your goodness, you pour out your grace upon us: it flows out of your being like water from a deep, pure spring, like love from a new mother, like light from the sun. As we look upon you in worship, "Light is shed upon the righteous and joy on the upright in heart" (Ps. 97:11).

I praise you, Lord Jesus, for you are the Light of life, the Radiance of perfection, the Illumination of the gospel, which you caused to shine deeply into our hearts. I praise you that you invite us into the light, to walk in the light of your presence, to live in the light of your Truth, to revel in the light of your love.

You, Lord Jesus, are so loving and kind, so gracious and pure, so giving and forgiving. To you belongs all glory, all honor, all praise, all exaltation, both now and throughout all eternity!

Prayer: "Lord Jesus, help me to walk in the light of your presence today, thinking your Word, living worthy of you, pleasing you in all I do. Amen."

April 27

"Put on the full armor of God so that you can take your stand against the devil's schemes."

Ephesians 6:11

In the cold of late December while I was talking in the hall with our upstairs neighbor about getting more fuel oil for the furnace, one of the landlords of the building walked by. I took the opportunity to talk with him about his share of the building's heating bill, which he had not paid. He was unreceptive to my suggestions, which meant that the rest of us had to shoulder his share of the cost if we wanted any heat in our homes. He was unaffected because he doesn't live here.

As he resisted all I had to say, I felt a hot flash of anger beginning to rise up in my chest at his imperious and negative replies. Knowing that if we talked much longer I was going to say something I'd regret, I abruptly and somewhat impolitely cut off the conversation and retreated into our apartment.

It was obvious, however, to all involved that I had become angry and I was chagrined about that. It was one of those instances where I hadn't seen one of Satan's traps coming my way, and fell right into it.

One of my regular prayers is that God would help me to see Satan's wiles before I fall into them, not afterwards. However, God does not always choose to answer in the way I'd like. In this case He helped my humility develop a bit more with a little humiliation, and, more importantly, without my knowing it, prepared me for a more significant event.

A couple of days later I was having a very difficult conversation with one of our teammates here, and the same hot flash of anger began to rise in my chest. The Lord used my previous failure to alert me so I could recognize what was happening. I could immediately turn to God for help, use His weapons of the shield of faith and the helmet of salvation and not fall into Satan's attempt to trap me in my natural temper.

This situation was much more important than the earlier one, and I am so thankful that the Lord chose to warn me as He did so I would not ruin several months of careful relationship building with one impatient response!

I am so weak and selfish, so impatient and self-willed. Praise God for His patient and gracious working in me (and all of us) to save us from our sinful responses and to keep us on the road of righteousness! "I will bless the Lord at all times; His praise shall continually be in my mouth" (Ps. 34:1).

Prayer: "Lord today help me to keep on the armor and see the wiles of the devil before I fall into them! Amen."

April 28

"Rejoice in the LORD, you who are righteous, and praise his holy name."

Psalm 97:12

You, Lord God, are good and pure and loving. As I think about the question, "Why does God allow evil?" I am impressed more and more with your great heart of goodness, of how you can take the wrong choices of people as well as the negative consequences that flow from them and turn them into good for the very rebels who shake their fists in your face!

You are so loving, so wise, so powerful, so creative. You rain down good on your evil creatures, you patiently wait for the right time to work in their lives, you wisely let them go off on their own ways so they can come to their senses and turn to you. You are always there, patiently waiting, and patiently suffering with them as they grieve your heart over and over, rejecting the work of the Holy Spirit, choosing darkness rather than light.

What a God you are, what grace and wisdom you display every day, what restraint and preciseness in your actions, what love and tenderness in your intent. And what joy you have in store for those who turn to you and bow before the King of the Universe.

What an encouragement to obey your command, "Rejoice in the LORD, you who are righteous, and praise his holy name" (Ps. 97:12). With eagerness we come to praise you, Lord Jesus, to extol your wonderful qualities, to exalt your great and pure and powerful name, to rejoice in you, the perfect and pristine One, ruling with wisdom and grace, coming with judgment and power to eliminate evil.

You alone are worthy of worship. As we look upon you in adoration, "Light is shed upon the righteous and joy on the upright in heart" (Ps. 97:11). This leads us to further understanding, insight, more grace and deeper worship.

Prayer: "Glory be to you this day, Lord Jesus, in our lives, in our thoughts, in our motives, in our words, actions and attitudes. May every moment bring honor to you, for you are worthy. Amen."

April 29

"Though we are outwardly wasting away, yet inwardly we are being renewed day by day."

2 Corinthians 4:16

The following thoughts flow from my beginning to lose hair and facing the possibility of becoming bald!

Aging is, to put it bluntly, the process of progressive deterioration of the body and loss of abilities and qualities. Hearing fades, eyesight dims, muscles lose strength, flexibility decreases, joints creak, energy wanes and the mind slows.

Many of these losses are more than physical, for they are also the loss of what has made us feel good about ourselves, of what gave us a sense of worth, importance and the ability to accomplish. Therefore the process of aging can be doubly devastating as things physical, mental and emotional are taken from us.

Looking at this from a different perspective, however, aging is an opportunity for a deepened life. It should force us to reexamine the values we have adopted, especially on an emotional level. As our ability to perform is taken from us by these losses, it is an opportunity to further turn our attention towards enduring values and truths.

It is an opportunity to affirm that our worth actually does not depend on our accomplishment but upon two unchangeable facts: as human beings we are made in the image of God and as believers we are redeemed by the blood of the Lamb. In addition, our significance does not come from what we can do with our bodies and minds, but from being given important and vital roles in God's overall plan for the universe: praise, prayer, persistence in doing what we know to be right and propagation of the gospel.

These can be carried out in old age even better than in our youth as we have had time to develop a character that reflects Christ. When we age to the point where we can do nothing else but exist, Christ's kindness, love and grace can still shine out of our lives as we continually offer the sacrifice of thanksgiving (Ps. 50:23).

In addition to worth, our sense of satisfaction does not need to come mainly from physical strength or mental ability or accomplishments. It should come primarily from the unending and unfathomable truth that we, as believers, belong to God.

He is carrying us through each stage of life, onward to a timeless and perfect relationship with Him in a sinless and overwhelmingly wonderful setting. "...our light and momentary troubles are achieving for us an eternal glory that far outweighs them all" (2 Cor. 4:16,17).

Aging, then, becomes an opportunity to further shift our focus away from the passing things of earth to a deeper and timeless mindset as seen in Psalm 72:25, "Whom have I in heaven but you and earth has nothing I desire besides you." This leads us to thinking Truth rather than half-truths, thinking eternally rather than temporally. "So we fix our eyes not on what is seen but on what is unseen. For what is seen is temporary, but what is unseen is eternal" (2 Cor. 4:18).

Aging is also a further chance to understand Paul's statement, "When I am weak, then I am strong" (2 Cor. 12:10). My increasing lack of competence in the natural realm is a platform upon which the grace of God can be displayed to all around me. It is an impetus to look forward to what God has for us as we age and can no longer depend on our own abilities!

Old age is the process of losing things; maturity is letting them go, embracing the truth that God has better things for us.

Prayer: "Father, help me to be continually moving from a natural mindset to a supernatural one, praising you in all, seeking to give you glory, seeing you as my all in all, letting go of what I can't keep, holding on to what I can't lose, and rising above the losses of life with joy. Amen."

April 30

"Shout for joy to the LORD, all the earth, burst into jubilant song with music...."

Psalm 98:4,5

We shout praises to you, O Lord God, the King of Glory, Ruler of all, we exalt your high and holy Name, "for he has done marvelous things;" (Ps. 98:1). You are the magnificent One, the powerful One, the loving One, the eternal King.

You, Lord Jesus, have worked salvation for your enemies. Your amazing love, your overflowing grace, your deep compassion and your tender concern for those who oppose and resist you, are astounding You are loving towards those who spit in your face, who insult you, who hate you, who spurn your direction, who deny your truth! In your compassion you are wonderful, deserving endless worship and praise and glory.

"...his right hand and his holy arm have worked salvation for him" (Ps. 98:7). You, Heavenly Father, brought about this salvation with your pure and powerful arm: with your sinless Son you reached down into the corrupt and putrid world, lived amongst your enemies, patiently revealing your glory one tiny step at a time. Then at the right moment, in a burst of blinding righteousness, you raised Him from the dead, defeating all foes, opening the way for all to receive power and wisdom and grace, ushering into your Kingdom all who believe.

Your work was finished, the shelter from your coming wrath was complete and the invitation went out to all, for "all the ends of the earth have seen the salvation of our God" (Ps. 98:3).

In your faithfulness and goodness you continue to call, woo, encourage and convict us sinners, pointing the way to the shelter where there is eternal life, unending joy, continual worship and on-going fulfillment in knowing you. You invite us--we who are the opposite of you in every way--to come into your family, into your Kingdom, into your shelter, into your fortress, into your loving embrace where you become our Father, Savior, Brother and King.

You made us to "dock" with you, to fit into a perfect relationship with the Triune God, and you have stopped at nothing to make that possible again after the fall. We must, "...shout for joy before the LORD, the King" (Ps. 98:6b).

Glory be to you: we exalt you in jubilant song, we sing to you for joy, we glorify you with music, with hymns and words of praise! We proclaim your goodness, wisdom and love! We marvel at your holiness, your perfection, your omnipresence, at your seeing all, knowing all, loving all.

To you alone belongs worship, to you belongs exaltation. We bow before you, O Great God, O Mighty Father, O Wonderful Jesus, O wise Holy Spirit and shout with praise, for you are worthy of glory.

Prayer: "Lord God, help me today to live in the wonder of who you are, of what you have done, of what you are doing in my life today. Help me to praise you in all things, to live the goal for which I was made: continually giving you glory in all and for all! Amen."

MAY

May 1

"The LORD has made his salvation known and revealed his righteousness to the nations."

Psalm 98:2

What have you saved us from, O Lord? You have delivered us from devilish deceit, from Satan's dominion of duplicity, from his dirty and damaging control. It is deliverance from darkness bringing us to the Kingdom of Light. We were blind, without sight, without knowledge, without understanding. We lived in the night of sin and condemnation, which was churning, oppressive, heavy, debilitating and enslaving. As your Word says, "The way of the wicked is like deep darkness, they do not know what makes them stumble" (Pro. 4:19). And we certainly stumbled, continually falling in every area of our lives, especially in relationships.

When we allowed ourselves to think of the darkness within our souls, it was overwhelming, revealing empty hopelessness, an uncertain future, a depressing despair, foundationless floundering and a bottomless mire into which we were sinking ever more deeply.

But, You, Lord Jesus, burst into our darkness with the light of your love, pushing it back, reaching out your hand of healing right down into our souls. You washed the darkness from within, you banished it from without. You set us on the path of the righteous which is "like the first gleam of dawn, shining ever more brightly until the full light of day" (Pro. 4:18).

Your face now beams light into our lives every day, giving depth to our vision, causing the obstacles of life to stand out clearly before us in this sinful, twisted world, allowing us to walk around them rather than falling over them or into them. No more continual stumbling, as long as we walk into your light.

You have filled our souls with hope, you have given us a certain future, a solid foundation, a pure love and a deep joy that continually washes away the vestiges of darkness as we walk with you in the light.

You are a marvelous Savior, brilliant in your plan, shining in your suffering, radiant in your resurrection. You are worthy of all worship and honor and praise, the Savior of Light, the Defeater of darkness, the Son shine in our souls.

"…shout for joy before the LORD, the King. Let the sea resound, and everything in it, the world, and all who live in it" (Ps. 98:6b,7). Yes! Let us rejoice for all that You have done, Lord Jesus, Savior of the whole of creation, Un-twister of the crippled universe, Redeemer of mankind, Lover of Your enemies.

Prayer: "May You be exalted and glorified in our lives today, Lord Jesus, as we walk in Your light, shunning the darkness, rejecting the invitation to look back at the looming, churning, destroying oppression Satan seeks to spread over the land and over our souls. May we never forget from where you have saved us, Lord, but may we ever look to you, at your glory and power. Help us to be ever living in your light, walking in your path that we may give you unending honor and praise. Amen."

May 2

"...put your trust in the Lord both now and forever more."

Psalm 131:3

We sat in the tiny crowded lounge of the Dushanbe airport in Tajikistan, waiting for our return flight home. I was reading in Psalm 131: "I do not concern myself with great matters, or things too wonderful for me." My thoughts went back over this trip to Tajikistan and the many aspects of it that were out of our control, but not out of God's.

The bus trip to a new airport 60 miles west of Ist.anbul was an example of this. We expected the bus to drop us off at the airport and were surprised when the driver pulled over to the side of the road at a junction and said, "This is your stop. Walk down that road and you'll come to the airport." There was nothing in sight: no house, no traffic, no airport, just a deserted road.

We gathered our luggage, got off the bus, prayed, "Well, thank you for this, Lord", and set off down the cold, empty road, not knowing how far we had to walk with our heavy load.

We hadn't made it 20 yards, however, before a taxi came along and picked us up. This might seem like a normal thing to happen on a busy road to an airport, but not this airport. We found later that only about five planes a week fly into it. The only reason the taxi driver happened to come by was that he had gone out to buy some cigarettes.

Things were so new at the airport that there were no services yet: no restaurants, no snacks, no newspapers, no tea, not even any cigarettes for the taxi drivers. While we were talking with some of the personnel, they mentioned that the shifts were changing and offered to give us a lift into town to get something to eat. Since it would be several hours before our flight left, we accepted.

After a bite to eat and a futile attempt to find some English language newspapers to take to our friends in Tajikistan, we started back. The weather had turned much colder by this time with a strong wind blowing. We asked a man on the street where we could get a bus back by the airport. He not only took us to the bus stop, but invited us into his shop, which was just around the corner, gave us tea and bought our tickets for us! We certainly were guided in asking the right person!

The bus dropped us off at the same spot, and we began the hike to the airport, this time knowing it was about a mile and a half. However, we were not dressed warmly enough for the sudden drop in temperature and the wind chill factor, so were freezing by the time we'd gone our 20 yards. I turned around to back into the wind and saw a small truck coming! The driver stopped and picked us up, dropping us off at the terminal.

An interesting coincidence, one might say. However, the whole time we were at the airport (several hours), we only saw five vehicles use that road, and two of them came along just at the time we needed help—and were willing to stop and pick us up! These matters, small as they are in the course of life, were too great and wonderful for me to orchestrate; these were God sightings, direct help from the hand of God.

Now in Dushanbe as I thought about the return trip and the uncertainties of what would happen when we arrived at that empty airport, two other verses in Psalm 131 spoke to me. First verse one: "My heart is not proud, O Lord, my eyes are not haughty; I do not concern myself with great matters...." So, if I fuss and worry about things out of my control, I am being proud and haughty, acting as if I could influence these factors. Worry is a manifestation of pride!

Verse two led me to the next insight: "But I have stilled and quieted my soul, like a weaned child with its mother, like a weaned child is my soul within me." My soul naturally craves the kind of security that being totally in control gives; but that is beyond any human being. Instead I must look away to the God who is actually in control, who brings what is good (which can also sometimes be what is very difficult) and rest in His embrace. It is up to me to quiet and still my soul, looking at truth, refusing to give in to fear and conjecture.

Verse 3 sums it up: "...put your trust in the Lord both now and forever more." Who do I trust? My level of worry certainly tells me something about that! This exposure of the sin of pride and its manifestations has been good. After taking care of what is my responsibility (proper preparation), then I must quiet and still my soul and rest in Him, not let it thrash about in a fit of worry and self pity. This rest is part of the lightness of the yoke Jesus offers us. Let us take it with joy.

Prayer: "Lord, in the difficulties of life, help me to look to you, to rest in the greatness of who you are, to trust instead of worrying, to believe instead of feeling sorry for myself. Give wisdom in how to move ahead in your power today. Amen."

Epilogue: upon arriving at the new airport, we were able to share a taxi with other passengers to get safely and inexpensively back to Ist.anbul. The Lord had it all in hand!

May 3

God "chose us in him [Christ] before the creation of the world to be holy and blameless in his sight. In love he predestined us to be adopted as his sons through Jesus Christ, in accordance with his pleasure and will."

Ephesians 1:4,5,

Praise be to you, Father in Heaven, for your perfect love, your perfect interaction, your perfect grace in our lives. You chose us before the foundation of the world, meaning that you wanted us to be your children and knew we would respond to your efforts to draw us to yourself.

You purchased us with the blood of the Lamb, paying a huge price to buy us back from the prince of darkness. You predestinated us to the adoption of children through Jesus Christ—"according to the good pleasure of your will" (Eph. 1:5b). It gave you pleasure to make sure that we became your children! It was your intense desire to adopt us! And this adoption was "to the praise of the glory of your grace, in which we are accepted in the beloved" (Eph. 1:6), as the KJV says so poetically. We are not just tolerated, we are fully, wonderfully, wholeheartedly embraced and enjoyed.

The most astounding thing about your love poured out on us is that you did this when we were your enemies: bitter, rebellious, negative, destructive, hurtful foes. Rightfully you could have immediately condemned us to hell, separating us from your presence for eternity. "But because of your great love for us," you, Lord God, who are rich in mercy, "made us alive with Christ even when we were dead in transgressions—it is by your grace that we have been saved" (Eph. 2:3,4).

We exalt in this, we rejoice in this and praise you, giving thanks from full hearts for the warm and wonderful love that you pour out on us every day—including your gracious rebukes and correction—and our response is to love you back by bowing in awe-filled submission to your mercy and by living in obedience to your Word.

According to Ephesians 1, your attitude towards us, your interaction with us, your words about us are filled with energetically positive and loving thoughts. It is a delight and pleasure to you when we come into your presence. It is not like when we knock on some people's door and they open it to say in a disappointed voice, "Oh, it's you." We were

not the person they were hoping for.

No, when we come into your presence in prayer, or worship or thanksgiving or thought, your response is, "Oh!! It's you!! I'm so glad you came!!! I am delighted to hear from you!! I was just thinking about you, how much I love you, how you are one of my favorite sons—of course, all my children are my favorites, but that doesn't diminish my love for you. I am so glad you are my child; I have no regrets about choosing, calling and adopting you; in fact every time I think of you I am pleased; I delight in you; you are fully accepted in my heart. It is such a pleasure to have you in our family, to know you, to spend time with you.

"Come to me more often, I enjoy your prayers, your intercession, your praise time, your thoughts of me throughout the day. I look forward to eternity where we can spend unbroken time together in heaven, where you will be continually in my presence spiritually, mentally, emotionally, and physically. Live now in my love, live in obedience to Truth so that we both may have more pleasure and joy." And my soul and spirit respond with, "Yes!"

Prayer: "We praise you, Lord, our heavenly Father, for your rich, warm love toward us. Help us to honor and glorify you by reveling in your love, rejoicing in your acceptance, responding to your desire to spend time with us in coming to you each day. Help us to live in the warm, light-filled, graceful beauty of your rich, deep, powerful, ever-flowing, enthusiastic love for and acceptance of us in Christ. Glory be to you in our lives every minute of today. Amen."

May 4

"Then Jesus told his disciples a parable to show them that they should always pray and not give up."

Luke 18:1

Sometimes we pray for years, and nothing seems to happen. The people we pray for seem to continue on the same path of negative, self-inflicted defeat. Behind the scenes, however, God is at work, bringing change in deep and powerful ways that will break through to the surface at the right time.

Recently I visited several families we had worked with in the beginning of our ministry. Each one was a pool of problems, seemingly bottomless pits of need. Now, some 15 years later it is astounding and encouraging to see where the Lord has brought them.

When we met Abraham, he was a small, sad boy of 14; he had dropped out of high school during his first year and was working as an apprentice to a glazier. Being from a family of 5 siblings with an absent father, he and his sister of 16 had to earn whatever they could to feed the hungry mouths. His future was dim.

The most important change in Abraham's life came when, at 15 as a new believer, he whole-heartedly forgave his father for abandoning the family. As he willfully followed the Lord in this counter-cultural, counter-emotional obedience, every area of his life began to go uphill. He went back to high school and finished while working part time. At 19 he became one of the "elders" of a tiny church.

Today he is a university grad with a degree in graphic arts; he finished number two in his class and is married to a girl he led to the Lord, another graphic artist who finished first in their class. The development of his character preceded development in other areas and is the basis of his effective ministry.

Abraham was for a time the assistant pastor of a growing church and is now the director of the national children's ministry. Naturally a very quiet fellow, he has developed the ability to lovingly but firmly confront people with the truth.

What a difference from the shy and sad apprentice we met so many years ago. And he continues on a upward path of growth and effectiveness for the King, because he is willing to deny self, obey the Word and do what is right.

A large part of this difference can be attributed to the faithful prayers of many who interceded for Abraham and his family over the years. We need to "always pray and not give up."

Prayer: "Father, help me to trust you through prayer, continuing on when I'd like to give up. Help me to remember that you are the God of Moses, the God of Abraham and the God of Jacob who hears our prayers, just as you did theirs, and will answer powerfully and definitely, eventually bringing the change you desire. I praise you now for what you will do. Amen."

May 5

"...sing before the LORD, for he comes to judge the earth.
He will judge the world in righteousness and the peoples with equity."

Psalm 98:9

We will sing for joy to the Lord! You, Lord God, are the just and holy One and you are on the move to correct the injustice in the world. You have laid the foundation of redemptive righteousness in your great and powerful sacrifice of Jesus and in your raising Him from the dead.

You are now waiting for the right time to come and deal the final blow to all evil in the world, acting in equity and justice. You will eliminate wickedness, banishing it to the lake of fire forever, and you will fully transform your stubborn children into sinless holy beings able to come into the Kingdom of Heaven and live with you for eternity.

What a wonderful God you are, so patient in waiting for the right time, so gracious in providing a shelter from your wrath for all willing to come, so firm in carrying out your good plan to untwist the universe and right all wrongs.

We praise you for the suffering you allow in your wisdom, for you use it to open the eyes of blind rebels, as you did with us, to help us see the choices before us, to help us choose for you.

We praise you that you have ushered us into the fortress of your love and grace where we are protected from the onslaught of Satan and his forces, as well as from the impending flood of righteous wrath you will pour out upon the world at the appointed time. Safe, protected, cared for, loved—this is what we are in you, Lord Jesus. That is what you desire for every human being, if they will only come to the Truth and enter your shelter.

Our response to your great love and provision can only be worship and praise, thanksgiving and gratefulness, leading to loving you back in obedience and humility.

Praise be to you, Lord God, that you have revealed yourself to us in your Word, both written and living. Praise you, Lord Jesus, that you are the Word of life, the Word of Creation, the Word of resurrection, the Word of prophesy, the Word of authority, the Word of finality.

In you we can trust, in you we can rest, in you alone we find life and love, grace and goodness, power and provision, tenderness and tenaciousness. In you we can exalt, in you we rejoice, in you we are glad. We commit ourselves to walk in the light and life of your love today, obeying you in joy, pleasing you in obedience, glorifying you in praise, for you are worthy of all we can give and more.

Prayer: "As I live before you today, Lord, the Mighty and Majestic Ruler of all, help me to live in the light of your greatness, in the shadow of your love and in the wisdom of your Word. I bow before you in awe and rise up to obey you today in love. Amen."

May 6

"God chastens us for our profit so that we might be partakers of his holiness."

Hebrews 12:10

Sin can slip into our lives on little cat's feet, entering unnoticed to sit quietly in a corner and grow. It can enter through the door of our old nature, or the window of the world's values, or the crack of rebellion.

Fortunately, the Holy Spirit is very much aware of these intruders in the Kingdom and knows when to bring which ones to our attention.

As we came home from the Middle East and had two weeks in the States to prepare for our classes, a serious sin crept into my life, disguised as diligence. This sin is a blatant one, yet was hard to discern without the X-ray vision provided by Scripture, so God had me meditating on Colossians 3 in preparation for the exposure.

After our arrival, I set to work on different projects, laboring from early morning until late in the evening. I got a lot done, but there were some danger signs that all was not well. Instead of slowly resting up as intended, I was becoming more and more tired; there was tension in my relationships; my quiet times were not as deep; and I wasn't sleeping well. Then the Holy Spirit turned on the lights and revealed that I had become an idolater!

Colossians 3:5 spoke clearly to this: "Put to death therefore, whatever belongs to your earthly nature," and then goes on to list four sins, adding at the end, "and greed which is idolatry." There it was: I was being greedy to accomplish more and more, focusing on the things not done rather than on "the things above," failing to turn goals, projects and desires over to God, instead seeking to do them in my own strength.

All the work I was doing was good but it was corrupted by my greed of wanting to do more and more rather than being thankful for what could be done in a normal workday. Doing the right thing for the wrong motive is not good. I was driving myself hard, as well as those around me, serving the god of accomplishment rather than the God of goodness and grace.

Praise God that He is able to break through our delusions and give us clarity of vision, bringing us to confession and repentance, thereby bringing cleansing and freedom from the tyranny of the flesh. And just to make sure I got the message that slowing down is important, He let me break my toe so I had no choice but to limit myself! God is good all the time and shows His love to us in so many ways.

Prayer: "Praise you, Lord, for the work of your Spirit to convict us of sin. Show me the next one I should confess and turn from. Make me sensitive to your leading and make me quick to repent. Amen."

May 7

"The LORD reigns, let the nations tremble...."

Psalm 99:1a

Praise be to you, Lord Jesus, that I feel far from you today—an opportunity to walk by faith, to know that, in spite of my feelings, you are near and that I am with you, for you are faithful. Praise you for the lack of feeling and the abundance of truth. I choose to live by truth today.

[The Lord] "sits enthroned between the cherubim, let the earth shake" (Ps. 99:1b). You, Yahweh, are the absolute ruler of the universe. You are the most High, the final Authority, the undisputed King. No one can oppose your decisions for long. You will win in the end, for you are God: your power is infinite, your understanding is unbounded, your knowledge is limitless, and your wisdom is unfathomable. No one can plan or attack or rebel without your knowing about it long before hand.

Your being such a powerful God means we must tremble and quake before you. We are tiny, powerless, ignorant, sinful and weak. There is nothing we can do to prevent you from carrying out your plans for the universe. You are sovereign: no matter what we or anyone else may do, you will bring your desires to pass in the end.

Yet in your sovereignty you have given us limited authority to make decisions in the immediate circle of our lives—moral and ethical choices carrying serious consequences. You have made it possible that we truly can love—or hate. In your wisdom and love you have made us in your image, and given us such power. Praise you for what you have done and planned, for it is the greatest good.

We give you glory for your great grace, your deep wisdom, your incredible patience, your unwavering firmness in carrying out your objectives. You will judge the world in righteousness, you will protect all who come to You. Evil will end, Heaven will rejoice, eternity will begin, and we will be your Bride. Great hope, Great truth, Great mysteries. Praise you for being such a Great God.

Prayer: "I bow before You today, my triune Creator and Lord, trusting in your goodness, your righteousness, your compassion and your grace. I rise up to obey you in order to bring you more praise before the unseen hosts and the people around me. Help me to live in obedience to your power and presence, your wisdom and direction. Amen."

May 8

"Forgive as you have been forgiven."

Colossians 3:12

The legalistic quest for perfection is a natural one in my life, but it is futile. Every day I fail multiple times to do what is right in my thought life, or in some words spoken, or in some choice, action or relationship.

On one hand this is part of being a fallen person living in a fallen world, (although I must hasten to add that this in not a valid excuse for choosing failure). On the other hand, our failures can be fertile ground for spiritual growth.

This past year, and especially this summer, I made a number of choices that did not work out for the best. Almost all of these were made with the intent of doing good, and many for doing what was best. However, there were also heavy strands of wrong motives woven into the fabric of the decisions, and these marred the final product. For instance, jumping in to give good advice to a person who is not ready to hear it. Many would not consider such failures to be all that bad, but when I consider how they affect outcomes, they are significant.

The bottom line, however, is what I do with my failures. For someone with my natural old nature's drive for success and fulfillment, these failures produce anger: towards myself, towards those who may point out my failures, and ultimately towards God who has "allowed me to be imperfect." None of this anger is righteous, but God uses it as a "prod" to help me take up and put on the second piece of His armor of Eph. 6:10-18, the breast plate of righteousness.

It is His righteousness that counts, not my being perfect, and He offers me His righteousness on a daily basis. I need to lay down my idol, my desire for the perfection that I seek to look good, even to myself, and instead affirm that only God does everything right.

God has, through Christ's sacrifice, forgiven me for my sins and failures, so I need to agree and forgive myself on the basis of Christ's work. Failure to appropriate this forgiveness is a greater failure than any of the other lacks I've mentioned!

Not everyone struggles with forgiving themselves, but many of us do so without realizing it. To accept God's forgiveness allows us to forgive ourselves on the basis of His work and then we are freed to forgive others.

My failures of this past year have been used to lead me into a deeper understanding of God's forgiveness, allowing me to see more of its many facets. Forgiving myself also reveals my anger for what it is, a deep vein of self-centeredness in my old man; this revelation then helps to free me from my anger through confession, especially confession in layers.

Our Lord knows what He is doing in our lives, often leading us by enlightenment as a result our failures. The ways of God are both inscrutably complex and marvelously simple. Are we following?

Prayer: "You, Lord, are the God of all forgiveness; give us grace to grasp how much we are forgiven so we can forgive ourselves and then forgive others. Then may we keep on the whole armor to be useful to you and bring glory to your name. Amen."

May 9

"Commit your way to the LORD; trust in him and he will do this: He will make your righteousness shine like the dawn, the justice of your cause like the noonday sun."

Psalm 37:5,6

Praise, You, Lord Jesus, that you are righteous and good. As an acquaintance of mine faces an unjust and potentially dangerous accusation in court, you brought some verses from Psalm 37 to mind: "Trust in the Lord and do good, so shall you dwell in the land and be fed." What wonderful commands, giving us direction and hope. You are the One we trust, not judges or court systems or lawyers. You give wisdom in what good to do and direction in overcoming evil with good.

"Delight yourself in the Lord...." You turn our focus from the intense desire for deliverance to you, the Source of all hope, the only Certainty that exists, and the One who gives us many reasons to delight, whether things go as we like or not.

"Delight yourself in the Lord and he will give you the desires of your heart." So when our delight is in you, you will put the right desires in our hearts and then bring them to pass. The greatest desire we can have is to glorify and honor you—no matter what may come to pass; that gives us the big perspective. Then we can let go of our own small desires and give you permission to bring whatever you desire into our lives. And you will bring to pass what is best.

"Commit your way unto the Lord, trust also in him and he will bring it to pass." We can surrender all to you, for you are trustable, wise, powerful, loving and true. You are the only One who can bring the right conclusion to pass.

"He will bring forth your righteousness as the light and your justice as the noon day sun." You, O Lord, can bring the justice that is so lacking in this world. You are the One who loves righteousness and justice, and our lives are full of your unfailing love.

To you be honor and glory for what you will do in my acquaintance's life, for I know it will be good, just as you are good. The outcome may be hard, for you allow suffering for high and wise reasons, but you will also give enough grace to move through the experience with power and wisdom and joy.

You are the True God, the only Wise One, the Source of all Good. We praise you now for what you will do before seeing any conclusion to this situation.

"The Lord foils the plans of the nations, He thwarts the purposes of the people. But the plans of the Lord stand firm forever and the purposes of His heart through all generations" (Ps. 33:10).

Prayer: "Lord God, King of the universe, help me to trust in you today, to praise you in all that comes, pleasant or not, desired or feared, for you have great plans which will always include difficulties designed to make us grow. May you be glorified in my responses to today's difficulties. Amen."

May 10

"For we fight not against flesh and blood but against principalities and powers, against spiritual wickedness in heavenly places. Put on the whole armor of God so that you may be able to stand in the evil day and having done all to stand."

Ephesians 6:11

While talking recently with a person struggling with feelings of inadequacy, any advice I gave proved to be totally ineffective. Then a thought came to mind that turned out to be the key to opening the door to this person's emotional prison.

"This feeling of inadequacy is exactly what Satan wants you to focus on. Of course we are inadequate; we are human beings and have limitations. In contrast, God wants us to focus on Him, to find our adequacy in Him, our acceptance in Him, our worth and joy in Him.

"Satan, however, wants us to focus on what we can't do; he wants us to work for our worth and to seek for the elusive happiness of accomplishment. So whose lead are you going to follow? Are you going to fall into his trap, or sidestep it with God's truth?"

Asking "What would Jesus do in this situation?" helps us think biblically. Adding the question, "What would Satan want me to do?" will bring even more biblical clarity. Paul refers to this in Ephesians 6 when he says, "Put on the whole armor of God so you will not fall in to the wiles of the devil."

The devil is clever and does not want us thinking about his desires; he wants us to unknowingly mix our personal and cultural bias in with a bit of Scripture and do things that make us feel good and please him. It is easy to fool ourselves into thinking that our preferences as Christians are the same as God's. For instance, in our culture we have come to confuse busyness with being spiritual, having results with being blessed and talent and training with being spiritually mature.

When faced with an opportunity for more ministry, we need to think about what Jesus would do, and what Satan would have us do. Satan is happy when we are striving to push ahead in our own effort, keeping very busy "for the Lord", wearing ourselves out for others. He is not happy when we spend time first in prayer and in the Word, seeking God's direction, weighing our motives before Him, waiting for His timing–and then working hard as He directs.

As a concrete example of this concept, here in the Middle East we have often had opportunities to help believers financially. "Of course Jesus would have us give to them!" we thought. Yet as we look back now, it is clear how in the early years of ministry, channeling funds to seemingly desperate needs produced far more bitter and dependent believers than anything else. Our help was toxic, not a tonic. We have to admit that our estimation of what Jesus wanted was not fully correct. Yes, it made us feel good to help and we got the believers out of binds, but also often prevented them from learning the lessons God had for them.

Later, when God had gotten our attention and made clear that we should step back from such rescuing attempts and let Him teach important lessons of character, believers matured and grew in new ways. There are times to help, but wisely, in cooperation with God, not with Satan's feel-good solutions. Let us ask for wisdom and discernment and be willing to deny self so we can truly obey God.

Prayer: "Lord, as we seek your will in situations, remind us to search Scripture, asking the question, "What would Jesus do?" and also add the question, 'What would Satan want me to do?' Guide us in cooperating with you in your intentions. Amen."

May 11

"We wait in hope for the LORD; he is our help and our shield."

Psalm 33:20

Life is full of problems, fear-producing events, the unexpected and the unjust—all results of sin warping the creation. But you, Lord Jesus, are the rescuing Savior, the One whom we can trust in the midst of this tragic twisting. You are at work to bring an end to the destructive effects of sin. You are the good One, you are the powerful One, you are the loving One, you are the wise One.

Your plan to restore righteousness is perfect: you move at the right speed to bring the right thing at the right time. You allow what is painful now to bring glory in the future. You are absolutely right and absolutely trustable, always providing much more grace than we need.

You are the One to be praised in the midst of difficulty because you are bringing us through it into a wider place. You have a plan and will bring it to pass.

We can trust you, rely on you, praise you; we can rest in you when all about us is falling apart. No human resource, no earthly power, no political plan can protect us—but you can, and you have made a way for all to escape the corruption and destruction of the world and to be transported into the glory of the next world, spending eternity with you—if we believe.

David had it right in Psalm 33:20-22: "We wait in hope for the LORD." There is no one else to wait for!

"…he is our help and our shield." You give us grace and protect us from what is truly harmful.

"In him our hearts rejoice." Your love, your kindness, your faithfulness, your power and goodness are more than enough reason to rejoice.

"for we trust in his holy name." You are the holy and powerful God, the most High whose might can accomplish all that is necessary to save us.

"May your unfailing love rest upon us, O LORD," Praise you for your love that never ends.

"even as we put our hope in you." The key to participating in your power, Lord, is to trust in you rather than in ourselves. Help us to do that consistently. Glory and honor be to you for the power found in hoping in you, the certainty that you will do what is good and right and best.

Prayer: "Today we go into the day with you, in you, by you, for you,
>   Lord Jesus. Help us to put our hope only in you, praising you
>   before any answer comes, giving you 'great faith glory' before the
>   unseen hosts. Amen."

May 12

"And ye are complete in him, which is the head of all principality and power…."

Colossians 2:10 (KJV)

In thinking about some conflicts we've been dealing with, and in meditating on scripture, the following insight surfaced. One of the deepest themes running through conflicts seems to be the struggle for significance. Lucifer wanted more significance, to be like God. Eve was tempted to be more significant in knowing good and evil independently of God. Cain wanted his sacrifice to accepted and to be significant on his own terms rather than God's. The builders of the tower of Babel wanted to make a name for themselves by their achievement, rejecting God's command to spread out and fill the earth.

So it goes through all of scripture and all of life. I see this in myself, being hurt and angry when someone does something to rob me of my dignity; striving for accomplishment to feel and look more significant.

What brought this out clearly was meditating on Colossians 3:12-14, "Therefore as God's chosen people, holy and dearly loved...." Here in this verse is all the significance that anyone will ever need. We are chosen before the foundation of the world to be a child of the Most High. We are made holy: forgiven, purified and commissioned for significant work. And we are dearly loved: sought out by the intense and pure desire of God the Ruler of all, unconditionally accepted, whole-heartedly adopted, deeply cared for and delighted in.

If we could just grasp this on a "whole person level"--that is, not just intellectually but also volitionally and emotionally--what a difference it would make. In fact, I think that is the whole point of the next part of the sentence in verse 12, since you are chosen, holy and dearly loved, "Therefore clothe yourselves with compassion, kindness, humility, gentleness [translatable as "sweet reasonableness"] and patience." When we are secure in Christ and all He has given us, then we can put on these qualities that He has already supplied for us (2 Pet. 1:1-4) and stop fighting with others for significance.

When we are able to begin grasping this, conflicts can immediately lessen. But we can only understand these truths with the power of God– it cannot be done in human wisdom, insight or strength. In Ephesians 3:18 Paul prays that God will give the believers POWER so they can understand the greatness of the love of God, to know the love that surpasses knowledge, and the result is "that you may be filled to the measure of all the fullness of God."

So we are thrown back on prayer, which is dependence on God. May we avail ourselves through prayer, praise and faith of all that our loving Father has prepared and presented to us.

Prayer: "Lord God, grant us the power to grasp 'how wide and long and high and deep is the love of Christ' so that we may reject the human struggle for significance, rest in who we are in Christ and clothe ourselves with the qualities you have bought for us. Amen."

May 13

"The Lord foils the plans of the nations, He thwarts the purposes of the people."

Psalm 33:10

It is wonderful to know, Lord Jesus, Heavenly Father and Holy Spirit, that you watch over all that is going on in our lives and overrule in what is harmful. What cannot be used for your purposes is prevented, as the above verse points out.

"The plans of the Lord endure forever and the purposes of His heart through all generations" (Ps. 33:11). You never tire of carrying out your plans; you never fail to attend to any detail; you never are caught by surprise. You are the God of completeness and competence, care and concern; you know exactly what is happening all the time.

"From heaven the LORD looks down and sees all mankind; from his dwelling place he watches all who live on earth—he who forms the hearts of all, who considers everything they do" (Ps. 33:13-15). Praise be to you, O Lord God for your omniscience, your omnipresence, your omnipotence. You see all, know all, calculate all, consider all and are able to do all that is good, no matter the cost to you.

"No king is saved by the size of his army, no warrior escapes by his great strength, a horse is a vain hope, despite its great strength it cannot save" (Ps. 33:16,17). It is not the seen that saves, but the unseen, the invisible power of the living, loving God. His eyes "are on those who fear him, on those whose hope is in his unfailing love, to deliver them from death and keep them alive in famine" (Ps. 33:18,19).

You are the One who saves, Lord Jesus. You saved us from all forms of death: eternal separation from you, emotional separation from ourselves, social separation from others, physical separation from our bodies—you are the Defeater of death, the Giver of life, the Provider of protection, the Shepherd of souls. You are trustable, you are wise, you are thoroughly good.

"We wait in hope for the Lord, he is our help and our shield. In you our hearts rejoice, for we trust in your holy name" (Ps. 33:20,21). Praise you for what will come today: good things from your hands, wise things from your mind, loving things from your heart, challenging things from your will, grace-filled things from your compassion. "May your unfailing love rest on us, O Lord, even as we put our hope in you" (Ps 33:22). Help us to hope in you alone.

You, O Triune King, are worthy of worship and praise, even before we see what will happen, for you are good and gracious, wise and wonderful, strong and sure, true and trustable.

Prayer: "You are worthy of receiving glory from my life today, Lord; may I be a glory-giver, by offering the sacrifice of thanksgiving, not a glory-stealer by complaining. May I hope in you. May honor flow to you today from my attitudes and actions, my words and worship. Amen."

May 14

"Purge me with hyssop, and I shall be clean: wash me, and I shall be whiter than snow. Make me to hear joy and gladness; that the bones which thou hast broken may rejoice."

Psalm 57:1,2

God has this wonderful and terrible way of keeping us accountable. He wants to make sure that I am applying what I am preaching. Earlier I wrote about how the struggle for significance is at the bottom of most disagreements. This was brought home again shortly after that letter was sent when I found myself so angry over something that I was literally gasping for breath.

Unfortunately in this instance I clearly made a choice to NOT offer the sacrifice of thanksgiving, but instead to speak words of anger, even though it was just to myself. These words pushed me over the edge of the cliff of self-pity and there I was, speeding down the slope of selfishness bracing myself for the crash on the rocks of depression.

What triggered this incident was a statement by a close friend communicating that I was incompetent (that is not what was actually said, but what I perceived). This understanding, unbeknownst to me, percolated in my soul for three days, and then a repeat of the statement brought out the anger.

After cooling off and spending some time talking with the Lord about this through journaling, it became clear that there is something even more fundamental than the struggle for significance: UNBELIEF. I had chosen not to believe what God said about significance (that He has already given every believer all the significance that he will ever need, having created us in the Image of God, redeemed us by the blood of the Lamb, adopted us as His children and equipped us for significant service, Col. 3:12).

Instead I chose to fight for my "importance" and succeeded only in creating friction and the need to go back and ask forgiveness, plus wasting a lot of emotional energy! It's much better to believe God and act on Truth than to believe my feelings and act on foolishness!

All this shows that knowing something intellectually doesn't change us on a heart-level, doesn't bring the needed transformation and worldview shift. Knowing is the beginning but then we must cooperate with God as He works to transform us through prayer, meditation on Scripture, reviewing truth, and applying it. A very important ingredient in this is to "process" our feelings before God through lifting our souls (journaling), surrendering our preferences and perceptions to His Word, not allowing our negative feelings to fester inside.

In the end we must say, "Praise be to you, Lord God, for how, in spite of what we are, you gave yourself for us, that we may know you and be conformed to your image." In Him there is hope and there is joy--and we can live in both.

Prayer: "Father, help me today to listen to your voice in your Word, in your cautions, in your children, to offer the sacrifice of thanksgiving at every point. Help me to live in and obey the truth that you know what you are doing, that you allow what I need to make me grow, and that you give grace enough to praise you in the midst of it. In spite of all, glorify yourself in my life today. Amen."

May 15

"Bow down and hear me, O Lord, for I am poor and needy."

Psalm 86:1 NKJV

Praise you for this word, Lord Jesus, as it clarifies what is happening in my life. There is too much to do and I do not have the strength to work hard at it, being so tired. I praise you for this situation for it reminds me that without you I can do nothing (John 15:5).

Thank you for my weakness, thank you for there being more work than time, thank you that I cannot handle it in my own strength. In my mind there is a jumble of things, giving me an underlying sense of unsettledness; this further saps my strength, confuses my thinking and works against my being disciplined in doing the next thing.

Yes, "I am poor and needy" but you, Lord, are rich and powerful. Being at the end of my fraying rope, I willingly switch to your strong, eternal, graceful rope. I praise you for your love and kindness in prodding me to surrender like this. Praise you for working to "preserve my soul, for I am holy, devoted to you," knowing that you "save your servant who trusts in you" (Ps. 86:2).

I praise you for all that is happening in my life, both positive and negative. Thank you that I seem to be catching up on my sleep. Thank you that I am making progress on the big writing project, endless as it appears to be. Thank you that my restless legs have returned, again a sign of unsettledness, a need to return to rest in you. Thank you, too, for the seeming failure of my mother-in-law's eye operation; you are doing something with that, something we can't see yet, but which you will use for good. Praise you now for how you will work this out. Thank you for my wife's illness. Thank you for the uncertainty about our going to the US, about what to do in the next two months, about the uncertainty in the church. Also for the three, possibly four tax problems before us.

I look away to you, for you are "good and ready to forgive and plenteous in mercy to all those who call upon you. ... In the day of my trouble I will call upon you for you will answer me" (Ps. 86:5,7). You are the trustable One, the wise One, the powerful One. In the seeming turmoil, failure and insurmountable tasks, you are at work, guiding, directing, helping, overcoming.

You are my Rock, worthy of praise and worship and I give those to you now before solutions come to pass. You are "full of compassion, gracious, slow to anger and plenteous in mercy and truth" (Ps. 86:15). Glory is due you, praise is our privilege, worship is our response because your character is holy. Thank you that you "grant your strength to your servant and save the son of your handmaid" (Ps. 86:16). Praise you that daily you give "a token of your love so that those who hate me may see it and be ashamed, for you, Lord, have helped and comforted me" (Ps. 86:17).

Prayer: "Give me your wisdom, Lord, that I may do what is on your agenda today. I lay down my will and take yours instead. Thank you for the guidance you will give, the ways you will open and shut, the protection you will provide, shielding my head in the day of battle. Amen."

May 16

"…the God of Israel gives power and strength to his people."

Psalm 68:35

The Lord is faithful in helping us apply the new things He's teaching us. Here's the story of a friend who had opportunity to implement God's teaching on how conflicts stem from our unbelief.

After a particularly hard week, this acquaintance of mine took his car to have the brakes fixed and then the car aligned. He had hoped to be on the road for a long trip by 4 in the afternoon. However, when he called at 3:30 to see if the car was ready, he found that the mechanic hadn't even finished the brakes yet. He went down and was finally able to pick it up at 5, only to find that the brakes weren't working properly. However, it was too late to do anything about them.

Then he discovered that he'd left his computer's adaptor at a church several miles and 20 stop lights away and would have go there before leaving on his trip. While double-checking his luggage, he found that he'd lost the cell phone he'd borrowed from his son. Now it was 6 pm, he was tired, cold, hungry and facing a long drive with an unhappy fellow passenger, also stressed by the delays.

At this point he was tittering on the edge of unbelief, tempted to feel sorry himself, to complain and snap back at his passenger's negative comments. However, he said that the Lord clearly brought to his mind this idea of believing what God said–that the Lord is his Shepherd and he would not lack what was necessary.

He made the decision to praise God whole-heartedly and think on the basis of Truth. He felt his spirits rise, responded with grace to his passenger, drew on God's supply of patience and did the things he had to before leaving on the trip.

One thing he said later was, "You never know what possible trouble the Lord protects us from when He allows our plans to go astray." I don't know what God protected him from, but do know that it is good and powerful to offer the sacrifice of thanksgiving when we least like it!

We have the marvelous privilege to, "Proclaim the power of God;" for "His majesty is over Israel, His power is in the skies. You are awesome in your sanctuary; the God of Israel gives power and strength to his people" (Ps. 68:34,35).

Prayer: "Lord, it is so unnatural for me to trust you under pressure. Forgive me for my unbelief. Help me today to praise you no matter what comes so I can give you glory and honor through the whole day. Amen."

May 17

"The LORD reigns let the nations tremble."

Psalm 99:1a

As we face the great uncertainties of the future with many negatives going on in the world, it is so good to know that you, O Lord, reign! You are mighty, powerful, strong, undefeatable, impregnable and untouchable--for you are the Most High, the Final Authority, the Measure of all truth. You will triumph, you will win, you will defeat your enemies, you will reign forever. You are unstoppable, unquenchable, unending. There is no wisdom, no insight, no plan that can succeed against you.

The nations, and we, must tremble before you, for you are our Mighty Ruler, our Judge, the One we will come face to face with to give an account of our lives.

"...he sits enthroned between the cherubim, let the earth shake" (Ps. 99:1). You are the High King, the One crowned with authority, power and wisdom. The cherubim--mighty angels far greater than we--serve and worship you. How much more should we--puny, weak, feeble, powerless, sinful creatures--worship and serve you with joy and trembling. If the earth, seeing you, trembles, how much more should we?!!!!

"Great is the LORD in Zion; he is exalted over all the nations. Let them praise your great and awesome name—he is holy" (Ps. 99:2). Truly you are worthy to be exalted over ALL the nations, for you are the maker of EVERY nation: "All the nations whom you have created will come before you, O Lord, and glorify your name" (Ps. 86:9).

Your name, Lord God, is worthy of praise, for it is truly great and awesome: Yahweh, the Holy One, utterly other, spotless, clean, free of any corruption within or without, unable to sin, shining in glorious purity, full of goodness, righteousness and love, empty of all evil, darkness and negativeness, Hater of sin and Lover of sinners. You,

LORD, are absolutely worthy of praise, because of your perfect character, your powerful deeds, your persistent love. We must worship you, we must honor and glorify you, for your holy character demands it: your intricate, inscrutable triune nature; your perfect justice and love; your overwhelming beauty and greatness.

We bow before you in humility, we rise up in obedience, rejoicing and delighting in being your children, in being held by your right hand, in being guided by your counsel, in being swept along by you to the end of history and into your heavenly home, to be there for eternity, worshiping, praising, glorifying the One True God!!!

Prayer: "Guide me in living in the truth that you, Lord God, reign! Turn my eyes from worries, fears and apprehensions to your might and wisdom, victory and future. May you be glorified in my life, my attitudes, thoughts, words and actions today as I trust in you! Amen."

May 18

"So then, those who suffer according to God's will should commit themselves to their faithful Creator and continue to do good."

1 Peter 4:19

It is amazing to see how the Lord skillfully weaves together various "event threads" to produce the fabric of our lives, intertwining different happenings, truths, failures, corrections and experiences to make us beautiful and effective in His Kingdom.

We have all had difficult relationships, some being resolved, others dissolving as one or both parties pull back. At present there are several painful relational problems in my life, which, in spite of all I could do from my side, remain unresolved.

This has been humbling for me. For one thing, I have fault in all of my broken relationships: mistakes I have made continue to be a barrier for the other person even though I've taken steps to correct them. I cannot make people reconcile. God has given each of us real moral responsibility and we cannot properly force others to do what is right; we stand weak and dependent on Him.

James 1:2 gives us our part in this drama: "Count it all joy when you fall into diverse temptations, knowing this, that the trying [stretching] of your faith produces perseverance...." We must see these events as positive tools God is using in our lives to make us grow.

The most important question to ask in a conflict is, "What is God doing in my life through this?" Is He, with my cooperation, producing a beautiful pattern of godly response no matter what the other person does? Or is He encountering opposition from me that produces snarled threads and an unpleasant spot in His weaving of my life?

One of the most positively powerful examples of cooperation with God in the trying of Joseph's faith: betrayed by his brothers, he is marched across the sands, his ankles chained, an iron collar around his neck, the sun beating down on him, his situation hopeless. Yet after being sold, he displays a sweet attitude of grace, being both a hard worker, and liked by all. His faith had been stretched, probably to the breaking point, but because of what he knew of God and His character, Joseph made the right decision to forgive his brothers and let go, thereby allowing God to weave into his life a picture to help us in our difficulties.

What God is after in His relationship with us is to have the warp of Scripture woven expertly with the woof of experience. His part is deciding what to bring into our lives for our good and His glory. Our part is submission, growing in the knowledge of the Word and in giving godly responses. The result of our cooperation is what Peter describes in his first letter, 2:12, "Live such good lives among the pagans that, though they accuse you of doing wrong, they may see your good deeds and glorify God on the day He visits us."

Prayer: "Lord, help me to cooperate with you as you bring to me events, people and experiences to make me grow and to give you glory. Remind me to respond positively in faith to your grace and power by praising you in all. Amen."

May 19

"The Lord reigns; Let the peoples tremble! He dwells between the cherubim; Let the earth be moved!"

Psalm 99:1

Praise be to you, Lord God, the holy One, our sovereign King. Praise you that I can give thanks in all things, knowing that you reign, allowing/bringing to us what is good. Thank you for last night's interrupted sleep, the restless legs, disturbing dreams, waking up often, being dried out and the resulting grogginess this morning. All this reminds me of my weakness, my inability to regulate even how well I sleep.

In reality there is not much that I can control, just a tiny sphere of "power" where I can make decisions, but not fully determine their outcomes. I can choose to go to bed early, but what comes afterwards is not in my hands.

Praise you for showing me again my powerlessness—it reminds me that most of the points in the beatitudes in Matthew 5 are a description of weakness. Beginning with, "Blessed are those who are poor in spirit, for theirs is the kingdom of heaven," Jesus went on to say, blessed are the meek (instead of those in control), those who hunger (instead of those with resources), those who are merciful (instead manipulating others), those who are peacemakers (instead of being dealmakers), those who are persecuted, insulted and lied about (rather than being able to protect their honor).

To be weak is good, it is honorable because it brings honor to you: "My power is made perfect in weakness" (2 Cor. 12:9). It is something to rejoice in, to delight in, to praise about (talk about supernatural thinking!). It is a chance to give you glory, to live by faith, to be a channel of power, a spring of grace, a beacon of hope, a demonstration of goodness, a witness of the One true God to all those around us.

Praise be to You, Lord Jesus, for showing us the way in this, as you, in your human weakness, suffered emotionally when you could have decided to avoid it, suffered physically when you could have called on angels to deliver you, suffered spiritually when you could have come down from the cross and left us to what we deserved.

Instead, you chose to be weak, to let the attacks of men and devils reach you, flow over you, defeat you in the moment, so that you could triumph in the end. Because of your willingness to be weak you could fulfill the demands of justice. You followed the unseen wisdom of God and brought redemption, salvation, glory for all who were to become your brothers and sisters and honor for yourself, which you will also share with us. Power alone could not do it; power in weakness was the way. Praise be to you for showing this to us.

Prayer: "Lord, help me to walk joyfully in weakness today, rejoicing in your strength, your power, your mightiness, your holiness, your greatness, to acclaim you in all I do, to walk in the light of your presence. Glory be to you. Amen."

May 20

"I form the light and create darkness, I bring prosperity and create disaster; I, the LORD, do all these things."

Isaiah 45:7

One of the hard-to-accept truths from Scripture is that God uses, even causes disasters where many people die or are hurt. From our "compassionate conservative" modern viewpoint, this is hard to understand; in fact, it is threatening. If God allows or wills this to happen to others, what will He bring into my life?

This is a question predicated on two non-biblical assumptions. First is that we deserve only good things, and second, that personal comfort is a higher value than our true goal in life--which is to glorify God through obedience.

A clue to understanding God's actions lies in the oldest book in the Bible, Job. After allowing great suffering into Job's life, God refuses to answer his question of "Why me?" Instead God points to His wisdom, power and grace. "Trust me to do what is best, not just what is comfortable," He says. Job chose to trust Him and has been a beacon of hope for millions since.

This question of tragedy and disaster came home to me during the earthquakes in the Middle East in 1999. Just after the first one occurred, I was reading in Revelation 9. Verses 18-21 describe how many people were killed by plagues God had sent and concludes with these words, "the rest of mankind...still did not repent of the works of their hands; they did not stop worshiping demons and idols.... Nor did they repent of their murders, their magic arts, their sexual immorality or their thefts."

God wanted these people to be saved (He had the long term in view), and brought about what was needed to get their attention; but still they refused His grace. God uses as small a stick as He can to get our attention and bring us to repentance. Many, however, do not listen and need a bigger stick; and even then many don't listen.

God's compassion, His wisdom, His understanding of eternity and His grace lead him to be as firm as necessary to bring as many as possible to repentance, yet leaves room for the operation of our limited will.

He does the same in bringing His children to maturity. If we pay attention to His still small voice, He won't have to shout to get our attention. He may still lead us through deep waters, but will carry us through in His power and grace. We can trust such a God to do what is best in our lives, seeing His love in what He allows or sends. We can praise Him in it and bring Him glory.

Prayer: "Lord, I cannot understand your reasoning but help me to trust your understanding, to rest in your wisdom, to grasp that in each difficulty of life you are at work to open people's eyes and bring them to repentance, then to mature them in Christ. Help me to cooperate with you in this by offering the sacrifice of thanksgiving at each juncture. Amen."

May 21

"The King is mighty; he loves justice—you have established equity;"

Psalm 99:4a

Praise be to you, Lord Jesus, King of Kings, Lord of Lords, Ruler of the universe, Creator and Sustainer of all. You are the star-Breather, the atom Keeper, the earth Spinner, the dawn Bringer. I exalt you, King

Jesus, for you are mighty and powerful, the most high, the immeasurably strong, majestically great and eternal God.

You are undefeatable, unconquerable, unlimited, unending. You are the Source of all strength, the Spring of all power, the Author of all authority. You are the Ruler who reigns in all regions of life. No bird flies without your knowledge, no man sins without your grief, no person acts without your seeing, and no evil is allowed that cannot be woven into your plan of redemption and revival.

Before you we all are judged by the same great and righteous sinless standard, for you are the perfect, holy and righteous Judge. You know all our thoughts, all our motives, all our secret acts, all our manipulations, all our rebellion against your standard of perfect goodness. You can, without dispute, pronounce what is evil, punish what is sin, banish what is wrong.

You, the sinless, pure, untainted and perfect God, will remove sin from your presence. And you will purify from sin all those who come into your shelter of salvation so we may live forever in holy and harmonious relation with you, eternally giving glory to you.

Lord, "…you have done what is just and right." Therefore we will "Exalt the LORD our God and worship at his footstool; he is holy" (Ps. 99:4b,5). We praise you, Lord God that we can bow before your footstool, that you allow us entrance into your presence, that as we come in the blood of Christ, our worship is acceptable to you.

I exalt you Lord God for what you are: pure and powerful, good and gracious, mighty and magnificent, wise and wonderful, holy and happy, eternal and ever-present, all seeing and all knowing, intimate and involved, caring and consistent, loving and lavish, rich and real, forgiving and forever. You, Lord God—Father, Son and Holy Spirit—are Triune and Complete in yourself; you are worthy of worship without considering how your qualities benefit me—and they certainly do!

Prayer: "To you be glory and honor today in my life as I live under the hand of your love and protection, deeply satisfied in you, Lord God, the great Shepherd and King of my life. Amen."

May 22

"My soul yearns, even faints for the courts of the Lord; my heart and my flesh cry out for the living God."

Psalm 84:2

There is in each of us that deep longing for something more than this earth can give. As one friend said recently, "There is a question that keeps coming up inside, 'Is this all there is?'"

God has given us a yearning for Him, a gift we often don't recognize. This longing can be disguised as an undercurrent of dissatisfaction, or a realization that no matter how well things go, there is still some emptiness inside.

We tend to confuse this longing for God with our desires for material things, accomplishment or human relationships. However, no matter what we do about it, this longing is there, showing us the emptiness of life without Him, pulling us towards Him.

If we pay attention to and cultivate this longing, it can become a positive passion, the burning "first love" that draws us deeper into our relationship with Christ. Ignoring this yearning means we will be like the Ephesians who, Christ said in Revelation 2, would be judged for losing their first love and falling from the high place God had for them.

Part of cultivating that passion is looking to see who God is. Psalm 84:11 gives us two pictures of our wonderful God: "...the Lord God is a sun and a shield...." Think about what the sun does for us. It gives warmth without which life can't exist. It is the source of light so we can see, and it makes many other things possible including life, food (light interacting with chlorophyll), energy (all usable energy has sun light as its ultimate source), clean water (the weather cycle providing clean rain comes from evaporation), the rhythm of the seasons (regulated by our distance from the sun), variety in weather (sunny days and cloudy days, calm and storm), direction (the sun rises in the East and sets in the West), discipline and rest (night and day), beauty (sunrise and sunsets, shadows to highlight the landscape), and consistency (it comes up every day). Our God is like this, providing all this and more for us. We are surrounded by His love and provision, but take most of it for granted.

God is also our shield, like the atmosphere filtering out what will harm us. There are many promises in Scripture of His protecting us from what is harmful (e.g., Ps. 23). He knows what is good for us and lets the pleasant and the difficult positives come through while keeping out that which will damage us spiritually. I am tempted to complain at some of what He allows to come through the filter of His love, but have to come back to His shielding us from all that is true evil with wisdom and power, and in praise bow before His will.

It is good to remember that our God is our sun and shield, to note what He does for us every day, and to cultivate the deep yearning of our souls for His presence and grace by spending time with Him, in worship, in the Word, in intercession.

Prayer: "Lord, help me to recognize your work in my life as my sun and shield, to be thankful, to give praise in all, to cultivate the relationship you have for me, for your glory and for the growth of all those around me. Amen."

May 23

"Exalt the LORD our God and worship at his holy mountain, for the LORD our God is holy."

Psalm 99:9

As part of your holiness, Lord, you are completely other than your creation:
- We are physical, you are spirit.
- We are limited to one place, you fill the universe.
- We must eat and sleep, you are never hungry or tired.
- We are mortal, you are eternal.
- We are sinful and sinners, you are pure and holy.
- We so easily sin, you are unable to sin.
- We are of the earth, you are of heaven.
- We create from materials here, you create from nothing.
- We are human, you are the most High.
- We are creatures, you are the Creator.
- We are your children, you are our heavenly Father.
- We live in time, you exist outside of time.
- We don't know what will happen in the next second, you know all that will happen in every second for all history.
- We can't control more than a few details of our lives, you are the sovereign God who has the power to control every event and detail in the lives of billions at the same time.
- We can focus on only a few events around us, you are intimately involved in the lives of every living person.
- We are tiny compared to this world, you are huge, beyond conception, larger than the universe.
- We are fragile and die so easily, you are mighty, powerful and eternal.
- We have sickness and suffering as the results of sin, you have no maladies, but do suffer grief when we sin.
- We are one person, you are three.
- We are dependent on you, you are totally independent of us, totally complete in yourself.
- We were made to need you, you do not need us but love us anyway.
- Our knowledge is limited, yours is limitless: you know everything there is to know.
- We are foolish and selfish in our thinking, you are wisdom itself, living in enlightenment and agape love.
- We naturally live in darkness, while you are light itself.

- We do not understand how things fit together, you have all understanding.
- We are jealous, hateful and selfish, you are love, light and life.
- We are impatient, you are slow to anger and plenteous in mercy.
- We love based on others responses to us, your agape love is dependent only on your character.
- We love only when it suits us; your love flows on and on no matter what the rebellious do.
- We are unfaithful, you are totally faithful in your Word and character, motives and actions.
- We are partial and prejudiced, you are just and righteous.
- We make decisions based on what we see, you judge from a full knowledge of all.
- We are weak in our ability to bring things to pass, while your plans and purposes stand firm through all generations.
Our desires are easily thwarted by events and people, but there is no wisdom or insight or plan that can succeed against you.

To you, O great and mighty Lord, the Creator, Sustainer and Ender of all, belongs glory and honor, praise and power, worship and wonder, surrender and obedience.

Prayer: "Be glorified in my life today, O Lord God, Ruler of the universe, King of the earth, Sovereign of my soul. Amen."

May 24

"I know that nothing good lives in me, that is, in my sinful nature."

Romans 7:18

Our son, Nat, wrote the following: "In looking back on the last few weeks, I can see that I've been learning the following: Indiana Jones and the Last Crusade have a good lesson for us.

"Remember what Jones was looking for in that movie? The Holy Grail. And can you recall in the final scene which of the various bowls and cups the Holy one was? The rattiest of them all. This is what God is showing me about myself.

"I thought I knew who I was. From other people's descriptions of me I'm a pretty nice guy. Clean. Religious. Gracious. And I thought to myself, after examining my actions from a distance, 'Yeah, that's what I am.' And I felt smug about it.

"However, 'Pride comes before a fall.' And I fell pretty hard. Over the course of the past two months the LORD showed me a very different Nat, one I feared to see. Little by little I noticed that much of what I do and say, even though the exact language and/or methods used weren't as bad as what my unbelieving friends employed, wasn't that dis-similar.

"At first my mind couldn't compute this paradox it was seeing in me: I'm 'good' but contrary to that I do bad things. I'd snap at people, join in on mockery, laugh at things that shouldn't be laughed at. This set forth a struggle within me which is best summed in Paul's statement to the Romans: 'I do what don't want to do and not that which I want to' (paraphrase).

"It's been very disillusioning to see this tendency and it provoked a sense of meaninglessness and failure within me, as well as a loss of identity to some extent. As a result I lost much of my desire to dig into the Word but still did it by the LORD's strength.

"Then after having watched the movie I mentioned and pondering my situation, a little light flickered on inside of me: "I'm not good!" Duh! Yes, I'm not good in myself nor any better than the others of this world. But just the fact of having been selected for the task of serving the LORD has made me holy, not what I do and say. Just like that cup. It was holy (set aside for special use) because it was a relic used by Christ, not because it was made of exceptionally expensive materials.

"This is a simple concept but for some reason it's hard to really grasp. Many of us say that we aren't good but don't really believe it. If we really want to be effective for the LORD, this must be understood internally, not just theoretically.

"I know that feeling worthless and seeing all of my failures drove me into His presence and got me to look at what was inside me, leading me to admit that I can't do anything in my own strength. Then He said 'Good, let me do it.'

"That was another door kicked down in the dungeons of my soul and another room illuminated. He's been cleaning up since then. God wants to turn our dungeons into palaces. But He can't do that unless we are willing to face the facts about ourselves and clean out the bones and other filth that is a common part of dungeons.

"He does the work but we facilitate in it by loving Him. And the more He works in us the more we love Him...."

Prayer: "Lord, help me to see myself as you do, to accept in mind, will and emotion that in my natural self there dwells no good thing (Rom. 7:18). Help me to walk in the newness of life with you, obeying you in all I know to be true. Amen."

May 25

"Exalt the LORD our God and worship at his holy mountain…"

Psalm 99:9

Praise be to you, Lord God, that you are such a loving Father, ever listening to us, ready to help, carefully prepared to do what is best in protecting us.

As it says in Psalm 99:8,9, "O LORD our God, you answered them [Moses, Aaron]; you were to Israel a forgiving God, though you punished their misdeeds." You, Lord, answered when they called: you protected and provided, you disciplined and corrected, you brought them to the promised land, and prepared the children of Israel to enter it.

You did all these things with them, not just for them. You were there, working to make them successful in following your commands. You required obedience, cooperation and faith from them. As they obeyed, you drove out the other nations by using the swords of the Israelites. You could have sovereignly done this with plague, famine or the angel of death, but you chose to give Israel a significant part, based on their faith in you. The battle had to be fought on a human level, while you worked on the supernatural level to make sure of your desired outcome. And when the Israelites didn't follow through, it didn't get done.

"...for the LORD our God is holy." Praise you that although you are holy, completely other and without any sin, you call us to yourself, we who are sinful by nature, rebellious in our hearts, resistant to your leadership. You have opened the way into the Holy of Holies and invited us to worship you. Praise you that you are our God, that we belong to you and you to us, that we are your beloved children.

Praise you that you invite us not only into your family, but also into your work, into your plans, giving us significant roles. You call us to obedience to your Word, to your Character, to your Spirit. You prepare all and then wait for us to obey. When we follow you, things happen; when we disobey, things don't happen--just as we saw in the lives of the Israelites.

What a privilege to live for and with you, the holy Lord God. What a wonder to worship you in obedience, in word and thought, in plan and deed. We lift up your name, we glorify you, for you are worthy of all worship.

Prayer: "Lord, may we follow through on the things you have for us to do today. May we give you honor in obedience and bring to pass what you have planned. We do exalt you, LORD, Jehovah, Yahweh, the great eternal I AM! May you be glorified in all that we do today. Amen."

May 26

"The Lord reigns, let the earth be glad...."

Psalm 97:1

As leaders of a new church planting team we have gotten to lead the charge in getting several aspects of a new ministry going. This has been both challenging and fulfilling.

However, after all team members agreed to the basic plan and we began to work on it, differences amongst us began to emerge. These differences were inserted into the situation by God who loves diversity. He has given each of us something to contribute, but sometimes they don't seem to be very complimentary.

My approach to work is, "Get the basics in place, start operating as soon as possible and add as we go along." Some of my teammates' approach, however, is, "Have everything (that means EVERYTHING!) ready and in place, then begin."

My approach on economics is: "Make it nice for the least amount we can spend; use what we save for other ministry." Some of my teammate's approach is: "Make it REALLY nice even if it costs us a LOT more; a good start means a good finish."

Perhaps you can sense the tensions inherent in these perspectives. Some differences may be from background, temperament or personal taste; others may be generational. Whatever the source, they resulted in some tense team meetings. I felt like I was being called on to bend too much, that my teammates' desires were unreasonable. None of us were very happy.

As usual when my emotions are in turmoil, part of my quiet time consists of writing in my journal, lifting my soul to God by pouring out my feelings before the Lord and then evaluating them in the light of Scripture. It is really important for me to get my feelings and thoughts out on paper, for then the full scope becomes clear, plus important insights come out as the Lord interacts with me on these things. As it says in Psalm 143:8, "Show me the way I should go, for I lift up my soul to you."

In this case He brought to mind the description of heavenly wisdom in James 3:17-18: "The wisdom that comes from heaven is first of all pure...." Thinking on this, I had to face the question, "Are my motives pure in these team debates?"

Knowing that in every instance my motives are mixed, I began to list them out in this situation: a desire for God's glory, doing things well, helping others grow...and then the most powerful one at work: feeling fulfilled. This one is always active in my life as it is both fundamental to my old nature and nurtured by our culture. Fulfillment is something God has for us, too, but it is meant to be the by-product of obeying Him, not a primary motive.

Doing things inexpensively, quickly and in a basic way is very fulfilling to me; spending what I consider extra on something is VERY UN-fulfilling. This, the Lord pointed out, is really what was driving me in this situation, not the other more noble motives I'd listed.

So here was another opportunity to grow; it was repentance time; self-denial time; obedience time. The Lord said, "Stop trying to bend yourself and let Me bend you!" Much against my personal desire, the Lord led me to give up my way and agree to let the team move in the direction it wanted. This brought instant resolution to the tension amongst us and in the long run brought more good then my stingy desires would have.

So the Lord is reminding me that being a leader is not just getting to forge ahead in shaping decisions and plans. It is also a call to deny self and often to let others' ideas prevail, not necessarily because their ideas are better but because relationships and godliness are more important than ideas, forms and structures.

We lead most of all by our example. I praise God that He got my attention and showed me my sinful primary motive so I could reject it. He thereby kept me from splitting the team over a relatively minor amount of money! He is good! All glory to Him! "The Lord reigns, let the earth be glad...Let those who love the Lord hate evil, for he guards the lives of his faithful ones..." (Ps. 97:1,10).

Prayer: "Lord, help me to lay out my motives before you every day, so you can sort through them, point out the negative and neutral ones for rejection, and affirm the godly ones for implementation. May I cooperate with you in this, being willing to deny self and follow you! Amen."

May 27

"Shout for joy to the LORD, all the earth."

Psalm 100:1

What a joy to know you, Yahweh, the completely other One, the Mighty God, the Holy Lord, the Hater of sin, the Judge of all evil, the Lover of sinners, the Provider of salvation to all your enemies.

What a great privilege to be called to you; what a wonder and joy to be chosen to be your child, to have you as the ideal Father. You are always perfectly balanced between love and discipline, grace and judging, warmth and firmness, forgiving and chastening, whole-hearted happiness and grief at our sin, unending correction and consistent cherishing.

The human mind could not begin to conceive of a situation better than having a God like you—and that is because you are beyond conception. No one has ever thought up a triune Creator, a three-in-one God who is our Father, Brother and Spirit at the same time. No one could imagine a God who loves those who hate Him, who redeems those who spurn Him, who woos those who reject Him.

After redeeming us, you patiently endure our grieving your Spirit every day with our sin, our quenching your Spirit with our refusal to obey your promptings. You graciously, patiently, firmly work to bring us to maturity in Christ—such a love is beyond our human experience, conception, imagination—and that is what you are, Lord God, far beyond anything we could imagine. In your eternal infiniteness there will be no end to knowing you, learning about you, rejoicing in your marvelous, majestic, mighty being.

You, Lord, have put us in the perfect position as your beloved children, giving us supreme support, continuous correction, lavish love, great goodness and unending, unlimited attention.

You are a marvel in your mighty majesty managing to love miniscule mankind, creatures of no consequence, especially in light of the immensity of the stars and the size of the universe. In spite of our microscopic size, to you we are valuable, precious and dearly loved. We bask in the warmth of your love, we dance in the light of your eyes, we rejoice in the strength of your embrace, we "worship the LORD with gladness" (Ps.100:2); what less can we do in the light of your grandeur?!!!

Prayer: "Lord, help me today to bask in the beauty of your being, to rejoice in the undeserved and lavish privilege of knowing you. May your greatness, glory and goodness fill my vision throughout this day. Amen."

May 28

"How many are your works, O LORD! In wisdom you made them all; the earth is full of your creatures."

Psalm 104:24

This morning for my quiet time I sat on the dock in front of our little house in Connecticut. The sun was rising over the forest to the east, warming the cool, damp air and sparkling on the heavy dew left from the embrace of the night. The morning breeze ruffled the waters, making intricate patterns from the reflections of trees along the edge. Stretching beyond the pond on my left, grasses of various shades nodded in the wind. On my right, trees crowded down to the pond's edge, some dipping their leaves into the water, each tree with its own shade of green, and different texture of leaf. At my elbow, tall grasses, headed out in rich grain, nodded in the breeze.

At the far end of the pond a pair of Canada geese kept a wary eye on me, ever protective of their four offspring. Nearer to me a muskrat swam across the pond carrying a load of freshly harvested grasses like a flag over his shoulder, his journey sending a "V" of ripples across the pond. A redwing blackbird perched among the cattails and chided me.

Closer to the dock, I looked down into the amazingly clear water and watched some fish swimming slowly in circles, their fins lazily sweeping from side to side. At times one would rush at another, chasing it away, then would rise to the surface and nip at something floating there, hoping that it was edible. Out of the deeper parts came larger fish, long and supple, swishing their powerful tails, moving through the water with a purpose. Along with them came a bass, swimming more sedately; suddenly he yawned, stretching his whole body–maybe he had just gotten up!

I had been reading in Psalm 104 the description of the wonders of the world God created. It concludes with, "May the glory of the Lord endure forever; may the Lord rejoice in his works...."

To sit and look at what God has created, to be reminded of how much He loves beauty and wants to share it with us is inspiring, refreshing, restorative. This is just a tiny glimpse of the splendors God has in store for us, first in our relationship with Him, then in Heaven beside Him. The question is, are we taking time to contemplate on who He is, to see His character as reflected in His creation and in His Word? I need to do that more. Soaking in these different aspects of truth brings transformation and a deeper love for Him. What are we doing with our time?

Prayer: "Lord, you are beautiful and you love beauty. Help me to consistently gaze upon your loveliness, to bring glory to you as I praise you for how I see you reflected in what you have created. May this beauty flow in, through and out of me to those I will meet today. Amen."

May 29

"Know that the LORD is God."

Psalm 100:3a

This verse above is a command. We are to willfully accept this truth, to grasp it and internalize it. This calls for bowing our intellect to Scripture, for we can only know God through revelation.

Praise be to you, Lord God, for giving this information to your tiny creatures limited by this natural world, unable on our own to see the supernatural. There are hints, but we guess wrongly without your specific revelation.

We praise you for your love that makes your person knowable: you are Lord, Yahweh, the holy One, great and glorious, powerful and pure, the righteous Judge and Hater of sin. You are God, Elohim, the powerful and faithful One, showing your power in creation and your faithfulness in fulfilling your promise to provide salvation. What a God, what a Lord: without fault, without lack, without sin, complete in your triune self, complete in full orbed wisdom, complete in everlasting love.

"It is he who made us, and we are his…" (Ps. 100:3b). You have created us—such a simple statement, but such complex beings you have made: miles of arteries, millions of nerves, trillions of brain cells, zillions of molecules all held together by your power. You have made us with self-healing parts, able to reproduce, to feed, care for ourselves, to think, plan, talk, see, hear, walk, carry goods, make tools—and to rebel.

We are also complex on other levels, being a trinity of body, soul and spirit, having in our soul another trinity of mind, will and emotions, all working together in some mysterious fashion to comprise a human being.

You have made us, and therefore we belong to you, the great Creator, the Lord God who fashioned us in your image: echoing your tri-unity, able to think, plan, love and choose.

"…we are his people, the sheep of his pasture" (Ps. 100:3c). Not only do we belong to you as a possession, you have made us your people, your chosen ones, purchasing us back after we had strayed away. And you have made us your sheep. You, the great and good Shepherd, watch over us, giving us what we need to prosper—green pasture, still waters, right paths, your presence in danger, protection from our enemy, blessings on our heads, goodness, mercy, and certain hope for life with you after death. To belong to you is a marvelous privilege, and you, in a way beyond our understanding, are delighted to have us as your sheep, as your children, as Jesus' brothers and sisters, as the bride of Christ.

Glory be to you, O Lord our God (Our God!!!), for your wisdom and grace in thinking up such wonderful possibilities and bringing them to share with your sheep. We worship you, glorify you, lift you up, exalt you today, for you, the Great and Mighty One are worthy.

Prayer: "May your name be glorified before the unseen hosts in my life today as I seek to obey you out of love. Amen."

May 30

"...as God's chosen people, holy and dearly loved...."

A new insight often has several levels of application, and so it is with the understanding that the "struggle for significance" lies at the root of most conflicts. Last month I accidently damaged an item belonging to a friend. The owner was understandably unhappy with my mistake, and expressed that with quite some forcefulness.

My mental response was, "Come on, it was only a small item I damaged, not something like your child!" And my emotional response was anger. Then the Spirit opened my eyes to what was happening: the owner's anger was expressed in a way so that I felt foolish, it snatched away my sense of dignity and significance, so I chose to be angry. This insight called me back to a higher reality: the significance I have in Christ is safe, untouched by anything I could do or this person could say.

Then came the new insight: knowing the significance Christ has given me also strengthens my grasp of the belonging, the worth and the competence He has bestowed on me (Eph. 1:18,19). Since all this is tied to God's character and strongly declared by Him to be Truth, therefore I can be free from others' negative emotions. "You will know the truth and the truth will set you free" (John 8:32). I can stand in His approval while letting the others' anger bounce off the shield of faith. I am not responsible for others' happiness, only for giving a godly response to them.

For someone with my fragile emotional makeup, this is a tremendous truth. So often when someone is angry with me, whether the anger is legitimate or not, I feel tied to that person's emotion. I allow it to drive me either to my own anger, or to trying to placate the person out of guilt. This stems from my selfish desire to protect myself, not from a desire to do what is right.

Now, however, knowing the dynamics of the situation, resting in my significance in Christ, I can accept the blame that is mine, ask forgiveness/make restitution and resolve the situation without being controlled by the other person's emotional state.

To be healthily emotionally independent of others means I must be fully dependent on God in every way, including emotionally. I must remember who I am in Him, know the spiritual battle we are in, and use the weapons of Truth God has given.

Jesus demonstrated this in John 13:3: "Jesus, knowing that the Father had given all things into His hands and that He had come forth from God and was going back to God [Jesus clearly knew who He was!], got up from supper and laid aside His garments; and taking a towel, He girded Himself...and began to wash the disciples' feet."

He knew His significance depended on who He was, not on what tasks He performed, so He was free to do anything He knew to be right, no matter what others thought. He was healthily independent of those around Him, while being fully dependent on His Father.

Here is freedom from the fear of man, from the guilt of our own inadequacies, from the judgment of others and from our own actual sin. What a wonder it is to know God. He has bestowed on us a relationship that is ever-growing, ever-deepening, ever-broadening. We must stand in awe of what He has done and is doing for us.

Prayer: "Lord, help me to give you glory by taking up all that you have provided, living out a life of wonder and freedom from the opinions and actions of others, the life you desire for us, living as sons and daughters of the King! Amen."

May 31

"The fear of the Lord is the beginning of wisdom."

Proverbs 9:10

Today marked my fiftieth birthday. Beginning a new decade is always a significant event. Turning thirty was a time of "jelling" in values and direction leading to ten years of vigorous activity. Turning forty opened a decade of working smart based on insights, skills and experiences God had given earlier and applied through delegation, partnering and self-denial.

Now at fifty there is another shifting of the gears, characterized by a voluntary reduction of speed. This is the direct result of God's good working in my life, mostly through insights provided by meditation on Scripture, and also by my little wife.

The first insight is the growing revelation of my innate depravity. This is easy to mention, very hard to experience. Just last Friday at a meeting I spoke unkindly to my dear wife; I wasn't even aware of it, but as she later gently pointed this out, it instantly became clear that I had spoken out of two wrong motives: fear of what might happen and the desire to control others. I was distressed by this—mostly because I had to admit that, no matter how hard I try, I cannot be good in my own strength, only in His! It was another opportunity to be broken (learning not to trust in myself but in God) and to praise God for the truth of His Word being validated.

The second insight is the realization that a lot of the hard work I have done springs from the motivation of greed! I am greedy for more accomplishment, for more fulfillment, for more recognition. Understanding this is very helpful now in evaluating what the Lord would have me do or not do.

The third insight I am embarrassed to even mention, as it reveals the innate self-centeredness of my being. It is now clear that I will never accomplish or become the things I had dreamed of, such as being successful and well known as Chuck Colson or Chuck Swindoll. I have to settle for a smaller sphere of responsibility—and that is good, for it helps me focus on what the Lord has for me, rather than toying with thoughts of grandeur.

Fourth is a simple truth that my dear wife has been telling me for years: take time to recover. I have always run from one event to the next. Now I am beginning to see how I have sinned in not taking a regular Sabbath to rest and be restored. This past Sunday after a nice afternoon of reading I went to prepare some tea for myself and noticed that the dishes needed to be washed. I washed them and enjoyed it! Always before this activity has raised my inner tension because the goal was to get it over with and move on to more important items. Today I enjoyed the warm water and the warm feeling of doing something nice for my wife. I am amazed at how God is changing me.

What does all this mean? God is moving me towards His mindset where life is more a rhythm than a race. Take time to savor things, especially relationships; work hard when there's work to be done, but don't let the wrong motives of greed, self-centered fulfillment and the desire for glory dictate my decisions; take time to be refreshed and restored. Simple, isn't it? Too bad it took me fifty years to learn it!

I am looking forward to the next decade of walking with God, if Jesus does not rapture us first. I think it is going to be much more of His working through me in quiet ways than me accomplishing much. And that's good because the glory needs to go to Him!

Prayer: "Lord, help me today to walk in the fear of you that I may be wise. Help me to choose to act out of godly motives, to do the work you have for me, not more. Help me to savor relationships and rest in you, for your glory. Amen."

JUNE

June 1

"Take up the shield of faith with which you can quench all the fiery darts of the wicked one."

Ephesians 6:14

The fiery darts, the negatives of life, may come *from* the hand of the devil, but come *with* the permission of God and God intends to use them to drive us into the Word and into the arms of Jesus. We get to choose whether to take His hand and cooperate with the Lord, or to let the flesh lead us into the swamp of self-pity, anger and despair.

Recently I visited Rick, a fellow I've known from his youth, now 40 years old. Humanly speaking he is in bad shape, and has been for years. Having severe genetic diabetes (even though he is not at all overweight), he has had parts of both legs amputated, first below the knees, then above them, as well as some fingers; his kidneys have failed so he is on dialysis 3 times a week; his arms are one mass of scars from infections from plastic inserts to deal with dialysis; he has continual reflux and scaring on his esophagus, partly from severe vomiting when he was poisoned by infections in his legs; in addition he has experienced heart attacks and insulin attacks and could die at any time.

My intent in visiting him was to give him some encouragement and perspective. How wrong I was! I came away so encouraged! Sitting there in his wheelchair, Rick was cheerful, upbeat and positive. He said that he is still alive because God has a purpose for his life. He believes that his job is to pray, so he intercedes about everything: what he sees on the news, what he hears from others, the people he has met in his medical world.

He may be handicapped humanly speaking, but he is focused spiritually on what God has for him. He has allowed these difficulties to drive him into the arms of Jesus, not into the swamp of despair and bitterness. I'm sure that he has had his times of discouragement and self-pity, but he has moved out of them into the light of God's continual presence.

I thought to myself, "If I were in Rick's place, would I think positively like that?" The answer is, humanly speaking, "No!" But if, like Rick, any one of us took up the grace of God and let these difficulties drive us into the Word and into a deeper dependence on God, we, too, could be joyfully useful in His hand.

Hebrews 12:15 says, "Take heed lest any man fail of the grace of God [meaning we fail to take up and use the grace that God offers], lest any root of bitterness springing up trouble you and many thereby be defiled." Rick is a living example of obeying this verse and principle.

He takes up the grace of God every day and rejects the temptation of self-pity and selfish thinking, instead praising God in and for all. Therefore, he is not bitter, and does not spread the poison of discontent to others; instead he is sweet and brings help and joy to all he meets. May we who have much easier lives, be and do the same.

Prayer: "Lord, help me to remember Rick whenever things don't go the way I would like. Help me to reject the temptation to feel sorry for myself, to be angry, and instead help me to take up your grace, to praise you, remembering that you will use my disappointment and discomfort for good, and to give you glory in the moment and throughout the day. Amen."

June 2

"Be strong in the Lord and the power of his might."

Ephesians 6:10

It is good to know you, Lord, my High and Holy Shepherd who hears and answers prayers. You are the same One who heard Moses' prayers and answered with wonders of power. So you hear and answer in my life, too, albeit in smaller ways.

Praise be to you, Lord, for your goodness and grace, your wonderful, warm love, your constant presence and protection. What a difference between just knowing truth about you, and thinking/resting in that truth. Lord, today I surrender myself to you, commit myself to obey you and give myself to bring you glory.

Help me to be strong in you and the power of your might today, to embrace my weakness and rejoice in your strength. Confessing my sin--basically unbelief and rebellion--I ask for your forgiveness. I ask you to be my Captain and Navigator, agreeing to obey your direction. Fill me with your Spirit, Lord, that I might be useful for you. Fill me to overflowing so that the Spirit spills over onto those around me, so when people meet me, they may meet you also.

Help me to put on the full armor of God so I can stand against the wiles of the devil; may I recognize his wiles before I fall into them and fight them with your full armor on. Help me to remember that I fight not against flesh and blood but against the forces of spiritual wickedness and do so with praise, prayer and persistence in doing what I know to be right. Help me to recognize that people are not my real enemy; they are just pawns in Satan's hands; help me to fight him with your whole armor on.

Help me to put on this whole armor of God every day so I might be able to stand in the evil day and having done all to stand. Help me to put on the belt of truth, remembering that all I naturally deserve is suffering, failure, punishment, pain and hell, plus eternal separation from you (Rom. 7:18; Eph. 2:1-6). But praise you for your eternal grace in which you chose me, called me, cleansed me, claimed me as your son, commissioned me for special service, and now I stand before you dearly loved, deeply cared for, doted on and delighted in (Eph. 1:1-10; Col. 3:12a).

In the same way, help me to put on the breastplate of righteousness, forgiving, accepting and loving myself as you do me. And to put on the shoes of peace, forgiving others as you have forgiven me.

In addition to all of these, help me to lift up the shield of faith by praising in and for all things so I can quench all the fiery darts of the wicked one.

Help me to put on and keep on the helmet of salvation, remembering/believing that my salvation, significance and security all depend on and flow from you, from your character and your provision, not from my performance or others' opinions of me and my work.

I also praise you, Lord that you have given us the sword of the Spirit: your living, powerful, transforming Word. Help me to soak in your Word, read it, to think it, pray it, live in it today. And then to pray with all prayer for all the saints continually, making intercessory prayer the foundation of all I do.

Thank you now, Lord God, for how you will answer these requests, for this is prayer according to your Word and will (Eph. 6:10-18)

Prayer: "Praise you, Lord Jesus, for your presence, your power, your provision prepared for this day. May you be glorified, magnified, lifted up, exalted and praised through your working in me today. Amen."

June 3

"When I thought how to understand this, it was too painful for me--
Until I went into the sanctuary of God; then I understood their end."

Psalm 73:16,17

It is now September 18, 2001 as I write this, just one week after the terrorist attacks of 9/11. The mental and emotional dust stirred up by these tragic events is still in the air, along with the uncertainty of what action President Bush will take.

How does one respond to these events? On the news, one of the first reports explored how Americans were suddenly feeling vulnerable and insecure. When people suddenly have their security ripped away without warning, one certain reaction is anger, anger at the attacker and at God: "Why did He allow this? Why didn't He prevent this?" There are good answers to these natural questions.

God is the author of good; evil has its other sources: the heart of Satan, his troops and sinful humanity. Scripture is clear that we live in a fallen world where distressing and deadly things happen. God also tells us that He uses evil for good and that He will end it at the right time. He delays so more people may come into the Kingdom: "The Lord is not slow in keeping his promise, as some understand slowness. He is patient with you, not wanting anyone to perish, but everyone to come to repentance" (2 Pet. 3:9).

God is at work plowing the hearts and minds of Americans. We are so comfortable and so confident that it takes a lot to get our attention; this did. Many, many people who, before Sept 11 had no spiritual interest at all are now open, searching, questioning. This is part of the answer to many of our prayers for revival in America.

The suffering of the world has been brought home to us in a powerful way. People in Sudan, Afghanistan, Somalia and other places suffer violence and the loss of loved ones daily–but it is hard to relate to this for those of us who live comfortable, safe lives. There are more refugees in the world now than ever before in human history. We now can feel in a small way the shock, the loss, the pain of being caught in conflict not of our own making.

We as believers are forcibly brought face-to-face with the truth that our only real security is God: "My soul, find in rest in God alone...He only is my rock, my salvation, my fortress, I will never be shaken" (Ps. 62:1,2). Although we may acknowledge this intellectually, we actually tend to draw our security from our surroundings, our successes, our possessions. This event of 9/11 should bring us to a greater dependency on God, focusing on Him as the truly Almighty One. One person summed it up this way: "Safety is not the absence of danger, but the presence of Jesus."

For many, this happening brought into focus what is really important in life. As our son, Nat, wrote, "Prior to all of this transpiring, I had been concerned about my injured leg, about my cross country season, and getting my homework done. As it seems to be with all of us, I felt like my agenda was the most important. Then the news came. Suddenly I felt insignificant...I suddenly found myself staring into the finite nature of our world, realizing all the worries I had prior to that moment meant nothing at all."

God is at work here to bring revival to believers and an awakening to America. Will we cooperate, or will we let the power of pain drive us primarily into patriotism, which leads to self-dependence, looking away from God to ourselves? Time will tell.

[Epilogue: looking back from several years later, it is clear that patriotism swallowed up the budding revival. Churches were full for a

few weeks, and then people went back to life as usual. What will it take to break through?].

Barbara pointed out to me that this is also an opportunity for us to implement some of the hard sayings of Jesus: "Love your enemies, pray for those who persecute you" (Matt. 5:44). In normal life we don't often have this possibility on such a large scale.

I'm sure all of us are praying for the President and his advisors. We also need to be praying for Bin Laden and the others involved in this horrific attack, or those cheering because of it-- praying for their salvation, for their seeing the error of their thinking and their coming to Jesus.

We also need be careful not to view Arabs, Middle Easterners or Muslims as all being evil; those who believe and act out the evil we have seen are a small minority. Even if these people were all our enemies, again we would be obligated, in obedience to Scripture, to pray for them and do good to them.

In the end times terrible things will happen. God is not the author of evil, but He allows it to draw people to Himself (Rev. 9:20). God is trustable; God is love; God is wise. He is taking us somewhere and will provide all the grace we need to move through the difficulties that will come upon the world. Ours is a greater hope, and we must look to it.

Prayer: "Lord, in the midst of unwanted, uninvited, unlovely happenings, help me to keep my eyes on you, my thoughts in your Word and my responses filled with praise that you may be glorified. Amen."

June 4

"Exalt the LORD our God and worship at his holy mountain, for the LORD our God is holy."

Psalm 99:9

You, O Lord our God, are wholly holy: you are completely other than your creatures and creation. Unlike us, you cannot sin, which means you cannot lie, or think an evil thought, have a bad motive, have a evil attitude, speak a bad word, gossip, slander or say too much. You cannot have evil plans or intent, you cannot be selfish, you cannot bring harm with hurtful intent, you cannot judge unfairly, you cannot have unrighteous anger, you cannot do anything wrong.

On the other side, this means that you always do what is right, you are always good, pure and positive; you are always loving, gracious and wise; you are always light, love, life and goodness. Your plans are edifying, your intents are positive, your motives are pure, your words are helpful, your thoughts are high and healing, your utterances are always true.

You judge in full knowledge and righteousness, your anger is pure and directed correctly against evil. You are perfect, without fault, solidly balanced, unchanging, utterly faithful and eternally without inner conflict or contradiction. You are the God we can trust-- completely, continually, constantly.

Truly it is right to exalt you, the Lord our God. You are worthy of worship, of obedience, of faith, of praise, of exaltation. Before you we bow in surrender, eagerly offering all that we are in worship, for you are the God of all creation who deserves full, wholehearted love, honor and glory.

Prayer: "This day, in all I do and say, may you, the great, wonderful and holy God--my God--be honored and lifted up before all the unseen hosts. To you be praise in my life both today and forever. Amen."

June 5

"'Not by might, nor by power but by my Spirit,' says the Lord."

Zechariah 4:10

One Friday evening our very religious neighbors came over for a visit. It was the end of a long and difficult day for me and I was tired. Near the conclusion of the visit Hasan brought up a favorite subject for Muslim apologetics.

"As you know, Steve," he said, "the coming of our prophet, Mohammed, was prophesied in the gospel of John. In the Greek it mentions the 'paraclete' but this is actually a reference to a similar Arabic word which is one of Mohammed's titles."

I had politely endured a number of other similar groundless beliefs during the evening, but this commonly voiced and totally fabricated proposition was too much. My reply was quick and strong: "Absolutely not! The text is perfectly clear that this is referring to the Holy Spirit. Just read it! I've heard that many times, have researched it and found it to be a complete hoax. Remember, this is a Greek text that has nothing to do with Arabic." I was intense and right!

Hasan smiled quietly and tried to smooth over the situation, "Well, I suppose there are some points we won't agree on, but basically we believe the same thing." I wanted to reply to that one, too, but thought better of it because it was clear that I'd already said too much.

After they left Barbara and I talked about the visit and it was clear that my impulsive response to Hasan's statement did not accomplish anything positive but rather put up a wall. The next morning during my quiet time the Holy Spirit crystalized in my mind the lesson from this situation: "My personal intensity does not accomplish the purposes of God." In fact, I had accomplished the exact opposite of what God wanted and created unnecessary tension.

Thinking back on other times of intensity, it became clear that although I may have felt better for pushing my point, winning the debate did not accomplish the desire of God. And, I wasted a lot of energy in the process.

The encapsulation of this concept in that sentence is helpful, one which can easily come to mind when I'm tempted again to push things in my own strength: "My personal intensity does not accomplish the purposes of God." The biblical text from which this springs is John 15:5 where Jesus tell us, "I am the vine, you are the branches. If a man remains in me and I in him, he will bear much fruit; apart from me you can do nothing."

Zechariah 4:6 gives further perspective: "'Not by might nor by power, but by my Spirit,' says the LORD Almighty."

So, when I am tempted to be intense, win the discussion by overwhelming the other person with logic and truth, or push as hard as I can, this phrase can direct me to the biblical goal of leaving a nugget of Truth with the person and let the Holy Spirit use it: "My personal intensity does not accomplish the purposes of God."

Prayer: "Lord, as I seek to carry the gospel to others, help me to rest in you, to live in the Truth that love and grace, wisdom and your Word, the Spirit and revelation are what will bring people to yourself, not my intensity. Remind me of this before I plunge into an argument, and then help me to share in your grace, not my power. Amen."

June 6

"I will sing of your love and justice; to you, O LORD, I will sing praise."

Psalm 101:1

Justice is a scary word when we are honest with ourselves. There is much in me that is wrong, unjust, negative, shameful. If not every minute, certainly every hour some ungodly thought, motive or attitude surfaces in me that is selfish, cynical, condemning, negative, competitive, lustful, proud, self-serving, slanderous or lying.

Any judgment of my life with any form of justice would bring clearly deserved punishment; it wouldn't need a life-long look, just taking a few minutes from my inner life would be sufficient to convict me. My flesh, my natural self is a swamp of evil, a poisoned spring, a thoroughly polluted well: "In my flesh dwells no good thing"

(Rom. 7:18). And the more the Lord reveals of Himself to me, the more I see how true this is.

You, O Lord, are just and you love justice; you will punish sin—and that is good, for without justice there would be no hope of ridding the world of sin and evil, no hope of protection, no hope of change. At the same time justice appears totally negative for us human beings who will be judged by what we have done—for we are naturally part of the sin and evil that will be eliminated from the new creation.

Praise you that justice is not your only quality, Lord, that you are also love. Just as your justice is unbending, uncompromising, unstoppable, so your love is eternal, overwhelming, utterly powerful and consistent. In your love, mercy is able to triumph over justice (Jam. 2:13). Your love has, at great cost, opened the way to escape the judgment to come, the judgment that has already begun against sin.

In Christ we stand sheltered from eternal separation from you, from endless punishment, from continual remorse at what we have done. Also in Christ, we are sheltered from the hopelessness that our struggle with sin brings, we are healed of our shame, we are freed from condemnation and worthlessness and cynicism.

You have brought us into a wide place, a beautiful dwelling, a lovely relationship with you: chosen because you loved and wanted us, cleansed from our guilt, transformed into a new creature, adopted into your family, made brothers and sisters to Jesus, delighted in and dearly loved.

We can now openly acknowledge to you our sinfulness, our shame, our inner struggles; we can allow you to shine the light of the Holy Spirit deeply within our souls (Ps. 51:6) and to eagerly confess what is revealed, knowing that in the security of your love, in the safety of your satisfied justice, in the warmth of your heart, there is no further condemnation, no reason to fear and hide.

You, Lord God, are love, you are light, you are healing; you are good and wise and right. We can revel in your words from Ephesians 1: "In Christ you are forgiven," and "I love you with an everlasting love," and "I choose you because it is the good pleasure of my will," and "I am delighted to have you as my child" (paraphrased).

Sinful thoughts, attitudes and motives still come, for the poison of the flesh is still there, but I can confess them right down to the root, be forgiven and walk in a growing freedom from them. In addition, Lord Jesus, you have given us hope, the certainty of eternity with you in a sinless place with the struggle ended and you to glorify and love.

You are all, Lord Jesus: our Hope, our Savior, our Love, our Transformer. In you is all we desire: acceptance, worth, meaning, security, growth and a future. Glory be to you for sharing these things with us, we who deserve the exact opposite. I lift you up, rejoice in you, exalt you and bow before you in thankfulness, praise and adoration.

Prayer: "Be exalted in my life today, Lord Jesus. Help me to live a life worthy of you, freely admitting my sin, joyfully accepting your forgiveness and whole-heartedly reveling in your great love and acceptance. May you be glorified as I am satisfied in you. Amen."

June 7

"…when I am weak, then I am strong."

2 Corinthians 12:10b

The wisdom of God is far beyond anything we can comprehend, therefore His answers to our prayers can be very different from what a human mind would expect. Lately Ephesians 1:12 has been one of my prayers for others as well as myself: "I keep asking that the God of our Lord Jesus Christ, the glorious Father, may give you the Spirit of wisdom and revelation so that you may know him better." As a result, I expected to see more of God's glory in the Word, to be more aware of His working in the world and of His greatness in creation. That, however, is not what happened.

First God began to point out how much I was relying on my own goodness, my own experience, my own spiritual insight—and then how inadequate these are. It was in just simple things, like my response to a disparaging remark touching on a sinful attitude of mine: I reacted strongly, defending myself.

At the bottom of each such incident was the same thing: failure to believe the Word of God. On one side I was rejecting the fact of my natural depravity. And on the other side, I was not resting in the truth that I am a son of the Most High God, chosen before the foundation of the world, cleansed, accepted, assigned to significant work and dearly loved. Why should I be upset at some mere human being's insult, especially when it pinpoints an actual sin in my life? The problem is I can't seem to remember these truths very well at the moment of impact!

Second, the Lord combined this frustration with 2 Corinthians 12:9, "… he said to me, 'My grace is sufficient for you, for my power is made perfect in weakness.'" With this, the lights came on. If I am content with my own efforts, growth and accomplishments, I will rely on myself. However, when God lets His children see more clearly the weakness, failure and sin of our natural side, then we can turn away from ourselves to Him. We can embrace this truth of our inadequacy in ourselves, confess our self-reliance, receive forgiveness and revel in His love, saying with Paul, "Therefore I will boast all the more gladly about my weaknesses so that Christ's power may rest on me" (2 Cor. 12:9b).

God has wanted to use the happenings of 9/11 in this way, I believe, for all of America: suddenly our weakness, our vulnerability was revealed and with that, how much we senselessly have depended on our own strength, cleverness and goodness to protect us from evil. May we turn to God in a new way, realizing our need for Him, and find new strength, new insight, new freedom to serve Him.

Prayer: "We pray, God, that you will give us the Spirit of wisdom and revelation that we might know you better, not for our own comfort and advantage, but that you might transform us so we can be more useful for you in what you plan to do in and through our lives. Amen."

June 8

"In the beginning you laid the foundations of the earth, and the heavens are the work of your hands."

Psalm 102:25

You, O Mighty God, are the Beginner and Ender of history. You formed the earth and hung it on nothing. You made the stars, the galaxies, the clusters of galaxies, the farthest reaches of space. They all belong to you and at the right time you will bring them to an end: "They will perish, but you remain; they will all wear out like a garment. Like clothing you will change them and they will be discarded" (Ps. 102:26).

It is hard to think of this great, expansive, majestic, far flung creation ending. Yet, it is not permanent, for it is a part of time. As it had a beginning, so it will have an end, an end brought about by you, Lord. The heavens and earth will come to the conclusion of their purpose and usefulness; they will "wear out" and you will remove them. All we know is temporary. Only you, Lord God are timeless.

You have something else in store to replace them, something perfect, untainted, untwisted by sin. You have a proposal, a plan, a purpose: a pure and pristine new heaven and earth, far beyond what any man could imagine in beauty, in greatness, in perfection—incorruptible and eternal.

"But you remain the same, and your years will never end" (Ps. 102:27). Yes, Lord God, in contrast to the temporariness of all in time, you, who are outside of time, are permanent, eternal, unending, unchanging, uncurtailed in your existence. As you were before time, so you will be after time: the perfect and pure paragon of all that is positive. In you there is no alteration, no shifting, no deterioration, no development, no growth, no vacillation--for you are already perfect.

We rejoice in your eternalness, in your enduring through all generations, in your permanency. You are the only stable, unchanging, certain thing in all of creation, in all of time, in all of existence. And you have made yourself our Rock, our Fortress, our Defender.

We glorify you, we rejoice in you, we exalt you, we lift you up. Our eyes are on you as we turn away from the things of this world to be enthralled with your dazzling beauty. It is true, as Asaph wrote in Psalm 73, that when we gaze upon you in worship, we must say, "Whom have I in heaven but you, and earth has nothing I desire besides you." As we worship you, learn of you, are drawn to you, what we have and don't have matters less and less, for you are our all in all. Glory be to your name.

Prayer: "Lord God, great Creator and Sustainer, help me today to live in your light, to value and obey your Word, to live for eternity. May your Spirit guide me in making wise and glory-giving decisions. May you be exalted in my life today! Amen."

June 9

"My salvation and my honor depend on God; he is my mighty rock, my refuge."

Psalm 62:7

Our team has been working through a book called *Search for Significance* by Robert McGee (Nashville, TN: Thomas Nelson, 2003). After establishing that our foundational significance comes from God (being made in His image, redeemed by the blood of the Lamb, chosen before the foundation of the world, and adopted as a child of the King), the author asks two questions.

First, "What do I have to do in order to feel good about myself?" This points us to where we actually draw our significance. If we are resting in the Truth of our being Sons and Daughters of the King, we don't need to add anything to "feel good" about ourselves. Our true source of stability, significance and "feeling good" is not what we do, but who we are in Christ.

God does want us to have satisfaction in a job well done, pleasure in doing what is right and joy in good relationships, but none of these are the source of the significance and worth that flow through a correct understanding of who we are.

As I honestly evaluated this, it became clear that there are a lot of items on my "to do list" which are there so I can feel good about myself; that is, my motive in doing them is wrong. These are things like: get up early, have a good quiet time, pray through my list, don't eat too much, exercise enough, be nice to everyone around me. All of these are good things, many of which I am responsible to do, but they are not to be the source of my significance, stability or sense of goodness. I must switch my motive from doing these to feel good, to doing them because I love the Lord and want to obey and please Him.

My wrong motives point to the disparity between intellectually grasping a truth and the deep implementation of it in one's life. To be aware of the tendency to look for significance in the wrong areas and to counter it with Truth is the way out. Memorizing verses that give God's viewpoint, such as, "Therefore as God's chosen people, holy and dearly loved..." (Col 3:12); "Chosen before the foundation of the world, accepted in the beloved..." (Eph. 1:4) and meditating on them certainly helps to internalize it. When trying to decide what to do, examining my motives and rejecting the wrong ones also helps.

The second question is: "Are you a 'have to' person or a 'want to' person?" If I can grasp my significance in Christ and rest in that, then I will "want to" do those things which are pleasing to Him, not "have to" do them in a legalistic, self-saving way.

This is part of the freedom of the abundant life Christ is calling us to: knowing who we are and, as a result, acting in obedience to Him for the right motives rather than just to make ourselves feel good. There are several very important consequences that flow from this.

First, instead of being pushed by the inner drive for gaining significance through getting this or that done, we can listen more quietly to what the Lord wants us to do.

Second, we can be more willing to do the unpleasant but necessary things that do not bring us any sense of significance.

Third, since we do less, (having eliminated the "have to" things) there is more time to do well the things God has for us.

Fourth, flexibility, grace and kindness can replace the harried, nervous, pressured attitude of the "have to" Christian.

These things I am learning. It reminds me that my walk with Christ is one long and wonderful process of growth, deepening and transformation. And we can constantly praise God for His wonderful, unending patience with us in it.

Prayer: "Lord, help me to regularly check my motives before you so I can deepen my rest in the significance you have given. Help me to be a "want to" believer, not a "have to" one. May I love you through obeying your Truth. Amen."

June 10

"Bless the Lord, O my soul; And all that is within me, bless His holy name!"

Psalm 103:1 NKJV

You, King Jesus, the mighty Ruler, administer a Kingdom of light where blessings flow all the time. You are the One who is to be praised! Without reservation, all of my being praises you, for you are worthy of total submission, absolute surrender and whole-hearted service: you are totally good, purely positive and persistently patient. Every part of me – my mind, my will, my emotions, my spirit and my body – rejoices in you, exalts you, extols you, exults in you: for You are worthy of this and far more.

"Bless the Lord, O my soul, and forget not all His benefits" (Ps. 103:2). You are to be praised and lifted up for your goodness shown in how you poured out your gifts upon your enemies: you have given us eternal life, eternal comfort, eternal provision, eternal presence, eternal joy.

"Who forgives all your iniquities" (Ps. 103:3a); there is not one unforgiven sin left in our lives—you took all our guilt, all our shame, all our condemnation, our full record of wrongs, and nullified their power to condemn us. Forgiveness sets us free, separates us from sin, superimposes your righteousness on our record. We stand in your righteousness before the great Judge who declares, "You are forgiven, enter into my joy!"

"Who heals all your diseases…" (Ps. 103:2b). You are the great Physician, the Maker of these bodies. You know just how to heal what you have created, even we creatures who are warped and twisted by sin. You heal some diseases now, some after teaching us, shaping us and changing us, and some you will heal at death. In your wisdom you do what is best.

"Who redeems your life from destruction…" (Ps. 103:4a). We lived in destruction, under the power of the destroyer, heading towards eternal devastation, existing only in the living death of time without you, Lord. But you bought us and snatched us off the disassembly line moving inexorably towards the pit; you translated us into the light of your Kingdom and made us your beloved, cherished children.

Your gifts are many, multiple, magnificent, and marvelous. You are the God of promise, persistence and provision. We lift up your name in praise for your gorgeous heart, your glorious love, your great and good gifts. You alone are worthy of worship all through today and every day.

Prayer: "May you be glorified in my life today as I live consciously in this lavish love of yours, O Lord God Almighty. Amen."

June 11,

"…those who suffer according to God's will should commit themselves to their faithful Creator and continue to do good."

1 Peter 4:19

For the last few weeks I've been reading Foxes Book of Martyrs, a most challenging book. It has certainly expanded my understanding of what suffering encompasses. The persecution of believers, starting shortly after the beginning of the church, and continuing right up to the present, is one long demonstration of the power of God in the lives of ordinary people.

In our age, the idea that God will protect us from evil is interpreted to mean that He will somehow remove from our lives what makes us uncomfortable. Much of what we would label as persecution in our own lives is really discomfort or harassment, (even including most of what we personally are experiencing here in the Middle East).

Biblical definitions are different than this. Evil is what will harm us spiritually. Suffering is what can make us grow spiritually. The vast majority of martyrs recorded in Foxes' book were killed for their stand on the Word of God as their authority; they rejected the additions and alterations to Scripture the church had made, and therefore were cruelly killed as heretics. They, almost to a person, demonstrated a courage and trust that allowed them to take up the grace of God and to die praising Him while praying for those who condemned them. Here is one example.

"When Mr. Hawkes was led to the fatal spot, he patiently prepared himself for the fire, and was bound to the stake by a strong chain, cast about his waist. Having promised his friends to show a disregard of pain, he agreed that, God helping him, he would, during his agonies, lift up his hands above his head towards heaven. After the noble man had been some time in the fire, his speech was lost, his skin thoroughly shriveled, his fingers burnt away to black stumps–yet mindful of his promise, he suddenly stretched forth his burning hands over his head and struck, or clapped them three times together; then sinking down in the fire, he gave up his spirit, June 10th, 1555." (*Foxes' Book of Martyrs*)

As horrendous as this is, let it be an encouragement to us of how we should endure persecution. "We wait in hope for the Lord, he is our help and our shield. In him our hearts rejoice, for we trust in his holy name" (Ps. 33:20,21).

Prayer: "Lord, I must confess that I know nothing of real suffering. Help me to praise you in the midst of the discomforts of this day so that I may be prepared to endure with grace whatever true suffering may come later. May I give you glory in all that comes. Amen."

June 12

"The LORD works righteousness and justice for all who are oppressed."

Psalm 103:6

Praise be to you, Lord Jesus, the King of Glory, for you have come to the help of all who are oppressed by the devil and his hordes. Caught in the net of Satan's design to destroy whatever is good, people are entangled in sin and self so they are unable to understand, to extract themselves, to know what keeps them making bad, harmful choices: "…the way of the wicked is like deep darkness, they do not know what makes them stumble" (Pro. 4:19).

Satan is able to oppress partly because this is what we human beings deserve: we are born in sin, we are naturally wicked in our hearts, we are separated from God; we are caught in the kingdom of the evil one.

But you, Lord Jesus, descended into this corrupt, poisonous, repulsive sea of sin; you made yourself weak, limiting yourself to a human body, opening yourself to attack and the possibility of failure— and in this weakness you worked righteousness for every person (1John 2:2).

You satisfied justice by taking the punishment we deserved. You were beaten, broken, became sin, became a sacrifice, became separated from your Father. You fought Satan and all his forces, you wrestled with death--and you defeated them all as you rose from the grave, rose from the earth and raised all believers with you.

Now you are seated in heaven at the Father's right hand: the Lamb that was slain, the Lion who was raised to reign forever. You bought righteousness and justice for all who were oppressed, for all those who will believe and also for all those who will refuse, even though you know they will never avail themselves of your gift (1 John 2:2).

You, Lord Jesus are worthy of praise and honor and worship and glory. At great personal cost you have done what no one else could do, or would do. You have triumphed over sin, selfishness and Satan!

Today you continue to deliver the oppressed, to set the prisoner free, to put the lonely in families, to care for the widow and the orphan.

You, Lord Jesus, are the freedom Bringer, the De-oppresser, the prison Breaker. You bring grace into our sin-filled lives, making it possible to let go of our destructive, self-centered, self-binding ways. You make it possible to hold on to the Truth of your love and forgiveness, your grace and goodness, and with the power of the Holy Spirit to rise above what would naturally tie us down in misery, unhappiness and foolishness.

You, Lord Jesus, King of Glory, Ruler of the universe, Deliverer of the miserable, Savior of the trapped, Adopter of your enemies,

Transformer of our souls—you are worthy of far more than our puny worship and praise can give. Yet you accept it, you welcome us into your presence, you delight in our being in your family, you give us your gifts every day.

I revel in your love, rejoice in your acceptance, celebrate your grace, extol your faithfulness and exalt your name, for you are the everlasting Yahweh, the undefeatable Adonai, the immeasurably powerful Elohim, the all-providing El Shaddai.

Prayer: "Glory be to you in my life, today, O Lord Jesus Christ, King of Glory. Guide me in being a glory giver, praising you in every difficulty, every disappointment, every pain as well as in every positive pleasure. May such responses of faith exalt you before all living creatures. Amen."

June 13

"I will bless the Lord at all times, His praise shall continually be in my mouth."

Psalm 34:1

We had just passed through the security check at the airport in N. C. I got Barbara seated at a restaurant for a snack while I went and checked on our gate. As I was leaving, I glanced at my shirt pocket, and saw that my passport and boarding pass were not there where I always keep them! Wow, that was a potential glitch! Immediately the Spirit spoke: "This is a test! Will you trust me in this?"

"OK, Lord, I praise you for this new challenge, for the chance to give you glory by trusting you. You know what you are doing and I can rest in you no matter what the outcome!"

I told Barbara about it, and went right back to security where all the bins were searched, but no passport or boarding pass. "Well, Lord, this is another chance to give you glory in praising by faith. Thank you for your goodness in this, for however you are going to work it out."

As I walked back to the restaurant, Barbara happily came towards me with my passport! It turns out that in the rush to get everything back in place after going through security, I had uncharacteristically stuck the passport and boarding pass into my backpack. "Thank you, Lord!" we both said.

Upon reflection, I realized this happened because I had been worried about getting through security quickly and was rushing, not being careful. Finding my passport was a great relief; however, there was more to come.

After arriving at our destination, while waiting for our luggage, I tried to call the office to see who would pick us up. If they came right away, there was time to make our two interviews scheduled for that afternoon. However, all I got was the answering machine (turns out I was using the wrong number).

I began to get irritated; worry and anger were not far behind. As I went out and looked up and down the line of waiting cars, again the Spirit spoke, "Can you thank me for this one?" My reply this time was more reluctant. "All right, Lord, I will praise you." My will engaged, but my emotions were elsewhere. I walked down to the end of the line of cars, and just at that moment the gracious folks from the office pulled up. When we arrived at the office, we found that the interviews had been rescheduled for the next day, so, although we were late, we didn't miss a thing. God had it all in hand!

The next morning in my quiet time, while thinking through these events, it struck me that my irritation and worry at the airport were "glory-stealers." That is, by my worry I was saying "The Lord isn't handling this well, so I'd better jump in and help Him out!" There was no faith in that response and thereby I was stealing His glory. But when He reminded me to trust Him and to rest in His strength, I was able to praise without any solution in sight-- that gave Him glory!

This insight opened up a whole new perspective for me: in every response I can steal glory from God or give it to Him!

The next morning there was opportunity to practice this. We were getting ready to go to the office; Barbara was carefully arranging everything in our room before leaving and I was getting impatient. Then the Spirit reminded me: "Isn't impatience a 'glory-stealer?'"

"Oh, right, Lord! I repent; thank you for this delay and the patience you offer me!" My heart calmed down, I relaxed, all went well, and most importantly, God was glorified before all the angels and demons watching us.

So I encourage us all to take a closer look at our reactions and be aware that sins such as worry, complaining, negativity and impatience are all glory-stealers. At the same time they are also opportunities to repent, deny what is natural and give glory to God through trust and praise. All the spiritual beings around us see it clearly, as do many human beings! "He who offers the sacrifice of thanksgiving honors me and opens the way that I may show him the salvation of the Lord" (Ps. 50:23).

Prayer: "Lord, help me today to recognize where I am being a glory stealer, not trusting, not praising. Help me instead to give you glory in praise, leading to being patient, kind, thoughtful, trusting and gracious. Thank you for how you are going to help me. Amen."

June 14

"He made known his ways to Moses, his deeds to the people of Israel...."

Psalm 103:7

You, Lord God, our Heavenly Father, are the God of revelation. You make known to your creatures what we cannot possibly learn from research, study or observation. You spoke to Abraham, you spoke to Jacob, you spoke to Moses and Aaron, revealing to them what was needed.

Praise be to you that you do not leave human beings in the dark about yourself. Praise you that you had Moses and others write it all down so we could learn these things, too.

You revealed to them your acts, your way of thinking and judging, your way of loving and directing—and through these revelations, you showed your character. You spoke through your mighty deeds done for Israel in bringing them out of Egypt: the 10 plagues; the pillar of cloud by day and fire by night; rescuing Israel from Pharaoh by opening the Red Sea; providing manna, water, birds and protection in the desert—we stand in awe of these displays of your power and wisdom and majesty.

"The LORD is compassionate and gracious..." (Ps. 103:8a). You are full of rich love, caring for your creatures with deep, overflowing, unending compassion. You are deeply concerned for each one and each situation. You watch, observe, protect, guide and reveal yourself to each one, calling them all to drink of your grace. You are the ever-giving, ever-sharing, ever-generous, ever-kind and ever-helping God. You provide air, sunshine, food, water, relationships, beauty, protection, guidance and wisdom. You generously pour out on us your goodness every day. When we awake you are there, while we sleep you watch over us. Your unending supply of all that is good never fails, you are graciousness itself and we exalt you for that.

"...slow to anger, abounding in love" (Ps. 103:8b). You, Lord God, are patient, working with your stubborn, rebellious, obstinate creatures over long periods of time. With Abraham you endured his fear of Pharaoh, his listening to his wife's cultural urgings, his repeated failures; you waited and taught, taught and waited. In the end, Abraham trusted you completely and became the spiritual father of faith for us all.

With Jacob you promised him all but he did not believe you. So you patiently waited while he manipulated, twisted and turned everything to what he thought was his advantage. You gently wrestled with him through his whole life, for 137 years, and in the end he finally bowed before you in worship. You are slow to anger, your love abounds, it is immeasurable, it is ever flowing.

Praise be to you, Lord, King of Glory, Commander of Compassion, God of Grace, Lord of Love, Revealer of Reality, Provider of Patience, Teller of Truth, Redeemer of rebels—for you are worthy.

Prayer: "To you be glory and honor in my life today, Lord God, the compassionate, gracious and patient One. I bow before you in adoration, I rise up to obey you in love. Guide me in doing all in your wisdom and power today. Amen."

June 15

"...you, O God, are my fortress, my loving God."

Psalm 59: 9b,10a

David wrote Psalm 59 during the time Saul sent men to kill him in his home. The reoccurring theme is "O my strength, I watch for you; you, O God, are my fortress, my loving God." David was giving a "response of faith" to a desperate situation.

The challenge came to me: do I give a "response of faith," thinking truth, speaking praise in daily life? For instance, how do I respond when I get interrupted in my reading; or the task I want to complete gets put off; or someone's derogatory remark strikes at my sense of significance; or I lose miserably in a game?

I can honestly say that my emotions certainly do not give a response of faith in any of these situations; my feelings encourage me to react naturally, according to what I can see: "He has no right to interrupt me!" or "I can't do anything right!" or "I'm such a loser!" I need to recognize the lie in these and replace it with truth.

A response of faith is not based on the situation but on God's character. In Psalm 59 David was still in danger, but he focused on what he knew of God and could say, "In the morning I will sing of your love, for you are my fortress..." (Ps. 59:16). He knew that God is loving and powerful. He could sing of God's love before the day unfolded, knowing that God would be at work to bring what is best, to bring him through whatever difficulties would come, to protect him from what was truly evil. The outcome could be death or suffering for David, but he would be safe from evil as he trusted God.

One of the most effective ways of giving a "response of faith" is to give thanks when the unpleasant appears. This is, in fact, how we lift the shield of faith, which can quench all the fiery darts of the wicked one. I'm not speaking of blind, rote mouthing of praise words, but of responding with our will to the great Truths we know of God.

He is our loving Father. He will give grace in each situation. He will protect us from true evil. He allows difficulty and disappointment to point us away from the chaff of life to the rich way of living for eternity. The question every day is, "How will I respond, in faith or in folly?"

Prayer: "Lord, I need your help to give a response of faith to difficult, distressing or disappointing situations today. Help me to remember that you are my fortress and that whatever comes is with your permission and love. May praise be the keynote of my life today. Amen."

June 16

"…he does not treat us as our sins deserve or repay us according to our iniquities."

Psalm 103:10

Praise be to you, O Triune God, Ruler of all, perfectly Just One, you who hate sin and will punish it—you have made a way so in your mercy you could avoid repaying us according to our iniquities. You did not treat us as we deserved—what we deserved was banishment from your presence, continual and total failure in life, suffering, agony, pain, fear, punishment, death and hell—but you loved us, died for us and rose out of the clutches of death for our salvation and your glory.

You work constantly to bring all who are willing into the shelter of your Kingdom. Thereby they can be protected from your just wrath that will be poured out on all sin and sinners who refuse to accept your offer of forgiveness and family. You have made it possible for mercy to triumph over justice, to treat us exactly the opposite of what we deserve! What a God, what a Lord, what a King!

"For as high as the heavens are above the earth, so great is his love for those who fear him" (Ps. 103:11). Your love is immeasurable. The heavens extend above the earth way beyond the conceivable limits of human understanding: the farthest known reaches of space are 14 billion light years away. No human being has ever traveled even one light year in distance. Your love is so great, so expansive, so all encompassing, so large that there is nothing in human speech or thinking that can measure it.

"…as far as the east is from the west, so far has he removed our transgressions from us" (Ps. 103:12). Your work, Lord God, is so complete, so powerful, so final that words fail in description. You have not only forgiven us, but you have removed our sins and taken them as far away as possible. They are wiped off your books, erased from our record, moved from your mind, put out of the picture, forgiven forever. We rejoice in your thoroughness, we praise you for your completeness; we exalt you in your faithfulness.

Prayer: "Lord, today help me to walk in the light of your greatness, your goodness, your power, your forgiveness. Help me to be a carrier of your grace to those I will meet today, being as forgiving towards them as you have been towards me. Amen."

June 17

"…let us run with perseverance the race marked out for us."

Hebrews 12:1

Growth involves motives. Knowing our motives is a significant and integral aspect of our walk with God, for then we can reject the negative and neutral motives, while affirming the positive ones. And one of our positive motives should be wanting to trust and please God.

This past week Romans 15:13 was my general prayer for all. It says,
"May the God of hope
fill you with all joy and peace
as you trust in him
so that your life may overflow with hope
by the power of the Holy Spirit."

This verse emphasizes that our responsibility is to trust this God of goodness, wisdom, power, mercy and justice. He will then give us the joy and peace He has prepared, plus cause an overflowing abundance of hope in our lives.

Such hope, of course, is not just airy, wishful thinking, but a certainty of what was accomplished at the cross and of what God will bring to pass—protection, provision, power, patience and His presence, to name a few. These promises are guaranteed with the Holy Spirit's indwelling in our lives.

While meditating on hope, other passages came up in my reading that show further how important it is. Colossians 1:5 speaks of the "faith and love that spring from the hope that is stored up for you in heaven...." I'd never noticed so clearly that faith and love flow from our hope. Our faith is based on the certainty of God's character and on what God has in store for us; our love then flows from God through us to others as we focus on our certain hope rather than on earthly things.

In a further insight, 1 Thessalonians 1:3 shows how this trinity of faith, hope and love should be foundational motives for all we do, especially in our service of obedience to God's leading. It says, "We continually remember...your work produced by faith, your labor prompted by love and your endurance inspired by hope in our Lord Jesus Christ." All we do should flow out of these three.

I'm sorry to say that faith, hope and love are many times not the motives I have; mine are more often the desire to feel good, the desire for significance, the desire for the approval and adulation of others. These verses, however, have clarified things as never before and have given a standard to measure my motives.

Contrary to the world's message, the bottom line is not our performance; instead the bottom line is our hope in God, our solid trust in His powerfully faithful, gracious character—all else will flow from that. We need to get to know better that certain hope and all it involves, to understand it and think in terms of it. This comes from knowing God Himself better: spending time in worship, in the study of His Word, in getting our eyes off the trivial distractions of this world and making prayer the foundation of all we do. In nurturing that trust we cooperate with the Holy Spirit to make us overflow with hope.

"May the God of hope
fill you with all joy and peace
as you trust in him
so that your life may overflow with hope
by the power of the Holy Spirit" (Rom. 15:13).

Prayer: "Lord, help me to pray this verse regularly for myself and for others. Help me to live it out, trusting you by obeying what I know to be true out of the motives of faith, hope and love. Help me to do this so that hope will overflow from my life to all those around me, bringing you more glory and them more grace. Amen."

June 18

"Find rest my soul in God alone; my hope comes from him."

Psalm 62:5

What an expansive, open-armed, loving, powerful and good God you are. I exalt you, Heavenly Father, for your provision; I praise you, Lord Jesus, for your presence; I praise you, Holy Spirit, for your power.

Your greatness, your wisdom, your strength, your understanding, your knowledge—they are all of immeasurable greatness and are unified and directed by what you are: Love. Therefore "my soul finds rest in God alone." All else in the world shifts, shakes, deteriorates, collapses or crumbles; in total contrast, you stand firm forever.

Psalm 61:1b says, "From you comes my salvation," so why should I look elsewhere? Yet in my sinful independence, my first reaction is to look to "Egypt," that is to other sources of help. Just as I read last night in Isaiah 30:1-2: "Woe to the obstinate children…who go down to Egypt without consulting me, who look for hope in Pharaoh's protection, to Egypt's shade for refuge."

You, Lord God, tower over, dwarf and eclipse the micro-power of any help we can find on earth. You are the One who deserves praise, trust and obedience. My hope comes from you and you alone. Forgive me for looking elsewhere

Psalm 62:2 has a trio of your qualities. You "only are my rock:" unshakable, unyielding to any force, firm, solid, enduring and trustable. When I stand on you, no tremor, no problem, no earthquake, no tragedy, no seismic shifting can shake me, for all is in your hand, all is under your power, and you never change, never alter.

"You only are my salvation": no one else can save from death, from sin, from hell, from sickness, from accidents, from eternal suffering--only you. As you stand beside me, with your great sword in your hand, no evil can come near me, no difficulty can approach without your permission, no harm can waylay me. Every weakness, hardship, insult, persecution and difficulty is a privilege, a blessing from your hand, a chance to praise, to trust, to give you glory.

"You only are my high tower": you stand there, immensely tall, strong and good; you reach down, lift me up and set me up on your shoulder. There I am close to you, can hear you, speak to you, and can see from your perspective: wider, longer, higher. No one can shake me there in this intimate, high level relationship with you, my God, my Savior, my Protector, my Brother, my King.

Truly, I will not be shaken when I am in Jesus, on my rock, surrounded by my salvation, up in my high tower. You, Lord Jesus, in your powerful love are worthy of worship, of glory, of unending honor for you are the Mighty Rock and Secure Refuge of the universe.

Prayer: "To you, Lord Jesus, be exaltation, majesty, strength, glory and praise throughout all eternity. I pray today that you will help me rest in your greatness, gaze upon your beauty, bow before you in obedience in each choice that comes up today. May you be exalted in my heart, in my thoughts, in my actions and words. Amen."

June 19

"Put on the whole armor of God so that when the day of evil comes you may be able to stand, and having done all, to stand."

Ephesians 6:13

At a prayer meeting in my home church, we were talking about a painful happening in someone's life when Marilyn spoke up to say, "Even in this we know that God is good and all He allows to come to us is good." Nice words, true words, easy to say, hard to live. But Marilyn knew what she was talking about.

When she was 32 her husband was diagnosed with cancer, and in nine months he was gone, leaving her with two small children. She had to go to work and support her family, which she did very willingly.

Then several years later, one Sunday on the way to sing at a convalescent home, her car spun on some ice, hit a telephone pole and her beautiful, angelic teenage daughter was killed. Marilyn said that God gave her a peace from the moment of impact and she was able to let go of any self-blame or bitterness.

Other difficulties followed: a son who left the faith and made poor choices in life; a deer that totaled her car; a mother who got cancer and died a long and painful death; a father who became ill and as a diabetic had several amputations. She took care of them all. Then she developed a serious, painful problem with her spine and yet remained sweet, trusting and full of praise. She met it all with genuine peace, acceptance and thanksgiving.

In her last years she came down with Parkinson's, which slowly robbed her of every ability; in her last year she could not do anything, not even talk. And yet she remained steadfast in her faith.

Her response to these human tragedies was the opposite of the psalmist who wrote, "When my heart was grieved and my spirit embittered, I was senseless and ignorant, I was a brute beast before you" (Ps. 73:21,22). He played the victim, while she chose the "more than a victor" role.

Why was Marilyn's response different? Because she was not willfully ignorant as the psalmist was (and as we are when we complain about things, forgetting the goodness and power of God). She had cultivated her first love for Jesus. She regularly spent time with God, worshiped Him and dwelt in the knowledge of His faithfulness.

In each difficulty she reached out and took the grace that God offered. This sustained her, deepened her and caused her to bear lots of fruit for those around her, all of it tasty. You would have to look long and hard to find another person who is so genuinely sweet. Truth is pure and powerful when we live it.

Prayer: "Help me to take this example of Marilyn, Lord, to spend that time with you every day, learning to think like you, filling the cup of my soul with the beauty of your Truth so when the day of testing comes I will be ready to trust and praise you in all. Amen."

June 20

"As a father has compassion on his children, so the LORD has compassion on those who fear him…"

Psalm 103:13

You, O Heavenly Father, are without fault, lack or error. You are the perfect Father: as loving, as firm, as gracious, as giving, as warm and consistent as is exactly right. You are the totally trustable One: always there, always at work, always good.

Compassion is one of your main character traits: you lean over the balcony of heaven, watching your children, cheering and encouraging them on, being intimately engaged in their lives for their good.

You are intensely on their side: lovingly, kindly, passionately working to help them move towards maturity in Christ. You help them make decisions in line with Truth and Righteousness. You pour out your grace on them every day. You are not interested in just their momentary, fleeting happiness; instead you desire long-term joy for them.

You work to move us ahead compassionately, caringly, carefully, "for he knows how we are formed, he remembers that we are dust" (Ps. 103:14). You are well aware of our weaknesses, our tenuousness, our feebleness and limitedness, of how our abilities are miniscule. As we walk with you, listening to and obeying you, you protect us from too much pressure, too much temptation, too much growth at once.

You are aware of our fleeting temporal nature, knowing clearly that, "As for man, his days are like grass, he flourishes like a flower of the field; the wind blows over it and it is gone, and its place remembers it no more" (Ps. 103:15). We can perish in a day, in a moment! If we live longer, what's 70, 80 or 100 years compared to 1000, to 10,000, to a million? Who remembers the average Joe from 100 years ago? From 500 years ago? But you do, Heavenly Father, even though for you 1000 years are like a day; how short our lives must appear in your eyes.

To compare our temporariness with your permanence brings perspective: "But from everlasting to everlasting the LORD's love is with those who fear him…" (Ps. 103:17). In the whole sweep of history, from the beginning of time until after it ends, your love and compassion have existed, are at work, and will continue to work.

You pour out your love on all, and especially on those who fear you--the Awesome, Mighty, Powerful and Great One. We who have taken shelter in your arms, in your love, in your grace, in your Word (living and written) are to fear you, stand in awe of you, bow before you, obey you. This is our privilege.

How great you are, how majestic in your love, how compassionate in your mightiness. Your love flows on from year to year: "and his righteousness [is] with their children's children—with those who keep his covenant and remember to obey his precepts" (Ps.103:17c-18).

Praise be to you, Heavenly Father, that you enable us to keep your covenant and to remember to obey your commands. In your compassion and grace is the possibility of walking in growing obedience, growing understanding of what we were (condemned criminals), what we are (children of the King), what we are becoming in you (more like Christ), what we will be in heaven (sinless and fully transformed).

It is possible to have joy unspeakable in knowing you in ever deepening, every widening, ever broadening ways, seeing more and more of how you are Marvelous in your compassion, Mighty in your love, Majestic in your perfection.

Prayer: "May glory and praise, honor and strength, obedience and worship be to you in my life today, Lord God, and in the lives of all your children. As you in your holiness are completely "other" than the twisted creation we live in, may we, too, be 'other,' positively different and thereby bring honor to your name. Amen."

June 21

"Trust in him at all times, O people; pour out your hearts to him, for God is our refuge."

Psalm 62:8

One of God's great gifts to us is an ever flowing, growing freedom from things that prevent us from having the abundant life. God is continually working to set us free so we can love Him more and serve Him better. He has a specific plan for this and at the right time points out the next thing that is binding us. Then, if we are willing to listen, to let go of what is binding us and follow Him, we can step up and out into a greater freedom.

He has done this again in my life recently, showing me how much unnecessary responsibility I take for other people's emotional balance. In a recent conversation I made an innocent observation that, surprisingly to me, deeply hurt the other person. Normally I would have been severely disappointed in myself, seeing myself as having failed in being godly. I would have agonized over the other person's pain, blaming myself entirely and would have tried to "fix it."

In this case, the Holy Spirit opened my eyes to a new objectivity. What I had said was thoughtless and I wish I hadn't said it; but it was not negative, it was not an attack, and certainly it was not the huge error the other person felt it to be. It had unfortunately tapped into the other person's insecurities, unfulfilled hopes and lingering frustrations. But I cannot prevent such wrong processing on his part.

I clearly confessed my thoughtlessness to this person and asked for forgiveness, dealing with my responsibility. "In repentance and rest is your salvation" (Isa 30:15a).

Unfortunately the other person's distress continued. But with the new perspective on what was my responsibility, I was able to let go of the other's distress rather than paralyzing myself emotionally as I usually did. This was application of the rest of Isaiah 30:15, "In quietness and trust is your strength." The other person needed time to work though this and I needed to let him have the time.

The next day as I was meditating on Psalm 62, the Holy Spirit again opened my eyes to how often I cripple myself because I seek for rest and peace in the wrong places. I try to find it in having everything go smoothly, in always doing the right thing, in trying to make people happy. I need instead to "find rest in God alone," and this incident helped me see that more clearly.

Prayer: "Lord, may we each continually grow in the freedom you have for us so we can serve you better. Help me to follow you today out into the greater freedom you have for me. Amen."

June 22

"The LORD has established his throne in heaven, and his kingdom rules over all."

Psalm 103:19

Praise be to you, O Mighty King, for you are the Ultimate Power, the Greatest Authority, the Final Judge, the Eternal Sovereign, the Lamb upon the throne. Your power is beyond comprehension, extending from pre-time to post-time, stretching from one side of the universe to the other—and beyond. You hold sway over all, from the magnificent clusters of galaxies filling the great expanse of the universe, stretching billions of light years across, right down to the sub-atomic parts of creation, dealing with every detail, while at the same time allowing us to make real ethical and moral choices.

Being completely different from every part of your creation, you tower over every other being in wisdom, might, ability, character, accomplishment and authority. No other power, strength or force can ever overcome you. "There is no wisdom, no insight, no plan that can succeed against the Lord" (Pro. 21:30).

You deserve praise, O Lord God; you deserve worship from all. "Praise the LORD, you his angels, you mighty ones who do his bidding, who obey his word. Praise the LORD, all his heavenly hosts, you his servants who do his will" (Ps.103:20,21).

When your awesome angels appear in their glory before men, they strike them with fear, awe, panic and quaking in their hearts; men fall to the ground, unable to stand in the presence of these mighty beings. So impressive are the angels that John, who knew Jesus intimately, was moved to worship one but was stopped only by the angel himself, who worshiped the only One truly worthy of worship: You.

These members of the heavenly host are far greater, far more glorious, far more powerful than we are, but they bow before and praise the Most High One: You, the Lord God, King of Heaven and earth, Ruler of all. You, O Yahweh-Elohim are worthy of their worship—and ours.

"Praise the LORD, all his works everywhere in his dominion" (Ps. 103:22a). Your rule, your authority, your power to order and control is so great that all you have created in every place must praise you, glorify you, lift up your name.

You are the ultimate One, unchallengeable, unconquerable, unending, inscrutable, unfathomable--the Source of all good, the Corrector of all error, the Righter of all wrong. To you belongs praise from every atom, every molecule, every creature, every feature, every river, mountain, sea, as well as the moon, sun, every plant and star. You are gloriously mighty, you are wonderfully worthy, you are to be eternally exalted.

"Praise the LORD, O my soul" (Ps. 103:22b). What is there to hold me back from joining this pageant of praise, and doing so with all my heart? "Praise the Lord, O my soul, and all that is within me, praise His holy name!" (Ps. 103:1). Your character of Love, Light, Life, Holiness, Wisdom, Power, Justice, Mercy and Grace deserves total glorification, total obedience, total worship, total devotion.

Prayer: "To you, O Mighty God, we lift our hearts, to you we pledge all praise, to you we bow down in worship, to you we rise up to obey, for you are worthy, you are endless, you are great. Glory be to you in our lives today! Amen."

June 23

"It is good to praise the Lord and to make music to your name, O Most High, to proclaim your love in the morning and your faithfulness in the evening."

Psalm 92:1

As we left our boys in the States for further education when we returned overseas, I found it very easy to worry about them. I know that God is good, and that He will protect them from evil ("though I walk through the valley of the shadow of death I will fear no evil, for you are with me" Ps. 23:4), but also know that God allows difficult things in our lives, albeit for good reasons. Suppose one of them has a car accident and is killed or maimed? Things like that do happen.

As I prayed about this, the Lord brought several things to mind, which laid these fears to rest. The first came from Psalm 92:15, where I was memorizing and meditating at the time; it says, "The Lord is upright, He is my rock, and there is no wickedness in Him." The Lord used this to show me that I have been thinking in very human terms, suspecting God of wickedness, of possibly bringing harm.

Actually what He brings is the best for His glory and our good. It may be painful, but it is an invitation to live out of His grace and do what we have been created for: giving Him glory. This helped me move out of the "defensive mode" of trying to protect my comfortableness, into seeing whatever may come as a positive challenge to my faith, an opportunity to grow and give Him glory.

The next thought was, "If He deems it best to take one or both of our boys, we can and must be thankful for each day we've had them." God shifted my attention away from looking at what we potentially wouldn't get if they died, to the good we have enjoyed. We have to trust His goodness. He will be our rock if such a thing happens.

And last was a letter from Nat telling of a trip he took where he had three close calls, and how the Lord protected him in each one. A little reminder that God will watch over them as He sees best.

We can proclaim God's love in the morning before any events of the day have come to pass, for we know He is good; and we can proclaim His faithfulness in the evening as we look back on the day and see how He has helped and protected.

It is good to get our fears out and look at them together with God in the light of His Word. Light will dispel the deceptive darkness of our old nature and free us to live in the Truth. "He has not given us the spirit of fear, but of power, and love and a sound mind" (2Tim. 1:7).

Prayer: "Lord help me to consistently bring my fears to you, to compare them with the truth of your Word, to repent of my doubt and trust in you by praising you ahead of time for what you will do. Amen."

June 24

"Praise the LORD, O my soul. O LORD my God, you are very great; you are clothed with splendor and majesty."

Psalm 104:1

Praise be to you, my God, the God of relationship, of intimacy, of personality, of interaction and communication. You, O Yahweh, I will praise with my mind, my will, my emotions, with my whole being; without reservation I will exalt you.

You are worthy of worship for you are great: you are mighty, immense, immeasurably great, filling the universe with your presence, knowing all, seeing all, performing all that is good.

You are glorious, clothed in garments of splendor and grace—rich, beautiful, gorgeous, lovely and majestic. You are lofty, high and lifted up, powerful, overwhelming and wonderful. As the Word says, "He wraps himself in light as with a garment" (Ps. 104:2a). Dressed in light, you are radiant, shining, sparkling, illuminating, revealing, glowing and glorious.

You are light itself, light to the core of your being, hiding no evil, covering no sin, harboring no darkness, for there is none of these to be hidden. You are what you are: good, holy, pure, positive, righteous, just, merciful, wise, patient, firm, unchanging, inexorably loving. No one can rightfully accuse you of any wrong, any injustice, any sin, any evil—your light would reveal such things if there were any, but there are not.

You are the God of goodness, the Lord of Love, the King of Kindness, the Judge of Justness, the Sovereign of the Supernatural, the Highest of Heaven, the Ruler of Righteousness, the Protagonist of Purity, the Adopter of antagonists, the Transformer of truants, the Spring of Spirituality, the Spirit of Sanctification, the Paragon of Patience, the Terminator of time, the Ender of the earth, the Extender of eternity, the Eliminator of evil and the God of Glory—you only are worthy of worship!

Words fail to express the greatness of your goodness, the perfection of your personality, the beauty of your being. In response to your love, I fall before you in wonder and weakness, I rise up filled with the Spirit, I move into the day in obedience. To you be glory and exaltation, joy and pleasure in my worship of you all this day.

Prayer: "May my attitude, my trust and my obedience give you the glory where my tongue fails. Honor and praise be to you, Lord Jesus, in my life today. Amen."

June 25

"Teach me Your way, O Lord; I will walk in Your truth; Unite my heart to fear Your name."

Psalm 86:11

God has such an ability to take us right through to the heart of a matter, making us deal with the next area of growth He has for us. As 2002 was drawing to a close, He brought me again face-to-face with my own weakness, imperfection and fallibility. It was another case of "humiliation is the shortcut to humility."

Twice in one weekend I was humiliated by my wrong choices. First I almost killed my whole family by making an impatient, unwise move while driving and only God's grace kept us from being hit.

Then, in doing an act of kindness to our destitute renter, I built a fire in his wood stove and I stacked extra wood nearby. However, later this wood fell over on the stove and caught fire, almost burning down the house!

In both cases God protected us and used my errors for good (in fact the fire at the renter's shook him up so much that he seems open to spiritual things and says he wants to make some very needed changes in his life). But it is not easy to let go of my self-image of being competent, wise, effective, and to see myself as God sees me: poor, needy, weak and faulty.

Interestingly my meditation ground at this time has been Psalm 86 where verse one begins, "Bow down and hear me, O God, for I am poor and needy..." How true that is! The psalmist doesn't stop there, however, but gives the other half of the story: "preserve my soul for I am holy...." It's hard to keep those two opposing truths in mind: our abject natural spiritual poverty and our shining, glorious acceptance in Christ. Yet the tension between the two is what God uses to keep us balanced.

This reminder of my fallibility and dependency on God is very important, and my prayer is that the rest of Psalm 86:1 will be true for all of us: "O my God, save your servant who trusts in you."

Prayer: "Lord help me to embrace the humbling, humiliating things that come, to accept that I am weak and needy. And at the same time help me to grasp that in you I am complete, that in Christ I am valued, belong, am competent and useful in your hands. Help me to keep that balance, seeing myself as you do. Amen."

June 26

"...he stretches out the heavens like a tent and lays the beams of his upper chambers on their waters."

Psalm 104:2

Praise be to You, Lord God, for your greatness as seen in your creation. To think of the expanse of the heavens, even if we limit that to only the earth's atmosphere, it is amazing. The layer of gases, stretching miles up from the surface, carrying water from one area to another, providing protection from harmful rays, burning up meteors before they hit us, giving the needed mixture of oxygen and other gases necessary for carbon-based life—this you just stretched out over the earth, and it stays there, preserving your creatures. And you did this simply by speaking! You are marvelous, incredible, a wonder, rising far above any created being in every aspect of your character.

"He makes the clouds his chariot and rides on the wings of the wind" (Ps. 104:3b). All the forces of nature are at your command: you can use them any way you choose. "He makes winds his messengers, flames of fire his servants" (Ps. 104:4). In Hebrews 1:7 this verse is referenced and clarified: "In speaking of the angels he says, 'He makes his angels winds, his servants flames of fire.'" You can somehow blend the material and the immaterial, wind being angels, angels being wind—you are inscrutable in your wisdom and your ways, you are worthy of worship.

"He set the earth on its foundations; it can never be moved" (Ps. 104:5). In this you have given us a powerful stability: only you can move the earth and until you do so, all will remain steady, reliable, with the earth rotating at the same rate century after century, circling the sun in exactly the same time each year—revealing your faithfulness.

"You covered it with the deep as with a garment; the waters stood above the mountains. But at your rebuke the waters fled, at the sound of your thunder they took flight; they flowed over the mountains, they went down into the valleys, to the place you assigned for them. You set a boundary they cannot cross; never again will they cover the earth" (Ps. 104:9). You commanded and the waters obeyed; you spoke and all stood fast.

You, O Lord God, are amazingly powerful. You are the final authority, you are fully in charge: when you speak, the universe responds; when you decide, and that is the way it is; when you set limits, nothing can cross them. You are mighty, great, strong, unconquerable, unstoppable and wise.

You only are worthy of worship, of praise, of honor—it is you only we should obey, it is you we should love with all our hearts as we see your greatness and your grace.

Prayer: "Lord, help me to glorify you today in my motives, attitudes, thoughts, words and actions, for you are the great One, totally worthy of worship in every sense of that word. May you be exalted in my life today. Amen."

June 27

"Rejoice the soul of your servant, O Lord, for unto you do I lift up my soul...."

Psalm 86:4

It had been a long day, much of it spent working out in the cold and snow. I had intended to quit at 4 pm and take care of some details for the evening's Bible study scheduled for 6:30 pm at our home, but then a neighbor came over and offered to pull our stalled tractor out of the field.

Darkness was coming on, but "Why not?" I thought, "it shouldn't take long." So I sent my boys home and went with the neighbor.

What ensued was not a few minutes of work, but almost 2 hours of arranging and rearranging a motley collection of chains between the two tractors, trying several combinations, each only giving us several feet of progress. As time dragged on my gloves got wet, my feet were soaked and freezing, my shoes were slick and I kept almost falling each time I jumped off the tractor. In addition, worries about being ready for the Bible study were churning about in my mind, stirring up negative emotions.

Finally we were done shortly before 6 and I trudged home in the dark. When I got to the yard, no one had moved the cars to make room for our expected guests, so I went in and said we needed to move them. After getting a grunt of acknowledgment, I went back outside to begin scraping the ice off a windshield, but couldn't find a decent scraper, so ended up using a stick.

I expected help any moment, but by the time I'd finished no one had shown up. As I stomped back to the house, the fire of frustration was burning hotly and by the time I opened the door, I'd "had it" so everyone inside "got it in the neck."

This brought, of course, an immediate response and the cars got moved pronto, but that minor victory was eclipsed by the wave of guilt for letting anger control me in an unhealthy way.

We made it through the Bible study, and afterwards I retreated to spend some time writing in my journal to "process" the event. As I wrote my feelings, it was obvious that I'd made several mistakes that led to my explosion. First, I was angry with myself for not taking a rain check on the offer to move the tractor and thereby bringing unnecessary stress on myself. Second, as time wore on I began to worry rather than trust God. Third, as I became colder and wetter, I began to feel sorry for myself. This was the "danger stage," opening myself to further attack by the dart of self-pity, which Satan uses very effectively in my life. From there on it went downhill.

After confessing and receiving forgiveness for my sins involved, I had to forgive myself and then talk with my family about it, asking their forgiveness for my ungodly anger. Two interesting and positive things came out of that.

First, Nat said he was glad to see that I could lose it sometimes, too, as he was feeling some pressure to be perfect! Second, I realized I'd had a low level of frustration with the boys on some issues and hadn't confronted them well on these, so stored up my anger. Now I have determined to take care of such issues earlier.

A failure, yes, but God turned it for good, deepened our family relationships and respect, and gave opportunity for humility. I am so thankful for regular meditation on Ephesians 6:10-18 which quickly brought things into focus and helped me to process it speedily by lifting my soul to God, "for you, Lord, are good and ready to forgive and plenteous in mercy to all those who call upon thee" (Ps 86:5), including the angry!

Prayer: "Lord, help me to lift my soul regularly to you, telling you what I am thinking, wanting and feeling so I can process it all and thereby hear your directions on what I should do. Amen."

June 28

God "alone is my rock and my salvation; he is my fortress, I will never be shaken."

Psalm 62:2

Your Word, Lord Jesus, is so rich and powerful, so comforting and healing. Psalm 62 continually comes to mind in the struggles of life: "My soul finds rest in God alone...." It is so natural to first try to find rest in other things: eating, relaxing, work well done, success, to-do lists accomplished, getting my way, reaching goals, having safety, being healthy, having good weather...there is no end to the things that help us to temporarily be at rest.

You, however, are the only source of true, ongoing rest. All these other things are gifts from you that should lift our eyes to the Source and cause us to place our hope in you, not these fleeting fixes to our feelings.

When I feel the desire to eat, or pace or otherwise uncreatively relieve inner tension and stress, anxiety and fear, I first need to come to you, lift up my soul and find that deep, abiding, sweet rest in you, rather than the restless, self-centered, shallow relief in my own resources.

You are so vast, so powerful, so good, so kind, so wise, so gracious, so compassionate, so firm, so sovereign. Therefore we can know that whatever comes to us flows from your hand of care and love. Whatever comes is for our good, for our growth, for us to give you glory, for your honor. We can therefore look at each event in a wider, deeper, longer way, in an unnatural, a supernatural way, and join you in what you are doing. And even in the most difficult circumstances, our souls can find rest in you.

"...my salvation comes from him" (Ps. 62:1c). This is the supporting truth: every solution to every problem comes from you. You are the Savior from sin and self, the Great Redeemer, the Rescuer from the dominion of darkness, and you have put us in the Kingdom of Light.

In your resurrection you began the untwisting of the universe, the righting of wrongs, the healing of hurts. Every day you are at work in this, rescuing us from our sinful nature by giving us opportunities to take up and use your grace, to reject the decision of Adam and Eve, to give you glory in praise, trust and obedience.

You, Lord Jesus, are all we need. In you, at the right time, all will come together, all will be resolved, all evil and sin will be eliminated. You are truly worthy of worship and glory, praise and thanksgiving, celebration and rejoicing, honor and exaltation.

Prayer: "I praise you, Lord Jesus, I lift up your name, I bow down before you, and surrender myself to you again, unreservedly, wholeheartedly, totally with all that is in me. Glory be to your name in my life today. Amen"

June 29

"Why are you downcast, O my soul? Why so disturbed within me? Put your hope in God, for I will yet praise him, my Savior and my God."

Psalm 43:5

The world is an increasingly dangerous place, and at the moment it is becoming potentially more dangerous from confrontations with Iraq and North Korea. Is there any safe place left? As the US prepares to invade Iraq, think of those living in the countries around Iraq and how unsettled they must feel, to say nothing of the Iraqis themselves!

What should our response as believers be to such a situation; what if you were living in a country bordering Iraq, as we are at the moment, well within the range of Saddam's missiles?

Certainly Satan would like us to worry and fret: his three major weapons are lies and fear, along with violence. But our weapons are more powerful: Truth, Faith and Love. Psalm 91 gives us some definite perspective here.

Verse 2 says: "I will say of the Lord, 'He is my refuge.'" Picture Him drawing you onto his lap where you are safe and dearly loved.

He is "My fortress." Picture a huge, solid castle wall surrounding you, keeping the enemy out.

"My God in whom I trust." Picture a huge and glorious being, standing there protecting you; He is so big that all you can see is the bottom of his big toe. No one can get to us without His permission. We are absolutely safe with Him no matter how things appear. Our eyes need to be lifted from the situation to God: He is the Almighty Ruler, the One who has never been defeated and never will be.

Verse 4 says, "He will cover you with his feathers and under his wings you will find refuge; his faithfulness will be your shield and rampart." As we seek our refuge in Him, He personally guarantees His presence and our protection all the time, everywhere. As someone said, "Safety is not the absence of danger, but the presence of Jesus."

This is followed by an implied "Therefore," and continues with "you will not fear the terror of the night"—for us this could be terrorists attacking; "nor the arrow that flies by day"—some missile falling from the sky; "nor the pestilence that stalks in the darkness"—a chemical attack; "nor the plague that destroys at noon"—a biological attack.

These are the things people fear today—and ones that are a threat to us where we live now—but God is greater than these and we can trust Him to protect us from all He knows to be harmful.

The conclusion is that we are immortal until our work for Him is done (although we should certainly live responsibly, not taking unnecessary risks, like overeating). We do not need to fear death, or troubles, or suffering. When any of those come—and they will—our Father will provide us the grace we need, save us out of it at the right time, and take us home when He is ready! No need to worry, fret or be afraid. Let us live in that assurance of his presence and protection.

Prayer: "When danger threatens, help me to flee to you in my thoughts, Lord Jesus, so that you may protect me. Help me to rest in you, in your great power, in your mighty love. May I give you glory today by trusting you in each happening. Amen."

June 30

"… and you have been given fullness in Christ,"

Colossians 2:10

Praise be to you this morning, Lord God, you who are the Creator of all, Preparer of each day, Provider of all that is necessary, Protector of all your children. I praise you for giving us the three things every human being needs and longs for: belonging, worth and competence.

You, Lord, gave us a longing to belong. We see this desire lived out as people desperately cling to being part of a group: extended family, tribe, city, nation, fan of some team, hobby groups, clubs, gangs—no one wants to be left out!

In Ephesians 1:19,20, Paul wrote, "I pray also that the eyes of your heart may be enlightened in order that you may know the hope to which he has called you…." You, Lord have given us the ultimate certainty of belonging—it is our hope (which biblically means something that is definite), for it is based on your action, your choosing us in Christ "before the creation of the world….In love he predestined us to be adopted as his sons through Jesus Christ, in accordance with his pleasure and will…" (Eph. 1:4,5). You have called us to be part of your Family, your Kingdom, the Church universal, the church local. We are part of your plan, we are your ambassadors, brothers and sisters to Jesus, and your friends. What more belonging could we want?!!!

To be a child and friend of the Creator of the Universe, the Sustainer of all life, the Beginner and Ender of time, the One who is always with us, always for us, always protecting us, the Pure, Holy, Powerful, Wise, Loving and Eternal One—that is really belonging.

Then there is worth; anyone who feels worthless is in trouble, for this unbalances us emotionally, and will lead to imbalance in every other area. We naturally seek worth in our work, our possessions, our relationships, our power, but it is all fleeting, unsatisfactory and worthless in the end. But you, Lord God, have declared "the riches of his glorious inheritance in the saints…" (Eph. 1:18b). We are your riches, your glorious inheritance!

You not only proclaim this, you have demonstrated it by your personally and powerfully redeeming us from the hand of Satan. And you did this at great cost. You said, "I value these my creatures so much that I will give all I have to buy them out of slavery and certain punishment. I will not only purchase them, but I will transform them and adopt them. They will be my treasure, my riches!"

When you, Lord, the ultimate authority, say that we have worth, then we have it, no matter how we may feel about it. Praise be to you for assigning worth to us who were your enemies, we who worked against your purpose, who rejected your rule. We praise you for buying us, we rejoice in the fact that we are chosen, cherished, dearly loved and delighted in. We revel in the warmth of your great love, the depth of your whole-hearted, total acceptance of us, affirming the worth you have given. Praise be to you, our Heavenly Father, our Brother Jesus, our Guide Holy Spirit.

And third there is competence. No one wants to feel like a klutz, a failure, a dummy. We either strive to be good at something, or we withdraw into the vague comfort of mediocrity and seek to ignore this desire for competence. But you, Lord God, have given us the potential for competence in granting us your "incomparably great power for us who believe." What you have given us in power is not something minor: "That power is like the working of his mighty strength which he exerted in Christ when he raised him from the dead and seated him at his right hand in the heavenly realms, far above all rule and authority, power and dominion, and every title that can be given, not only in the present age but also in the one to come" (Eph 1:19-21).

Plus you have given each of us natural abilities and spiritual gifts with which to utilize your strength. We can draw on your power, joining you in prayer, in knowledge and implementation of your Word, in loving one another, in building each other up, in being diligent workers, creative parents, gracious spouses, faithful friends, loving neighbors, wise counselors, loyal citizens, effective witnesses, fruitful church members…and the list goes on. You not only give us commands, but the power to carry them out.

Yes, you, Lord God, have thought of everything, provided everything. In you *we belong, we have worth, we have competence*. We have what all people long for. We thank you, we praise you, we glorify you for your wonderful love and grace and goodness demonstrated in this. Truly you are worthy of our worship and we give it to you today.

Prayer: "Lord, today help me to live in the belonging, worth and competence you have provided. Forgive me for my unbelief when I let my feelings tell me that I don't have these three wonderful gifts. Help me to live by volitional faith, believing you no matter what I feel. Amen."

JULY

July 1

"Look to the LORD and his strength; seek his face always. Remember the wonders he has done, his miracles, and the judgments he pronounced."

Psalm 105:4,5

Life is often a succession of emotional ups and downs, which hopefully lessen somewhat as we mature. But of late I've been reminded of how much of our emotional stability really lies in our own grasp, determined by our point of focus in life.

There have been a number of very exciting developments here resulting in ten locals coming to Christ in five weeks! This is a huge increase over the one-a-year we've been seeing. It is God's powerful working amongst us.

These events are so exciting that if I think about them too much, the motor of my mind threatens to rev itself right off into oblivion! And that's the point I want to make: as we focus on the exciting or depressing events swirling around us, our emotions tend to follow the course of these happenings: up or down.

Some folks always have a new answer to prayer, or a powerful display of God's power to tell about. That's wonderful, but the question to ask in this is: "Am I focusing on the events or the author of the event?"

In my own life I tend to let the event fill my vision, not my Lord who has done it. And the Lord Jesus has recently reminded me of the importance of looking to Him by praising Him in both plenty and poverty. One of the wonderful aspects of praise is that it keeps us focused on the Creator, not on the creation, ushering us into the peace of His presence no matter where we may be emotionally.

He has also reminded me of the need to praise with my whole heart, something I can do if I want: "I will praise you, O Lord, with my whole heart...for your love and your faithfulness, for you have exalted above all things your name and your word" (Ps. 138:2).

Lord, help us to make you our focus, not the ups and downs in our lives. Then, Lord, as we remember the wondrous works that you have done, your miracles, and the judgments you uttered, may you, O Triune God, be the One we seek, not just your acts. And we do seek your face, O Lord, for there is no one like you, the Almighty God, perfect in power and purity, greater than all in the universe, uninfluenced by anything, unswayable by anyone, the same yesterday, today and forever!

We glory in your holy name: we rejoice, exalt, delight, bask in and revel in the wonder of your great and pure, powerful and authoritative name. Let the hearts of those who seek the LORD rejoice!

Prayer: " Lord, we commit ourselves to seek your presence continually today, to worship, exalt, honor and extol you in our thoughts, actions, words and motives, for you are our Lord God, the almighty King and tender Shepherd. Amen."

July 2

"If you make the Most High your dwelling—even the LORD, who is my refuge--then no harm will befall you, no disaster will come near your tent. For he will command his angels concerning you to guard you in all your ways."

Psalm 91:9-11

It was late evening. A local believer, Earl and an expat worker stood looking at the mess: paint splashed on the walls, windows broken, the furniture and curtains a charred mass in the center of the room and water damage from the fire department. After two weeks of getting the newly rented building ready to serve as a church, this was disheartening, especially since it was the second such attack.

Then, hearing a noise, Earl turned to see a hulking fellow step into the room. The newcomer began uttering threats, his slurred speech showing that he was at least partially drunk. He then pulled out a knife to back up his words. Earl and the worker were able to disarm the man and hailed a passing police car, which took the attacker to the local police station.

They went, too, to give a statement to the police. The attacker told the captain that Earl had called him in and offered him $100 to become a Christian; this had made him so mad that he took Earl's knife to threaten him! And the police captain not only believed the attacker, but said he would crush Earl and what he was trying to accomplish in starting a church!

A couple of days later as two believers were repairing some of the damage done to the building, the thug returned with some friends and a foot-long knife, again attacking them, this time much more fiercely. After escaping, they went to the police station to file a complaint, but after scolding them for bothering him again, the captain only wrote down that the attacker had scratched one worker's car, but refused to document the knife attack. Later more damage was done to the building, and when they tried to hire a local welder to come and repair it, he refused, saying he'd been told to stay away from the church or else.

So the prediction of one worker has come true: when legal channels fail to stop the growth of the church, the opposition will resort to violence. This is probably the work of just one police officer (it appears that he put the thug up to the attacks), but is indicative of what may come in the future. Are we ready for suffering?

All this must be looked at from a Scriptural viewpoint. As Psalm 91 tells us, God will protect us from true harm, His faithfulness is our shield. However, we must realize that God's definition of harm may be different than ours, that is, harm in His mind is what will damage us spiritually. Suffering can be good rather than harm. "Consider it pure joy, my brothers, whenever you face trials of many kinds, because you know that the testing of your faith develops perseverance…" (Jam. 1:2-3) We need to trust, pray and act in wisdom.

Prayer: "Lord help me today to look to you in the difficulties that come, to praise you for what you are going to do whether it lines up with my desires or not. Be glorified today in my trust of you through praise. Amen"

July 3

"He remembers his covenant forever, the word that he commanded, for a thousand generations…."

Psalm 105:8

This morning I woke up late, have a headache and a scratchy throat, had disturbing dreams and am groggy. This is a great chance to praise you, Lord Jesus, for your unchanging, ongoing, immutable, eternal faithfulness, your consistent character and beautiful being.

I change, vacillate, fail and am fickle, but you, Lord Jesus, are rock-solid, reliable, never wavering, fully faithful, always true, reliably righteous, ever the same, ever perfect.

My ups and downs become an impetus to praise you, Lord Jesus, as they highlight the unwavering majesty of your mighty and magnificent character. You are the perfect One whose plans stand firm forever and whose purposes continue through all generations. You promise, you follow through, you fulfill--always.

I think of the time gaps between the giving of prophesies in the Old Testament and the fulfillment in the New: the promise given in the Garden of Eden of your coming as the Deliverer from the curse; the promises to Abraham some 2000 years before your coming; the Psalm 22 prophetic poem of David, written 1000 years before your incarnation, detailing your death on the cross long before crucifixion was known; the clear declaration in Isaiah 53 of the details of your work of salvation, written 700 years before you accomplished them. So sure was the carrying out of your plan that you are called the Lamb of God, sacrificed before the foundation of the world.

Today, as we see the increase in earthquakes, in political turmoil, in immorality, in rampant self-centeredness, in the coldness of believers—all prophesied in your Word—we remember how faithful you are in fulfilling what you promised as you carry us on towards the conclusion of history.

In our daily life you, in your faithfulness, prepare, protect and propel us forward in our walk with you. Whatever comes, whatever happens, whatever failures, problems, difficulties, insults, weaknesses, persecutions, sicknesses, hurts, losses or tragedies come, you are there. You are our Refuge and Strength, an ever-present Help in trouble (Ps. 46:1). You are our Shepherd and Shield (Ps. 18:1-4), leading us forward, fulfilling our needs, giving us rest, restoring our souls, protecting us from the enemy, providing peace, giving grace, manifesting mercy—all out of your faithful and sure character.

As I go into this day with a headache, I want to praise you, Lord God, for you are worthy of worship, glory, honor and obedience at all times, in all circumstances. You are to be lifted up, exalted and honored and I commit myself to do that today.

Prayer: "You are great and glorious, Lord Jesus; may my love for you today also be great, demonstrated in obedience and praise when I don't feel like it. Amen."

July 4

"Be still before the LORD and wait patiently for him; do not fret when men succeed in their ways, when they carry out their wicked schemes.... For evil men will be cut off, but those who hope in the LORD will inherit the land."

Psalm 37:7,9

My recent trip to our Middle Eastern country was a very interesting one. While I expected to spend a lot of time with teammates and believers, I ended up in the middle of a power struggle among the residents of the bookstore's building.

The building's administrator has been having a running battle for years with a retired, mentally unstable lady lawyer who lives in the building. The lawyer decided to get back at the administrator by investigating each business in the building to see if she could find anything to use against us. And she found something amiss in each one's papers, including ours.

In our case, I had accepted help from a person in the city government while setting up our bookstore, but unbeknownst to me, that help turned out to amount to fraud on my part! This is a crime with a two-year jail sentence for punishment! So the lady lawyer has a threat to hold over us.

After much prayer, seeking of advice and many meetings with those involved, the issue seemed to be resolved, with the lady lawyer finally signing new papers for all the businesses in the building—this was a great answer to prayer and demonstration of both the Lord's grace and His protection.

Then it all erupted again with the administrator winning a court case the lady lawyer had opened against him. This set her off on another rampage.

We have thought very seriously about moving to a new location that opened up on our street, but in the end were convinced by Psalm 37:1-2 not to go yet. It says: "Fret not yourself because of evil doers...for they shall be cut down like the grass...Trust God and do good, so shall you dwell in the land and be fed."

If we moved, we would do so out of fear and a desire to do good to ourselves, not thinking of our landlords or the other people in the building. Our being there is a blessing to all involved because we bring light and truth. So we decided to stay and share Psalm 37 with each person involved to show the basis of our decision, a good chance to witness.

Epilogue: *The Lord worked it all out through one of our landlords, who is also a lawyer. He came and put the unstable lady in her place. Since then she has been very quiet. And now, after more than 14 years of various believers renting the bookstore's place, it is still being used for the Lord's work. Thus far it has been the launching point for three church plants! Satan's opposition can often be the opportunity for God's advances as we rest in and follow His Word.*

Prayer: "Lord, help me to look with your eyes at the difficulties, problems and people Satan seeks to use in my life for negatives. May I view Satan as the real enemy, not these people. Help me to praise you, to trust you to use them for good, to cooperate with you in bringing good to those who oppose you. Amen."

July 5

"Glory in his holy name; let the hearts of those who seek the LORD rejoice!"

Psalm 105:3

These are commands, giving us opportunities to choose obedience in praise, or rebellion in complaining. And we *can* obey in praise, not because of our situations, our strength of will or our freedom of choice, but because of who you are, Lord Jesus: God of Glory, King of kindness, Potentate of power, Lord of Love, Ruler of Righteousness, Paragon of Perfection, Judge of Justice, Light of life, Wonder of the world and Savior of sinners, especially of all those who believe.

You are the Focus of eternity, the Fulfiller of prophecy, the Finisher of time, the Final Solution to sin and evil. In you all comes together, all holds together, all works together. In spite of its twisted and cursed condition, the universe continues to operate as you hold the stars in their places, the planets in their orbits, the atoms in their makeup, the details of our lives in line, the timing of events in sequence and the tide of evil in check.

You are the One to rejoice in, the One to glory in, the One to rest in. What a privilege, what a possibility, what a power, to be able to choose to praise you in and for all, to glorify you, thank you and revel in you at all times.

"Seek the LORD and his strength; seek his presence continually!" (Ps. 105:4). We can obey this command for you are always there, the way into your presence is ever open, the invitation to come is continually extended to us.

Praise be to you for your open offer of partnership, the way you call us to cooperation with you, giving us the power and possibility of deciding. As Pascal said, you "instituted prayer in order to lend to [your] creatures the dignity of causality."[5] We can consciously and continually practice your presence with praise and prayer. Along with joining you in your work, this is acknowledging the reality of who you are: the All-present, All-powerful God of Creation.

"Blessed are those who have learned to acclaim you, who walk in your presence, ever praising your name" (Ps. 89:15). To acclaim you, to acknowledge your presence and power in all that happens--this is a wondrous privilege we can practice every day. In our weakness we can seek your strength, in our ignorance we can seek your knowledge, in our foolishness we can seek your wisdom, in our smallness we can seek your great presence.

You, Lord Jesus, are truly worthy of worship, of glory, of honor. We exalt you today by choosing to praise you, to seek you and your strength in prayer, to practice your presence in our thoughts and attitudes, to honor you in our words and work.

Prayer: "May you be richly, powerfully, visibly exalted in my life today as I choose to live for your glory by praising you in all. Amen."

---

5 Quoted by C.S. Lewis in *The Atlantic* Vol. 203, No. 1, pp. 59–61

July 6

"For our struggle is not against flesh and blood, but...against the spiritual forces of evil in the heavenly realms."

Ephesians 6:12

As part of a trip we stopped in Gettysburg to attend my 35th college class reunion, the first one I've attended. Our plan was to join my class social on Friday evening. As time for this approached, I found myself being uptight and disagreeable with Barbara.

Stepping back from my negative interaction, I asked the Lord what was happening here and almost instantly realized that the insecurity, fears and anxieties that had been part of my life in college were being triggered by the familiar surroundings and the anticipation of seeing my old classmates. College was not a positive experience for me, especially socially. My time there had been one long struggle to maintain an emotional balance.

Now these emotional monsters from the past were clutching at me, trying to drag me back into the old traps--but I am no longer the same person I was 35 years ago. For one thing, I was probably not a believer while at Gettysburg. For another, the Lord has been at work over all these years, freeing me from wrong ideas, perceptions and emotions, equipping me to avoid these "wiles of the devil."

With this in mind, I could take up the armor, step out in freedom and with Truth beat back these ghosts from the past. As a believer I am "chosen before the foundation of the world...predestined to the adoption of children by Christ...and accepted in the Beloved" (Eph. 1:4-7); He has given me a basis of worth, significance and belonging that tops anything I could have gotten from whatever approval the world can give. Standing on the Truth, I could banish these negative feelings and thoughts and move forward secure in Him.

The end result was a great evening of sharing with my old classmates, renewal of two significant friendships and opportunities to share some "nuggets of Truth" with folks. Praise God that He is in the business of setting us free to be all He intends. Then we can do all He desires!

Prayer: "Lord, help me to recognize the wily attacks of the enemy, to keep on the armor and fight in your power with truth. Help me to stand in the wonder of being your child and reject the withering force of the fear of man. May you be honored today by my resting in you. Amen."

July 7

"Remember the wonders he has done, his miracles, and the judgments he pronounced, O descendants of Abraham his servant...his chosen ones."

Psalm 105:5,6

Good morning, Lord Jesus. Praise be to you this day, for you are worthy of worship and I acclaim you King, Ruler, Lord and God. It is good to, "Remember the wondrous works that you have done, your miracles, and the judgments you uttered" (Ps.105:5). And to think on how you faithfully "remember your covenant forever, the word you commanded, for a thousand generations..." (Ps. 105:8).

You, Lord God, are the marvelous One, for you are able to weave the evil decisions of all people and the conditions of this warped and twisted creation into the detailed plan for your recovery of righteousness and holiness in the universe.

In your wisdom you got Jacob, that stubborn, self-centered, rebellious, underhanded man, to move to Egypt, to where he didn't want to go, so that his family line could be preserved and produce the mother of the Messiah. "You called down famine on the land and destroyed all their supplies of food..." (Ps. 105:16). The far-reaching features of the famine (foodlessness and fear) drove Jacob to leave his beloved land and go where you wanted him.

And you didn't leave him unprotected: "... and you sent a man before them—Joseph, sold as a slave" (Ps. 105:17). He didn't go on a camel as an esteemed emissary, but as a slave, in chains, cut off from hope, experiencing the death of his vision to be a ruler.

It was no pleasant position, being a slave: "They bruised his feet with shackles, his neck was put in irons..." (Ps. 105:18). As he trudged across the sands of the desert, the shackles cutting into his ankles, the iron ring on his neck burning in the sun, you spoke to him, you brought him to surrender, burned the bitterness out of him, saved him from his self-centeredness, prepared him for being a productive person.

Then the years of service, of disappointment, of imprisonment (a second death of his vision), then of abandonment as Pharaoh's servant forgot Joseph's help and his plea for reciprocal help, leaving him to rot in jail for another two years (a third death of his vision). You kept him there "till what he foretold came to pass, till the word of the LORD proved him true" (Ps. 105:19). You refined him, broke and reshaped him, taught him to trust you no matter how bad it looked.

Then when things were ready, when Joseph was fully prepared by you, "The king sent and released him, the ruler of peoples set him free. He made him master of his household, ruler over all he possessed, to instruct his princes as he pleased and teach his elders wisdom" (Ps. 105:20-22).

At the right time you elevated him from the lowest position, a slave in prison, to the second highest position in the kingdom, Prime Minister, as it were. And he was ready to rule: having learned obedience and submission to you, he was able to lead others.

You, Lord God, are wise, all-knowing, all seeing, ever looking at the goal, always weaving every detail of life into the fabric of your plan, bringing history to the conclusion you desire: the exaltation of your Name, the elimination of evil, the elevation of the saints and an eternity full of praise, worship and glory.

Your wisdom is wonderful, your strength is sure, your love is long-lasting, your grace is ever good, your plan is perfect, your execution is excellent, your greatness is gracious, your workings are wondrous—you, O Triune God, the Excellent One, are worthy of worship and whole-hearted obedience through all eternity.

Prayer: "May I remember your wonderful workings in the life of Joseph, taking him through suffering, through waiting, through breaking, through disappointment, on to equipping and effectiveness in the kingdom. Help me to grasp that you are doing the same in my life, so that today I will praise you in problems, trust you in trials, exalt you in extremes and glorify you in your goodness. Amen."

July 8

"Blessed is the man" who delights "in the law of the LORD, and on his law he meditates day and night."

Psalm 1:1,2

Lately I've felt somewhat spiritually dry. I realize that such times come to everyone and we need to just press on through. However, it's also important to see what may contribute to this dryness and learn to deal with those factors or avoid them, if possible. In praying about the situation, it became clear that certain items played a part in my dryness.

First, right now we are winding down from our time in the States after a very good year, so there is a "giving up" again, leaving all this comfort, beauty and ease, as well as family and friends for something difficult and demanding. We need to acknowledge the loss and embrace the change. We will praise God for moving us on to what He has for us.

Second is the realization that all we had hoped to do will not get done–and that there are a lot of people we'd liked to have seen but we won't reach because of time constraints. There is the need to give up to the Lord what we can't do and praise Him for what was accomplished.

Third is the flurry of activity right here at the end, with a lot of giving out; this can contribute to feeling somewhat depleted. There is the need to take in more.

Fourth, and most importantly, for the last three or four weeks I've not been keeping up my habit of meditating on a new passage of Scripture. Actually I am constantly meditating on passages memorized earlier, but there's nothing like sinking one's spiritual teeth into a new passage from which flows powerful spiritual nourishment. As we grow spiritually there is a need for more input to maintain the advances made; riding on our past achievements only goes so far. Again I stand in wonder at what God does through meditation (memorizing a passage, personalizing it, then praying through it daily for several weeks).

This morning I started memorizing 2 Corinthians 4:4-18. In just the first day, the Lord began pouring nourishment into my system again. It is good to have that input to replenish what has been given, to fill up new places and to provide new resources to share with others.

So in the end I am thankful for this dryness, which has sparked anew a commitment to meditation–the Lord has a way of turning every problem into a blessing!

Prayer: "Lord, help me to be diligent in meditating on your Word, soaking in it through memorizing, personalizing and praying the rich and powerful passages you have given. May I thus be a more effective instrument in your hand. Amen."

Upon Returning to the Middle East
At the End of Our Furlough:
A Poem of Thanks to Those Who Help Us.

We stand on the threshold
of departure
again called to leave
the beauty,
the comfort,
the closeness
of home
and launch out
into the battle anew.
We do this
gladly and
not alone.
We go with God,
and also with you,
that is,
accompanied by
your prayers,

> *thoughts*
> *and support.*
> *So we give thanks for you*
> *and to you*
> *for your faithfulness*
> *in responding to God,*
> *in joining Him*
> *in what He's doing*
> *in the Middle East.*
> *Blessings be on you*
> *and all you do.*

July 9

"Have mercy on me, O Lord, for I call to you all day long. Bring joy to your servant, for to you, O Lord, I lift up my soul."

Psalm 86:3,4

I praise you, Lord God, for your warm and loving heart which makes it possible to always come to you and tell you what is bothering me, where I have failed, where I am uncertain, where I am angry, upset and hurting. You are pleased when your children transparently pour out their hearts to you. We can be fully honest, "for you are good and ready to forgive and plenteous in mercy to all those who call upon you" (Ps. 86:5).

What a full-orbed God you are! On one side you are pure and perfect, high and holy. On the other, you are loving and merciful, gracious and gentle, kind and forgiving, faithful and tender. There's a tension between these two aspects of your character—your being the firm Judge and the kind Justifier, the stern Punisher and the gracious Pardoner, the awesome Mighty One and the approachable Merciful One, the fearsome sin Condemner and the tender Savior of sinners. Both sides are always present, showing the beautiful balance of your character, kept in place, at least in our minds, by the tension between the two aspects: your "firm side" and your "tender side."

This balance helps us respond to you well. Your unbending justice inspires a holy fear of you: awe, respect, a fear of firm consequences if we sin. And your all-encompassing compassionate side inspires love, trust and joy. Together they nurture worship, self-denial and obedience. Seeing this perfect balance in your character brings security, rest and contentment. In you we belong, in you we have worth, in you we have competence.

Your balance also reminds us of the positive tension that you desire in us: the remembrance of where we have come from (out of the dominion of darkness where we were condemned criminals before the court of Heaven, trapped in net of the enemy) and who we are in you (the beloved children of the King, brought into the Kingdom of Light, living in your love and grace).

In our natural selves we are sinful, rebellious, negative, selfish, unbelieving and destructive. But in you we are cleansed, forgiven, justified, equipped for special service, accepted, dearly loved, and delighted in. Keeping both in mind means we are able to be truly humble—that is, seeing ourselves as you see us. Keeping both in mind protects us from being depressed in the negative and from being proud in the positive.

Only you could bring us to such a balance, lifting us from the level of natural thinking to heavenly seeing, from a self-centered viewpoint to a Christ-centered understanding.

You, Lord, are our wonderful God: High and Mighty, Wise and Wonderful, Pure and Powerful, Eternal and Perfect. In you all is brought together in marvelous balance. May we live there with you constantly.

Prayer: "I bow before you in worship, Lord; I rise up before you to obey. Help me to see myself as you see me: being your beloved son while being a sinner whom I can't trust. Helpl me to trust you instead. May you be glorified in my life today as I live in this positive and constructive tension, resting in your love. Amen."

July 10

"…I will boast all the more gladly about my weaknesses, so that Christ's power may rest on me."

2 Corinthians. 12:9b

Barbara just shook her head when I asked her. She had handled so many items in packing and unpacking that she could not remember the whereabouts of the book and the adaptor I wanted. I accepted that and went to the living room to have my quiet time.

First came some "lifting of my soul to God", telling Him what I was thinking, feeling and wanting. In journaling with Him about not finding those items, out came some anger–and it was more than I expected!

Confessing the selfishness and impatience under my anger then led to another thought. This is a situation where I am weak: we have no idea of where those things are, and are dependent on God's help. To be weak is an opportunity to see God's power at work, and I should be delighting in this weakness, as Paul did in 2 Corinthians 12:9-10! He wrote, "That is why, for Christ's sake, I delight in weaknesses, in insults, in hardships, in persecutions, in difficulties. For when I am weak, then I am strong."

Wow, what freedom that Truth brought. I could relax from the inside out, thank God that we couldn't find those things and know that at the right time He'd show us where they were–or enable us to get along without them. Plus, He had me deal with that anger before it popped out in some relationship and caused damage. He is really goodness itself.

The postscript is that later that morning Barbara found the adaptor and the next day the book. The lessons learned, however, were far more important than finding the items. To see and admit our weakness is such an opportunity for growth.

Prayer: "Lord, I do not like to be weak, it is unpleasant. Transform my thinking on this point, help me to rejoice in my weakness so your power may be made perfect and so you can get glory as you work to bring the right things to pass. Amen."

July 11

"Praise the LORD. Give thanks to the LORD, for he is good...."
Psalm 106:1

You, Lord Jesus, are powerfully, deeply, broadly, thoroughly, completely good. There is nothing in you that even remotely resembles rebellion, or rejection of what is right, or any relaxing of your righteousness. You are purely, positively, perfectly, powerfully good: you reject sin, you abhor sin, you cannot sin, and we praise you for it!

You love righteousness, you love purity, you love light: in you there is no darkness, no evil, no shadow, no turning from good, no twisting of truth, no scheming, no inconsistency, no contradiction, no sneakiness, no double-mindedness, no self-centeredness, no egoism, no wrong motive, no mistake.

You are the Rock of Righteousness, the Lion of Light, the Lamb of Love. In your goodness you are unshakable, unstoppable, unquenchable, unending: "...his love endures forever" (Ps.106:1b). From eternity to eternity, through blessings and difficulties, through our obedience and rebellion, through pleasure and tragedy, your Love goes on and on, flowing like a mighty river, unending, unceasing, unwavering.

In your mighty flood of majestic ministry to your creatures, your gracious stream of Love sweeps over sinful people, transforming those who yield to the current of your grace, while sweeping aside those who resist in their rebellion and rejection of righteousness. Your Love endures forever. Hallelujah!

"Who can proclaim the mighty acts of the LORD or fully declare his praise?" (Ps.106:2). Your powerful acts are as many as your multifaceted Character is marvelous. Your praise is ever expanding, ever growing, ever widening, ever deepening, filling the universe because you are absolutely worthy.

No matter how much we praise, you deserve more, for you are infinitely good and great: there is always more to learn about you, giving us more reason to exalt you. Your light that reveals much about you also blindingly hides aspects of your being which you will reveal to us only in eternity, the unending display of your marvelous, majestic, multifaceted, mighty Character.

Truly you are worthy of endless praise, ever-flowing glory, ever expanding exaltation, full trust and complete obedience. You are great, gracious, gorgeous, glorious and good, worthy of the worship of every creature, every feature, every measure of creation—and that's not enough, for you deserve more!

Prayer: "May you be glorified through praise and obedience in my life today before the unseen hosts, before the unseeing peoples, before your saints, before the Throne of Grace, for you are worthy, O Lord our God, our Savior, our Sanctifier, Supplier and Shepherd, the King of Glory, Lord of Hosts and Ruler of All. Amen

July 12

"My salvation and my honor depend on God; he is my mighty rock, my refuge."

Psalm 62:7

It is amazing what a pair of glasses can do. After arriving here in the Middle East where the sun is so bright, new sunglasses were in order, and I found a pair that were, in my opinion, well, cool. This was confirmed when someone asked me if my sons had picked them out for me! I felt good in them, handsome, with it.

Now there's a subtle difference between feeling good in something and drawing your worth/importance/status from them. Unfortunately I crossed that line and actually began to use those sunglasses as a barrier between myself and others, acting distant and, well, cool. No one knew this but God and me, but that was enough.

The Spirit quickly convicted me of my "standing in the way of sinners" (Ps.1:1,2), so I could repent and look to the Lord instead for my status. That desire for worth/importance is a strong one in all of us, and my old nature is good at pulling me in the direction of wanting worth from the wrong source. My attitude had to change. I still wear the glasses, but they are now only a source of good things for me: shade for my eyes, and a reminder of my dependence on God.

This whole experience was an effective encouragement to think according to the Word, which means thinking out of the "world's box." We need to recognize and reject ungodly advice, especially when it comes from our own heart.

This brings to mind the results of a survey done of believers in America which was summed up with a statement something like this: "Never have so many, who claimed to be born again, had so little effect on the society in which they live." Failure to recognize unhealthy conformity to our society results in our lives being tasteless and fruitless for those around us.

In contrast, when we think God's Word and live it, we become salt, bring refreshment and make others thirsty for Truth. We need to live according to a different standard and do that for the right reasons.

Prayer: "Lord, show me where I am drawing my worth and importance from the wrong sources. Help me to repent and draw significance and security only from you, that you may be more powerfully glorified through my life. Amen."

July 13

"Blessed are those who have learned to acclaim you, who walk in the light of your presence, O Lord."

Ps 89:15,16

Praise be to you Lord Jesus, King of Glory, God of Greatness, Ruler of Grace. In you all holds together, in you all is moving towards a conclusion, in you all will be judged righteously. Praise you for the shelter you have provided from the wrath to come, and from the attacks of the enemy, as well as from our own rebellious, independent selfishness.

Glory be to you, for your promise in Psalm 91 that we can "dwell in the shelter of the Most High"—that shelter is you, Lord Jesus, the Most High King, the Most High Lord, the Most High Ruler, the Most High Creator—there is no one else like you, no one greater.

There is no one who can contest your righteous rule, for you are both powerful and perfect, the Paragon and Potentate of good. The shelter you provide is like you: effective, good, strong, right, undefeatable and everlasting. He who dwells in this shelter, "will rest in the shadow of the Almighty."—that's you, too, Lord Jesus: the incredibly powerful One who spoke the stars into existence, who holds every atom together, who can bind up every wounded heart.

You, Lord Jesus, are the all-sustaining One, giving what is needed and more in abundance. You are the delightful One, reveling in your creatures, providing for and protecting them. You are the faithful One, always keeping your Word, always leading your sheep, always doing what is good.

Psalm 91:2 says, "I will say of the Lord, he is my refuge." You are the One I can flee to, whose lap I can crawl into for comfort and warmth when life is too much, too cold, too harsh.

You are "my fortress"—I can know that you are strong enough to hold off the great attacks of the enemy, the foe which is too powerful for me. You let through only those difficulties that will bring growth to me, glory to you and goodness to those around me. You are "my God in whom I trust."

You are the God in control, moving all to a conclusion and taking us with you. You are the future Maker, the time Ender, the eternity Bringer. We can look away from every difficulty to you, and as we take the hand of help you stretch out to us, we receive power for living, which you give through our offering praise. As Paul said in 2 Corinthians 12:9 "I will boast all the more gladly in my weakness so that the power of Christ may rest on me." In you, Lord Jesus, we can be more than conquerors in any situation, for you are the true GOD!

Prayer: "Lord, help me to acclaim you today, to walk in the light of your presence, remembering that you are my shelter, my protector, my King. Help me to walk in obedience so I can bring honor to your name today."

July 14

"…our struggle is not against flesh and blood, but against the rulers, against the authorities, against the powers of this dark world and against the spiritual forces of evil in the heavenly realms."

Ephesians 6:12

It was the perfect situation for a family fight. On our way back from a nice week of vacation we stopped off to visit friends. We were running late and weren't sure how to get from the main road to our destination.

Barbara thought that we should turn off much earlier than I thought we should, but knowing she is the better navigator, I took her suggestion. We immediately found ourselves in unfamiliar territory on a small street that curved through an obviously non-central part of the city; it looked like a wrong move to me.

The longer we wandered the unhappier I became and the riper I was for speaking some sharp words of criticism and complaint. But even before I prayed for help, the Holy Spirit brought to mind what was happening.

First, my security had disappeared because we were lost and late. Second, my sense of significance was gone because I was following Barbara's directions and she didn't know where she was either.

This loss of security and significance was the result of my natural, faulty viewpoint: I was looking at the situation, not to God. These responses were occurring largely on an emotional level, but needed to be dealt with in the mind and will.

Once these sources of my distress were out in the open, I could remember the truth: all the security and significance I need is mine in God right now; He knows where we are and will guide us. Then I could lean back to say, "Thank you, Lord, for this opportunity to trust you, to be weak and see what you have for us."

All credit to Him, the inner tension went right down and I could think clearly again. The Lord had again answered one of my daily prayers: "Lord help me to see the devil's wiles before I fall into them!"

We wandered around for a while longer, then came to an intersection with a familiar landmark, and we were immediately on course. This was a graphic illustration of how true Proverbs 4:18-19 are: "The path of the righteous is like the first gleam of dawn, shining ever brighter till the full light of day, but the way of the wicked is like deep darkness; they do not know what makes them stumble."

As we continually walk with Him, we come more and more into His light so we can see the things we are tripping over (the wiles of the devil, our own wrong values and ideas, the world's values, to name a few) and can avoid them. Life is so much easier when I respond in the Spirit rather than follow my own ideas and stumble around in the dark!

Another aspect of this was that our purpose in visiting our friends was to deal with some of their delicate interpersonal issues – can you imagine how effective we would have been had I arrived all bent out of shape, angry with Barbara, with God, with the events, out of communion with the Spirit? That is what Satan wanted, but God intervened and produced exactly the opposite situation, leading to a very productive visit! Praise God that He kept me thinking Truth and utilizing the armor--wonderful!

Prayer: "Lord Jesus, help me to keep on the armor and to see the wiles of the devil before I fall into them and to thereby avoid them. Amen."

July 15

"They grumbled in their tents and did not obey the LORD."

Psalm 106:25

Lord God, our heavenly Father, you are so patient as you observe the continual stream of wrong, rebellious decisions your creatures make, both believers and unbelievers. We reject your Word and Way in favor of our own feeble ideas of human reasoning, and for philosophies built on a foundation of toothpicks and empty tin cans. We ignore the light you give and walk in darkness, thinking this is the right and normal way.

What is especially sad is when we, as your children, citizens of your Kingdom, members of your family, choose every day to follow those around us rather than your Spirit and the wisdom of your Word.

As it says in Psalm 106 of the Israelites, "...they mingled with the nations and adopted their customs" (Ps.106:35). We so often have no discernment, no understanding of how the culture around us influences our thoughts, perceptions and choices. We don't evaluate by the Word, judge by your commands, or act out of your principles.

"They worshiped their idols, which became a snare to them" (Ps.106:36). We worship the idols of leisure, comfort, possessions and food. Entertainment, sports and hobbies occupy our thoughts and hearts. We follow the crowds around us; we fail to ask you the way and so get lost in the swamp of culture.

"They sacrificed their sons and their daughters to demons. They shed innocent blood, the blood of their sons and daughters, whom they sacrificed to the idols of Canaan, and the land was desecrated by their blood" (Ps.106:37-38). How terrible, we think, how could the Israelites do such a horrible thing? What kind of parent would sacrifice their own children to an idol?

Yet in our culture unborn babies are sacrificed every day to the idols of convenience, comfort and individualism--aborted because the mother or father or both don't want to be bothered with another child. Every year millions are killed, and our government not only condones it, but encourages it. Truly the land of America is desecrated by blood, by the slaughter of the defenseless.

"They defiled themselves by what they did; by their deeds they prostituted themselves" (Ps.106:39). As a nation we have been unfaithful to you, Lord God, choosing instead to worship self, Satan and sin. Forgive us, help us to abhor and reject our sin, to live instead for you.

"Therefore the LORD was angry with his people and abhorred his inheritance" (Ps.106:40). You must judge our sins, Lord God, for you hate sin, you are the righteous Judge--and yet you wait, you are patient, you have your time set. We praise you that you are at work and that you will do what is right. Give us wisdom in joining you in what you are doing.

Prayer: "We pray that you will guide us in rejecting the negatives of culture and in joining you in stopping this slaughter of babies; give us your wisdom; give us your direction that we may follow. "Save us, O LORD our God...that we may give thanks to your holy name and glory in your praise" (Ps.106:17). We are weak and helpless, but you are mighty and powerful. Act, O Lord, give glory to your name, for you are worthy. "Praise be to the LORD, the God of Israel, from everlasting to everlasting. Let all the people say, 'Amen!'" (Ps, 106:48).

July 16

"But the wisdom that comes from heaven is first of all pure; then peace-loving, considerate, submissive, full of mercy and good fruit, impartial and sincere."

James 3:17

Each week I take a passage of Scripture and pray it every day for everyone on my list. Recently the passage was James 3:17, the description of heavenly wisdom. My prayer went something like this: "Lord, help each of us to be pure, examining our motives before You, rejecting the wrong ones, affirming and acting on only the good ones; may we be peace-loving, considerate, submissive to Your Word and each other, full of mercy and good fruit, impartial and sincere."

Since these are things the Lord wants, He is going to answer this prayer. However, one answer I didn't expect came as an idea to pray this for one young pastor, but from a negative viewpoint. "Lord help him to see where he is not pursuing peace and begin doing so, where he is not considerate and learn to be so, to see where he is not submissive to your Word or to older, wiser believers and the needs of his people as he should be and to change. Help him to see where he is not full of mercy but is judgmental and legalistic and be willing to change, to see where he is not full of good fruit and begin to bear the fruit of the Spirit, to see where he is partial and begin to be impartial, to see where he is being hypocritical and to become sincere. Help us each to also conform to heavenly wisdom in every one of these areas."

As part of answering my prayer, the Lord began to show me where I was not being peace-loving or considerate myself. This came out mostly in my relationship with Barbara: the Lord pointed out my thoughtlessness and my laziness in not doing things that promoted peace. Amazing: I had thought I had been doing pretty well, but it had more to do with Barbara's mercy than my maturity!

And He showed me other points where my life was not reflecting heavenly wisdom. This, of course, was a somewhat painful answer to prayer, but praise God that He is moving us along, not letting us stagnate in our delusions of spiritual maturity, but is leading us to pray His Word and then He answers powerfully.

Prayer: "Lord, help me to be pure, examining my motives before You, rejecting the wrong ones, affirming and acting on only the good ones;

may I be peace-loving, considerate, submissive to Your Word and others, may I be full of mercy and good fruit, impartial and sincere. Show me where I need to change to have Heavenly Wisdom. Amen."

July 17

"The Lord is my shepherd…he makes me to lie down in green pastures."

Psalm 23:1,2

Praise you, Lord, for you do not take our advice on where we should be at each stage of life. Instead you *make* us lie down where you know it is best—you don't ask us or suggest or advise, you make us stay there.

That green pasture could be a moment of great success—or of monumental failure; it could be great comfort—or painful suffering; it could be in wonderful health—or in severe sickness; in rich, positive relationships—or in continual conflicts; in having plenty of money—or in pitiful poverty; in being wonderfully fulfilled in work—or living in futility and frustration; in having warm, supportive relations—or in being cut down, wounded and rejected.

You know what is best, Lord Jesus, you make us lie down in this green, sustaining, place of growth—a place where we can feed on your Word, drink from your presence, rest in your love. If we cooperate in this way, then this pasture becomes one of learning, growing and deepening until we internalize what is necessary.

The pasture we find ourselves in may look brown and desolate to us, but it is exactly what we need at the moment to drive us into your embrace where we will be transformed for the next step up in our life with you.

That is what you did with Joseph, taking him from his comfortable life of being the favored son, to making him lie down in the green fields of slavery, of false accusation, of unjust imprisonment, of being forgotten for a final two years—all to prepare him for the great task of saving many people.

I praise you, Lord Jesus for what you are doing in my life right now, making me lie down in situations where you can make me grow, situations I'd rather ignore or escape from, but you know the best for me and for your glory.

Your wisdom is wonderful, your plans are positive, your grace is grand, your ministry is mighty, your goodness is great, your presence is powerful, your guidance is grace-filled.

You are trustable, you are followable, you are lovable—we bow down before you, the Great Shepherd, the King of Kings, the Lord of the Universe, giving you glory and honor and praise, exaltation, power and obedience, for you are worthy of this and more.

Prayer: "May you be glorified in my life today; show me where I am glorifying myself or others instead of you, and bring me to the surrender of trust, obedience and praise. Help me to willingly lie down in the pastures you pick for me and to praise you for what you give. Amen."

July 18

"I pray that out of his glorious riches he may strengthen you with power through his Spirit in your inner being, so that Christ may dwell in your hearts through faith."

Ephesians 3:16b,17

Every morning we face a new day, another week, another month, another year, another decade, each one of which is full of uncertainty. We have hopes that things will go well from our perspective, but they may not. God may have other, greater plans, and we need to be ready to join Him in those, living out our purpose of giving Him greater and greater glory.

Recently a friend was giving away books, and I got one called *Don't Just Sit There, Have Faith* by Ron Dunn. Faith, the author points out, is our response to the revelation of God's character (the Almighty One, the Holy One, the Faithful One, the Just One). Faith is looking beyond the visible to the unseen: "My grace *is* sufficient for you" no matter how things seem (2Cor. 12:9,10).

Here's a quote from the book, telling the story of a pastor's wife's illness and death, an illustration of walking in faith. The pastor wrote: "I had hoped for the miraculous healing of Sara and that we might bear a dramatic testimony to the direct intervention of God. I had a sermon ready. But it was not to be....

"My disappointment was intense but sober thinking has changed my view. If a dramatic experience of healing had been ours it would have been sensational, but.... Most of us do not have such miracles. Our loved ones die...and we need a word for those who walk the Valley with no happy ending to the story on earth.

"So I preach and write for a host of fellow travelers through the Valley whose hopes, like mine, were not realized and whose deepest wish was not granted. If we can move through the Valley and come out in victory, we have found a greater blessing than if our personal wish had been fulfilled in some miraculous way." (*Don't Just Sit There, Have Faith* by Ron Dunn, Here's Life Publishers, 1991)

Knowing God is enough for joy, period. If He answers our prayers with "Yes" or "No" or "Wait," faith says, "Fine, Lord, I trust you to do what is best." Our focus must be on Him rather than the answer. Then, in the light of His wisdom, goodness, power and grace, we can accept with praise what He gives.

Prayer "Lord, may this day be one with my knowing you better, and growing in faith, living a life with the keynote of praise. In my exercise of the faith you've given me, may I be an encouragement, beacon and help to all those around. Amen."

July 19

"…he leads me beside the still waters., he restores my soul. He leads me in paths of righteousness for his name's sake."

Psalm 23:2b

Glory be to you, my Good Shepherd, my Lord Jesus, for leading me beside the still waters. Every day you call me to your Word to drink deeply from the waters of Truth, to be refreshed with the revelation of your character, to be washed with the water of the Word.

I don't see a great deal of change on a daily basis, but you are definitely at work, altering my soul, bringing growth, deepening and transformation. You are restoring my soul, moving it in the direction of its original, pre-fall condition so your relationship to me can be more profound, more transparent, higher and deeper.

Praise be to you, my Great Shepherd, my Heavenly Father, my Heavenly Brother, my Heavenly Spirit, for this faithful, powerful and wonderful work in my life. As I spend time with you in worship each day, you have been giving me strength in my soul, you have been quietly transforming my being into the likeness of Christ, so that when the disappointments of life come, there will be strength in me to pass through them with your endurance.

As a result of your work, my soul in no longer weak and flabby, able to be pushed this way and that by circumstances, feelings, and discouragements that come in life. You are making my soul strong, firm, muscular, able to stand in the face of opposition.

You are removing my fear of man, empowering me to make tough decisions for the good of the people involved without letting fear of how they will react control me. You are teaching me to think like you, rather than being swayed by my feelings. This is your doing, to your glory, in line with your greatness. I praise you for your faithful, deep work, your gracious goodness in bringing this change as I spend time gazing upon your marvelous Character. You truly are Glorious, Great and Gracious!

You lead me in paths of righteousness: warning, guiding, teaching, disciplining. You nudge me when I am about to say something negative, out of bounds, unhelpful or gossipy. And when I heed your warning, there is a sense of freedom—freedom from the selfish desire to give myself a thrill by being the one to pass on information or to be the authority in some matter. To deny self, to obey you, that is following you in the paths of righteousness.

I praise you, Father, for you have set your Spirit in me to lead. I praise you for your great patience in working with me to help me to quit worrying, to reject complaining, to refuse to feel sorry for myself, to walk away from disappointment and discouragement, choosing instead to walk with praise in the demanding paths of righteousness that you have prepared and where you lead me.

I praise and thank you for your wonderful shepherding, for your faithful goodness, for your continued, gracious patience. You are marvelous, merciful and magnificent in your persistent, powerful, positive transforming work in the lives of your children.

As the Great Shepherd, you are leading, guiding, disciplining, protecting, providing, commanding—therefore you are worthy of all exaltation, worship, glory, honor and praise. It will require more than eternity to give you what you deserve, and I glorify you for that!

Prayer: "Today, may my drinking of the pure waters of your Word and my walking in the path of righteousness you have prepared, bring glory to you, Lord, and transformation to me so that I may give you more and more honor each day. Amen."

July 20

"I will love you, O Lord, my strength."

Psalm 18:1

Psalm 18 has been a great encouragement in the last few weeks as I've been meditating on its first few verses: after the initial statement "I will love you, O Lord, my strength." come a series of strong images communicating God's power and protection:

"The Lord is my rock,
my fortress,
my defender,
my God,
my strength in whom I trust,
my shield,
the horn (power) of my salvation,
my high tower."

As I face difficulties and problems, these truths remind me of where my true help lies, of where to go for help first, right away.

While in the States we went with the boys to see the final "Lord of the Rings" movie. I was struck again with the clear and constructive "evil versus good" theme and how victory came from good character, courage and obedience to truth.

The scenes in the movie of the besieged city on the mountainside gave a graphic illustration of those verses from Psalm 18: "The Lord is my rock" (the city was built on the mountain and around a great blade of rock jutting out of its side),

"my fortress" (there was a high strong wall protecting the city),

"my defender" (there was a warrior king),

"my God" (this element was explicitly missing in the movie, but there was always a sense of someone working behind the scenes)

"my strength in whom I trust," (in the end reinforcements came)

"my shield" (each warrior had one for personal defense),

"my power, my high tower." (the enemy was unable to penetrate the upper reaches of the city).

The scenes from the movie were, of course, only a feeble illustration of our God whose power far exceeds that of any creature here on the earth. He is the One who created the universe by speaking, controls history by his sovereignty and will bring it all to an end at the proper time. There is no one else like our God!

The scenes from the movie help me to picture that, even when things appear dark and hopeless, we can trust in our Almighty God and move forward in the responsibilities He's given us, knowing that He is our Defender and Deliverer.

I can say in my experience that "He reached down from on high and took hold of me; he drew me out of deep waters. He rescued me from my powerful enemy, from my foes, who were too strong for me" (Ps.18:16,17). He is the One whom we can trust totally.

Prayer: " Lord, help me to run to you right away when trouble comes; may I take refuge in you, seek your power through praise, prayer, trust followed by obedience to what I know to be right. Deliver me from my enemy who is too strong for me. Thank you now that you will do that. Amen."

July 21

"I, even I, am he who comforts you."

Isaiah 51:12

Praise you, my Heavenly Father, the King of Glory, Creator and Sustainer of the universe, Guide and Lover of my soul. You are wonderful in your words of comfort: "Who are you that you fear mortal men, the sons of men, who are but grass, that you forget the LORD your Maker, who stretched out the heavens and laid the foundations of the earth..." (Isa. 51:12-13).

You are the Mighty One who made the measureless heavens, stretching them out light year after light year, in length and breadth, height and depth. You filled them with stars and galaxies, light and dust, space and nebulae. Your love of beauty, your enjoyment of variety, your penchant for order and the vastness of your power are all on display there.

You number the stars and call them each by name. The scope of your power is overwhelming: the power of planning to lay it all out; the power of creativity to make them out of nothing; the power of greatness to make stars so gigantic; the power of memory to know each one by name; the power of faithfulness to keep each in its place. You, Lord God, are marvelously, amazingly powerful.

Then on a much tinier scale, in a little place tucked under one arm of the Milky Way Galaxy, you laid the foundations of the earth. You made the molten core, you clothed it in its mantle of minerals and metals, then you laid over it the garment of water and crowned it with a transparent atmosphere. You placed it in just the right spot, provided it with a sun, a moon and sister planets, gave it just the right tilt, orbit and speed of rotation. Then through the years you have sustained each of those so that your creatures are able to live on it. You, Lord God are marvelous in your creativity and wisdom, might and imagination.

You "who churn up the sea so that its waves roar—the LORD Almighty is your name" (Isa. 51:15b) -- your power is unlimited, your wisdom is boundless, your greatness is without end, your glory is eternal, your holiness is without change. You are worthy of glory and fear, of worship and honor, of praise and obedience.

Although you are so great and we so small, although you are so powerful and we so weak, although you are so holy and we so sinful, yet you proclaim, "I am the LORD your God" (Isa. 51:15a)! What a wonder, what a joy, what a foundation for life, what a comfort! You who are so mighty and marvelous, managing the vast expanses of space, stoop down to make yourself our God: personal, knowable, loveable, trustable.

To have such a great and personal God means an end to fear: the fear of man, the fear of the future, the fear of failure, the fear of loss, the fear of suffering…no need to "live in constant terror every day because of the wrath of the oppressor…" (Isa. 51:13). You are greater than the old devil, greater than miniscule men, greater than puny people who seek to control, hurt, manipulate or use us.

"I have put my words in your mouth and covered you with the shadow of my hand…" (Isa. 51:16). All that comes to us flows with your permission, and you will give us grace to pass through it with power, to grow and mature in it with wisdom, to shine in it like stars in the darkness.

You are the One to be feared, to be reverenced in awe and love. To obey you is an honor: it is freedom, it is joy. To lift our eyes from those who threaten us to the One who protects us, to think Truth, to live in your Light, to bask in your Love—these privileges are what you, the Almighty One give to your people in the Kingdom of your Son. Praise be to you.

Prayer: "May this day be one long stream of honor to you through obedience in my life, O LORD my God! Help me to live in the light of your greatness and to fear you well. Amen."

July 22

"The path of the righteous is like the first gleam of dawn, shining ever brighter till the full light of day."

Proverbs 4:18

From all outward appearances it had been a good day: a couple of positive discipleship lessons, business goals accomplished, and a warm, productive team meeting. However, inside I was in turmoil: dissatisfaction, anger, jealousy and negativity swirled around in my heart.

As soon as we got home from the team meeting I got out my journal and began to write about what I was feeling, lifting my soul to God. A string of emotions poured out on the page where I could look at them more objectively and begin to examine them in the light of Scripture.

The last few weeks Psalm 27:1 has been my springboard for worship: "The Lord is my light and salvation, whom shall I fear...." God is the One who brings light into our darkness; He illuminates our way, showing us what is causing us to stumble; He shows us the next step. Then, as we let Him, He moves to save us from what is threatening us.

In this case what was threatening me was my old self. After letting God shine the light of His Spirit down into my soul, what emerged as the root of all the turmoil was, surprise (!), my desire to be significant, and after our return from America I was having trouble fitting into things again.

This uncertainty was manifested by my craving to have control over the events and people around me, to be important because I was in charge. This desire is ungodly and destructive. Plus having control of everything is, of course, an impossible goal, so I naturally ended up frustrated and angry.

Having shown me the source, God then led me to confess my unbelief and rebellion against the Truth, to reject this desire to be important through power and to surrender to His Word. He has already given me all the significance anyone could ever desire: created in the image of God, chosen before the foundation of the world, redeemed by the blood of the Lamb, adopted into the family of God and equipped for special service to Him. I needed to start thinking and acting like who I am in Him!

Another factor is that we were still in jetlag and had not recovered from a very intense, one-month trip. Low emotional and physical resources can lead to a skewed view of things. So after dealing with the root cause, I took the evening off and did some relaxing and profitable reading before going to bed early.

Life is so complex from our viewpoint, while it can be quite simple when we look at it from God's perspective. He gives light from His Word and Spirit. We need to take the time to look and listen through lifting our souls to Him and then obey what we know to be right.

Prayer: "Lord, help me today to walk in the light of your Word, to think your thoughts, to make decisions that please you. Help me to continually surrender my will to yours. Amen."

July 23

"Hear, O LORD, and answer me, for I am poor and needy. Guard my life, for I am devoted to you. You are my God; save your servant who trusts in you."

Psalm 86:1,2

Praise you, Lord, that in the midst of a struggle to come to an agreement on policy, you are directing my attention to Psalm 86:15-17 where the focus is on you, on your goodness.

The essence of this Psalm is a cry for help and an appeal to your mercy—I praise you that you are a merciful God whom we can trust in trouble, for you will answer us!

"…you, O Lord, are a compassionate and gracious God, slow to anger, abounding in love and faithfulness." Praise be to you, Heavenly Father, Lord Jesus, Holy Spirit, the Almighty Three-in-One Creator God, that you are compassionate -- "full of compassion" as the KJV says.

You are the One who pours out mercy on us every day, protecting us in the small and great events of life. You have mercy on us by not punishing our sins, by not bringing us what we deserve, by not treating us as we treat others, by not allowing the enemy full access to us. You are wonderfully merciful and will continue to overflow with mercy through the rest of our lives.

In addition, you are gracious; this is another "overflowing word." Your nature is one of giving, for you are Love itself, outwardly focused, desiring to do good to all around you, not for what you get back, but because your essence is Love. You give and give, and then give more: the sun rises every day, there is air to breathe, food to eat, shelter for living; and you give clothing, relationships, protection, guidance, grace and goodness.

Your presence, your power, your purpose, your persistence are all poured into our lives every day. We rejoice in your love, we bask in your favor, we rest in the shadow of your might; we are renewed in your strength, we delight in your being. And all you do, Lord, you do graciously, with kindness, wisdom and thoughtfulness. You are beauty, grace and goodness. You are worthy of trust and praise.

You are "slow to anger." You don't just give us another chance, you give us a thousand more chances! You call to us, you remind us, you tap us on the shoulder, you give us hundreds of little messages to alert us to where we are going wrong. And when we don't listen, you patiently wait for the right time to come down hard.

You are "abounding in love and faithfulness." The measure of your love is beyond anyone's conception—only words of limitless dimension can express the greatness, the fullness, the expansiveness of your love—the highest heavens, the deepest deep, the endlessness of eternity. And because of your great love, your faithfulness also overflows on us: unmeasured, unbounded, fathomless and deep. You are faithful to your character, to your Word, to your purposes, to the intents of your heart, and to your children.

You will not fail, you cannot fail, for you are so full of faithfulness that there is no room, no possibility of failure in your plans. We can trust you entirely, completely, fully, endlessly, whole-heartedly, forever. What you bring to pass will be good in the fullness of time, no matter how it appears in the present. We can praise you now in faith for what you will do.

So as I cry, "Turn to me and have mercy on me; grant your strength to your servant and save the son of your maidservant," I am appealing to the essence of who you are: the Loving, Gracious, Patient, Faithful God, who will answer me in my day of trouble. My part is to cry out to you, to appeal to your character, to your name and to praise you ahead of time for what you will do.

Prayer: "Glory be to you, for you are a merciful God, full of compassion, slow to anger and plenteous in mercy and faithfulness. Answer my cry for mercy so that your name may be lifted up, so that the devil and his forces may cry out in anguish at the victory you are bringing. May it be a victory marked by unity among your children, a unity based on you, your Word, Truth and obedience. Amen."

July 24

"May all those who seek you rejoice and be glad in YOU...."
[Emphasis added]

Psalm 40:16

Superficially everything seems to be going well, but underneath things have been in a different state. The major hint of trouble is that I've been waking up at 2 am and can't get back to sleep for 2 or 3 hours. Although this is a great time to pray and do other things (I'm writing this at 3 am), a few nights of this makes one really tired.

The cause of this insomnia seems to be having a lot of irons in the fire while the fire is going out! On a number of fronts things are not going as I'd like: Light Church is experiencing only miniscule progress; some of our leaders are being tested in dangerous ways (tempted to marry unbelievers); plans for our multi-church Easter celebration are stymied by lack of a venue and vacillation in the commitment of our closest partner. In our business platform, which provides a legal entity for doing ministry, the coffee sales are expanding very slowly, held up by delays in production of our coffee-cup-top filter; advertisements for our tours have brought in zero results; and cash flow in the business is a problem. Then the nation-wide men's conference, for which I am primarily responsible, is looking like it may bomb out with low attendance; and there are a number of other projects that aren't getting sufficient attention from me because of time crunches. And the list goes on.

In all this, the Lord has reminded me of the need to constantly lift my soul to Him, journaling regularly and processing my thoughts, desires and emotions, but this has not been sufficient. Tonight as I was meditating on Scripture trying to get back to sleep, Ps 37:4 came up: "Delight yourself also in the Lord and He will give you the desires of your heart." There it is! The deeper cause of my sleeplessness jumped out at me: my focus has been on these events and desires, not on God.

I was subtly trying to draw my delight from things going well, not from God Himself. This is putting the cart before the horse, actually preventing things from going well! So now I am in the process of unhitching the horse of praise and re-harnessing it in front of the cart of ministry: deliberately finding my delight in God, in His character, in His revealed Word while giving up my desire to see each of these things go my way. May He work what is best in each one, bringing glory to Himself, whether that be through what I consider failure, or through it going well. That releases me from a whole unnecessary load and will make me easier to live with!

Prayer: "Lord, alert me to when I am finding my delight in anything other than you. May I enjoy what you give, but reserve true delight for you. May glorifying you be my highest value, goal and desire. May you be exalted today in my life. Amen."

July 25

"Among the gods there is none like you, O Lord; no deeds can compare with yours."

Psalm 86:8

As I face a difficult situation, praise be to you Lord God, Ruler of all, King of Glory, Master of the universe, Lord over every circumstance. I praise you that your hand is mighty and that you are the eternal Sovereign, Lord over all that goes on, all that comes into my life. Each thing arrives with your permission, with your goals, with your purpose.

Therefore, I can praise you for my present difficulty, trust you in it, rest before you in the help you will give before I can see it. This is setting my heart on things above, on your things, your outcome, your decisions, your plans.

Praise you that in the unresolved situation before me, I can praise you for the outcome now, while things still look dark and the horizon is disturbingly empty. Our hope is in you, Lord God, Lord Jesus, Heavenly Father, Triune Lord who helps us at break of day.

"Rescue me from my enemies, O LORD, for I hide myself in you" (Ps.143:9). Yes, I come to you, asking you to fight for me, guide me, give me wisdom.

"Teach me to do your will, for you are my God…" (Ps. 143:10a). I do surrender myself to you in this situation, I commit to doing your will rather than following my own.

"May your good Spirit lead me on level ground" (Ps.143:10b). I praise you that you are only good, that you will lead me on good ground, in a grace-filled way, in paths of righteousness.

"For your name's sake, O LORD, preserve my life; in your righteousness, bring me out of trouble" (Ps.143:11). Yes, do this to bring glory to your Name, do this according to your character, only you can correctly bring me out of this swamp of turmoil.

"In the day of my trouble I will call to you," [this is my response: to come to you] "for you will answer me" (Ps. 86:7). This is certainty, you are trustable, you will act and help in the way and in the time you know is best. I can praise you for that now before any resolution comes.

"Among the gods there is none like you, O Lord; no deeds can compare with yours" (Ps. 86:8). I can trust you because you are so great: great in character, in integrity, in wisdom, in power, in goodness, in the certainty that you will act. You are worthy of worship, wonder and waiting for. Glory be to you today in my life, Lord.

Prayer: "Lord, help me to bow before you, to revel in your goodness, to delight in your holiness, to rejoice in your powerfulness, and to rest in your perfectness, for this brings you glory. I ask today for your direction, your guidance, your bringing to pass what is good and I praise you now for what you will do. Amen."

July 26

"...He restores my soul, He leads me in paths of righteousness for His name's sake."

Psalm 23:3

Being unjustly accused really bothers me. A healthy sense of justice and indignation at injustice is a good thing, but in my case most of the "unjust accusations" have been revelations of my selfish "seeking of significance" in the wrong places. Such accusations upset my inner balance and anger wells up within.

God has made me to lie down in the green pasture of unjust accusations because He wants to set me free from the sins that lead to my wrong, unhealthy and destructive responses. Instead of protecting myself, running away or ignoring the problem, I must remain where He puts me until He's ready for me to move on, having learned the lesson prepared for me.

In this green pasture the Holy Spirit is using Scripture to give me a growing grasp of how my significance flows from God's character and what He grants us in Christ, rather than from my "being right." This allows me to let go of my demand for justice and frees me from the fear of man. As a result, there is an observable character transformation going on inside: my touchiness towards "unjust accusations" is diminishing.

This past week in two separate incidences, people incorrectly accused me of saying something negative, but the normal strong urge to rise up and defend myself was muted. The accusations were not important and I could easily treat them as such--even though I was really tired and stressed. This is God's deep work in my life to free me from the chains of my old nature, a freedom that flows from His Word and Spirit at work on the inside. As a result, I could let go of what people think, hold on to what God has to say and rise above my natural reaction.

Praise God that He is the Good Shepherd, doing what is right whether we like it or not, whether it is painful or pleasant. He has larger goals for us than our comfortableness and success. Am I willing to put down my puny, selfish desires and take up His grand and glorious, powerful and perfect desires?

Prayer: "Lord, help me to stay put in the green pastures you give me. Help me to learn all that is needed. Help me to empty my hand and heart with confession and surrender so that you may fill them with the great and glorious things you have for me, both here, now and in eternity. May I give you glory in this. Amen."

July 27

"He is a shield for all who take refuge in him.

Psalm 18:30b

Jesus was a master at using the events around him to illustrate the truths he was teaching. At times he helps us in the same way, giving "life examples" to drive home a point we've just been taught. Today we had a very graphic example of this.

This morning two believing ladies came to Barbara for a Bible study where she taught a lesson on the importance of thanking God in and for all things (Ps. 50:23). Barbara emphasized that only good things come from God, but at times He also allows Satan to bring along a seemingly bad thing so God can work some good from it in our lives.

I arrived home from teaching at the university at about 1 pm, just as they were finishing the lesson, so Barbara asked me to drive one of the ladies, Nadia, down to the local share taxi stop because this was the first time she'd come by herself and she wasn't quite sure of the way.

Since the main road was very busy, I drove to the other side so Nadia wouldn't have to cross. I explained this to her and pointed out where she should wait for the share taxi. But, when she got out of the car, she began to cross the road; somehow she had it in her mind that she was on the wrong side. I was now waiting at the red light to cross and called her to come back and wait.

Instead of coming back, for some reason she hesitated and went first one way and then the other, not aware of a truck that was rapidly bearing down on her. I could see the accident coming, but could do nothing to prevent it. The driver obviously expected Nadia to get out of the way because he just flashed his lights and kept coming, but she had her back to him, and then wham, he hit her. She flew into the air and landed in a crumpled heap on the pavement.

I shouted "Oh, no!" I leaped out of the car and ran to her side. I was sure she was dead from that tremendous impact. However, she only had the wind knocked out of her and was conscious. With the help of others we carried her to my car and I took her to the hospital. She was spitting blood and moaning, while at the same time thanking me for helping her and apologizing for causing me trouble! It turned out that there were no broken bones, only bruises.

Such an incident is hard to thank God for, but he brought several good things out of this. The first, and somewhat comical, was that her crooked nose was straightened out on impact! More importantly, God used the accident to heal some broken relationships. Because Nadia and her family had become Christians, her brother-in-law and family had not been speaking to Nadia's family for three years, which was a great grief to her. But the brother-in-law sent his son to the hospital to see how Nadia was doing! Then two believing women who had been very condemning of Nadia showed sympathy for her in this situation.

Nadia herself was praising God for how He was using the accident even before she saw all the positive results. Not bad for a believer of only four months! How about us?

Prayer: "Lord, help me to also be a person who in faith gives thanks in all things so that you may be honored before men and angels. Amen."

July 28

"I will extol the LORD at all times; his praise will always be on my lips. My soul will boast in the LORD; let the afflicted hear and rejoice."

Psalm 34:1,2

This year's Men's Conference for all the workers in our country turned out to be the toughest, most problem-ridden conference I've ever been involved in. Humanly speaking, the basic reason was the attitude of the hotel and its staff. There were also logistical problems with not enough elevators and floors that didn't match up (to get to the 9th floor—one meeting area—from the 8th—our dining area—you had to go down to the 6th and follow a labyrinth to the other side and go back up). Plus the meeting rooms were not adequate and many hotel rooms were small, airless and hot.

Second and more importantly, the hotel management was not cooperative: they over-booked both rooms and meeting rooms, kept moving us around, tried to double charge us on a number of items (once for over $800), didn't provide the tea breaks as agreed upon, etc. One morning we came down to find they had filled our book display room with dining room tables! Then the manager got upset and abusive about the books that were for sale, being Christian books—even though we had been very up front about who we are and what we would do. In addition there were problems with the AV equipment, with translation, with communications and with over-crowded rooms.

It was enough to make one want to complain. As one person put it, the conference was one long episode of spiritual warfare! Fortunately the Holy Spirit kept us thinking in warfare terms, so each of these problems became an opportunity to praise God, to rely on Him, to give a positive response, and at times to "wash the feet" of the hotel staff by agreeing to changes to make their work easier/possible.

Most of the attenders were unaware of many of these problems except when we had to ask for prayer about them, or shift meeting places and times, but in the end several folks said that the way the situations were handled was as much a teaching as what the speakers had to say! Being weak is more powerful than seeming to be strong!

What makes me shudder is to think of how difficult it would have been if you and we hadn't prayed so much for the conference! The final outcome was a good year of foundation building; God is able to use all for His glory!

Prayer: "Lord, help me to consistently think in terms of spiritual warfare, keeping on the armor, fighting with praise, prayer and persistence in obedience. May I bring you honor today by living in the light of your presence. Amen."

July 29

"Be still before the LORD and wait patiently for him….For evil men will be cut off, but those who hope in the LORD will inherit the land."

Psalm 37:7a, 9

Praise be to you Lord God, King Jesus, Shepherd of my soul, for your reign, your rule and your righteousness. Praise you for your call to surrender, to follow, to trust and obey; you are more than worthy of our obedience, our worship, our awe and fear. So in the midst of ponderous problems staring me in the face, I choose to believe your Word instead of my feelings.

I praise you for the clarity of your Word, which says in Psalm 37:2-8 "Trust in the LORD and do good;" I bow before you, Lord God, agree to trust in you, and will do the good you show me to do, no matter how I may feel about the situation.

"Dwell in the land and enjoy safe pasture." I can choose to settle in quietness in the green pasture you have given, knowing that you will provide all, prescribe all and protect in all.

"Delight yourself in the LORD and he will give you the desires of your heart." Lord, you are delightful. To revel in you is not hard if I am willing to get my eyes off my "problems" and onto you, the great and mighty God of Glory. And then it is a certainty that you will put your desires into my heart and fulfill them at the right time and in the right way.

"Commit your way to the LORD;" I surrender to you, bowing to your lead, believing in your goodness and wisdom.

"trust in him," I agree to trust you rather than my instincts, my ideas, my thoughts. I submit my intellect to your Word.

"and he will do this:" what a statement of certainty--in response to my obedience and prayer you *will* act.

"He will make your righteousness shine like the dawn, the justice of your cause like the noonday sun." You will bring out what is right, you will expose error, you will be the One to bring true resolution. Help me to know how to walk in step with you in this, to not run out before you, but to trust you in all.

"Be still before the LORD and wait patiently for him; "I can rest in you, be quiet before you, be confident in you, knowing that you will act in the right time, in the right way. I can wait patiently because it is clear that you know the correct time to act. I only can guess while you know exactly, so it is proper to wait for you, the Omnipresent, Omniscient, Omni-loving God.

"Do not fret when men succeed in their ways, when they carry out their wicked schemes." This will happen, but my trust is in the Lord and what He will do; my primary tactic is praise, then prayer, then persistence in doing what is right.

"Refrain from anger and turn from wrath; do not fret—it leads only to evil." I want to be far from evil in this, so I agree to reject anger and wrath, to refuse to fret and be anxious, to fear. Perfect love (your love) obliterates all these.

Yes, Lord, to bow before you, to revel in your goodness, to delight in your holiness, to rejoice in your powerfulness, to rest in your perfectness--this brings you glory, this brings me peace. I commit myself to doing this.

Prayer: "I praise you now for what you will do in the problems that face me; I ask for your direction, your guidance, your bringing to pass what is right, what is good, glorifying and godly. Amen."

July 30

"My grace is sufficient for you, for my power is made perfect in weakness."

2 Corinthians 12:9

As we stood in the long line for security check in the Frankfurt airport, I was getting more and more agitated. We'd arrived 3 hours early, thinking we'd have plenty of time, but it was almost boarding time, there were still 20 people in front of us and we had at least 3 more control points to go through! The baggage check-in had had a huge line, but it had moved right along, quite in contrast to the present line, which was barely moving at all. It seemed that the security people were intentionally making long, long pauses between each person so in the end it took about 45 minutes to put 20 people through.

In order to pass the time profitably I was trying to meditate on the armor of God passage in Ephesians 6. Coming to the verse on the belt of Truth, the Holy Spirit reminded me that what I actually deserved was not getting what I wanted when I wanted it (as was happening now), but to suffer condemnation, suffering, pain and failure.

Suddenly I realized that my present discontent came from my feeling I had the right to have things go my way and those stupid security people were keeping me from my rights! OOOH, a further revelation of my self-centered view of life! Here was another chance to confess sin, deny self, trust God and praise Him for what He was going to do before I could see the results.

He did get us through in time and onto the plane at the last moment, but more importantly He showed me again how ingrained my natural, self-centered thinking is, which stems from believing the world rather than the Word.

It actually took me several days to work through all the sludge of my discontent with that situation, but the Holy Spirit patiently led me through the process of lifting my soul to Him in journaling, ending again with 2 Corinthians 12:10, "Therefore I will delight in weaknesses, insults, hardships, persecutions and difficulties, for when I am weak, then I am strong." There is such freedom in embracing that Truth rather than fighting for my supposed "rights."

Prayer: "Lord, help me to think your Truth, to consistently meditate on your Word, to absorb your thoughts and to live them out. Help me to delight in being weak, remembering that you are incredibly strong. Amen."

July 31

"…set your hearts on things above…."

Colossians 3:1

As I face this difficult situation, I praise you, my Lord, Ruler of all, King of Glory, Master of the universe, God over every situation. I praise you that your hand is mighty, that you are the eternal Sovereign, Lord over all that comes into my life. Each happening arrives with your permission, with your power, with your purpose. Therefore I can praise you for it, trust you in it, rest in you for the outcome before I can see it.

Doing this is actively setting my heart on things above, on your things, your desires, your decisions. Praise you that in the situation before me, I can praise you now for the outcome, when things still look dark, and the horizon is hopelessly empty. I can do this because our hope is in you, Lord God, Lord Jesus, my Heavenly Father, the Triune Creator who helps us at break of day.

"Rescue me from my enemies, O LORD, for I hide myself in you" (Ps.143:9). Yes, I come to you, Yahweh; fight for me today, guide me, give wisdom.

"Teach me to do your will, for you are my God" (Ps.143:9b). I do surrender myself to you in this difficult situation, Elohim, I commit to doing your will.

"may your good Spirit lead me on level ground" (Ps.143:10). Praise that you, Adonai, are only good, that you will lead me on good ground, in a constructive way, in paths of righteousness.

"For your name's sake, O LORD, preserve my life; in your righteousness, bring me out of trouble" (Ps.143:11). Yes, do this to bring glory to your Name, the great I AM, do this according to your character. Only you can bring me out of this swamp of turmoil correctly.

"In the day of my trouble I will call to you," this must be my response, to call to you first, "for you will answer me." (Ps 86:7) This is a certainty—you will answer—for you are consistent and faithful, you will act to help in the way and in the time you know is best. I can praise you now for that before any resolution comes.

"Among the gods there is none like you, O Lord; no deeds can compare with yours" (Ps. 86:8). I can trust you because you are so great: in character, in integrity, in wisdom, in power, in goodness, in the certainty of your faithfulness.

To bow before you, Lord Jesus, to revel in your goodness, to delight in your holiness, to rejoice in your powerfulness, to rest in your perfection—this brings you glory, especially when I do so before having any answers.

Prayer: "I praise you now for what you will do in the unresolved difficulties before me; I ask for your direction, your guidance, your token of good, your bringing to pass what is best. And I thank you now for the answers you will send, O Faithful Father. Amen."

AUGUST

August 1

"Fret not yourself...."

Psalm 37:1

Praise you, Lord Jesus, for as I awoke, you were there, waiting for me in your great Goodness, your shining Glory, your immense Power, your perfect Wisdom, your rich, immutable Love. You are the One to delight in, you are the One to obey, you are the One to rejoice in, you are the One to trust. I praise you that you have revealed yourself to us in your Word which is rich, deep, full, powerful, transforming, eternal and trustable.

Praise you that you are moving history to a conclusion and taking us with you. In all that swirls around us, events that are beyond our control, that humanly speaking are distressing, we can trust you to be weaving all into the fabric of your plan for the ending of history. You will then begin eternity, cutting off all evil, and initiating a sin-free existence for all who have come into the shelter of your righteousness and love. Praise be to you!

Thank you so much for your Word, which gives me guidance. Psalm 37:3 says, "Dwell in the land and befriend faithfulness...." This is a command to be faithful to your Word, to your stated desires, to my brothers in this conflict.

Psalm 34:4 continues: "Delight yourself in the LORD, and he will give you the desires of your heart." The call is to make you my focus, my delight, my worship, my center, my primary thought—this is what I must do and want to do. Thereby my heart will be conformed to yours, wanting what you want, living for you, thinking with you your thoughts, working with you, obeying you—all for the proper motives.

Lord, thank you for the talk yesterday with my colleague about our opposing views. Thank you that you are working in this, advancing things forward in ways we cannot see. In this conversation, you have brought me again face-to-face with my failure to trust you—I am fretting, anxious, thinking too much about the issue. I confess to you that this failure to trust you is a serious and dangerous sin: it flows from rebellion, unbelief, pride and selfish independence. I confess these, ask for forgiveness and repudiate them.

Guide me, Lord, in leaving these behind, in submitting to you, trusting you, delighting in you, rejoicing in you, resting in you, obeying you. Guide me, Lord, in knowing what I should do and what I should let go. I praise you, Heavenly Father, that in this I am weak and that you are at work. Show me how to join you in your work in me. I thank you for the outcome now.

Thank you for the certainty of your doing what is right, for your perfection, your power and your wisdom. I can delight in these aspects of your personality even when nothing works out as I desire, even though I lose all, am forced out of where I want to be and fail totally—knowing you is enough for joy.

So I will "Commit my way to you, LORD; I will trust in you, and you will act: you will bring forth my righteousness as the light, and my justice as the noonday sun. I will be still before you, LORD and wait patiently for you; I will fret not myself over the one who prospers in his way, over the man who carries out evil devices! I will refrain from anger, and forsake wrath! I will fret not myself; it tends only to evil" (Ps. 37:5-8 ESV).

Prayer: "This, Lord, is where I want to be: in the center of trust in you, in the center of your will, of your love, wisdom and power. You are to be the Focus, the One lifted up. Then you will work. Help me to join you in this. My work is primarily worship and prayer; help me to know how to pray, may your Spirit pray through me, in me, for your will today. Amen."

August 2

"Set your heart on things above...."

Colossians 3:1

Being of Scottish ancestry and a natural penny pincher, spending money is an unpleasant event for me. What gives me much satisfaction is getting a great bargain, or better yet getting something for free. On the other side of the coin, it is painful when I am overcharged or get cheated in some way. I tell you this so you can better appreciate how the Lord is working to expand my perspective.

We recently stopped renting half the space we had for the bookstore in Ankara. We left everything in much better shape than when we rented it, got back all our deposit and thought all was taken care of. However, this past week I got news that the landlord had come and demanded that we fix the heating system for the new renter.

Since we had left the heater in at least as good a condition as when we moved in, the landlord's request was unjust and, I think, illegal, but my partner and the bookstore manager agreed to pay for it anyway. This did not make me happy.

However, as I prayed about it, obediently thanking God for the situation (although I was not joyful about it), a new thought came to mind, triggered by Ephesians 6:8, "...you know that the Lord will reward everyone for whatever good he does...." As we use the resources God has given us for the Kingdom, we are investing in eternal things. Going the extra mile, paying for a repair we are not legally responsible for is a concrete witness to the landlord (with whom we have shared a good deal of Truth). This is an investment here and now, plus in the eternal, laying up of treasure in heaven. This is a new and freeing emphasis for me!

Author Randy Alcorn has written a book called *The Treasure Principle* dealing with how we invest what God has given us. What we give to the church, to missions, to help others, is a double investment: once to help God's work here, but again in eternal rewards for using resources wisely to advance His Kingdom.

It seems that in our evangelical culture we don't talk much about this type of investment or of the rewards He has for us – it seems a bit self-serving, thinking of what we will get out of it. But perhaps that's why the average evangelical believer gives back less than 2% to the Lord rather than the minimum of 10% encouraged in Scripture.

God is so generous in what He pours out on us; and I am thankful for His patient working to give me His perspective on the handling of His money so I can reject my natural worldview and give Him more glory in generous, trusting obedience.

Prayer: "Lord, help me to remember that all that I have is actually yours, that I am only your steward, not the owner of anything. Help me to use it as you desire, to give as freely as you want. Help me to be faithful in consistently giving at least 10% to your work. Amen."

August 3

"Wait for the LORD and keep his way."

Psalm 37:34

Praise you, O Lord my God. At the dawn of today there you were, as always, waiting for me: faithful, ever-present, loving, wise, kind, and powerful. You are perfect: you never fear, never fail, never are flustered. You are the Rock, the Wall, the Shield, the Shepherd of my life. In you there is what we all desire: security, significance and salvation; there is meaning, hope and a future; there is love, peace and joy. I lift up your name, I glorify you, honor you and exalt you, for you are worthy of obedience, praise and worship.

Lord, yesterday I failed again in not asking you for guidance during my conversations—this shows a dependence on self, a failure to join you in what you are doing, a confidence in my own abilities, wisdom and insight rather than reliance on the all-knowing, all-seeing, all-wise God. Forgive me for such arrogance, independence, rebellion and unbelief. I praise you that you are "ready to forgive and plenteous in mercy to all those who call upon you" (Ps. 86:4b KJV). Thank you for your powerful and rich forgiveness.

Thank you also that when I am unfaithful, you continue on in your faithfulness, in your grace, in your goodness. You will never fail to act with exact timing, and you always live according to your perfect and positive character. You will move inexorably to bring righteousness and no one can stop you; you will act in the right moment to bring out truth and no one can block you; you will consistently defend those who hide in you and no one can overcome you. Praise be to you!

You are faithful: to your character, to your Word, to your promises, to your salvation. When you give your word about something, there is the certainty of hope: it will come to pass in your time, in your way, in your power, period! So I can trust you now in this difficult situation before me to do what is right, knowing that you will lead me in paths of righteousness.

Praise you that in spite of what we are in our natural depravity, you call us to walk with you, to join you in your great work, to be effective instruments in your hands. What a wonder that you are able to draw straight lines with crooked sticks. May your name be exalted before all.

Prayer: "Lord, I lay before you the outcomes I want, I give you my desires, I surrender my will and take your will in its place. I trust you in your greatness to work out what is best and glorify yourself in it. Amen."

August 4

"Set your heart on things above, not on the passing things of earth...."

Colossians 3:1

For our team's conference one summer we all read the book *Peacemaker* by Ken Sande. One thing in this book stood out to me starkly: the biblical concept of idols. The author gave a clear definition: "An idol is anything apart from God that we depend on to be happy, fulfilled, or secure." Wow, that is really easy to grasp.

He continues, "In biblical terms, it is something other than God that we set our hearts on (Luke 12:29, 1Cor. 10:19), that motivates us (1Cor. 4:5), that masters and rules us (Ps. 119:133, Eph. 5:5) or that we trust, fear or serve (Isa. 42:17, Matt. 6:24, Luke 12:4-5)."

He went on to say, "Idols always demand sacrifices. When someone fails to satisfy our demands and expectations, our idol demands that this thwarter of my pleasure should suffer.... As James 4:1-3 teaches, inflicting pain on others is one of the surest signs that an idol is ruling our hearts."

Shortly after reading this, the Holy Spirit brought into sharp focus one idol in my life. We were due at a meeting and Barbara wasn't ready at the time I wanted to leave, so I began to get restless and irritable. She calmly went about putting things in order while I stood at the door fiddling with my keys. When she finally came I made a cutting little remark concerning our being late.

There it was: I was demanding that we leave at a certain time in order for me to be happy, and when that didn't happen, I punished the offender with a sharp word!

The Lord used this definition of idol worship and this experience with my sinful impatience to expose in me a number of other areas where I am an idol worshiper. Ken Sande said idols are often hard to discern because what has become an idol is often in itself a positive thing (getting to meetings on time is good), but when we demand it to be happy, fulfilled or secure, then we are misusing a healthy thing.

The author ended the chapter by saying, "When you find yourself in conflict, work backwards...to identify the desires that are controlling your heart." Idol-destruction is the key to removing the source of many conflicts from our hearts and homes. This is very good advice, but only if we are willing to admit that we have a wrong attitude and want to correct it.

Fortunately the Lord gave me a willing heart, so that when He revealed to me how my selfish desire (idol) led me to be unkind, demanding and negative, it was a quick and clear step to confess this idolatry and be free to proceed with grace, asking forgiveness from Barbara. And, by the way, we did get to the meeting on time!

Prayer: "Lord, expose in me the idols that compete for my affection. Help me to confess and repudiate them, to make you the true and only God in my life. Amen."

August 5

"With my mouth I will greatly extol the LORD....For he stands at the right hand of the needy one, to save his life from those who condemn him."

Psalm 109:30,31

My prayer in distress, based on Psalm 109:20-23, 26-27.

"... O sovereign LORD" You are the LORD, Yahweh, the Great and Holy One, the Sinless One, the Mighty I Am, without beginning or end, without negativeness or evil, without sin or selfishness, the Perfect Judge of all and the Lover of sinners. You are the One to whom we can appeal.

"...My Lord," you are Adonai, the One who has the right to demand complete obedience, for you have purchased us at great cost, in great pain, through great suffering. You also promise complete provision for us to be able to obey you, serve you and love you well.

"...Deal on my behalf for your name's sake." I am weak, I can only appeal to you to contend with those who oppose me. And my motive is that your Name be honored.

"...Because your steadfast love is good, deliver me!" I turn to you, for your love is sure, your power is unlimited, your wisdom is boundless, your influence is endless, your work is flawless.

In contrast, "...I am poor and needy, and my heart is stricken within me." I cannot open people's eyes, I cannot convince them when they've made up their minds, I cannot bring change—my ability and resources are extremely small—micro-power when what is needed is macro-power, which you have. You are the Star-Breather, the Earth Spinner, the Dawn Bringer, the History Ender, the Eternity Beginner.

"I am gone like a shadow at evening; I am shaken off like a locust." The contrast between you and me is stark:

- you are from forever to forever, I last only an instant;
- you are the undefeatable One, I can be shrugged off with one small move;
- you are the all-knowing One, I live on tiny crumbs of knowledge;
- you are the Rock, immovable and unassailable, I am a molecule of dust, easily swept away by a tiny breeze.

Praise you, Lord God, for your great love for one like me who in myself am such a weak, insignificant, useless, ignorant creature!

"Help me, O LORD my God! Save me according to your steadfast love!" Without you nothing will happen, O Yahweh, my Elohim, the Supreme God, strong in love, mighty in power, faithful in promise, trustable in your strength and wisdom. You answer me according to your unwavering love, which you demonstrated in the garden of Gethsemane. When faced with such suffering, such evil, such awfulness, you faithfully, fully fulfilled your promises because of your steadfast love, your kindness, your mercy, your pity for your rebellious creatures.

As you showed your love then, so now, for your glory, for your honor, for the sake of your Kingdom, for the sake of your desire to have more worshipers, answer us!

"Let them know that this is your hand; you, O LORD, have done it!" Act in a way so that all will know it is unmistakably your work, your desire, your perspective that prevailed.

I think of the way you have worked in the past with the many difficulties of my life and how you moved, overruling the perspective of people and brought your desire to pass. I praise you now for what you will do in the problems, the threats, the fears that are before me.

Prayer: "Now in this situation that faces me, Lord, bring glory to yourself, honor to your name and praise to your character. I commit my way to you, I trust in you and wait for you to bring to pass what is best.

And I praise you now for the outcome, even though it may not be what I prefer, for you are good! Amen."

August 6

"God said to Abraham, 'Take your son, your only son, Isaac, whom you love....Sacrifice him there as a burnt offering....'"

Genesis 22:2

One of the basic principles of walking with God is to hold all we have with an open hand, being willing for God to take and give as He sees best.

Since returning to the Middle East in late July, the Lord has been taking things from us one at a time. First was Freedom's going to Germany. He has been such a good help in both business and in the church: energetic, insightful, eager to help, visionary and a leader. I had to put him on the altar of my heart, telling God what I wanted (for him to stay), but being willing to accept the opposite (for him to go).

Then there was a period of sickness (health taken for a while), then disappointments in business. Then a larger issue: losing our apartment. The landlord's son wants to move in; legally we could resist this for at least 6 months, but both of us believe our witness is more important than our rights.

Then while looking for apartments Barbara fell down a full flight of stairs, landing on her face and hitting her head against the marble wall and breaking her right wrist. This was the biggest test for me, as I rushed down the stairs to get to her, seeing blood all over, not knowing if she were dead after hitting her head so hard, or if she had a broken neck, or some other serious injury. Praise God that He protected her from major, permanent damage.

This incident then forced us to give up or postpone a number of planned items (our vacation, Barbara's trip to see her mother, a trip for business), and brought a good deal of change in our life style for a while (because of her broken wrist, I learned how to put bobby pins in Barbara's hair, among other things).

Then while helping to lead a small tour on the Black Sea coast, the authorities pursued and interrogated us, leaving us with the threat of investigation, harassment and perhaps expulsion.

Beyond this are happenings in the lives of friends here, which involve us to some degree: terminal cancer, financial problems, persecution, a death in a traffic accident, and other difficulties--things we'd just as soon not deal with, but things God has allowed to come for good reasons known only to Him.

All these events involve giving up: relationships, convenience, desires, what is familiar, security. But they also involve gaining much more: a deeper surrender, a better understanding of His Word, the opportunity to praise in the midst of disappointment, a greater grasp of God's character, the opportunity to see Him powerfully answer prayer, the possibility of being a witness to those who watch us go through these times with grace.

These positives were especially true with Barbara's accident. Very obviously God protected her from permanent damage in the fall; why, then, didn't He protect her fully by preventing the fall? Barbara answered this question herself: "God is doing something through this that we can't understand yet. Look at all the new people we've met with whom we can now share the Truth!"

What summarizes all this for us is Psalm 50:23 "He who sacrifices thank offerings [giving thanks when we don't feel like it] honors me and prepares the way so that I may show him the salvation of God."

Prayer: Lord, help us each to be people characterized by holding all with an open hand, by praising in all circumstances, trusting you, glorifying you, resting in you. Amen"

August 7

"Your face, O Lord, I seek."

Psalm 27:8

As I set the phone down I was shaking and my heart was pounding. That had been one of the most difficult conversations in my life; I felt ripped up, abused, stomped on and belittled. The anger vented by the other party had been of hurricane force in my emotions and I had to get up and walk around to try and relieve the tension. And all this over a little misunderstanding! The other person, a mission leader from another group, felt betrayed and foolish because I had misunderstood him; unfortunately I had, in the end, also replied in anger to his charges.

With trembling hands I opened my Bible to Psalm 37, my refuge in times of conflict, especially verses 1-3: "Fret not yourself because of evil doers, neither be envious of workers of iniquity, for they shall be cut down like the grass and wither as the green herb" [KJV]. Good perspective on how God will deal with things. I can trust Him to work them out. "Trust in the Lord and do good, so shall you dwell in the land and be fed. Delight yourself also in the Lord and he will give you the desires of your heart." Great words; healing words; encouraging words. The question was: how can I now do good to this man?

It did not help that I got a follow up email from him that evening, full of anger, accusations, demands and threats. I never wanted to see or hear from him again; I wanted to tell everyone what a terrible person he was; I wanted to hurt him like he hurt me!

But the Holy Spirit kept bringing Psalm 37 to mind, prompting me to delight in God, to do good, to take the low road. So, beginning with forgiving the man in my heart as I have been forgiven, and after much prayer for wisdom, I wrote a short email expressing my distress at the way things had gone, and apologizing for my impatience and for interrupting him in our phone conversation. It was hard to write that when it seemed to me mostly his doing, but I did have a part and the Spirit led me to take responsibility.

This event was a challenge to the truth I often repeat: "Knowing Jesus is enough for joy!" And, like Habakkuk, I chose to rejoice in my God.

It took two days for the vibrations in my being to settle down, and I felt no joy, just hurt. But beyond what I felt was the Truth that God's joy was waiting for me at the end of the tunnel of obedience, palpable through faith.

A couple of days later the response came from the fellow; I saw it when getting email in the morning, but didn't open it, not wanting to ruin my day with more anger and accusation. I should have read it, for it was a humble admission of his being the cause of the conflict, asking forgiveness and wanting a new start! It was amazing! It showed again the power of prayer and following God's principles, no matter how illogical they may seem.

The man also humbly asked if there was anything else he should deal with. It was at that point where I began to realize one of the reasons God had allowed this painful happening into my life. This man had responsibility for a good number of workers in his organization; if he poured out such anger on me when I inadvertently didn't meet his expectations in a small matter, what will he do to his "sheep" when they disappoint him? Now I could help him see and deal with his anger before he hurts others.

I, too, have struggled with the same sin of unjustified angry responses, and am learning that it usually stems from failure to be a "grace receiver." When I am trying to earn significance or security by performance or to get it from others' opinions, I am not receiving grace from God, so I cannot be a "grace giver." I demand performance from others as I do from myself. And when they fail, they feel my wrath.

However, when I begin to understand how much I have been forgiven, and how much I am unconditionally accepted by God, then I can pass on this grace to those around me no matter how they act.

Prayer: "Lord, I am in myself so weak and fragile. Help me to rest in the shadow of your Almightiness, to trust you in each storm that comes into my life, to flee to your Word, to praise you and obey so you may work freely, bringing the good fruit you desire. Amen."

August 8

"Therefore as God's chosen people, holy and dearly loved, clothe yourselves with compassion, kindness, humility, gentleness and patience. Bear with each other and forgive whatever grievances you may have against one another. Forgive as the Lord forgave you."

Colossians 3:12-13

Shortly after the painful, difficult, attack described in yesterday's entry, I was the receiver of rich, healing grace from my teammates.

The local brothers had postponed a leaders' meeting from Saturday evening to Sunday. However, I forgot to tell my two teammates, both of whom went to great effort to get there (getting a baby sitter, traveling 45 minutes by bus, being away from their families on Saturday evening). I met them separately as I was leaving the store and when I apologized for my failure in communication, each said the same thing, "That's ok, we all forget at times." And they meant it.

Grace flowed; goodness welled up, joy rained down. They didn't say the words, "I forgive you" but they certainly acted it out. If they had been measuring me by performance rather than grace, they certainly would have had the right to rake me over the coals. Instead, they were living demonstrations of being "grace receivers" and "grace givers," forgiving others as God has forgiven them.

C.S. Lewis declared that every believer should be a grace receiver and giver, describing it this way: "To be a Christian means to forgive the inexcusable, because God has forgiven the inexcusable in you."

Counselor David Seamands summed up his career with this insight, "Many years ago I was driven to the conclusion that the two major causes of most emotional problems among evangelical Christians are these: the failure to understand [and] receive...God's unconditional grace and forgiveness; and the failure to give out that unconditional love, forgiveness and grace to other people..."

Both quotes come from the book, *What's So Amazing about Grace?* by Phillip Yancey (Grand Rapids, MI: Zondervan, 2003), one I recommend.

How are you doing at forgiving and extending grace in the conflicts in your life? Take a look at Psalm 37:1-10 with its admonitions to "fret not" "trust in the Lord and do good," "delight in the Lord" and "wait on Him." It will help!

Prayer: "Lord, help me to be a grace receiver and a grace giver, forgiving others as you have forgiven me. Help me to remember how much I am forgiven, and in actuality and comparison, how small are others' offenses against me. Help me to live the truth that your death and resurrection bought forgiveness for every sin committed against me. Who am I to not forgive?! Praise you for the grace you give. Amen."

August 9

"The LORD says to my Lord: 'Sit at my right hand until I make your enemies a footstool for your feet.'"

Psalm 110:1

You are wonderful, O LORD, our Heavenly Father, the One glorious in holiness. You work hand in hand with the Lord Jesus, the Sovereign One, Master, Owner of the universe, King of glory, to bring about your plan of redemption and restoration of all.

What power, what ability, what glory is at work, for you are the LORD (*Yahweh* whose glory is in your holiness) and the Lord (*Adonai*, the Owner of all who has the right to demand obedience and promises to supply all so we can obey). You will defeat evil and rebellion, eliminate lying and unbelief and bring about beauty and perfect righteousness. Your enemies will be forced to bow down before you, before Truth and Righteousness, before Justice and Mercy, before Goodness and Grace.

"The LORD will extend your mighty scepter from Zion; you will rule in the midst of your enemies" (Ps. 110:2). No enemy can resist you, Lord Jesus, no evil can stand against you, no rebellion can succeed against you. You will prevail!

"Arrayed in holy majesty, from the womb of the dawn you will receive the dew of your youth" (Ps. 110:3b). You, Lord Jesus, are gloriously dressed in your pristine, majestic, marvelous holiness. You, the eternal One, who has died once for all and rose to live forever, you will always have the dew of your youth, the vigor, strength and power of the ageless God of Creation. You are able to act in might and majesty, to accomplish all that your holy heart desires. You are trustable: completely, wonderfully, firmly trustable.

"The LORD has sworn and will not change his mind: 'You are a priest forever, in the order of Melchizedek'" (Ps. 110:4). You, Lord Jesus, are, by virtue of your nature as God and by virtue of your vow and promise, our Priest forever. You are utterly, entirely, totally faithful so you will never change your mind.

"... because Jesus lives forever, he has a permanent priesthood. Therefore he is able to save completely those who come to God through him, because he always lives to intercede for them. Such a high priest meets our need—one who is holy, blameless, pure, set apart from sinners, exalted above the heavens" (Heb. 7:24-26).

You, Lord Jesus, are the exalted One, the Most High, the Everlasting One, the Blameless One, Pure in heart, in motive, in thought, in action. All you do is good, and all you will is good. You are the Pinnacle of greatness, the Paragon of goodness, the Prince of graciousness. All must bow before such purity, such holiness, such perfection. You are worthy of praise, of trust, of obedience both now and forever more!

Prayer: "We give you glory, Lord God, Yahweh and Adonai. We bow before you and exalt you in our thoughts, words and actions. Praise be to you in my life both today and forever and ever! Amen."

August 10

"All the Israelites grumbled against Moses and Aaron, and the whole assembly said to them, 'If only we had died in Egypt! Or in this desert!'"

Numbers 14:2

A dragon's egg hatched in my heart. I was unaware of this, as the egg was hidden under the bush of busyness, the one with the broad leaves of distraction. Even after the event, not much grabbed my attention, for newly hatched dragons are small, unable to do much. I think it spent much of its time munching on the plants of discontent and selfishness.

However, as time went on and the little dragon grew, it began to dig around and do some damage in my heart and in my life. Things began "innocently" with my becoming more and more intent on seeing justice done both for me and in the world around me. The biased, negative reports in the news were more irritating; everyday difficulties in life bothered me more; problems with the banking system I used brought out more and more negative thoughts and words.

Finally, Someone pulled back the leaves and revealed the dragon there among the bushes of my heart and I saw its name written between its' eyes: "Grumbling." This is a destructive dragon, a serious sin, one that angered God in the lives of the Israelites and led them into deep trouble. In fact, it is the significant second step away from God in the downward spiral of sin described in Romans 1:21, "For although they knew God, they neither glorified him as God nor gave thanks to him..." I was grumbling instead of giving thanks.

Fortunately, this dragon was still small and I was able to seize it by the neck, bring it, scratching and biting before the Lord and with the knife of confession dispatch it on the altar of Truth and surrender.

This was followed by a willful commitment to think in faith and to act in praise, thereby repairing the damage done to my heart by the habit of grumbling. Every time thoughts of the many unjust, distressing and evil things happening out there in the world came to mind, I chose to remember that our Loving God is at work. He is using the evil of man and Satan to advance the cause of His Kingdom, to prepare hearts to believe, to strengthen and mature believers. We can trust Him in this turmoil and replace grumbling with grace leading to praise and prayer.

I am not talking about "Pollyanna" thinking here, but about using faith to see the larger picture and joining God in His plan through intercession. This is expressed in the Ephesians 3 prayer of Paul: "I pray that out of his glorious riches God will strengthen you with power through his Spirit in your inner being so that Christ may dwell in your hearts by faith." This refers to God empowering our faith, so we go from being people of feeble faith to people of *great* faith.

Grumbling certainly works against this, keeping us focused on the temporal and visible. Faith, in contrast, focuses on the eternal, on the invisible and powerful Truths that set us free, such as knowing that God works all things together for good (Rom. 8:28) and that when we seem the most weak then we are strong (2Cor. 12:9-10). This is where I want to go and live for the rest of my life!

Prayer: "Lord, help me to listen to myself talk and be aware of what predominates: grumbling and complaining or praise and thanksgiving. Help me to daily slay the dragon of grumbling with confession and repentance. Help me to walk in the light of Truth and Freedom, to live in the Joy and Faith you have given us. Amen."

August 11

"I love you, O LORD, my strength. The LORD is my rock, my fortress and my deliverer; my God is my rock, in whom I take refuge. He is my shield and the horn of my salvation, my stronghold."

Psalm 18:1,2

What a challenge this weather is: cold, cloudy and continual rain for weeks—although the calendar says it August, it's more like November! It would be easy to complain and gripe, as most here do, but when we have Sonshine inside, it is not so important to have sunshine outside.

The more we are tied to Jesus, the more healthily independent we are of the weather, of circumstances, of our surroundings—for we then live in the unseen, which is higher, more real and more powerful than what we can see and touch.

Praise you, Lord Jesus, for your reality, for your true, strong presence in our lives. Praise you that we have the assurance of your protection, your purpose, your power at work before us, in us, around us, over us, through us.

You are the Rock in our lives, never shifting, never changing, never shaking. You are our Salvation: from sin, from ourselves, from harm, from evil, from fears, from frivolity, from negatives, from human thinking, from complaining, from idol worship, from laziness, overwork, burn out, selfishness, pride, manipulation and greed--to name a few.

You are the mighty Tower: strong and sure, standing high over the dangers and demons of this world. You are our ever-effective Refuge and Redeemer. As our high Tower, it is as if you lift us up, set us on your shoulder, make us safe, give us a wider view, bring us understanding, hold us near your heart, and give us wisdom and advice.

With you, in you, by you, all is good. We can rejoice, we are protected, our future is secure, we are set free to obey you with joy, to worship you with all our hearts, to love you with all our mind, strength and will.

When we look to you and truly see you in your beauty and glory, greatness and goodness, we are dizzy with delight, for you are beyond what we could possibly have thought up in our limited imaginations. We tend to think of you in human terms, which are far below what you really are. Where we imagined tinsel, you are like titanium; where we imagined plastic you are like the pure power of steel; where we imagined smallness you are immense; where we imagined earning righteousness, you give grace; where we imagined ourselves somewhat good, only you are perfectly pure; where we imagined you like us, you are completely other: holy, sinless, entirely good, perfectly balanced, immensely powerful, totally independent, full of contra-conditional love, ready to forgive and plenteous in mercy to all who call upon you. You are a wonder, you are wonderful, you are fully worthy of our worship.

Prayer: "Glory be to you, Lord Jesus, my God and King, for you are worthy of all my wonder and worship! Help me to follow you into the freedom you have prepared for your children. Amen."

August 12

"Hear my prayer, O LORD God Almighty; listen to me, O God of Jacob."

Psalm 84:8

It's been a long road for our son, Josh, in his bid to get back to the Middle East. We all thought that he would be able to quickly raise support since he is fully equipped to immediately enter ministry—when he steps off the plane he will be further ahead in his language and cultural knowledge then we are after 25 years! But the Lord has something else in mind, so Josh is still in the States. Here is what he wrote about it

Despair, Hope, and Psalm 84

This morning, as I was preparing to write this letter, I found myself suddenly feeling very depressed at where I am currently in my journey back to the Middle East. Things are moving much more slowly than I wish they would, and, as usual, I was blaming myself and my fears and weaknesses for that. But the Lord reminded me of 2 Corinthians 12:9-10 where Paul is assured that God's power is made perfect in weakness. And he exclaims triumphantly, "Therefore I will boast all the more gladly about my weaknesses, so that Christ's power may rest on me." (NIV) And that was encouragement. God never discourages, but I think He allows us to feel that way so we'll turn to Him, and when we ask, He encourages.

Then, my daily reading ended up in one of my favorite Psalms, Psalm 84, where it says: "How blessed is the man whose strength is in You, in whose heart are the highways to Zion! Passing through the valley of Baca they make it a spring; the early rain also covers it with blessings" (vv.5-6 NASB). The strength I find is not in me, it's in Him, and in my heart are the highways, or the desire of pilgrimage, to the place where He wants me to go. The blessings will flow, the strength will come, and this valley of tears (which is what "Baca" may mean) will become a place of peace and a resource of comfort for me and for others in the future. That's what it's all about."[6]

Humanly speaking, if 100 people gave up a pizza a month (about $10) and gave that to Josh, his support would be complete. But God rarely works in such a neat and logical manner (although if He's calling you to give up a pizza and give the money to missions, please do so!).

He is eagerly awaited in the Middle East where the Education Team has projects for him, a church planting team could use his teaching and discipleship skills, and other ministries could use his expertise. The passage above shows, however, that the Lord is using this time to deepen Josh's character, to make him more effective in the long run, so we are confident that in the right time his support will come in.

Prayer: "Lord, thank you for the delays in my life, for the times of waiting when you are working deeply to bring needed transformation. Help me to cooperate with you in praise, consistency in my daily time with you and obedience to what I know to be true. Amen."

---

[6] Source: http://www.wolfhawke.com/ptm/viewentry.php?e=200412

August 13

"May the God of hope fill you with all joy and peace as you trust in him so that your lives may overflow with hope by the power of the Holy Spirit."

Romans 15:13

Praise you, Lord God! You, like the sun, are there every day, shining in perfection, in power, in wisdom and goodness. You are empty of negatives, full of positives, perfect in character, overflowing with promises.

Praise you for your Word, always ready to pour its riches on us and into us as we delve into it every day.

Praise you for your Spirit who stands ready to teach us what we need today, guiding, warning, encouraging and protecting us.

Romans 15:13 says, "May the God of Hope...." and that is what you are, Lord, the God who is the source of hope, who offers hope to all, who calls us to hope. And your hope is not a "maybe," "perhaps," or 'I wish it were so" uncertainty. It is a rock-solid surety—you promise, you carry through, you deliver.

You desire to fill your children "with all joy and peace...." This says so much about you, my Lord God. You desire good for us, to give us the joy and peace that every person longs for. We desire a joy that is unquenchable, undefeatable by the difficulties, tragedies and suffering of life; and we can have it because you, the unchanging God, are its source. You don't do things half way: you don't offer just some joy but ALL joy.

You give us a purchased peace: sure and sound, deep and dynamic, restful and responsible. We can have peace with you by eagerly confessing our sin and sins, then receiving your rich, healing forgiveness.

We can have peace with ourselves by forgiving ourselves as you have forgiven us.

And we can have peace with others by forgiving them as we have been forgiven.

This is true peace, a vibrant peace, a renewable peace—each time we sin, it can be restored. You are the God of hope, giving us in abundance the deep things every person longs for. Praise you for your generosity, your graciousness, your overflowing heart of love!

There is, however, a condition in this: you promise this joy and peace, "as [we] trust in him...." Our part is to believe you, to live in the truth of what you are. As we look away from the aggravations, disappointments and difficulties of life to you, it is clear that we can trust you, the Great Shepherd.

In trust we can respond with praise, no matter how painful the situation is, because you, in your wisdom, grace and mercy have allowed this for good in our lives and for glory in yours. Forgive us for the many times each day we trust ourselves instead of you. Help us to ever grow in our trust as we see you in the Word, in your work, in the world.

Trusting then brings more grace from you for us to live in and to pass on to others: "trust…so that your lives may overflow with hope by the power of the Holy Spirit." Here is your plan: the more we know you, the more we can trust you; the more we trust you, the more joy and peace you give us, and the more hope we can have.

This hope is the certainty of your goodness, power, wisdom and love surrounding us, guiding us, protecting us, filtering all that comes to us, carrying us through to the end and then will come our translation into your presence.

As we trust, the Holy Spirit will, by His great, all-present, immeasurable power, cause this hope to overflow from us onto those around us! When we trust in you, we become the source of hope, the spring of hope, the stream of hope, the river of hope to everyone we meet, for it will flow out in our attitude, in our words, in our actions, in our reactions.

Those around us are thirsty for hope, and we can bring it to them by trusting in you.

Glory be to you, O Great and Powerful One, our Wise and Loving, Just and Merciful Lord and God, for you accomplish exactly what this verse says so that we may give you ever increasing glory before the world!

Prayer: "Forgive us, Lord Jesus, for being busy here and there with this and that, and not spending time with you. Help us to be daily in the Word, in personal worship, in prayer, in confession, living in the light of your presence all through the day. May we trust in you so that all peace and joy and hope may overflow from our lives onto those around us, giving you growing glory. Amen."

August 14

"For our struggle is not against flesh and blood, but against the rulers, against the authorities, against the powers of this dark world and against the spiritual forces of evil in the heavenly realms."

Ephesians 6:12

The flood of anti-Christian articles and TV shows in our Middle Eastern country this past month has driven us again to that high and golden standard: "Blessed are you when people insult you, persecute and falsely say all kinds of evil against you because of me…Love your enemies, pray for those persecute you…" (Mat. 5:11,44).

Criticism by itself is hard to take, but when it comes in the form of vicious slander from ignorant, hateful, bitter and vengeful people, it is much harder to respond in a godly way. Yet God calls us to give a superhuman reply to persecution, rather than feeling sorry for ourselves.

Just this morning I was reading in Acts 3 where, after the initial arrest, interrogation and release of Peter and John, the church meets and prays, "Now, Lord, consider their threats and enable your servants to speak your word with great boldness." That's the opposite of whining!

Then came another blow here: one who had been a pastor renounced his faith—the outcome, I believe of the unhealthy practice of workers giving a young pastor a salary; when the salary was stopped, the pastor "lost his faith." He went on several national TV talk shows where he reinforced all the lies others had been telling (people become Christians for money, the workers' aims are all political, they want to take land away from the country, etc.). He went on to name specific workers, projects and events, exposing many to possible attack. He also has the addresses of many correspondence course contacts he'd been following up on, placing these seekers in danger.

Again, Jesus' words about such happenings came to mind: "Rejoice and be glad, because great is your reward in heaven, for in the same way they persecuted the prophets who were before you" (Mat. 5:12).

We are confident that God will somehow use this for good, for spreading His Word across this land. I've been praying Psalm 140 for the situation, especially verses 8 and 9: "...do not grant the wicked their desire...let the heads of those who surround me be covered with the trouble their lips have caused...let not slanderers be established in the land."

One answer to this prayer came in an interesting way. A reporter for a major newspaper challenged those making outlandish accusations against Christians: "If you say there are 89 house churches in this one area of our city, show them to me one by one, and if you can't, I'll call you a liar before everyone!" Unbelievers end up defending us!

With God's grace we will continue to rejoice in such persecution while recognizing that in this serious situation we need prayer for His protection and the outworking of events for good.

Prayer: "Lord, we need to think your thoughts consistently and constantly; keep us in the Word, responding in faith, in praise and in grace. May you be glorified in every situation. We are weak and that is good; make your power perfect in our weakness. Amen."

August 15

"When I am weak, then I am strong."

2 Corinthians 12:10b

Facing me is a situation where others, who are at odds with me, are going to decide my future. In this I am weak, and that is good—good, but uncomfortable. Praise you, Lord, that being comfortable is not the measure of anything important, spiritual or significant. Knowing your Word, trusting you, living in praise, obeying what we know to be true, these are important. We need to train our faith to respond biblically to whatever comes. As Lilias Trotter, pioneer evangelist in Algeria in the 1800s, said, "Swinging out over the abyss without anything other than you, Lord, rejoicing in this need to trust in you and your power, praising for your goodness before any solution can be seen, this is trained faith."[7]

Praise you, Father that you are at work in ways I cannot see or foresee. I praise you for what you are doing and what you will do in this, for you are great, you are good —you are God.

"Taste and see that the Lord is good, blessed is the man who trusts in Him" (Ps. 34:8). I have certainly tasted and seen your goodness over and over again, Lord. You have protected me many times in near accidents; you have provided an inner stability that in my youth prevented suicide, relational crashes and personal failure.

You have also guided me through a maze of difficulties in my life: the journey through depression, adjustments in marriage, transition to life in the Middle East, dark days of deprivation and difficulty, accidents and expulsion, team turmoil, arrests, trials and uncertainty. You not only carried us through, but strengthened, deepened and matured us while utilizing us in your Kingdom. What a privilege to walk with you, to join you in the great plan you are carrying out to bring history to a conclusion and take us with you.

I have tasted and seen that you are the King of kindness, you are the Lord of love, you are the Ruler of righteousness and the Sovereign of selflessness. I praise you that you are only good—in you there is no wavering, no toying with the fate of people, no partiality, no failure to pay attention, no being late, no compulsiveness, no capriciousness, no mood swings, no lack of knowledge, no hesitation, no uncertainty, no inconsistency.

You are the God who is pure in motive, perfect in planning, persistent in values, perceptive in understanding, purposeful in love. You are flawless in execution, abundant in mercy, rich in resources, overflowing in love, generous in giving, gracious in provision, limitless in creativity, slow in anger and positive in patience. You are a marvel, you are majestic, you are trustable, you are great. To you be glory both now and forevermore.

---

7 *A Passion for the Impossible: The Life of Lillias Trotter* by Miriam Huffman Rockness

Prayer: "Lord, I praise you now for how you are going to work things out in my present uncertainties. I give you honor without seeing the end, for you are absolutely trustable. Keep me thinking these truths, help me to respond with love and grace and goodness, to fight the real enemy with praise, prayer and persistence in obedience. Amen."

August 16

"…set your hearts on things above, where Christ is seated at the right hand of God."

Colossians 2:1b

As I was driving my very basic 12-year-old rusty Fiat one morning, I suddenly became aware of the locals around me driving their shiny, new, beautiful Mercedes, Volvos, BMWs, Opels and Fords. And just as suddenly I experienced a strong surge of jealousy.

Jealousy also comes up in me in other instances, such as when I think about how many local businesses are doing well and ours never really takes off.

Jealousy is a selfish, bitter, negative and destructive response to others' success. It is no surprise that such a response would arise from my old heart, that swamp of foul desires. Praise God that it is easily taken care of by immediate confession and focus on Truth.

Confession, however, is more than just admitting being jealous; I must also look at and deal with the layers of sin hidden under jealousy:

- selfishness,
- accepting worldly values,
- believing lies,
- rejection of God's standards,
- pride,
- rebellion and unbelief—to name a few.

I find myself encouraged to continue in these sins every day through a multitude of stimuli from my environment. These reinforce the lie that significance and security come from success and other's opinions of me, as opposed to standing in awe of God and His unconditional love for me, in believing His Word and living to please Him.

As I've worked through this, the Holy Spirit has regularly brought to mind the principle of setting our hearts on things above (Col. 3:1,2), especially as it is explained in Matthew 5:19-21: "Do not store up for yourselves treasures on earth, where moth and rust destroy and thieves break in and steal. But store up for yourselves treasures in heaven…for where your treasure is, there your heart will be also."

This reinforced the realization that when I feel I must have something in order to be happy, I have set up an idol for myself. In reality I do not need a shiny new car, or a prospering business, or to arrive somewhere on time to be happy, content or fulfilled. God's gift to us is joy in Himself, as well as peace in our relationship with Him, with ourselves and with others as we trust Him (Rom. 15:13). That is more than enough for life.

Spotting and rejecting our idols (whatever we demand to be happy) opens the way for grace to flow in us and through us. As it says in Psalm 146:7 and 147:11, "The Lord sets prisoners free....The Lord delights in those who fear him, who put their hope in his unfailing love." He wants to set us free from the traps of the enemy, from the idols of our own hearts, and from the values of this world. We need to be cooperating with Him in this process by soaking in the Word, replacing lies with Truth and choosing to live in praise.

Prayer: "Lord, help me to see the traps of the enemy, the idols that are set up in my heart. Help me to immediately confess and forsake them so your Holy Spirit can have free reign in me so you may have more glory. Amen."

August 17

"Hezekiah received the letter from the messengers [of the attacking king, Sennacherib] and read it. Then he went up to the temple of the LORD and spread it out before the LORD. And Hezekiah prayed to the LORD: 'O LORD, God of Israel, enthroned between the cherubim, you alone are God over all the kingdoms of the earth. You have made heaven and earth.'"

2 Kings 19:14, 15

Thank you, Lord, for drawing my attention away from the issues before me to yourself. King Hezekiah is my example; he went to you with his problem of the attacking armies, as did King Jehoshaphat when he was in the same situation—and you protected both. Part of tasting and seeing that you, Lord, are good is remembering how you have answered prayer for others in the past.

Praise you, my Heavenly Father, that you work what is right and good in our lives: you lead us in paths of righteousness, you warn us, convict us of sin, show us where we need to change, and give us the strength to cooperate with you.

I praise you for your help, your direction, your insights, your understanding of what you share with us in your Word and through your Spirit; I praise you for the power you provide to increase faith, bring transformation and give us your view of reality.

You are wonderfully patient with us, graciously kind to us, faithfully firm with us. I praise you for your rod with which you keep back the enemy, and for your staff with which you keep us in line—we need to be protected from both the enemy and from ourselves!

I praise you for your infiniteness, working in so many lives simultaneously, listening to so many prayers at the same time, being able to weave our wrong and sometimes right choices into the fabric of your plan. I praise you that in you all will work out somehow in your time, in your way.

I praise you that your goodness and mercy are always there. You stoop down from on high and hear us, for we are poor and needy. You are Glorious, you are Good, you are Gracious, you are Great. Only you are worthy of worship!

Prayer: "I bow before you, Lord God, eagerly agreeing to follow and honor you today in obedience, in right thinking, in right priorities. Guide and empower me in this for the sake of your Name. Amen."

August 18

"Commit your way to the LORD; trust in him...."

Psalm 37:5a

After months of negotiation, planning and prayer for launching our internet-based English tutoring sales, a big red flag appeared on the horizon. Since we as foreigners are not allowed to sell educational materials here directly, we are required to partner with a local company. This we have done and things seemed to moving along quite well with agreements on pricing, marketing, commissions and advertising all in place. The owner of the company has lots of experience in marketing, has a wide circle of influential acquaintances and business people, and was willing to put up all the capital needed for the venture.

However, after all the good progress, contrary to his word, he suddenly switched printers (he'd promised to use our friend) and then became unreachable. If he made such a move with the printer, what might he do with the rest of his commitment?

We had to bring this whole venture before the Lord and surrender it again, coming to the point of being willing to give up this partnership if that is what the Lord wanted. The Lord brought to mind George Mueller's prayer principle, the gist of which is, "When asking the Lord for something, I bring myself to the point where if He gives me a 'yes' or a 'no', to me it is the same."

After all the work, the emotional investment and the high hopes we had for this project, it was a challenge to come to such a surrender. In reality, God was showing us that here was an idol in the making, something we were demanding to be happy: were we willing to have it sacrificed so that God's higher purposes may be accomplished?

The Spirit reminded me that this was another opportunity to be weak (we could do nothing until the man decided to contact us again), to live the truth of 2 Corinthians 12:9,10 where God said "...my power is made perfect in weakness..." and follow Paul's example in his response, "...therefore I will delight in weaknesses, hardships, insults, persecutions and difficulties, for when I am weak, then I am strong."

We had to wait several days for a resolution to the impasse, and during that time had the opportunity to rest in God and think Truth ("My soul finds rest in God alone," Ps. 62:1), continually surrendering our desire to Him. In the end things worked out and all was resolved—but more important than the resolution is the deeper surrender and new breaking God brought into our lives through this. May His will always prevail.

Prayer: "Lord, point out the idols in my life, help me to hold all with an open hand, to be willing to accept whatever you desire for me, to praise in and for all that you bring into my life. Amen."

August 19

"For the word of God is living and active. Sharper than any double-edged sword, it penetrates even to dividing soul and spirit, joints and marrow; it judges the thoughts and attitudes of the heart."

Hebrews 4:12

Praise you, my Lord God, for your wonderful Word which works widely and deeply in my life. Last night as I was wrestling again with the conflict before us, thinking of arguments and ways of presenting things, you brought Psalm 62 to mind again, drawing my churning thoughts away from my microscopic focus to your great overview: "My soul finds rest in God alone."

I don't have to wait for resolution of this conflict to have peace and rest, for you are the One who is in charge, who will work this out as you desire whether it be in the direction I think it should go or not. In your great plan you have reasons for allowing men to make willful choices against your Word. If the outcome is the opposite of what I desire, you are still sovereign, still worthy of praise and will use it all for good.

Psalm 62 continues with, "My salvation comes from you." All my striving and anxiousness, fears and scheming will do nothing unless you move. I must be quiet and follow the leading of your Spirit, working with you hand-in-hand. In doing this, I can relax in the knowledge of what a wise, gracious and powerful God you are.

Psalm 62:2-6 leads me in the right way. "You only are my rock"—you are my stability, not the decisions others make; "my salvation"—repetition reinforces right thinking and I must be looking only to you to be saved from evil; "my high tower"—in you I have both protection and a lofty and wide view of things, if I look at things from your perspective; "I will never be shaken"-- it is not the outcome that determines my rest, but it is you who are my stability

"How long will you assault a man, would you cast him down, this leaning wall, this tottering fence?"—a good reminder of my weakness, my inability in my miniscule strength to stand against the onslaughts of Satan and his hordes.

"Surely they intend to topple him from his lofty place. They delight in lies; with their mouths they bless, but in their hearts they curse." I must remember Satan's tactics and goals: lies, worry, fear, anxiety, unbelief. I must keep on the armor of light, trust in you, O God, and you will act to protect me. You are Truth, you are Good, you are the One who lifts me up.

"Find rest, my soul, in God alone,"—again repetition reinforces, this time as a command. I must obey and choose willfully to find my rest in you long before any decision comes to pass—"for my hope comes from him." Again, it is not my perfect performance which will bring good results but you in your wisdom, your power, your opening of eyes and your turning of hearts to what is needed. "You only are my rock, my salvation, my high tower, I will never be shaken."

What assurance, what confidence, what stability, what joy there is in knowing you, Lord Jesus, my God, my Rock, my Ruler, my King. You are certainly worthy of all worship and obedience.

Prayer: "Praise be to you throughout eternity, and throughout today. May the meditation of my heart and the words of my mouth be pleasing in your sight, my mighty Rock and my Refuge. Amen."

August 20

"The entire law is summed up in a single command: 'Love your neighbor as yourself.' If you keep on biting and devouring each other, watch out or you will be destroyed by each other."

Galatians 5:14, 15

The conference speaker had one of the worst deliveries that I'd ever seen; he certainly would have flunked any hermeneutics class. But his message was compelling and part of the power of it was his lack of polish.

As I listened to the speaker, the Spirit spoke to me, "Notice how judgmental you are of this man? That's because you have a critical spirit!" Then He brought to mind several people who had hurt me, whom I had forgiven, but who still irritated me every time I thought of them.

Two of these were at the conference and as the Spirit effectively convicted me of my criticalness, He then made me realize I needed to go to these two men to confess and ask forgiveness. Here I resisted, "Isn't confessing to you enough, Lord? They don't know of my attitude; it will be humiliating to ask forgiveness...."

"Yes," said the Lord, "it will be humiliating; don't forget that the short-cut to humility is the road of humiliation, the one I walked."

Finally I relented and went first to one, then the other; each time I was overcome with emotion and had a hard time speaking, but each willingly forgave me. I must admit it was freeing and cleansing to receive forgiveness. But then I realized I needed to also confess my critical attitude to the speaker.

In that confession came a realization: I have high standards for myself—and for others—so when those standards are not kept, I take a judgmental stance towards that person. My standards, good as they are (mostly biblical, as a matter of fact), are not the ones God puts at the top. He is more interested in mercy and love and grace being shown before He is interested in seeing discipline and diligence. He definitely wants both categories, but there is a godly order to them: "Wisdom is first of all pure, then peace-loving, considerate, submissive, full of mercy and good fruit" and after all that comes, "impartial and sincere" (Jam. 3:17).

In the next few days, more light shone from the Spirit into my heart, revealing criticalness crouching in every corner. I never realized how judgmental my general thoughts have been! Now I have chances every day to draw back from saying or thinking something negative about another person or an action. My thoughts and words are generally accurate and are about things done wrongly, but my attitude tends to be one of condemnation instead of redemption.

This is another revelation of my weakness and the need to depend on God rather than my own mind, might and measures. It is another chance to be broken and reshaped into a more useful instrument for God. Breaking comes in many ways, but always, as Paul says,"...that we might not rely on ourselves, but on God who raises the dead" (2 Cor. 1:9).

Prayer: "Lord, I want to be a positive person because you are my focus. Help me to spot and reject any critical, judgmental spirit. Help me to bless those around me with good, biblical thoughts and words, confronting only when necessary in love and grace. Amen."

August 21

"I will extol the LORD with all my heart in the council of the upright and in the assembly. Great are the works of the LORD; they are pondered by all who delight in them."

Psalm 111:1,2

Lord God, my Triune Elohim, praise be to you this morning, praise be to you forever. You are marvelous in your character, beautiful in your desires, lovely in your grace, and astounding in your wisdom. You deserve that I extol you, the LORD, with all my heart, for who and what you are. As it says in Psalm 111:2-9,

> "Great are the works of the LORD
> Glorious and majestic are his deeds,
> and his righteousness endures forever.
> He has caused his wonders to be remembered;
> the LORD is gracious and compassionate.
> He provides food for those who fear him;
> he remembers his covenant forever.
> He has shown his people the power of his works,
> The works of his hands are faithful and just;
> all his precepts are trustworthy.
> They are steadfast forever and ever,
> done in faithfulness and uprightness.
> He provided redemption for his people;
> he ordained his covenant forever—
> holy and awesome is his name."

What a list of greatness! You, O Lord Jesus, tower far above all creation; you are so perfect, so pure, so powerful, so priceless—you deserve eternal praise, daily obedience, moment-by-moment trust. To live otherwise is an insult to your character, to your person, to your being. To see in Word and deed such a God as you, to know such a Lord as you, to walk with such a Savior as you—these are great, awesome, overwhelming, totally undeserved privileges.

Truly, "the fear of the LORD is the beginning of wisdom; all who follow his precepts have good understanding. To him belongs eternal praise" (Ps. 111:10).

Prayer: "May I fear you, follow your precepts and walk in good understanding so you may be glorified in my life today and for eternity. Amen."

August 22

"...my God is my rock, in whom I take refuge. He is my shield and the horn of my salvation, my stronghold."

Psalm 18:2b

A good friend and I were talking about likes and dislikes, and I mentioned that a recent gift was not to my taste. My friend responded with something like, "You're so fussy, why don't you stop whining and grow up!" and walked out. I was amazed and hurt at this fierce response, especially since my friend's opinion is important to me.

As I sat there overwhelmed with feelings of self-pity, almost immediately the Holy Spirit again brought to mind Psalm 62:1, "My soul finds rest in God alone...." Then 2 Corinthians 12:9-10 flashed into my thoughts, "...my power is made perfect in weakness...therefore I delight in weaknesses, hardships, insults...."

Those verses, coupled with a willful giving of thanks for this happening brought a sharp change in my emotions, swinging me up to a fierce kind of joy at facing a rebuke and profiting from it. It was like first being swept off the cliff of touchiness and tumbling down towards the valley of self-pity, but on the way down grabbing onto a branch of the tree of Truth and climbing back up to solid ground.

Using another analogy, the Spirit led me to let go of my natural thinking and negative emotions (self-pity, pride, anger) so I could hold on to biblical Truth (I am forgiven, accepted in Christ, secure in Him, His love, His affirmation), allowing me to rise above the attack of the world, the flesh and the devil and thereby profiting from my friend's rebuke.

At first I fell into a trap of the devil, but with the Spirit's help and guidance, was able to immediately escape by raising the shield of faith, getting on the helmet of salvation and taking the sword of the Spirit. It was a small incident, lasting only a few minutes, but was a powerful example of how clinging to Truth in the face of life's negatives frees us to soar above the mundane and to look with spiritual eyes on the eternal. If I hadn't done this, I would have struggled with my hurt, probably then hurting others by my poor responses.

Being in Scripture and knowing the Word is such an important part of this. Without the every-day soaking in Truth I would not have escaped. The weapons have to be at hand in order to have victory in the attacks.

Prayer: "Lord, help me to be consistent in my daily time with you, worshiping you, reading, memorizing and meditating on your Word, and praying in line with your will, so that when the attacks come, I may be able to cooperate with the Spirit and defeat the enemy, for your glory. Amen."

August 23

"Even in darkness light dawns for the upright, for the Lord is gracious and compassionate and righteous."

Psalm 112:4

Praise you, O Lord God, the Great Savior, the Good Shepherd, the Gracious and Most High King. To you belong honor, glory, praise and thanksgiving at all times. In you alone my soul finds rest; at this time of uncertainty in my life, the powerful truths of Psalm 62 hold me, keep me from falling into the abyss of anxiety, a place where you are dishonored by unbelief and rebellion, by trusting in myself and by the fear of man.

Your greatness, your goodness and your graciousness all surround me, keeping me safe from the attacks of the enemy. No matter how things may appear, your shield of faith, raised by praise, wards off every assault of the enemy and extinguishes every flaming arrow. Because of your mighty Love, my soul is at rest in you: quiet, calm, trusting, accepting.

In the words of Psalm 112:1-3, "Blessed is the man who fears the LORD...." You are the One to be feared: honored, respected, obeyed, loved, considered above all in every decision.

"Blessed is the man ...who finds great delight in his commands." Your commands are delightful: based on your character, full of Truth, designed to protect, complete in understanding, beautiful in intent, powerful in outcomes, lovely in expression. In meditating on your commands, we can see more and more of your wisdom as your Spirit transforms our thoughts, our wills, our emotions, our understanding. Your commands are delightful because you are delightful and you are to be delighted in: the Gracious, Wise, Loving, Powerful, Good God.

What wonderful promises you give us as we trust in you, delight in your Word and obey your precepts. As we fear you, our "...children will be mighty in the land; the generation of the upright will be blessed." What a joy it is to see our children, both physical and spiritual, walk with you, rest in you, love you more and more.

As we are upright because Christ dwells in us, we are certainly blessed with many, many things: a walk with you, your continued presence, the certainty for a future with you, provision for living, grace in every circumstance, a wide and high perspective on life, your daily protection and your continued goodness to us.

Other blessings mentioned in Psalm 112 are: "Wealth and riches are in his house," –we think immediately of money, but don't consider ourselves wealthy; however, in relation to the poor in the world, most who read this have much more than we need to exist. And the spiritual wealth and riches we are given are far more than any material possessions. You, Lord, have given us peace, joy, hope, patience, power to live, the Spirit's continual transformation within, safety in you, goodness to give to others and love never ending. And in addition, "… his righteousness endures forever." We have the absolute certainty of eternity with you because you, Lord Jesus, live forever to intercede for us, to supply your righteousness in far greater abundance than our sin can ever be. To you be glory forever and ever!

Prayer: "Lord God, praise you for your provision. Help me to live in the riches of your grace, thinking Truth and rejoicing in your greatness throughout the day. Help me to have a Psalm 112 perspective to pass on to others. Amen."

August 24

"Then Jesus told his disciples a parable to show them that they should always pray and not give up."

Luke 18:1

Long term prayer is a delight to God; He speaks of it fondly in Luke 18:1-8 in the parable of the persistent widow. Prayer is a confession of our weakness and a declaration of God's greatness, faithfulness and goodness. For us it can be dull and boring, praying for the same things over and over, but as we persist in faith, God sends the answers at the right time.

One request that's been on my list for years is out of a Gordon McDonald book, *Ordering Your Private World*. "Lord, help me to discern and repent of these four 'spirits:' the spirit of jealousy and competition, of criticalness and negativeness, of the fear of man, and of the fear of averseness (being opposed in my wishes)."

God has been answering this prayer powerfully over the last three months, bringing to mind incidents from the past where I acted out of these wrong motives. And, in His grace, He has given opportunity to make these things right.

During the four-week-long Christar conference attended by about 230 of our workers, there were four people with whom I had had difficult times in the past (and they with me!). The Lord prompted me to speak with each one, to reject the idea that I had a right to protect myself by remaining distant, and instead to be willing to suffer the humiliation of asking forgiveness for my self-protection in the relationship, and to wish them well.

Each conversation was painful, but God knows what is right and best: He wants freedom for us, and persists in cutting the cords of jealousy and competition, of criticalness and negativeness that bind us.

It is good to have those relationships now cleansed and to be able to move on. The pain of having procrastinated will certainly help me to be quick in remedying any further manifestations of these negative spirits!

Prayer: "Lord, help me to be alert to the conviction of your Spirit, to see where I am jealous instead of rejoicing, competitive instead of cooperative, critical instead of kind, negative instead of nice. Bring surrender, transformation and freedom so I may give you more glory each day. Amen."

August 25

"Praise the LORD. Blessed is the man who fears the LORD, who finds great delight in his commands."

Psalm 112:1

Praise and glory be to you, Lord God, my Lord and Savior, for you are the unchanging One, ever good, ever faithful, ever righteous, ever pure. You are stability itself, manifest in your bringing your promises to pass at the right time. Truly you are good, great, gracious, generous, and gorgeous in your faithfulness.

I awoke this morning, tired and worried about today, about what to do, about the difficult meeting next month. But, as I look away to you, and with the guidance of your Spirit and your Word, as I choose to trust in you by giving thanks instead of worrying, your loving kindness is proclaimed to my heart and there is joy.

Today, in your provision, I choose to walk in the light of your presence all day long, trusting you, rejoicing in you, praising you. I am so thankful for the freedom to do this, bought by your blood, Lord Jesus, poured into our lives by the Spirit, flowing down and through our being, bringing transformation and joy as we choose to obey what you have taught us.

Psalm 112:5-8 says, "Good will come to him who is generous and lends freely, who conducts his affairs with justice. Surely he will never be shaken; a righteous man will be remembered forever." As we live in your perspective, Lord, obeying you, using the resources you have given us as you desire, living as you want, then you pour out extra blessings on us. In your wisdom you always seek such a partnership with us; as we obey, you bless.

"He will have no fear of bad news; his heart is steadfast, trusting in the LORD." Bad news will come—sickness, loss, death and disappointments--but we do not need to fear it, for we trust in your good character, your good heart, your good will. What comes will be carefully crafted to give us opportunity to glorify you, to encourage those around us, to be further transformed into the image of Christ. We can know that this is another adventure with Jesus, another possibility for power to flow into our lives to give you more glory.

As we look to you, the Creator, the Sustainer, the Ender of time, our "heart is secure, we will have no fear; in the end we will look in triumph on our foes." You have told us the outcome of the story: the defeat of the enemy, an end to evil and eternity with you. You are our security, you are the fear-killer, for your perfect love casts out fear.

I bow before you now and worship you richly for all that you are and for the deep, powerful, wonderful privilege of being your child. I praise you for the years of walking with you, of getting to know you, of being challenged and changed by your Spirit, and for however many more years there are to come of living with you here on earth.

Prayer: "Lord, keep my eyes on you today. May praise flow from my heart, my mind, my lips. May I live worthy of you, bringing you honor, joy and pleasure. Amen."

August 26

"…to know this love that surpasses knowledge, so that you may be filled to the measure of all the fullness of God."

Ephesians 3: 19b

The man I saw in my mind was jumping and leaping and shouting for joy! He was euphoric, having been saved from an awful execution. He had not only been pardoned but his former enemy, a kind, wealthy and influential person, had adopted him.

That rejoicing man was me—as I saw in a new way, on a higher level the wonder of what Christ has done in saving me from eternal condemnation, giving me grace that flows from His character, the opposite of what I deserved.

If anyone wants to insist that life is unfair, I would happily agree, for I much prefer mercy and grace over getting what is fair—which would be an immediate exit to hell!

This vision of ecstatic rejoicing came while meditating on Ephesians 6:10-18, putting on the armor of God, as I have done every morning for the last 35 years. It was a new breakthrough to grasping in a greater way on an emotional level how much I am undeservedly loved by God.

It is also an answer to my consistent prayer for myself and all the people on my prayer list, that we "may have power together with all the saints to grasp the length and breadth, the height and depth of the love of Christ and to know this love that surpasses knowledge, so that [we] may be filled to the measure of all the fullness of God" (Eph. 3:18,19).

As someone who is insecure and not willing to take risks in looking foolish, I am not inclined to be exuberant, to shout and dance except in the one acceptable arena of sporting events. But, in grasping how GREAT is the Love of God towards us, we certainly have a much bigger reason to leap and shout, to rejoice and celebrate than any sporting event could ever call for—and I want to do that more.

Prayer: "Praise you, Heavenly Father, for the great pardon you have bestowed upon your rebellious and unthankful children. Help me every day to grasp more of your greatness, more of my natural depravity and how much I have been forgiven, so that I may be 'undone and redone' and thereby become a more useful instrument in your hands. Amen."

August 27

"God is our refuge and strength, an ever-present help in trouble."

Psalm 46:1

Lord, as we face a number of difficult and significant issues and situations, I praise you that you are the Sovereign God, Director and Coordinator of all that comes, all that happens, all that works out. You use every event for good, for drawing people to yourself, for bringing your purposes to pass. Your power alone is enough to do this; add to that your deep wisdom, your knowledge of all including the future, your goodness, your righteousness, your grace and your love—this is a picture of the One who can be trusted.

Your name, Elohim, reflects this so well, Lord. You are the potently powerful One, capable of speaking substance out of nothing, of creating life, of stretching out the heavens for billions of light years, of filling it with countless stars, and on the other end of the scale, of knowing every thought before we ever form it. You turn the hearts of kings, you set up rulers and you take them down. You work your purposes and no one can hold you back.

The name Elohim also speaks of your faithfulness: you bind yourself with a promise, and you deliver. You commit yourself to your children and you protect. You predict the future and you bring it to pass. You give your Word and you come through. Psalm 46:5 says, "God is within her [Jerusalem], she will not fall. God will help her at break of day." Today you live in us as you did in Jerusalem in O.T. times and you protect us in the same way, bringing help at just the right time.

You are our trustable Lord, the Only One we can be sure of—all others are too small, too fallible, too vulnerable to forces beyond their control. But as you, Lord God, are the Creator and Controller of all such forces, nothing can thwart you, nothing can foil your plans.

Praise be to you, Lord Jesus, faithfulness incarnate, the One who followed through on providing salvation; you are the Promiser and the Keeper, the Denier of Self and Lover of rebels. And you continue to love your redeemed and rebellious brothers and sisters, faithfully working in us to bring surrender and growth, obedience and fruitfulness.

Praise be to you for your shining, glorious, awesome, powerful example of living out your character before us. You did this in forsaking the wonders, beauty and joy of Heaven, in your descent to this sin-twisted earth, being confined to a body, living among sinners (how your soul and spirit must have been distressed every day!), suffering the weakness, hardships, insults, persecutions and difficulties of this world, enduring (that is, moving through with power) the anguish in the garden in your final surrender, accepting the horrors of the beatings, of crucifixion, of becoming sin (the Holy One becoming sin for us!!!), the ripping of the fabric of the Trinity as the Father turned away from you, the descent to hell and the battle with the devil and death.

This was all faithfulness to your character: you are righteous, gracious, compassionate, pure, humble, kind, forgiving, holy and loving. This, the greatest drama of the universe, shows clearly that you are the One to be exalted, lifted up, honored and obeyed. To trust you is to worship you, to believe you when all seems to contradict your Word is to honor you, to praise you when there is no discernible reason to glorify you is lifting up your Name. You are worthy of exaltation always!

Prayer: "May there be trust, belief, obedience and praise in my life today so that you will be worshiped, honored and glorified before men and angels. Amen."

August 28

"...my God is my rock, in whom I take refuge."

Psalm 18:2b

As the chill wind buffeted our hair and whipped our coats about us, we watched an eagle soar through the blue sky above. His wings caught the up draft of the wind that stressed us and it held him effortlessly aloft. To us the wind was at best a discomfort, at worst a threat to our progress and health, while to him it was a chance to soar. He knew how to take an adverse thing and use it to rise above.

The verse from Isaiah came to mind,"...those whose hope is in the Lord will renew their strength. They will soar on wings like the eagles..." (Isa. 40:31). Like that eagle, I need to stretch my wings of faith to ride the winds of opposition, not let them beat me down.

We got a chance to practice using the wings of faith while we visited in Germany in early September and there got news of the possibility of being denied entry into our Middle Eastern country of work, because of our residence permit problems. As it had happened to others, it could happen to us. Imagine what it would be like, after a long trip, to come to the passport booth and be told you can't enter; what would you do then?

During this time of waiting, my "daily blanket prayer" for all on my prayer list was 2 Corinthians 12:9-10. I prayed, "Lord, help us to boast all the more gladly in our weaknesses (rather than complaining and being fearful about them) so that the power of Christ can rest on us. For Christ's sake, may we delight in our weaknesses (excitedly expecting you to do something powerful in them), in insults, hardships, persecutions and difficulties, remembering that when we are weak, in you we are strong." God heard and answered.

On the morning of our last full day in Germany, in my quiet time, the words of Ps. 31:4,5 stood out to me: "Since you are my rock and my fortress, for the sake of your name lead and guide me. Free me from the trap that is set for me, for you are my refuge. Into your hands I commit my spirit; redeem me, O Lord, God of Truth." He gave me confidence that He, the God of Truth, would work this out.

The next day we were ushered through the passport check in record time without a hint of suspicion! We could sing with the Psalmist, "How great is your goodness which you have stored up for those who fear you, which you bestow in the sight of men on those who take refuge in you" (Ps. 31:19).

Prayer: "Lord, help me to praise you in the midst of any threat of opposition, disappointment or difficulty, and may I do this before the solution comes, that I may give you great glory, praising in faith. Amen."

August 29

"The true light that gives light to every man was coming into the world."

John 1:9

What about those who have never heard? Do they have any chance? Does God not care about them? God is Himself light, and Jesus coming into the world brought light, not just to those who would believe, but to every person, as the above verse declares. If we respond to the light given, He will give us more. Following here is a conversation I had which illustrates the giving of light, the desire for more, and God then sending a person to provide what is needed.

The man leaned forward, looking at me intensely over his greying beard. "I was an atheist with no interest in any religion before the dream," he said.

"Tell me about it," I said.

"In my dream I died and found myself in a room with several others who had also died. They were all discussing how old they were at their death: this one 8 years old, another 50. I told them I had been 41.

"There was an open door in the room and a very bright, intense light was shining through it. Then a person came through the door, but I couldn't see his face because of the light radiating from it. He began to talk with the others in the room about when they had believed in him. Then I woke up. I somehow knew this was Jesus.

"So, the next day I called a friend in who knew where to get me a Bible--from the Bible Society. They sent me one and I read it from cover to cover in the next two months. During that time someone in the Bible Society told your employee in your bookstore about me and he came and led me to Christ. At that time my wife was in a deep depression, but as we began to go to church and read the Bible, she got better and better."

What a story! This is an exact answer to our prayers that God would bring the elect to us, giving them spiritual sight, causing the light of the Gospel to shine deeply into their hearts (in his dream he saw the light, literally!), for conviction of guilt and revelation of Himself to them.

I encourage you, also, to be praying for God to prepare the elect-- those who will believe, Rom. 8:29--and to bring you into contact with those who are waiting for a "light bearer" to come.

Prayer: "Lord, help me to pray consistently for the salvation of those around me. Help me to be alert to opportunities to share Truth, and to be bold and wise in taking them at the direction of the Spirit. May I be a faithful instrument in your hands. Amen."

August 30

"The righteous man may have many troubles, but the Lord delivers him from them all."

Psalm 34:19

Idolatry in my life has been steadily losing ground.   Ever since learning that concise definition of an idol (whatever I demand to make me happy), the Lord has been pointing out one idol after another. The first one was the "need" to be on time to everything, followed by the "need" to look good in what I did, and it went on from there.

The best antidote to idolatry is knowing God better—no idol comes across well in His presence! This month while re-memorizing and meditating on Psalm 33, the rich depth of God's character stood out clearly: "The word of the Lord is right and true, he is faithful in all he does... let all the people of the world revere him, for he spoke and it came to be...the eyes of the Lord are on those who fear him, on those whose hope is in his unfailing love" (Ps. 33:4,8,9,18).

Standing in the presence of such heavenly light frees me from the clinging, whining manipulation of the idols of my soul, and sweeps me up into the joy He bought for us: "In him our hearts rejoice, for we trust in his holy name" (Ps. 33:21).

Lord, you are an active God, a caring God, a powerful God, a delivering God. I praise you for what you are doing in my life, delivering me from many troubles, including my idols. You transform each difficulty into an opportunity to see you at work, to trust you, to rest in you.

Each thing we do is an adventure with you, a chance to do what is fine and right and good. I give you honor for your wisdom, your care, your grace, your active, intimate, incisive, positively invasive interaction with us, your children, in all things of life. You are good and I praise you for it.

Prayer: "Help me to be alert to your pointing out idols in my life; help me to abandon them and to run to you, the God who delivers. Help me to see each problem as a potential adventure with you. Amen."

August 31

"My grace is sufficient for you, for my power is made perfect in weakness."

2 Corinthians 2:9

I sit in a cage of weakness and watch things develop around me, powerless to influence most of them. I see people making unnecessary mistakes and can't stop them. I see others making decisions that are going to impact me negatively and can't prevent them. I see things I've worked for sliding towards disaster but can't counter it. The bars of my cage (lack of influence/being far away/having no access) prevent me from reaching into the situations to bring the change I'd like to see.

This is a picture of the inherent weakness we all have. We like to live with the illusion that we have significant control in our lives but, in actuality, we have very little beyond leading ourselves well. What will come to us tomorrow? An accident? Cancer? Loss of our job? A huge medical bill? Loss of a loved one? No one knows.

I made a list of the events and situations that are before us, over which we have no control. Among many other things, these include my mother-in-law's future, how long we will be in Germany, Barbara's health, where our ministry will go, the sale of my book and the outcome of work in the Middle East.

We are weak. But we also belong to the One who has plenty of power to change things. We not only know Him, but He calls us to join Him as He shapes the future. He gives us three powerful means of doing this: praise, prayer and persistence in obedience.

Praise brings us to a deeper surrender (Ps. 50:23) and opens the way for Christ's power to flow (2 Cor. 12:9). Prayer brings us in line with God's will and plugs us into His great strength. Obedience to what we know to be true opens the way for Him to work powerfully in us and through us.

So being weak is, in fact, wonderful. It is the way to real power. It is the recognition of reality. It is the privilege of humility. One definition of sanity is to live in what is true (that we have very little control), as opposed to living in an illusion (that we are in charge). God calls us to reality: weakness in ourselves, power in Him.

Let us choose Truth, and praise God for every weakness we find ourselves in so that His power may work for us. "That is why, for Christ's sake, I delight in weaknesses, in insults, in hardships, in persecutions, in difficulties. For when I am weak, then I am strong." (2 Cor. 12:10).

Prayer: "Lord, help me to reject my natural tendency to find security and happiness in having an illusion of control. Help me instead to embrace and rejoice in my weakness so that the power of Christ may rest on me, and so that you may be glorified rather than me. Amen."

SEPTEMBER

September 1

"But the wisdom that comes from heaven is first of all pure...."

James 3:17a

Motives make a huge difference in outcomes. Recently Barbara was away for the weekend at a women's conference; I was home alone, sick with a stomach bug. The whole time she was gone I did not wash any of the growing pile of dirty dishes in the sink. Sunday evening I decided to pull myself together enough to deal with this stack of desecrated china.

In preparing myself to get out of bed and do the washing, two motives surfaced in my heart. The first (natural one) was the self-defense motive: if she walks in and sees all these dirty dishes, she's going to be disappointed and let me know it, so I'd better protect myself from that potential attack and wash them.

The second motive was presented to me by the Spirit; it was an "other-centered" thought: It would be nice for her to come home to a clean kitchen, knowing that my love for her was strong enough to overcome my weakness and get those dishes washed. I chose this motive as the reason for doing the dishes while rejecting the first, negative motive.

Barbara would never know which motive was selected without my telling her, but she would definitely feel the difference. One results in "adversarial thinking," touchiness and negativeness. The second brings openness, grace and joy in the other's happiness.

It is a significant practice to sort through our motives, letting the Spirit shine His light on what's in our hearts. Proverbs 16:2 says, "All a man's ways seem innocent to him, but motives are weighed by the Lord." I find that my motives are always mixed, and I need to sort them out before God, to consciously reject the negative and neutral ones and to affirm the purely positive ones. It takes time, but is worth it. More than anything else, motives determine the outcome.

Doing things with heavenly wisdom brings lots of glory to God: doing the right thing, for the right motives, in the right way and at the right time. Check out James 3:13-18 for some more thoughts on this.

I'm sure glad that the Lord got my attention on that Sunday night and had me act from good motives! Barbara was happy and so was I.

Prayer: "Lord, help me to discern my motives, taking time to write them down, to sort out and reject the negative and neutral, to affirm the godly and good ones. Help me to do this so that I may bring you more glory. Amen."

September 2

"The righteous man may have many troubles, but the Lord delivers him from them all."

Psalm 34:19.

You, Lord, are an active God, a caring God, a powerful God, a delivering God. I praise you for what you are doing in my life, delivering me from many troubles, transforming each one into an opportunity to see you at work, to trust you, to rest in you. You help me to see that each thing I do is an adventure with you, an opportunity to obey you in what is best and right and positive.

Praise you, Lord God, for your glory, graciousness, and greatness: all that you do is full of powerful goodness. You pour out your riches on us daily, giving and providing, helping and guiding, teaching and loving, convicting and forgiving. You do all this in wisdom and might, in deep knowledge and completeness of understanding.

You are Elohim, the Triune One who is immeasurably powerful and unbendingly faithful to your character, your Word and your ways. Nothing can stop you, no happening can change you, no one can hamper you, no being can prevent you. Your plans will come to pass. You can use any evil of man, any attack of Satan, any failure on our part and transform them into an advance for your Kingdom.

Your wisdom, your purity, your power, your goodness and your greatness are beyond our comprehension both in quality and scope: you can do immeasurably more than all we can ask or imagine; your glorious riches are infinite; your purity continues forever, your power never diminishes.

You are the Measure of all good; you are the Means of all righteousness; you are the Master of all the universe. To you belongs all glory and honor and worship. To you we must bow down, to you we must surrender, to you we must give praise, for you are worthy of all glory, both now and forever more.

I lay down my superficial strength and take up your supernatural power; I lay down my worthless wisdom and take up your wonderful wisdom; I lay down my pitiful patience and take up your powerful patience; I lay down my puny plans and take up your perfect plans. Rule in my life today, help me to join you in your work, use me to bring honor to your Name.

I praise you that as I start this day, tired, with lots before me, I can know that you will carry me through, giving me enough grace; you will prepare, protect and provide. I praise you now for what you are going to do and allow today, for what you are going to prevent and what you will accomplish. You are the Great High God who does what is righteous, wise and wonderful. I will praise you in and for all today.

Prayer: "May you be glorified in my life, O Triune God, may you be exalted, honored and magnified by my thoughts, words and actions. Guide me, protect me, teach me and use me. I praise you now for your answers to come. Amen."

September 3

"Sing joyfully to the LORD, you righteous; for the word of the LORD is right and true; he is faithful in all he does. The LORD loves righteousness and justice; the earth is full of his unfailing love."

Psalm 33:1,4,5

A recent conversion went this way: "Hi, Steve. What's been happening in your life?"

"Well, my work visa was canceled, my residence permit was denied, the police say they won't give any extensions on our tourist visa, I was sick for 5 weeks straight this fall, our business is out of money, we lost a team family and I've got more on my plate than I can handle!"

My friend didn't quite know what to say!

However, this list of difficulties does not weigh on me much at all. The reason: worship and the Word. Every morning's quiet time starts with worship, looking at who God is, reveling in His character: All-present, All-powerful, All-knowing, All-wise and All-gracious, completely Just and Merciful (Ps. 33). This changes one's perspective on happenings in life. When we have such a God in control of our situations, we can trust Him in all He brings instead of complaining, worrying or being unthankful.

Add to this a recent Bible study we did on suffering and the wonderful things God does in our lives through it, and my list of difficulties is transformed into a list of opportunities. Suffering is the doorway through which He brings us maturity & equipping (Jam. 1:2,3), deepening (1Pet. 4:12-14), purification of our faith (1Pet. 1:5-7), correction (Heb. 112:5-8), rewards (Mat. 5:10-12) and powrer (2 Cor. 12:9,10).

Now when things seem to "fall apart," the thought comes, "Aha, God is at work—I am eager to see what He's doing here and I'm going to praise Him for it before I can see the outcome."

Recently we went to visit a friend who has miraculously recovered from cancer. Her adult daughter greeted us at the door, all happy and thankful. An interesting thought came to mind, "What a shame that the daughter was so depressed and stressed before news came of the healing—she missed a big opportunity to trust, to give God glory and to grow herself in grace and wisdom by resting in Him before any healing came." Even if God hadn't healed her mother, we can trust Him to do what is best, letting go of all we are holding onto and give Him glory now.

Prayer: " Lord help me to stay in the Word, to be a worshiper and trust you so that you can transform me more every day and I can give you more and more glory. Amen."

September 4

"Blessed is the man who fears the LORD, who finds great delight in his commands."

Psalm 112:1

Praise be to you, O God, my Heavenly Father; to you, the Lord Jesus, my dear Brother; to you, Holy Spirit, my indwelling Teacher. You are the Magnificent, Marvelous and Majestic Triune God. You are the Great Creator, the Mighty Manager, our All-powerful Authority, the Righteous Ruler, our Loving Leader and our Wise and Gracious God. You are worthy of worship because of:

- your great Character (perfect in every facet, balanced in every way, full orbed and completely developed),
- your great Goodness (pure, clean, positive, immeasurably great, powerful, wise and deep),
- your great Faithfulness (unending, unalterable, full of integrity, perfect and powerful),
- your great Love (rich, strong, ever-flowing, unquenchable, unimaginably great, unconditional, contra-conditional).

You are the One to be exalted, trusted, praised and obeyed.

As your Word says in Psalm 112:7-10, the righteous man--the one who believes in you and has been given the righteousness of Christ-- "*...will have no fear of bad news."* This is because he knows you, the Great Shepherd, the Sovereign God and the Eternal King who filters all that comes to him and gives grace and preparation for whatever challenges you allow or send.

"...his heart is steadfast, trusting in the LORD." The God-ward orientation opens the way for a deep, abiding trust.

"His heart is secure," because he is focused on, founded on the eternal rock of Jehovah's unchanging, holy character.

" he will have no fear...." for fear is defeated by love, and your love, O Heavenly Father, is perfect, powerful, unconquerable, ever-flowing and pure;

"in the end...." You give us the eternal perspective, you tell us the conclusion of the story.

"he will look in triumph on his foes." In the end no one and nothing can frustrate you and your plans—or us as we abide in you.

You, O Eternal, Immutable, Omnipresent, Almighty God, are a marvel; from a human perspective, you are too good to be true! But you are true, you are Truth itself and you are worthy of all our worship, our honor, our praise, our exaltation.

Prayer: "May you be greatly glorified in my life today, Lord, in my thoughts, attitudes, words and actions. Help me to walk in obedience, in praise, in truth. Glory be to you forever. Amen."

September 5

"Finally, brothers, whatever is true, whatever is noble, whatever is right, whatever is pure, whatever is lovely, whatever is admirable—if anything is excellent or praiseworthy—think about such things."

Philippians 4:8

While sitting in a meeting, something the speaker shared struck me as odd, and I made a note to NOT say something about that to my wife. That really is backwards, isn't it? Since naturally I am quite critical, spotting things that are not quite right and commenting on these to Barbara is normal for me. But, since God powerfully convicted me of my critical spirit last spring, the Spirit has been coaching me on filtering out my negative talk.

This is an answer to prayer, for I have regularly asked for Philippians 4:8 to be a reality in my life— I was never sure how to think JUST on things that are true, noble, lovely…but now I'm learning as the Spirit has guided me through this process of editing out the negative, critical things I think and then tend to say.

There have been interesting side benefits of rejecting the negative and thinking the positive. For one my life seems lighter. Being critical of others is a burden, carrying around those negative thoughts uses energy. Criticalness also darkens our minds, preventing us from seeing good which may be hiding behind someone's sloppy dress or poor speech habits.

Another benefit is that it reminds me of Jesus' words, "…it is what comes out of a man that makes him unclean" (Mar. 7:15). As I consciously set aside a judgmental perspective and in my thoughts extend to others the grace that God consistently gives me, I find that my mind and heart are cleaned out. This allows love to flow more freely and leads me to be more of a help to others rather than a judge. It is wonderful to be a grace-giver as well as a grace-receiver.

A third benefit is that I no longer plant negative impressions and thoughts in the minds of those around me. Instead of being a bringer of darkness and condemnation, I bless both the hearer and the person I'd like to judge by saying nothing negative and instead seek to speak positively.

I've definitely got more to learn and implement in this area and praise God that He is patient with me and persistent in His gracious work.

Prayer: "Lord, help me to spot and reject negative, critical thoughts before I speak them. Help me to be a grace receiver and a grace giver. Amen."

September 6

"Let the name of the LORD be praised, both now and forevermore."

Psalm 113:2

Praise be to you, Lord, for your gracious provision: a good night's sleep, hope for the day, grace for living, wisdom for decisions and peace for my soul. You are good and gracious--wonderful beyond comprehension.

To awake and find myself with you, the Eternal, Almighty, All-knowing God, is an astounding privilege, especially when I remember that what I deserve is the exact opposite. You are so gracious, forgiving and merciful.

Today in the meetings I am attending we will continue the discussion of significant points of contention. This is important from a number of perspectives: biblically, spiritually and organizationally; it is important also for it to be a positive, up building, gracious, loving discussion.

Lord, I pray that you will guide us in how to proceed, in how to speak and how to move ahead. I pray that you will overrule, undertake, protect, glorify your name, lead us to surrender. Only you can bring these things to pass. Guide me in cooperating with you, in being wise and gracious; keep me from being a hindrance to the outcome you desire.

In the midst of this battle, which is not against flesh and blood, but against spiritual wickedness in the heavenly realms, we must focus on you, Lord God, Lord Jesus.

In the words of Psalm 113:1-4, "Praise, O servants of the LORD, praise the name of the LORD." This is a command, not a suggestion, for you, Lord, are worthy of praise, exaltation, worship and glory, no matter what you may allow into our lives.

"Let the name of the LORD be praised, both now and forevermore." Since you are eternal, unchanging, ever perfect, you are worthy of worship at every moment, and will continue to be throughout eternity; your names are worthy of praise--Yahweh, Elohim, Adonai-- full of meaning, revealing your character, giving light.

"From the rising of the sun to the place where it sets, the name of the LORD is to be praised." You are the ruler over all the earth: everyone everywhere should praise and glorify you, for you are the only One worthy of this.

"The LORD is exalted over all the nations, his glory above the heavens." You are the One who created the nations, they exist with your permission and for your purposes; they are dependent on your grace without knowing it. You are far above them in power, wisdom, goodness, righteousness, purity, holiness and grace. In your character, essence and power you are also far above the heavens, far beyond any heavenly beings. You are worthy of worship, obedience, honor and praise at each moment today and throughout eternity.

Prayer: "Lord, help me to remember how great you are, to join you in what you are doing, to keep on your whole armor and to fight against the spiritual forces of evil, not against people. May you be glorified today as I trust in you. Amen."

September 7

"Sacrifice thank offerings to God, fulfill your vows to the Most High, and call upon me in the day of trouble; I will deliver you, and you will honor me."

Psalm 50:14,15

I could feel the old, familiar tension rising as I approached the traffic light: would I make it through before it turned red? If I didn't make it, I'd have to stop and wait, losing precious seconds! Worry, impatience, discontent all started to flow. Then the Spirit brought to mind the verses in Ps. 50 I'd been meditating on, highlighting the privilege of giving thanks no matter what happened. "He who offers the sacrifice of thanksgiving honors me and prepares the way so that I may show him the salvation of God" (Ps. 50:23). This was followed by some insights on patience which came because the light did turn red and gave me a chance to think.

Patience is more an outcome than a quality: it flows from our relationship with Jesus. The more intimate our relationship is, the more patience will flow. This is because patience comes from knowing the character of God, from exalting Him in our minds and hearts, grasping ever more deeply how big, powerful, wise, just and merciful He is. It comes from knowing that He is in control and is working things out on His time table, not ours.

Patience comes from trusting Him instead of trusting our own judgment which leads to worrying. It comes from accepting that He is in control, protecting us from what is truly evil, developing our character, carrying us forward to His goals. It comes from laying aside the idea of getting our plans accomplished and seeking instead to join God in what He is doing. It comes from setting our hearts on things above. It comes from abiding in His love, obeying the Truth He has given us.

That is why there is no place in Scripture where we are told to pray for patience. Rather, we are told to be worshipers and confessors. When we exalt God for His greatness and power, and in the light of this, confess our lack of trust, our fears, our selfishness and instead focus on Him, our impatience melts away in the light of Truth. So when the traffic light turns red, instead of groaning, we can say, "Thank you, Lord, for what you are doing with this interruption."

Romans 15:13 sums this up powerfully in Paul's prayer for believers: "May the God of hope fill you with all joy and peace [especially at traffic lights] as you trust in him [this is my part], so that you may overflow with hope by the power of his Holy Spirit." [Where hope overflows, there is no room for impatience!]

Prayer: "Lord, today I want to walk in the Truth of your character. Help me to remember how great and good you are when I am tempted to be impatient. Help me to rest in the knowledge of your power, your perfection, your patience at work in my life and move through whatever comes, trusting you to work what is best. Amen."

September 8

"He [the Holy Spirit] will bring glory to me by taking from what is mine and making it known to you."

John 16:14

Praise be to you, this morning, Lord Jesus, for your great and good character: pure, positive, powerful and perpetual.
- You are the Way, laying down your life to pave the path to the Father.
- You are the Truth, revealing to the world the face of God.
- You are the Life, bringing resurrection to the spiritually dead.
- You are the Light, bringing sight in the land of darkness.
- You are Love, pouring acceptance out to your enemies.
- You are Goodness, giving sun and rain to all the undeserving.
- You are Grace, bestowing help on those worthy of rejection.

- You are Faithfulness, following through no matter the cost.
- You are Wisdom, understanding what is best in each situation.
- You are Righteousness, being consistently right and spotless in Word and deed.
- You are Lovely, being totally beautiful and pure.
- You are Eternal, having no beginning or end.
- You are Just, leaving no sin unpunished.
- You are Gracious, providing salvation for all while knowing many will reject it.
- You are Trustworthy, being unable to lie, ever keeping your Word and being eternally good.
- You are Great, having created the stars by the breath of your mouth, the earth with the Word.
- You are Powerful, holding together all things, including every atom in the universe.
- You are Glorious, being exalted above all in your holiness, power and love.
- You are God, eternally the Son in the Trinity, the One to be obeyed.
- You are our Savior, our Lord, our Intercessor, our Shepherd, our big Brother, our Friend who loves to spend time with us.

You, Lord Jesus, are worthy of worship for you are Marvelous, Majestic, Mighty and Master of all. You are to be obeyed as the Holy Spirit glorifies you. We bow before you, Lord Jesus, we exalt your Name, we lift you up, we magnify you, we love and glorify you, for you are worthy of all honor, power and praise.

Prayer: "You alone are the One to be obeyed. This day may you be lifted up in my life, worshiped in my words, magnified in my mind, glorified in my goals, exalted in my emotions, submitted to in my soul, praised in my whole being. Amen."

September 9

"Be very careful, then, how you live—not as unwise but as wise, making the most of every opportunity, because the days are evil."

Ephesians 5:15,16

When we entered the restaurant, I asked for the nonsmoking section and we were directed upstairs. Five minutes after being seated, the man at the next table took out a cigarette and the waiter stepped up and lit it for him; when I protested, the waiter said, "There's no law forbidding smoking here!" The waiter went on to bring us the wrong food, charged us for drinks we hadn't ordered and was very slow in bringing us our tea.

These events were a gift from God, a chance to practice the concept of offering the sacrifice of praise. As you've read several times here, Psalm 50:23 says, "He who sacrifices thank offerings honors me and prepares the way that I may show him the salvation of God." This command is echoed in several NT passages. Hebrews 13:15 states it very clearly, "...let us continually offer to God a sacrifice of praise, the fruit of lips that confess his name."

A sacrifice costs us something; the sacrifice of thanksgiving is offering praise when we naturally would like to do the opposite. Such praise by faith is lifting up the shield of faith, which quenches all the fiery darts of the wicked one (Eph. 6:16).

And why can we do this? Because the God we serve is wise, loving, disciplined, gracious and powerful. Thanking God for uncomfortable, painful or disturbing events He allows in my life is joining Him in His work, it is embracing the power He offers in the plan He has for this event; and it gives Him much more glory than our thanking Him after He answers my prayer for help.

Right now I have the privilege of living this out in relation to a big project we're undertaking for the business. Money was wired to us several weeks ago, but the bank here will not release it. At first I found myself complaining inside, and it showed as I interacted negatively with the bank personnel. Then as I worked through this in my journal and went over verses like Psalm 37:1-7 ("Trust in the Lord and do good...commit your way to the Lord, trust in him.... Be still before the Lord and wait patiently for him... refrain from anger and turn from wrath; do not fret—it only leads to evil…"), God changed my perspective.

As I confessed my unbelief, my lack of trust in God, there came a release of anger. That evening as I went to bed, a spontaneous thought accompanied by joy rose in my mind: "This is another adventure in which to see God bring glory to His name, growth in all of us involved, and direction in the work."

Those events in the restaurant were also opportunities to glorify God, grow in grace and set my heart on things above— these inconveniences made very little difference in my life, really, but what a difference godly responses make, especially to the local believer I was having lunch with.

The money still has not been released by the bank, but in the meantime the value of the dollar has risen making each dollar more valuable. God knows what He is doing. Am I willing to believe that and offer the sacrifice of thanksgiving to Him in whatever He allows into my life?

Prayer: "Lord, thank you for the opportunities to give you glory by offering the sacrifice of thanksgiving. Help me to do this in the face of every difficulty, disappointment and discouragement. Help me to reject the temptation to grumble and to live instead in the light of your love. Amen."

September 10

"'To whom will you compare me? Or who is my equal?' says the Holy One. Lift your eyes and look to the heavens: Who created all these? He who brings out the starry host one by one, and calls them each by name. Because of his great power and mighty strength, not one of them is missing."

Isaiah 40:25, 26

Last night, Lord, I thought about context, and how important it is in our walk with you. When we fall into troubles, if all we see is that trouble, we are disappointed, frustrated and discouraged. But if we have the larger context of you in the situation, then our response is couched in your perspective and can bring glory to you.

The larger context is this: You are the Great, Glorious, Gracious Creator of all, the Breather of stars, Maker of the solar system, Spinner of the earth, Bringer of the Dawn. You are the Sovereign God: All-powerful, Almighty, All-knowing, All-loving.

When your creatures rebelled against your goodness, you in your rich grace and love, entered this sinful world, suffered greatly and bought us back. We deserved Hell, but instead you gave us Heaven. You chose us before the foundation of the world in spite of the great cost to you.

You called us, you cleansed, forgave and transformed us. You assigned us to and equipped us for special service wherein we are empowered to do things that have eternal importance. You gave us significance and security in yourself. You made us your beloved children. You delight in us, rejoice in us, cherish us.

Everything that comes to us is filtered through your love and power. You give us opportunity to glorify you by faith. You give us opportunity to be weak so that your power may be seen in our lives. You are moving history to a conclusion and taking us with you.

What a difference knowing this context makes! *Wow!* To live with you, to live for you, to be your child, your ambassador, your herald, your workman, your messenger, your servant, your partner in work, your fellow heir, your brother, and in the end, your bride—what great and marvelous privileges.

You are a wonder, O God, for all these gifts you have given to me, your enemy, the one who rebelled against you for so many years, who is stubborn in selfishness, slow to learn, who gives you pain every day in my willfulness, my self-dependence, my trusting myself instead of you, in my grieving and quenching your Spirit. How great is your love, how great is your forgiveness, how great is your grace.

You, as my Savior-Shepherd, have now allowed a new difficulty (challenge, adventure) in my life. Looking at it from your perspective, it is good thing. You give me the grace, not to just cope with it, but to more than triumph over it and to give you honor and glory through praise in the midst of it.

No human being could ever think up a God like you; you are too good to be true! And yet you are more than true as you are Truth itself: pure, clean, shining, solid, sure, unchanging. You are the only One to be trusted fully. We glorify you, we lift you up in praise, we rejoice in you and in your making us your beloved children. Great are you, Lord and wonderful is your name.

Prayer: "Today may you be lifted up in my life, glorified in my living, exalted in my being, my Lord Jesus, King of Kings, Lord of the universe, Shepherd of my soul. Amen."

September 11

"Put to death, therefore, whatever belongs to your earthly nature…evil desires and greed, which is idolatry."

Colossians 3:5

The loss was staggering—Barbara and I both felt it like a punch in our stomachs, and for days we grieved. I wrote a poem about the death, and cried when I read it to a Turkish friend. He, of course, did not understand, because it was just a dog that had died.

Why did our dog's death hit us so hard? Part of it was that she had been such a source of joy: happy, full of energy and love, beautiful, intelligent and faithful. But for me there was more; as I thought about it, shockingly, this death was harder for me than if Josh or Nat had died. Why?

Years ago God had brought me to face my fears of my family's possible deaths; it was a crisis of surrender, "Lord you have loaned me Barbara, Josh and Nat to care for and love, to enjoy and work with. If you choose to take them now or at any point, I will praise you for the time you have given us together, and will praise you for knowing the right time to take them."

The Spirit has prepared me for their potential deaths by letting go of those relationships now. Therefore, an essential part of the grieving cycle (letting go, dealing with anger and shock, adjusting to the thought of loss) has already been worked through; I hold them with an open hand, trusting God to do what is best.

However, I had not done that with my dog; it hadn't entered my mind to do so—although it should have! I had been holding her with a closed hand, expecting to have her in our family for years to come and when she went, I was not prepared. Therefore, I had to work through the whole grieving process from the beginning.

During this time Colossians 3:1-4 was an encouragement and challenge: "Since you have been raised with Christ, set your hearts on things above, where Christ is seated at the right hand of God. Set your minds on things above, not on earthly things."

When I surrendered Barbara and the boys to God, He was leading me to set my heart on things above. This is freeing and conquers a lot of my natural fears. We need to do this with everything we "own." In actuality, everything we have is loaned to us, we own nothing ourselves, we are just stewards of what God has given, He owns it all. This incident has prompted me to again formally surrender to God all that I have: people, possessions, positions, and possibilities. Setting my heart and mind on things above certainly helps in offering the sacrifice of thanksgiving when the need arises.

Such a surrender, by the way, is good preparation for martyrdom—when our hearts are set on things above, the things of this realm pale in importance and it is easier to let go of everything, including our own lives. Most of us will not face physical martyrdom, but we do face the call each day to think on and pursue what is above, rejecting the values of the materialistic, self-centered, pleasure-oriented society we live in; let's not settle for anything less!

Prayer: "Lord, help me this day to begin setting my mind and my heart on things above, to live according to your values. Help me to hold all you have given me with an open hand, ready to accept what you take and give. May you be glorified in my attitude as a steward. Amen."

September 12

"The righteous cry out, and the LORD hears them; he delivers them from all their troubles."

Psalm 34:17

The description of you, Lord God, in Psalm 34:18-22 reveals to us your great heart, your loving kindness, your faithful follow-through and your total trustworthiness—all reasons for worship, praise and exaltation.

"The LORD is close to the brokenhearted and saves those who are crushed in spirit." You know those who are in such situations; you don't draw back from them, but in compassion come close, tenderly drawing them to yourself, flooding them with forgiveness, healing and grace. You, Lord Jesus, are good!

"A righteous man may have many troubles, but the LORD delivers him from them all;" Your Word, Lord, is realistic: this world is full of troubles, flowing out of the well of sin, permeating all aspects of this twisted and broken creation. But you are there, at work in each trouble, bringing the deliverance that is right and positive, constructive and helpful.

"…he protects all his bones, not one of them will be broken." What a beautiful reference to your own suffering, Lord Jesus—you, too, had many troubles in your time on earth; you were willing to suffer them, and you were delivered from them--just as you do for us. No one can ever say to you, "But you don't understand!"

"Evil will slay the wicked; the foes of the righteous will be condemned." The outcome of their lives is certain. Their own decisions will bring about their own end. You are just, O Lord, you are wise in your statement, "I gave them over to the desires of their hearts."

"The LORD redeems his servants; no one will be condemned who takes refuge in him." We say "redeemed" so easily, but it cost you so much. The result of your great willingness to purchase your enemies is that no one who takes refuge in you will be condemned. You know all, you see all, you love all, you save all who are willing to come to you. You alone are worthy of our love, our worship, our obedience, our praise.

Praise be to you, Lord Jesus. You fill my vision, you color my world, you overrule every event, you guide in strength, you protect in power. You are unwavering in purpose, you exude faithfulness. You are perfect, pristine, powerful, passionate, priestly and permanent. You are worthy of worship for your marvelous makeup, your wonderful Word, your awesome acts, your perfect person.

Prayer: "May you be exalted in my life today, O Great and Mighty Lord. Amen"

September 13

"Nebuchadnezzar king of Babylon came to Jerusalem and besieged it. And the Lord delivered Jehoiakim, king of Judah, into his hand…."

Daniel 1:1b,2

I've been going through the book of Daniel, which reveals a great deal about God and the way He works. The Lord accomplishes much with one stroke: in bringing judgment on Israel and sending them into captivity, He brought the Word of Life to a king and then to an entire empire.

Chapter four is clearly King Nebuchadnezzar's personal testimony sent out to his whole expansive kingdom and beyond, urging others to believe: "To the peoples, nations and men of every language who live in all the world...It is my pleasure to tell you about the miraculous signs and wonders that the Most High God has performed for me....Now I, Nebuchadnezzar, praise and exalt and glorify the King of heaven because everything he does is right and all his ways are just" (Dan. 4:1,2,37).

Look at how God accomplished this. He had, among the captives taken to Babylon, four young men who were fully submitted to Him. They very obviously knew the character of God and trusted Him to do what was right no matter what the consequences were for them—even though they had been captured, marched as prisoners to a foreign land and were forced into situations they hadn't chosen. When three of them faced the fiery furnace they replied, "Our God is able to save us....But even if he does not...we will not serve your gods..." (Dan. 3:18). They did not complain, gripe or feel sorry for themselves—we can tell this because they were respectful and gracious in their interactions with those in authority.

And what means did God provide so they could be a witness? Crises: life threatening, impossibly difficult crises. In each one Daniel and his friends trusted God, offering the sacrifice of thanksgiving, and saw God answer in spectacular ways, displaying His glory before many.

What does this say to us? How do we respond to crises? Do we know the character of God well enough to trust Him in the impossible, to turn to Him in prayer rather than to frantic action? Are we willing to be thrust onto the stage of witness where only God's power can save us, seeing the unseen as reality? Or are we those who live in the natural: complainers, whiners, self-pitying victims, seeking to escape what is uncomfortable, unwilling to see how we are called to play important roles in the grand scheme of God?

One of God's purposes in giving us the book of Daniel is to give us a sense of how He is moving history to a conclusion. He is able to weave into His plan even the myriad sinful actions of human beings done against His will, moving things inexorably towards the culmination of His goal.

Now when we see crises in our own lives, in the church or in international events we need to remember that we can trust God to use both the good and evil of man for His purposes. A fresh read through the first 6 chapters of Daniel does wonders for recalibrating our thinking on God's working in our everyday lives.

Prayer: "Lord, help me to grow in the knowledge of your character. Help me to respond in faith to the small every day crises and the big ones in my life with the sacrifice of thanksgiving so I may be a witness for you, opening the way to others for belief and growth. Amen."

September 14

"Tremble, O earth, at the presence of the Lord, at the presence of the God of Jacob…"

Psalm 114:7,8

You, O Adonai, are the One to be feared—your power, your purity, your presence are overwhelming, overarching, overcoming all opposition. When you manifested yourself in leading the Israelites, "The sea looked and fled, the Jordan turned back; the mountains skipped like rams, the hills like lambs" (Ps. 114:3,4).

Your power and presence caused the earth to writhe, the seas to flee, the rivers to cease flowing. You, O Elohim, the powerful and faithful One "…turned the rock into a pool, the hard rock into springs of water."

You are Mighty and High. To view the earth from your lofty position you must stoop down; yet you do that willingly, lovingly, sacrificially. You call yourself the God of Jacob, identifying yourself with that rascal, that rebellious and unrepentant, self-serving sinner and his descendants. You watched over them; you opened the way, prepared help, protected, guided and loved the Israelites, even though you knew they would rebel, disobey and bring disgrace to your Name.

What a great heart you have; what a mighty love flows from your being, bringing the possibility and power of change to all in this fallen world. Praise be to you for the many who embrace your love, are transformed and become your children.

Praise you for your working with all, even with those who will reject your grace (John 1:9;16:8-11), who choose to remain in darkness and spend eternity without you. Praise you for your pity on them, your death for them (1 John 2:2), your love for them (John 3:16).

You are the God of mercy, triumphing over justice, offering an umbrella of forgiveness to all who come. And you will judge sin and evil because you are just, for without justice there can be no holiness, no peace, no freedom from sin.

Praise be to you, O Perfect God, Lord and Savior, Sovereign and King, the Wise and Loving One—to you belongs worship and praise, honor and glory, exaltation and obedience.

Prayer: "I bow before you today. Use me, glorify yourself through me in a way that will make you stand out and me fade from sight. May I be the paint on the wall; may you be the house itself, the one who gets the honor today. Amen."

September 15

"I will declare that your love stands firm forever, that you established your faithfulness in heaven itself."

Psalm 89:2

Every week someone tells me that all their problems would be solved if only they had more money, or a house, or a car, or a better job. The pull of the human heart is ever towards comfort—we may enjoy a challenge for a while, but eventually we want to get to a position where we can kick back and relax. We want to get rid of pressures as much as possible. For many this means having a substantial nest egg so they can live any lifestyle they please. For others it may be a less stressful job.

For us believers, however, the situation should be different: our hearts and minds are to be set on things above (Col. 3:1-2). Our desire is really the opposite of the world's desire to be independent; we want to grow in conscious and committed dependence on God.

It is in the midst of uncomfortable situations that we can mature in this, choosing to give Him glory in our weakness and in His strength. One author puts it this way, "We must get away from the idea that deliverance from trial is the highest form of spiritual blessing. We learn more in a few days in the fiery furnace than we would learn in years out of it." (J. Oswald Sanders. *Spiritual Maturity*. Chicago: Moody Press, 1962, p. 64.)

Life gives us plenty of opportunities to live this way, but I, for one, often find myself shrinking back from many of them. Scripture, fortunately, reminds me of the reality I need to embrace: "Yea, though I walk through the valley of the shadow of death, I will fear no evil, for you are with me" (Ps. 23:4).

There are dark valleys, and we will go through them, but never alone—and if we enter them with faith in God's goodness, we will come out of them deepened because Jesus, our Shepherd, is there every day, every moment, every step of the way, leading us on. In the midst of difficulty He offers us grace, love and joy in our relationship with Him, something that material security can never give!

It is up to us to take up His grace and love, to live in them, meeting with Him each day, soaking in the Word, joining Him through prayer. He's waiting there every morning to spend time with us, His beloved children. Are we as eager as He is to meet?

Prayer; "Lord, help me every day to meet with you so I can better live out the words of Psalm 89:15, 'Blessed are those who have learned to acclaim Him, to walk in the light of His presence.' Amen."

September 16

"Not to us, O LORD, not to us but to your name be the glory,"

Psalm 115:1a

What a privilege: to reject the desire to gain glory for ourselves and to give it instead to you, Lord Jesus--to be the vehicle to carry honor to you, to be the sign pointing to you. You are the Source of all that we have: all the abilities we possess, all the insight, wisdom, creativity and energy we have—every bit of it comes from you, belongs to you, is to be used for you.

However, as human beings, it is so easy to live in the illusion that what we do comes from our own abilities and drive, that what we possess is the result of our own efforts. The truth is that without you we can do nothing of any significance. When we act without you, we are producing wood, hay and stubble, we are standing on mud, slime and quicksand. Our choices apart from you are uninformed, weak, self-centered and destructive

But in you, Lord Jesus, we have guidance, wisdom and power to do what is right. This is "because of your love and faithfulness" (Ps. 115:1b). You do not abandon your children in spite of our rebellion and unbelief; instead, your Spirit works unceasingly in us to teach and direct, break and reshape, transform and empower. It is a seeming paradox but a great truth that the more we embrace our weakness and depend on you, the more we are empowered.

I praise you for your great love, Lord Jesus, as you pour out on our rebel souls your grace, goodness and guidance, patiently correcting, disciplining and leading. You persist as we resist: when you call us to the light, we naturally turn to darkness; when you beckon us to good, we turn to selfishness; when you point us to obedience, we turn to rebellion. But in your firm faithfulness, you consistently convict, convince, and bring to contrition. You are a marvel in your majestic, mighty patience.

"Why do the nations say, 'Where is their God?' Our God is in heaven; he does whatever pleases him" (Ps. 115:3). You, O Lord God, are the final authority—no one can tell you what to do; you can, literally and truly, do whatever pleases you, and all that pleases you is good, pure, positive and holy. You are never tempted to do anything wrong, anything selfish, sinful or negative. All that is evil is totally repulsive to you; you are incapable of doing what is unholy, impure, unloving or ungracious.

No, what pleases you is always lovely, true, noble, right, pure, admirable, excellent and praiseworthy (Phil 4:8). It is according to your character, to your name, to your being, to your essence. You are Love itself, you are Life itself, you are Light itself--you are literally lovely in every aspect of your being.

What pleases you is going to please us, too, in the long run. Your will is what we would want if we had all the facts, which we never do, but we can trust you to have them and act accordingly.

What a joy to be your child. You have given us great privileges: to look to you, to behold your beauty, to revel in your holy highness, to rejoice in your graceful goodness, to marvel at your glorious greatness, to rest in your full faithfulness, to bow before your pristine purity, to obey in your powerfulness, to act in your graciousness—these are the great riches of your children.

I lift you up, exalt you, honor you and praise you, Lord God, King of Glory, Lord of Love, Ruler of Light, Redeemer of rebels.

Prayer: "In all I do, say, think and desire today, may I direct all glory to you, Lord Jesus. May I live the fact that you are my mighty Rock and my Refuge. Amen."

September 17

"Yet I hold this against you: you have forsaken your first love.... Repent and do the things you did at first. If you do not repent, I will come to you and remove your lampstand from its place. "

Revelation 2:5

Revival has such a positive, attractive ring to it: spiritual breakthroughs, excitement, growth and a renewed closeness to God. In my home church they are praying for revival, first individually and then corporately - a great prayer - so I've been thinking about revival and what it looks like. And God gave me a little experience of revival this past week.

I responded with impatience to a comment from Barbara, and both she and the Spirit convicted me that this was wrong. Because I had been nurturing my first love for Jesus, He made me open to embracing this painful revelation of my sin. Confession and repentance then brought peace in both relationships. It also made me more open to God.

That is what revival looks like: first seeing more and more of God's goodness; then the uncomfortable conviction of sin which should lead to repentance; and then into the pleasant part, a renewed love for God, a wider understanding and wonder of His forgiveness, and deeper joy in my walk with Him.

In my life God uses three things to expose my sin and sins: conviction from the Spirit and the Word, interpersonal conflict, and "care-fronting" from others. If I don't respond to these, God will use a bigger "hammer" to get my attention.

Biblically I think we should be experiencing revival daily as Paul talks about being renewed in his inner man every day (2 Cor. 4:16).

That's part of the reason for having a quiet time, so the Spirit can bring to our attention things we need to confess and forsake.

Starting with a time of worship (exalting God for His character without thinking of how it benefits me) nurtures my first love for Him. This brings me into the light of His presence where the Spirit can easily point out sin—often the hidden, subtle sins of attitudes and motives.

After confessing and repenting from what the Spirit has revealed, I am more sensitive to the Word's direction and conviction. Then as I go through the day, I can be more attuned to the Spirit's guidance, can better spot the wiles of the devil before falling into them, and can draw on Jesus' strength instead of living in our own proud illusion of power.

In addition, if we are having a daily revival, it is going to spill over into the lives of those around us and help them grow, too. When our cup overflows with teachableness, repentance, surrender, grace and humility, all our family and friends will benefit and God gets more glory. Revival is a good thing to pray for!

Prayer: "Lord, help me to cooperate with you in your work in my life, spending time in worship, confession, reading the Word and prayer each day, so that I may have an ongoing revival, and thereby bring you more glory. Amen."

September 18

"I love the LORD, for he heard my voice; he heard my cry for mercy."

Psalm 116:1

Praise be to you, Heavenly Father, the Great I Am, the Creator of all and the Director of Life. You are the glorious One, worthy of praise, worthy of honor, worthy of love, for your ear always "is open to my cry and your eye is on the righteous."

There is not a second when you are not focused upon each individual in the world, especially your children. "From heaven the Lord looks down and sees all mankind" (Psa. 33:13). No event escapes your notice, no happening comes without your permission.

You do not prevent every difficulty or trouble from coming to us, for in your wisdom you know that our growth comes in and through problems and hardships. And each uncomfortable, unwanted situation is another chance to honor you with faith and the sacrifice of praise. It is an opportunity to dance with joy on the stage of life, clothed in grace, energized with truth, surrounded by the light of your love.

My response should be the same as David's in Psalm 116:1 "I love the LORD, for he heard my voice; he heard my cry for mercy." Your love, O Lord, your care, your compassion for me in and through difficulty awakens in me more love for you.

To look away from our personal situation to the great context of your wisdom, your power and your grace frees us to reject self-pity, anger, rebellion and unbelief. As you did for Elisha's servant, you open our eyes to see the forces of the Lord surrounding us: "The angel of the Lord camps around those who fear him and he delivers them" (Ps. 34:7). When I think back in my own life, there are many examples of your surrounding me with your protection in the midst of difficulty.

- When we were traveling through Greece, an oncoming car had its left front tire blow out and was drawn into our lane, but you caused me to respond and avoid a head-on collision. The result was minimal damage, and great memories of your provision and grace.
- When we were expelled from the country, we were able to come right back and stay another 12 years.
- When I was turned in to the police by a believer, fired from my job, put on trial, shunned by fellow workers and threatened with the loss of our apartment, you brought acquittal, a statement of greater religious freedom and protection to stay in the country—plus I no longer had to work as a teacher but could work full time to plant churches!
- In a summer of tremendous stress, you used the pressure to reveal that I needed a stent in my heart, and used the ensuing pain to bring me into contact with my doctor friend in Germany who has poured blessing after blessing over us in his generosity.

With the psalmist, I can shout, "Because he turned his ear to me, I will call on him as long as I live" (Ps. 116:2). You, O God, are faithful, you are good, you are wise, you are wonderful. To come into your presence is a privilege, a joy, a grace.

I can rest in your goodness, I can rejoice in your power, I can exalt in your faithfulness, I can praise you for the unknown that is to come today, this week, this year, for what you bring will be used for good. Glory be to you forever and ever!

Prayer: "Lord God, King of the universe, help me to remember your greatness, your glory, your goodness so I can rest in your power, provision and protection in the midst of distressing happenings. Help me to do this so I may give you ever increasing honor and glory. Amen."

September 19

"Keep your tongue from evil and your lips from speaking lies. Turn from evil and do good; seek peace and pursue it."

Psalm 34:13,14

"You don't tell me as many things as you used to," Barbara observed as we drove along. I was silent for a minute, and then replied, "That's because I'm editing out most of my negative comments!"

That was a startling thought: probably fifty percent of what I used to say was negative! Much of it was just observations, like: "What an ugly coat;" "Look how crooked the windows are in that building;" "I'd never get a haircut like that!" Others were judgmental, such as: "Where did that idiot get his driver's license?" "That's the worst job of painting I've ever seen;" "Who'd ever want to buy something like that?" None of these comments were necessary. Even correct comments, like how society is going downhill often end up dragging us down with them.

Think of all the time, breath, energy and brain cell-space I'm saving by eliminating those unnecessary, unhelpful utterances! And just by being quiet on those points I am influencing people positively, eliminating another unedifying force in their lives.

This is not to say that we should never utter anything negative; there are definite times to point out, judge and condemn what is wrong, such as this statement: "Being negative about your wife is not going to help you love her more! Rather than dwell on what you don't like about her, make a list of her positives and your own negatives that she has to deal with!" We need to be positively sure that a negative statement is constructive in nature and intent.

Now when I do express an unhealthy negative thought, I am convicted quickly by the Spirit of my judgmental attitude. The other night we were watching a movie, and the last scene was a very improbable combination of events, including huge birds able to fly in superheated air. I pointed out how scientifically impossible this was—a correct observation—but in the process tarnished the enjoyment of the film for Barbara and Josh. And why did I say that? To show my superior knowledge and logic in comparison to the filmmaker! Not a very good motive.

It is necessary to consistently remind myself to not give vent to negative statements, and the Holy Spirit certainly prompts me to edit them out—if I am open to His leading.

Memorizing and meditating on Scripture helps. Right now I'm working on 1 John 3, which starts with: "How great is the love the Father lavishes on us that we should be called children of God. And that is what we are!" There is beauty, edification, joy and stimulating truth all wrapped up in two short sentences.

John goes on to say, "No one who knows God keeps on sinning; no one who continues to sin has either seen him or knows him." These two good negative statements give correct judgment and are designed to keep us on track.

Let's cooperate with the Spirit and move towards Truth which is twinkling on the pathway ahead: "The path of the righteous is like the first gleam of dawn, shining ever more brightly until the full light of day" (Pro. 4:18).

Prayer: "Lord, make us sensitive to the leading of the Spirit in avoiding speaking and thinking negative, destructive, selfish, judgmental statements that lead us and others away from the light. Amen."

September 20

"…you, O LORD, have delivered my soul from death, my eyes from tears, my feet from stumbling, that I may walk before the LORD in the land of the living."

Psalm 116:8,9

Lord, today is the important meeting, long anticipated, long prayed for. I want to thank you now for the outcome of this—whether it be what I desire or the opposite—for you, the Sovereign One, the King of Glory will guide and direct in this. Praise you for your goodness, your power and your love.

I can be confident in your help, although not in the outcome—you will decide what you will allow, and you will have your reasons for that. We cannot question your will, but we know it to be the best in the overall situation. Praise be to you.

As the Psalmist wrote in 116;3,4, "The cords of death entangled me, the anguish of the grave came upon me; I was overcome by trouble and sorrow. Then I called on the name of the LORD: 'O LORD, save me!'" In the worst of circumstances, in suffering and anguish, we can call on you, and you will answer.

We can trust you because of your great and wonderful character: "The LORD is gracious and righteous; our God is full of compassion" (Ps. 116:5). Whatever you choose to do, it will be out of graciousness—good, kind, positive, empowering—and will be aimed to bring righteousness in the situation.

You are not distant and cold, untouched by the plight of people; no, you are full of compassion—concern, care, involvement, desire for the welfare of your children. You are the trustable God who deserves praise in every circumstance.

"The LORD protects the simple hearted; when I was in great need, he saved me" (Ps. 116:6). You call for faith, and you answer our prayers in faithfulness. "The righteous cry out and the Lord hears them and delivers them from all their troubles" (Ps. 34:17). What a wonder to know you, Lord Jesus.

When we cry out, when we seek you, when we stop trusting in ourselves and the solutions of this world, of the flesh and the devil, then you reach down and save us in your timing and your way.

We can praise you ahead of time for such salvation, long before we may see it, for you, Lord God, are good, gracious, great and glorious. Praise be to you for the privilege of walking by faith today as I wait for the outcome of the meeting.

Epilogue: *The meeting did not bring the results we'd hoped for, nor did subsequent steps. We had to surrender to the Lord our understanding of the situation, praise Him and move on. He is good.*

Prayer: "Lord today help me in getting up the shield of faith by praise, offering the sacrifice of thanksgiving, trusting you in the midst of trouble and thereby giving you glory before the unseen hosts. Amen."

September 21

"O LORD, truly I am your servant; I am your servant, the son of your maidservant; you have freed me from my chains."

Psalm 116:16

The sickness dropped on me suddenly, like the onset of darkness on a winter evening. Chills, fever, severe diarrhea; I was in bed for five days. It was painful, powerful—and productive. During those days in bed there was a lot of time for prayer about what was on my heart: revival for myself, for all the workers here, for all the believers. And God answered: He pulled back the curtain of my soul, revealing, in new understanding, the depth of the sins I thought I'd pretty much conquered. Yes, humanly speaking I was doing quite well in these areas, but God's standards are much higher. If I want revival, it is going to be on His terms, not mine.

The Holy Spirit brought out, one by one, nine sins (mostly attitudes), which needed to be dealt with more severely—and I was glad to confess and surrender each on a new and deeper level. The Holy Spirit went on to point out that even in wanting revival in my life some of my motives were not pure. Along with wanting a fresh filling of the Spirit and desiring to be more useful in God's hand to give Him glory, there was also the wish to be spiritually powerful so that others would admire me. That had to be confessed and repudiated. If I grieve the Holy Spirit (by sin) or quench Him (by not obeying His promptings), He will not work powerfully through me. He wants a clean channel in which to flow.

After this initial surrender, God tested me on one of these nine sins: the competitive desire to win. At the baptism picnic I got into a discussion with a philosopher-type visitor. The conversation got intense as he outlined how God wanted evil in the world so people can contrast it with good; shortly I realized we had stepped into an intellectual swamp where I was trying to compete against him on an intellectual level, but to no avail.

Abruptly I withdrew from the discussion and emotionally limped away. With reflection it became clear that I was out to win in my own strength, while the fellow was just having fun; it wasn't a serious discussion for him at all. I had not been listening to the Spirit but trying to bring conviction with my words and intellect: what a foolish mistake! Winning is nothing, being used by the Spirit to bring conviction is far more, and this requires denial of self.

In this working of God to bring revival in my life, no big, visible event occurred, but there was a worldview shift that made me more useful for Him. I went from trusting myself less to trusting the Spirit more to do the work.

This change was noticeable in a conversation I had in the following week with a 65 year old man who had declared he could not possible accept the deity of Christ. We took a look at Philippians 2, then I answered a few questions, and he said, "Now I can believe that Christ is God!" That wasn't from me! No argument, just the word of God and following the Spirit's leading. What a difference: joy in God's working, no glory for me and not even a thought of it! This is the powerful freedom God wants us all to live in.

Prayer: "Lord, work in my life to bring revival: higher revelation of your holiness, wider recognition of my sin, deeper realization of how much you have forgiven me. Amen."

September 22

"Be at rest once more, O my soul, for the LORD has been good to you."

Psalm 116:7

Your character, O Lord, is the basis of rest for us. Your goodness surrounds us, giving us air to breathe, food to eat, a place to sleep, clothes to wear, sight, hearing, taste, smell, touch, love, life, light and loveliness. You have shared yourself with us in your creation, which reflects your character in complexity, beauty, practicality, variety, continuity and faithfulness to laws you laid down.

As you open our eyes to your goodness, and through praise turn our focus away from the many blessings you give us to your lovely, pure, mighty and faithful character, the worries, desires, lusts and cares of this broken world fade into the background. They become opportunities to be transparent before you in confession, chances to praise you by faith, possibilities to triumph in your provision, situations to demonstrate your grace on the stage of life.

You are moving us towards living in the truth uttered by Asaph in Psalm 73: "Whom have I in heaven but you and earth has nothing I desire besides you." The lust of gluttony for more and more entertainment, excitement, food, things and self-centered attention is defeated by an ever-clearer view of you. I say to my soul, "find rest in God alone, for my hope comes from Him, He only is my rock, my salvation, my high tower, I will never be shaken" (Ps. 62:5).

Psalm 116: 8, 9 continues, "For you, O LORD, have delivered my soul from death,"—by your own death and resurrection, Lord Jesus, you have freed us from the fear and power of death so my soul and spirit can live forever. And you save me daily from untimely death physically.

"…you delivered …my eyes from tears…" Knowing you takes the sting out of many painful events—you, as the Sovereign God, rule over the happenings of my life, so I can praise you for what would normally be a burden, a sadness, a problem, a tragedy. Instead of mourning self-centeredly, I can praise Christ-centeredly.

"…you delivered …my feet from stumbling…" You give light, you show the way so that I can avoid the pitfalls, the problems, the traps which the world, the flesh and the devil set for me. You also give strength so that when I am weary, in you I can be refreshed and press on without stumbling.

"…you delivered [me]… that I may walk before the LORD in the land of the living." You do all this so that in this world I may walk in the light of your presence all day long, calling on your name, exalting you, praising you, thanking you for the great abundance of your love that pours out upon us moment by moment. What a wonderful God you are, worthy of praise in each minute, each event, each thought. .

Prayer: "May you be praised continually in my heart, mind and words today. Keep me from complaining, keep the praise flowing, help me to hold your name on high in all that comes today. Amen."

September 23

"Show me the way I should go, for to you I lift up my soul."

Psalm 143:8b

The power of "lifting my soul" to God never fails to amaze me. In Psalm 86:4,5 it says, "Rejoice the soul of your servant, for I lift up my soul to you, O Lord, for you are good and ready to forgive and plenteous in mercy to all who call upon you." Telling God what I am thinking, feeling, wanting and then evaluating these in the light of God's Word brings clarity, peace and grace. Following is a "soul lifting" entry in my journal. Note the insight, resolution and application that come in the end.

"I was grumpy and dissatisfied during the last day of our trip—it came out when we missed a turn and ended up in the industrial section of the city we were visiting. I really don't like getting lost—it makes me feel inadequate, insecure and a fool.

"This precipitated a 'discussion' with Barbara. Then I failed to follow the prompting of the Spirit and apologize for being grumpy; Barbara had to point out that I was not speaking kindly to her—not good!

"In looking back over this day, Lord, now I see that there were a number of niggling things that I was discontent about:
- all the red lights over the last 100 kilometers—seems they were just waiting for me!
- worry about the car (front end shimmy, whine in the differential, lack of power);
- not being able to have a shower for 3 days;
- tiredness from 4 days on the road, lack of eating;
- the intense conversation with staff at the hotel on 'has the Bible been changed' and my not listening to God during it;
- feeling sorry for myself for all the difficulties;
- grumbling in my heart and worrying about being late to pick up Barbara;
- failure to believe God and praise Him from the heart.

"Lord, forgive me for my sinful focus on what bothered me rather than surrendering each item to you with the sacrifice of thanksgiving. Thank you now for reminding me that knowing you is enough for joy. In you, Lord Jesus, we:
- have an unconditional love-filled relationship with the Creator of the universe;
- have the Holy Spirit living within;
- are watched over, protected and guided every minute;
- have continual, instant access to God's full attention;
- have eternal life;
- have meaning in life: ultimate meaning as well as meaning in daily events;
- are equipped and called to significant work (no secular/spiritual divide here);
- have all events filtered through God's hands;
- have every event designed for our growth and maturity;
- are a child of God, a child of the King;

- have the possibility of a life filled with love and grace.

"And the list goes on. What reason do I have to complain?!!! Forgive me, Lord, help me to live in the light of your powerful and beautiful presence."

As you can see, lifting my soul in journaling allowed God to bring all into focus, revealing the sources of my grumpiness and free me from my discontent. Lifting my soul brings out into the light the chains that bind me so God can set me free, again.

Prayer: "Lord, I praise you for the wonder of your pure and positive Being. Help me to lift my soul to you often; help me today to think of the many positive things you pour into my life all day long, and to praise you continually. Amen."

September 24

"The LORD is my rock, my fortress and my deliverer; my God is my rock, in whom I take refuge. He is my shield and the horn of my salvation, my stronghold."

Psalm 18:2

I praise you, Lord Jesus, for your great and constant love, always flowing in spite of the weaknesses, sin and inconsistency of your children, especially in me. Praise be to you that, as it says in Psalm 62, you "only are our rock" (never changing, always stable, always strong, always good). You "only are our salvation" (always at work to protect us from the attacks of the enemy, from assaults of the accuser, from daily harm, from our own poor decisions). You "only are our high tower" (our place of refuge spiritually, intellectually, emotionally and physically as you protect us, give perspective, guide and lead us).

Compared to our natural ups and downs in mood, in sharpness of mind, in quality of judgment and obedience, you, Lord Jesus, are wonderfully, marvelously, majestically stable. In your might and power you are always faithful: consistently, constantly, persistently, perfectly ever the same. You are the only One to be fully trusted—all others in our world are capricious, selfish, sinful and shifting.

I praise you, Lord Jesus, that you are at work, preparing to recreate this broken, twisted creation into a pristine, perfect, pure and positive place. You began this process with the plan revealed in Eden, you followed through with the selection of Abraham, the protection of the line of David, your arrival on earth in the incarnation, your living a perfect, holy life, your willing demise, your defeat of the devil and death by your resurrection and your present intercession at the right hand of the Father.

Now we await the fulfillment of this process: the judgment of all evil and its confinement to hell, the end of this earth and heaven, the creation of a new heaven and earth, and the beginning of eternity with you.

What a wonder that will be: a life without sin, always having pure motives, always desiring to do what is pleasing to you, always knowing what is right and doing it because we will love what is righteousness. It will be a life totally focused and centered on you, Lord Jesus, giving you glory, honor and praise at each moment—no distractions, no competition, no attacks from the enemy or our flesh.

This plan is a reflection of your good character--taking your enemies and making them model citizens of a new paradise: chosen, transformed, blessed, protected, equipped, commissioned, guided, dearly loved and delighted in at each moment.

The incredibleness of these truths is too much to comprehend, too much to believe, for they are far beyond our human experience, far beyond what we know we deserve.

These truths highlight what you are, Lord God: so gracious, so kind, so patient, so contra-conditional in your love for the rabble you have called to be your children. You are forever worthy of wonder and awe, honor and glory, worship and obedience. Therefore, I bow before you in eager submission, I rise up in overflowing joy and go forth in wholehearted obedience that you might be exalted in all today.

Prayer: "May you and your name be lifted up in my life, Lord God, through my transformed motives, thoughts, intents, words and actions. Amen."

September 25

"As for God, his way is perfect; the word of the LORD is flawless. He is a shield for all who take refuge in him."

Psalm 18:30

Recently I listed out the difficult events that have occurred among us here in the last 4 months:
- one family had to go home because of their small daughter's serious medical problems;
- another of our workers lost his brother (39) to a heart attack in July;
- and then his father died unexpectedly in October;
- A believer had a serious operation and then died at age 33;
- my father died the same month;
- another of our fellow workers had emergency quintuple by-pass surgery;

- three weeks later I had emergency double by-pass surgery;
- the unbelieving brother of a local pastor was killed in a car accident, age 39;
- one of our old believers was just diagnosed with colon cancer and will have surgery.

These events came one after another, with hardly any time to recover in between. If they were attacks by Satan, God was certainly not taken by surprise and is using each one for good. FB Meyer is credited with saying: "Trials are God's vote of confidence in us."[8] The Lord knows that if we take up the grace He offers, with His power we will be able to move through whatever trials He allows.

Trials are intended to drive us into Scripture and to expose our wrong thinking so we can be aligned with God's thoughts. Difficulties are to deepen us and to demonstrate to the world how we can take God's help and move through stress and mourning with grace. We can skip the early stages of grief (shock, anger at God, bargaining and denial) in dealing with such events, and we can move through the later stages (acceptance, adjustment, establishing a new norm) more quickly with power and healing.

In Psalm 3 David talks about his own trials, "...how many rise up against me, many are saying of me, 'God will not deliver him.' But you are a shield around me, O Lord, my Glorious One, who lifts up my head." Our confidence is in the goodness, power and meticulous love of our Sovereign God; He helps us to turn away from the negative thinking of the world (such as Murphy's law) to praising Him in the midst of whatever comes.

This has had personal application for me. As I was wheeled into the operating room for my emergency double by-pass surgery, a comforting thought came: "This is really a win-win situation. If I die, I get to go to heaven; if I live, I get to stay with my wife, my family and friends!" I had no fear or anxiety whatsoever, just a rich, settled peace. It is great to be a believer in Christ and to know where we are going!

Prayer: "Praise you for the peace you offer us in every circumstance, Lord Jesus. Help me to continually look to you in each event, to take refuge in you through praise and thinking your Word. Amen."

September 26

"As the heavens are higher than the earth, so are my ways higher than your ways and my thoughts than your thoughts."

Isaiah 55:9

---

8 Quoted in Daily Heartburn at http://www.dailyheartburn.com/genesis-22.html

Praise be to you, O Heavenly Father, our wise and all-knowing God. Your perspective is high and wide, long and deep. You understand and know all the aspects of every situation. You have seen all the past, you already see what will happen in the future. You know all the facts and your will is fully informed. Therefore whatever you decree, whatever you allow, whatever you choose to bring is good, a part of your overall plan. Your decisions may be painful to us, the opposite of what we desire, but because you are God--the Good, Great, Glorious and Gracious One--we can trust you in each situation.

Psalm 116:5 says, "Precious in the sight of the LORD is the death of his saints." Most of the time, death is a bitter experience for human beings; for many it is an end without hope. In you, however, there is death is full of hope.

You, Lord Jesus have defeated death, you have broken through the wall of hopelessness, making a doorway into eternal life. In God's eyes, the death of a believer (all of whom are saints) is a precious and wonderful thing. He is in the process of bringing them from a narrow, restricted, painful, difficult situation into a rich, broad, powerfully pleasant, gloriously positive, wonderful place.

To move from this sin-shackled, superficial, sullied and selfish world, twisted and warped by the fall, into the perfect, sinless, holy and pure heaven, into the presence of the Great King of all, the Creator, the Sustainer, the Ender of time—what a wonderful happening the death of a saint is! God knows the contrast: to bring another one of His children out of the darkness and dust of the dungeon of death on earth into the light and lavishness of the loving Lord—what better thing can He do for us?

It is hard to understand why some active, godly, useful servants of God are taken in their youth. We think in terms of their loss of years on earth, of our loss of their presence, help and service. But God has a much higher and broader view. He knows what is coming in the future and makes preparation. As it says in Isaiah 57:1, "The righteous perish, and no one ponders it in his heart; devout men are taken away, and no one understands that the righteous are taken away to be spared from evil."

A child dies, a teen-ager is taken in an accident, cancer strikes down a young mother, a heart attack kills a father not yet forty. Tragedy on a human level--but a rescue mission on a Heavenly level. God knows what evil awaited that person and those around him; so He protect them all by taking that person home—and does so in the best way and at the right time.

Those saints left behind are heir to God's rich grace to carry them through the loss, to be deepened spiritually, to see all their needs provided as they trust and praise Him by letting go of the loved person now departed.

Failure to let go can bring more evil. When King Hezekiah was fatally ill, he begged God for more years, and God gave him fifteen more. But during that time Hezekiah fathered the boy who became the worst king that Judah ever had, an evil God was seeking to avert. To pray for someone seriously sick, "Lord spare his life—but not my will, let your will rule," is a prayer of trust, of humility and wisdom, just as Jesus prayed in the garden, "Not my will but yours."

Lord God, you are the only truly wise One, you are the only Knower of the future, so we can trust you in your Goodness and Grace, your Revelation and Release of your children from this world.

Praise you for this high and holy perspective you give us on death. It is not the end, but the beginning of all the goodness you have stored up in eternity for those who love your Name. Glory be to you for your great goodness and graciousness.

Prayer: "Lord, my Lord, help me to have your perspective on death, to look forward to it as moving into your Kingdom in a complete way. Help me to let go of those around me, to hold them with an open hand so when you choose to take them I'll be ready to let them go. Help me to be a more effective witness to those who don't yet know you so they, too, can live and die in this hope. Amen."

September 27

"This is what the LORD, the God of the Hebrews, says: 'Let my people go, so that they may worship me.'"

Exodus 9:1

In some of my classes I've been teaching about worship. We often think of music being the main aspect of worship, but actually everything we do can be worship: when we do what is pleasing to Him, we give Him glory. That is worship.

In spoken worship there are two main aspects: thanksgiving and praise. Thanksgiving focuses on what He has done for us, and praise on who He is in His character.

I suggested that my students write their thoughts of worship in their journals. Here are some thoughts from mine, both praise and thanksgiving.

"Praise you, Lord God, Creator of heaven and earth, the sea and all that is in them. Truly you are high and powerful, majestic and loving. I praise you, O God, for your great and rich love, for your wide wisdom and positive power. You are able to bring together those aspects which are opposites and seem to contradict each other: unity and diversity, truth and love, justice and mercy, righteousness and forgiveness. Praise you, Lord God, that you have revealed this in your Word.

"Thank you that you have given us the tremendous privilege of being your children, transforming us from your enemies ensnared by sin and transforming us into your sons and daughters clothed in righteousness. To know you is a stupendous privilege beyond value; we are overwhelmed by this high and undeserved grace.

"Thank you that you have watched over us through a very difficult year, one in which your grace, protection and guidance have shone in the dark events that surrounded us, that could have overwhelmed us but your shining grace carried us through.

"Thank you for the future ahead—nothing guaranteed, of course, for all is in your hands, not our plans--but all is in your heart of love, shown in your doing what is best and good for us, although it may be hard. Truly, God, to live with you is a never-ending opportunity for growth and deepening."

Prayer: "Lord God, help me to praise you in my quiet time, to praise you throughout the day. May praise be the keynote of my life, for you are worthy. Amen."

September 28

"I will lift up the cup of salvation and call on the name of the LORD."

Psalm 116:13

Praise be to you, Lord Jesus, that I awoke and remembered that you are Sovereign, that all is in your hands, that all the things that weigh on me, that trouble me, are all within your power. You are at work in them and with them to accomplish your greater purposes. This is beyond our knowledge and understanding, but we can trust you in it all.

In Jeremiah there is chapter after chapter describing the disasters you planned to bring on the nations (Judah, Moab, Egypt, the Philistines, Babylon), punishing them for their sins, striking down their peoples because of their rebellion against you and refusal to repent.

What a powerful description of human tragedy and Divine justice (refusal of the refuge and therefore unnecessarily suffering just punishment); it is a description of human suffering and Divine love (difficulties brought on by poor choices, while the Lord is near to the broken hearted and saves those who are crushed in spirit).

We struggle to grasp this truth, for our senses overwhelm us with the immediate stimuli of suffering; we fail to see the bigger picture and therefore do not trust you in difficulty. Forgive us for our failure to think Truth, to see from your perspective.

Praise you for your revelation of Truth in your Word that gives us enough to go by: the wonderful beauty of your character, the examples of your gracious dealing with your rebellious people in the past, the forgiveness you have prepared for all who will respond. This allows us to connect the dots of your goodness and our sin and suffering with those of forgiveness, salvation, grace and glory.

Psalm 116:8-14 speaks to this: "…you, O LORD, have delivered my soul from death, my eyes from tears, my feet from stumbling, that I may walk before the LORD in the land of the living."

In the midst of all difficulties we can say, "I believe," even while I say, "I am greatly afflicted." When all is falling apart, when no one is trustable, when we are alone and forsaken, even then we can believe you, trust you, follow you, obey you.

As David said, "How can I repay the LORD for all his goodness to me? …I will fulfill my vows to the LORD in the presence of all his people."

We can and must praise you before the peoples, no matter what comes, for the measure is not what we see, but what you are. The beauty, power, goodness, wisdom, grace and purity of your character shine the light of understanding on all that comes to us. They give us clues that bring an understanding of the future, of how all will fit together in your creative, powerful, loving hands.

Glory be to you, the Great and Mighty One, King of Glory, God of Goodness, Lord of Love and Ruler of Righteousness. Praise you that you hold back the tide of evil, exposing what is harmful, guiding in what is confusing, protecting in what is negative and loving in what is difficult.

You, Lord Jesus, have suffered the ultimate in living out your love for your rebellious creatures, so we can trust you when suffering comes to us and those around us. Glory be to you, continually, every day, all the time, throughout eternity.

Prayer: "Lord Jesus, you know all about suffering. When it comes to me and mine, help me to trust you, praise you, obey you instead of following my own understanding which leads to self-pity, anger and rebellion. Protect me from myself! Amen."

September 29

"You give me your shield of victory, and your right hand sustains me…."

Psalm 18:35

After leaving the confines and concrete of the capital city in the Middle East with its five million people, heavy traffic, polluted air and brown landscape, everything here on the farm in CT is so refreshing: lush green trees, acres of grass, the still pond, fields with blue jays and cardinals flitting about, all wrapped in a peaceful quietness. There is almost no noise except for the occasional passing car and the twittering of the birds. It is another world to which we must adjust. As Barbara is fond of saying about international travel: it will take a few days before our souls catch up with our bodies.

As usual, our quiet times with God provide the stability we need in transition. Psalm 18 has been my meditation ground: "I love you, O Lord my strength. The Lord is my rock, my fortress, my deliverer. My God is my rock in whom I take refuge." Here is Truth to carry us through any difficult time—we just have to think it and believe it.

One way that God has been working as my Deliverer is by giving me a new way to combat temptation. This came out first in the war against impure thoughts, but is applicable to most any sin. It is the prayer of agreeing with Truth:

"Lord, I agree with you that this thought and desire of mine
- is totally selfish (I am thinking only of pleasing myself, not caring how it affects others),
- is destructive (taking me away from you and injuring relationships),
- is caustic to my soul (burning it with evil desire, scaring it for months to come),
- is pleasing to Satan (I am doing exactly what he wants, I am cooperating with him)
- and is grievous to you! (causing you, the One who loves me and died for me, pain and grief in your great, gracious heart. It is paying you back evil for the great goodness you pour out on me every day!)"

If prayed with wholehearted thoughtfulness, this prayer strips away sin's mask of potential pleasure and shows the yawning pit of ensnarement underneath, waiting to swallow us up. Do I want to please Satan?!! Do I want to grieve God?!!! Absolutely not!

When I pray this prayer I often get the chills at the revelation of how evil my sin is, and find myself wholeheartedly pulling back from the temptation, remembering that powerful verse, "You shall know the truth and the truth will set you free!" I want to live in Truth, not temporary pleasure.

Then after confessing my sin, repenting and receiving forgiveness, I continue with, "In the name of the Lord Jesus Christ I withdraw any ground I've given to Satan in this sin and ask that the Holy Spirit would fill this area of my life anew." That's joining God in what He wants to do in my life—just where I really want to be, in His green pastures!

Prayer: "Lord help me to quickly see where I am tempted and to expose the evil by remembering how this would lead me to please Satan and wound your heart so I can quickly step back from sin and draw close to you. Amen."

September 30

"I will sacrifice a thank offering to you and call on the name of the LORD."

Psalm 116:17

This morning, Lord, I feel far from you. Thank you for this opportunity to walk with you by faith, not feeling close, but knowing that you are there, within me, around me, loving me, even though I don't feel this.

As you have been transforming me through worship, you have deepened my emotional grasp of your love for me through lifting my soul to you. This strongly reinforces the intellectual knowledge of your gracious acceptance of me as your dearly loved son in whom you delight.

In this growth you give a rest, a security, a certainty of my relationship with you which is filled with forgiveness, gracious correction, firm direction, deepening knowledge, a joyful walk and light-filled days. This all gives me a desire to obey you, to please you, to love you, to avoid grieving you.

Praise you, Lord Jesus, for your great heart of love, continually overflowing on us who daily cause you pain with our rebellion and unbelief. We must confess our selfishness, our pride, our fascination with the material, our devaluing the spiritual, our worship of idols (focusing on what we demand to be happy), our impatience and self-centeredness.

You are the opposite of what we are: so patient, so kind and firm, graciously correcting us a thousand times a day, giving us direction, helping us to see our mistakes, our sin, our rebellion so we can repent and surrender. Praise you, Lord God, for your great, undeserved love.

Psalm 116:16-19 speaks to this: "O LORD, truly I am your servant; I am your servant, the son of your maidservant;" There is no doubt that I belong to you, you are my Master, my King, my Lord and my Brother. You will not abandon me.

"…you have freed me from my chains." Many were the things that bound me, and more that still do: fear, selfishness, pride, ambition, the desire to earn my own significance and security, greed, gluttony and lust, to name a few. You, Lord Jesus, in your death and resurrection bought my freedom from these and you are gradually walking me out into the actual experience of that freedom.

My response? "I will sacrifice a thank offering to you and call on the name of the LORD." I will praise you at all times, thank you for things which, humanly speaking, would lead me to complain, to be angry and bitter. In the light of your Word it is clear that these come with your permission, grace and kindness. They come so I can trust you with all my heart and give thanks for the good that I cannot yet see.

" I will fulfill my vows to the LORD in the presence of all his people, in the courts of the house of the LORD—in your midst, O Jerusalem." With your strength and grace, I can obey you, following through on my surrender. I can live for you, before all, giving them further glimpses of your glory, of how your grace helps us in every circumstance.

What more can we say but, "Praise the LORD!"

Prayer: "Lord Jesus, my Shepherd and King, I bow before you today, and ask that you will help me to listen to the leading of your Spirit, to think your Word, to obey what I know, to bring glory to you. Amen."

OCTOBER

October 1

"Praise the LORD, all you nations; extol him, all you peoples. For great is his love toward us, and the faithfulness of the LORD endures forever. Praise the LORD."

Psalm 117:1,2

I praise you, O Lord, for your great work in our lives to transform us into the image of Christ. This is your work, but requires our cooperation. Yours is the power, ours is the decision. Transformation comes from you, surrender comes from us.

This partnership is your gift to us, a wonderful invitation to the upward trail of spiritual adventure. On one hand, this involves difficulty: death to self, denial of ungodly desires, rejection of selfish motives, being totally transparent before you and surrendering all.

On the other hand, it involves endless positives: receiving grace, accepting love, believing truth, letting go of what binds, being set free, walking in the light, experiencing inner transformation, having joy and peace, overflowing with hope, dwelling in God's shelter, resting in His shadow, being His beloved child, being delighted in and richly loved, rejoicing in Jesus, fearing God, loving God, praising God, and obeying God. The right choice is obvious!

Psalm 117:1-2 says it all: "Praise the LORD, all you nations; extol him, all you peoples. For great is his love toward us, and the faithfulness of the LORD endures forever. Praise the LORD."

And we do praise you, O Lord God, the Triune King, Lord of all, for your powerful love, which, humanly speaking, is illogical—there is no reason for you to love us rebels. Yet, in your marvelous love for even your enemies, you have wrought a wonderful place of grace within a world of woe. As we pass through the difficulties of life, we see your faithfulness over and over: you are never late in helping, you are never short of grace, you are never lax in listening, you are never reluctant to respond.

Your wisdom and goodness as well as your love and grace allow what is for our good and growth along with displaying your glory and greatness. Each happening, pleasant or painful, happy or hard, delightful or difficult, is a gift from your hand, the opportunity to focus on you and to respond with thanksgiving.

This can be the thanksgiving of joy, the overflow of seeing your goodness poured out on us. Or it can be the thanksgiving of sacrifice, offering praise in faith when we'd rather complain, feel sorry for ourselves or rebel. Each possibility has its positives; thank you that you give both opportunities. You, Lord God are trustable, your faithfulness endures forever, praise be to you.

Prayer: "Today may your name be lifted high in my life, and may those around me see this. May they be drawn to you, Lord Jesus. You are the One worthy of glory, of honor, of exaltation and of obedience. I surrender to you, and declare you to be my Captain and Navigator today, the One to be followed and obeyed. Amen."

October 2

"Sacrifice thank offerings to God, fulfill your vows to the Most High, and call upon me in the day of trouble; I will deliver you, and you will honor me."

Psalm 50:14,15

A big problem appears on my radar screen. I ask God for help. He sends me another problem. He then uses the second problem to solve the first. This is a pattern: the important question for me is, will I trust Him in this process?

We've been having problems with our van for the last two years: among other things, it quits periodically on the road. Usually it starts again after a rest, but in January as we were driving to Reading on a dark, frigid Sunday night, it lost all power and slowed to a crawl. PTL, we had just joined AAA two days before, so were towed the last 80 miles without extra charge. And the next day the van worked fine! The mechanic could find nothing wrong with it. This was perplexing.

We prayed with friends for a solution. Then my computer began having similarserious problems, slowing to more than a crawl. Fortunately there is a computer expert in the office who is very willing to help in such situations. As I was chatting with him about the computer, I mentioned my troubles with the van, and he gave me the name of his mechanic, whom I called. He was willing to take me the next day, diagnosed the problem and solved it (needed a new fuel pump).

Now both my computer and van are working just fine—to God's credit. He is wonderful and worthy of praise. The question is, in the next difficulty will I praise Him before the answer comes? And when He sends another problem which He intends to use to solve the first one? I want to respond in line with our oft-mentioned verse, "He who offers the **sacrifice of thanksgiving** honors me and prepares the way that I may show him the salvation of the Lord" (Ps. 50:23).

Prayer: "Lord, your ways are so different than mine. Help me to trust you when things seem to go from bad to worse, knowing that you are far wiser than I am. May you be glorified by my giving thanks when I don't feel like it today. Amen."

October 3

"Give thanks to the LORD, for he is good; his love endures forever. Let Israel say: 'His love endures forever.' Let the house of Aaron say: 'His love endures forever.' Let those who fear the LORD say: 'His love endures forever.'"

Psalm 118:1-4

Thanks be to you, my Heavenly Father, for your grace-filled work in my life; you are so faithful, so kind, so patient, so wise. You are the One whom I can trust. In contrast, my own thoughts, feelings and perspectives are so up and down, so unstable, so easily influenced by circumstances.

You, being perfect, are unchanging: always good, always wise, always loving, always firm, always gracious. You are continually at work for the good of your Name, the good of your children, the good of every living being on earth.

I praise you for the power of your Name, the might of your Arm, the strength of your Character. There is nothing that can resist your plan, prevent your proposals or withstand your purposes.

Yet in your total Sovereignty, you allow us to make genuine, significant moral and ethical decisions that affect eternity for us and for you. You give us a sphere of responsibility where we can decide to follow you or not.

Your Spirit does the work of giving spiritual sight, shining the light of the gospel into hearts, convicting of sin, righteousness and judgment, revealing the need of all for a Savior, working through blessing and difficulty, goodness and tragedy, dreams and visions, questions and statements. And in the end you offer us repentance and faith. But still, we must respond: "…as many as **received** Him, to them He gave the right to become children of God, to those who believe in His name…" (Joh. 1:12).

You want us as unbelievers to come to you out of love, out of admitting our need, out of seeing your greatness, out of a desire for you. You woo and wait; then we respond and rejoice, or we reject and will be rejected at the last day.

You are awesome in the opportunity and responsibility you give to your enemies, your torturers (every refusal to listen, to obey, to respond grieves your Spirit), your antagonists, your rebels, your accusers (unjustly blaming You, the perfect One for what we ourselves have brought about). Your love is unbelievable, beyond conception, way above human thought, unexpected, incomprehensible, humanly speaking illogical, and amazing.

Praise be to you, the Lover of your enemies, the Redeemer of rebels, the Forgiver of your foes, the Transformer of the intractable, the Adopter of your antagonists. What a God, what a Creator, what a Forgiver, what a Leader, what a Lord, what a King, what a Father, what a Brother, what a Spirit! You are worthy of all worship, adoration and praise.

Prayer: "We give you glory and honor, O Lord; we bow before you, incredulous of your forgiveness and amazed at your grace; we rise up, rejoicing in your redemption and exalting in your love; we stand before you, surrendered in wonder, thankful in obedience. May you be exalted, magnified and lifted on high in our lives today—for you deserve it! Amen."

October 4

"How great is your goodness, which you have stored up for those who fear you, which you bestow in the sight of men on those who take refuge in you."

Psalm 31:19

Do you remember the concept of "God Sightings?" That is, being aware of God working in an obvious way in your life? Recently I've had some very clear smaller ones, (about a 2.3 out of 5), but so obvious and practical that I wanted to share them with you.

Knowing that we'd be home for furlough this year, last summer I thought about buying an old pickup truck to use around the farm in CT. A Dodge 4-wheel drive was what I had in mind. So I'd prayed about it and looked at ads in the paper and almost bought one or two, but in the end decided to wait. Then just before we returned to the Middle East last July, a good friend called to say that he wanted to give me a pickup truck! That was music to my Scottish ears!

I didn't have time to get it before leaving, so Nat picked it up for me and it sat there until we returned in January. And guess what? It was a Dodge 4-wheel drive! That was the first "God Sighting:" He gave me the desire of my heart (Ps. 37:4).

The tires on the truck were worn out, so I decided to switch them with ones from my father's defunct Ford Explorer. That meant dismounting the four tires from each vehicle and then remounting them on the appropriate rims. As I was getting ready to do this I decided, just for kicks, to see if the rims from the Ford would fit on the Dodge. As a former tire dealer, I knew the chance of this working was very slim; even if the holes lined up, the configuration could be wrong, causing the wheel to rub on the front brakes. But, praise God, I was wrong: they fit perfectly! The Ford rims were better, the tires were better and I had much less work! There was the second "God Sighting."

Then a young mechanic friend who was out of work came and tuned it up for me. One brake line was broken, so after repairing it, we worked at getting the air out of the lines. However, he couldn't get the bleeder valve loose on the front brake. I prayed and asked God to help us, but He didn't answer in the way I'd hoped. Because we were unable to get the bleeder valve loose, we ended up having to take the whole mechanism apart—and saw His grace: it was frozen up and broken; if we'd just bled the brakes and tried to use it, we would have ruined the rotors and perhaps had an accident. God's timely answer of "No" to my prayer, forcing us to dig deeper was the third "God Sighting."

These are very mundane happenings, aren't they? There's no obvious spiritual significance to fixing brakes or switching tires. But God was at work and wants us to recognize how He is involved with every aspect of our lives, fitting things together for us in the right way.

To pray about all things and then note how He protects, guides and answers brings great glory to Him. And that's what our lives are all about: worship! Let's not miss the opportunity to glorify Him in the everyday little things of life.

And one last thought: I've found that recognizing and relating "God Sightings" to my unbelieving friends (and calling them "God sightings") often opens up profitable conversations.

Prayer: "Lord God, I praise you for your intimate interest in my life, for your wisdom in wonderfully providing for me. Help me to see the "God Sightings" you insert every day into my experience so I can praise you and share about your love with others. Amen."

October 5

"Let those who fear the LORD say: 'His love endures forever.'"

Psalm 118:4

Praise you, Lord Jesus, that you are my Shepherd, that we can know that whatever comes, you have led us into it, as you led your disciples into the storm on the lake, into the opposition of the crowd, into the pain of your death. You have the larger picture, so we can trust and follow you as you walk with us into the future.

Psalm 118:5-9 says, "In my anguish I cried to the LORD...." This is the proper response to any situation, going right to you, O God, fleeing from self-pity, worry, fretting and anger to embrace your goodness, wisdom and love.

You will respond to our prayer: "In the day of my trouble I will call on you, for you <u>will</u> answer me" (Ps. 86:7). And your answer begins inside: "I sought the Lord and he heard me and delivered me from all my fears" (Ps. 34:4). "In my anguish I cried out to the Lord and he answered by setting me free" (Ps. 118:5).

You, Lord God, are the Freedom-giver—freedom from eternal death, from punishment, from condemnation, from selfishness and Satan, as well as from fretting and fear. You are always at work to set us free from things that bind us, on a deeper level, in a higher way.

Praise be to you for your wisdom, your insight, your understanding. You operate with full knowledge, certain of which thing to work on next, which enemy to defeat, which sin to reveal, which point to camp out on until we respond. You don't guess and fumble as we do in life; you know exactly what is wrong and you know exactly how to deal with it, for you are the Creator, the Healer and the Freedom-bringer.

"The LORD is with me; I will not be afraid" (Ps.118:6). As we look away to you, fear is defeated, fretting is routed, worry is wiped out, unbelief is banished. They cannot stand in the light of your mighty, majestic, magnificent power, of your gracious, great and good heart, of your perfect, powerful, positive character, of your deep, dynamic, everlasting Love.

Seeing you more and more clearly through worship, we can say, "What can man do to me? The LORD is with me; he is my helper. I will look in triumph on my enemies" (Ps.118:6b,7). The certainty of victory in the end, the knowledge of your present and sure help, your understanding of the fickleness and feebleness of man—this knowledge gives us the freedom to trust you in all, to praise in difficulty and disappointment. The victory you promise may come after death, but it will come.

"It is better to take refuge in the LORD than to trust in man. It is better to take refuge in the LORD than to trust in princes" (Ps.118:8,9). You, Lord God, are absolutely trustable while people are ever fickle; you are mighty, people are weak; you are eternal, people are fleeting; you are infinitely wise, people have very limited understanding and knowledge; you see all, people see only a tiny portion of reality; you know the future, people can only guess; you are good by nature, people are evil by nature; you are loving, people are selfish. So who are we going to trust?

To trust in you is always wise, to take refuge in you is always good, to rest in you is always right. Praise be to you, Lord Jesus: Creator and King, Lord and Savior, Judge and Victor.

Prayer: "To you be glory in my life today and forever more. Help me to flee to you with each challenge, problem and difficulty, so the answer can come from you and bring you glory. Help me today to distrust myself and to trust in you instead. Amen."

October 6

"After they prayed, the place where they were meeting was shaken. And they were all filled with the Holy Spirit and spoke the word of God boldly."

Acts 4:31

Their hands and feet were tied to their chairs, their mouths gagged, their throats slashed. By the time the police arrived and finally got the door open, two of them were dead and the third was barely alive. They rushed him to the hospital where he was immediately taken into the operating room. However, his injuries were so extensive that they could not save him, for he, like the others, had been stabbed repeatedly as well as having his throat slit. Killed for their faith in Christ, these men, two of them my friends, had become martyrs.

How are we as believers in this Middle Eastern country to react to these chilling events? The most natural reaction, and the one Satan wants is fear and withdrawal.

Instead we need to ask, "What does God want in this?" His Word speaks clearly: "Blessed are those who are persecuted because of righteousness, for theirs is the kingdom of heaven....Rejoice and be glad, because great is your reward in heaven..." (Matt. 5:10-12).

He desires that we have the attitude of the early disciples who reacted to arrests with this prayer: "'Sovereign Lord,' they said, 'you made the heaven and the earth and the sea, and everything in them'" [first they remembered who He was]... "'Why do the nations rage and the peoples plot in vain?'" [no one can defeat Him] "'Now, Lord, consider their threats and enable your servants to speak your word with great boldness.'" [advance, not retreat was on their minds] (Acts 4:24-30).

In and through this tragedy of our friends being martyred, God wants to awaken and strengthen the church, to deepen unity, to defeat fear and to see the gospel spread more quickly.

If we don't give in to fear, we can be a witness in whatever difficulty comes our way. And this is what is happening among the believers here. Even the tender girl who worked for us in the bookstore, after hearing of these murders said, "I'm no longer afraid to die; death is the doorway to heaven. I just hope I don't die like they did!"

Prayer: "Lord, help me to walk closely with you every day, thinking your Word, obeying your truth, offering the sacrifice of thanksgiving, so that when big challenges come, I will not react in fear but in faith, praising you and moving forward for your glory. Amen."

October 7

"...choose for yourselves this day whom you will serve....But as for me and my household, we will serve the LORD."

Joshua 24:15

Praise you, Lord God, for the many opportunities you give us each day to choose for you or others, for good or evil, for positive or negative, for what is constructive or destructive. Many of these choices seem innocuous and unimportant, but are steps towards or away from where we should be.

To choose to read email before doing my quiet time, to choose to have extra helpings regularly, to choose to look at pictures, images or people which stimulate negative thinking, to choose to speak selfish words—these all move me in the wrong direction.

They bring a sense of guilt and remorse, of emptiness. Over time these build up in my soul, clogging the flow of grace, sapping energy, bringing discontent, discouragement and possibly depression.

Praise You, Lord Jesus, for the continuous working of your Spirit to both convict and guide, to teach truth and encourage, to give perspective and heal.

When I have chosen what is wrong, and feel bad about it, you bring me to confession and cleansing. You forgive me, reminding me of your full rich love and how each failure is a potential doorway to deeper surrender, further breaking and spiritual growth. You remind me of the effectiveness of your death in bringing forgiveness, of your unending love for me, of you knowing all about me and still delighting in me—illogical as that may be, it is full of grace.

Praise you, Lord Jesus, the Lover, the Liberator, the Leader of my soul. You are a marvel, so different from any human being, so pure, so persistent, so powerful, so perfect in your character. You never change, you never vacillate, you never alter your ideas. You are rock solid, ever loving, ever correcting, ever forgiving. With you we can move through the valleys of failure and selfishness, sin and poor choices and still come out to a good place. You faithfully work to convict us, guide us, warn us, call us, protect us, chasten us—with you there is hope for growth and progress. You reverse the second law of thermodynamics, bringing order out of chaos!

I give you honor and praise and glory, Lord Jesus, for to know you is to be given stability in your love, grace in your commitment, hope in your power, peace in your forgiveness, joy in your presence, delight in your beauty, wisdom in your word, strength in your might, help in your compassion and guidance in your wisdom. Your goodness and desires for us are summed up with this: "May the God of hope fill you with all joy and peace as you trust in Him, so that you may overflow with hope by the power of the Holy Spirit" (Rom. 15:13).

Prayer: "Glory be to you, honor be to you, obedience be to you in my life today, Lord God, that your Name may be lifted up before men and angels. Help me to hear you, to comprehend and obey you for your glory. Amen."

October 8

Elijah "came to a broom tree, sat down under it and prayed that he might die. 'I have had enough, LORD,' he said. 'Take my life....'"

1 Kings 19:4

Revival continues in my life: meaning, God is revealing new sins to confess and forsake, and thereby bringing greater freedom and joy. I have a friend whose duty in this process, it seems, is to speak to me in accusations and negatives; this has been helpful in revealing one of the most insidious, joy-stealing sins in my life: self-pity.

Yes, I know, most people wouldn't even consider this a sin; however, it is a statement of unbelief. Is God lovingly in control or not? Giving in to self-pity says, "No. I have to watch out for myself, grabbing what encouragement I can from the words and actions of people around me. If I do well, life is fine, but if I fail, there is no comfort." It also betrays an attitude of entitlement: I deserve to have things go well. This is human thinking: unbelieving and destructive.

God calls us to a higher level of living. When negative, accusatory words are spoken, we can take up grace and truth with thoughts like these: "Thank you, Lord God, for this opportunity to live by faith, remembering that your love and acceptance are sufficient, remembering that to know you is enough for joy, period.

"Thank you for the challenge to rise above and live in the unseen, to rise on the wings of faith above the fiery darts of Satan and to soar in the security of your love. Help me to learn from the truth in this accusation, and to give you glory in my response!" I am slowly learning to do this.

One of my favorite verses for combating self-pity is Psalm 62:5, "My soul, find rest in God alone, for my hope comes from Him." The question for me is this: "Where am I trying to find rest, from where do I expect help?" Hopefully not from people or success or possessions, for those are fickle sources. God only, "is my rock and my salvation, my high tower..." If I live in that truth, "I will never be shaken" (Ps. 62:2).

Prayer: "Lord, when the accusations, difficulties and disappointments come in life, help me reject my tendency to self-pity and instead to think your Truth, praise your name and rest in you. Amen."

A Further Thought on Revival:

Lilias Trotter, a pioneer worker in Algeria in the late 1800s, speaking about a revival among the few workers there said, "There were those who had come longing for blessing…and yet who had not known that God must first break down before He can build up."[9] And so it is true in our lives. Are we willing to be "broken" by seeing our sin, then confessing and repenting so we can be reshaped into a more useful instrument in the Master's hand?

October 9

"This is the day the Lord has made. Let us rejoice and be glad in it."

Psalm 118:24

The above verse is a comprehensive statement, including all kinds of days. It points us to you, Lord, the Sovereign God in whose hands all days are made, whether they are in our eyes good or bad, restful or extremely challenging. You in your wisdom allow, create or send events which are going to be used in your great plan. You allow people to carry out their schemes within certain boundaries, allowing evil people to do evil things, but only within limits. You are able to use their evil to advance your plans and Kingdom (Rev. 9:20).

In the meantime, you continually pour out good on all your creatures, giving us air to breathe, food to eat, friends to share with, work to do, eyes to see, ears to hear, feet to walk, hands to use, skin to protect and feel. You give meaning, direction, provision and protection. You give grace and goodness in the midst of trials and challenges, problems and solutions. You use difficulties to chasten, punish, correct and restore.

You are above all, guiding in all, moving history forward in wisdom and power. In good ways you shake the foundations of our thoughts, the presuppositions of our worldview, the smugness of our systems, the security of our material comfort.

You are intent on greater things than what is on our small minds. You are focused on things of the heart, of the spirit, of eternity. You are working to change us through our problems today to prepare us for our marriage to the Lamb. You know how every detail works towards this and are not reticent to send or allow the storm, the flood, the famine, the fight, the upheaval, the war that will open eyes, plow hearts, draw

---

9 *A Passion for the Impossible: The Life of Lillias Trotter* by Miriam Huffman Rockness

our attention to eternal things, reveal our being poor in spirit, and bring us to our knees before Truth.

You, Lord God are wise, fully informed and aware of every detail of how it will work out. You are determined to do what is good and will do so while being unbending in both mercy and judgment.

Praise be to you for your greatness and goodness, your power and your patience, your persistence and your passion, your lavish love and your consistent correction. You are our Rock, you are our Salvation, you are our high Tower of safety, you are our Shield, you are our Shepherd. You are all that we need, for we were created to partner with you, to work with you.

Praise you for your persistence in pursuing us, possessing us, perfecting us for our future marriage with you, the Lion and the Lamb, our Lord and Leader, our Liberator and Lover.

You have provided us with all we need to live for you; you are so generous and gracious in your provision. We praise you, the totally trustable God, the fully followable King, the completely compassionate Ruler, and the wonderfully wise Leader. Therefore we can say without reservation, "This is the day the Lord has made. Let us rejoice and be glad in it."

Prayer: "We know, Lord God, that all you do is good, and we can praise you for it, with or without understanding what you are doing. Help us to learn your perspective and give thanks with faith in whatever comes. Praise be to you both now and forever. Amen"

October 10

"All men are like grass….The grass withers and the flowers fall, but the word of our God stands forever."

Isaiah 40:6b,8

As part of the revival God began in my life last fall, two of the sins He clearly convicted me of are fear of man and speeding.

Fear of man is basically putting some person's evaluation above what God thinks, while fear of God is carry deeply what He thinks about each thing. I can grasp that pretty well.

That speeding one, though, is a tough one for me. Our house in Connecticut is located on a back road where the speed limit is 30 mph. However, most people drive 50 or 60, some 70. It just gripes me to have to drive so slowly. When I'm driving fast, I feel more in control, more manly, more powerful. Slow driving feels like someone else is in control! Hmmm, come to think of it, that sounds like biblical reality!

In spite of my natural desires, however, in obedience to God, I decided to drive approximately the enforced speed limit, giving myself at least the 5 mph margin that police give drivers in a radar trap.

So here I am driving along sloooowly and up behind me zooms somebody in his shiny new SUV. I can see the driver in my rear view mirror, fretting at getting stuck behind this slow driver—and there's nowhere to pass on this road, so both of us have to suffer with this until we reach the highway 3 miles away.

On top of this I can hear my father's voice from the past commenting on slow drivers: "Well, there's grandpa, out on the road but going nowhere. Why doesn't he just get off the road and let those who have somewhere to go get by?!!!!"

I'm shrinking down inside, embarrassed and frustrated. And what is this embarrassment? It is fear of man. If God says to obey the law, should I let some kid who's in a hurry to hang out at the mall push me to disobey the Creator of the Universe?

As I've stuck to the speed limit with God's help, denying self, driving slowly and ignoring those eager beavers behind me, two things have happened. First, it doesn't bother me so much anymore to drive the speed limit. And second, the thought of what those behind me think also is losing its power. By my refusing to obey my fear of man, it is fading.

There is a lot of freedom in fearing God rather than man; as it says in Proverbs 29:25, "The fear of man brings a snare, but he who trusts in the Lord is safe."

Psalm 62:5 sums up both lessons: "Find rest, O my soul, in God alone, for my hope comes from Him."

Prayer: "Lord, help me to find my rest in you alone, to reject the pressure of the world and those around me to conform; help me instead to live according to your Word, your thoughts, your standards. Amen."

October 11

"The LORD is my strength and my song; he has become my salvation."

Psalm 118:14

You, O God, are the One worthy of worship! "Shouts of joy and victory resound in the tents of the righteous: 'The LORD's right hand has done mighty things!'" (Ps 118:15). You are incredibly Great, completely Sovereign, compassionately Gracious and incomprehensibly Glorious. Your balance of qualities is marvelous, your perfection is magnificent, your complexity is majestic.

In a word, you are Holy: you have no imperfection, no lacks, no foibles, no hang ups, no imbalance, no over-emphasis, no under development, no negatives.

Your individual characteristics seamlessly fit together, complementing each other, working in absolute harmony. Your power acts out of love, your decisions flow from wisdom, your motives are formed in grace, your mercy precedes judgment, your wrath works with love, your glory shines in goodness.

All that you accomplish is done, not just well, but perfectly, without error, without failure, without mistake. You are always right: your desires are right, your motives are right, your timing is right, your actions are right.

You are so great that you can see every detail in every second of every situation, right down to the sub-atomic particles involved. You mind is so expansive that you can comprehend every implication of every decision, from the next second, right on into eternity. You are aware of all that has and will happen in time. You always know what is best and will do it with perfect timing.

You are the God to be feared in awe, to be loved in obedience, to be honored in thanksgiving, to be obeyed because of your wonderful, marvelous, overwhelming, beautiful, and perfect character. To you be honor and glory today in my life and forever, for "The LORD's right hand is lifted high; the LORD's right hand has done mighty things!" (Ps 118:21).

Prayer: "Lord, may the marvel of your majestic character overwhelm me each day. May I love you back with wholehearted obedience. Amen."

October 12

"The fear of man brings a snare, but he who trusts in the Lord is safe."

Proverbs 29:25

"Why didn't you do it this way?" "Why can't you get it right?!!! " How often has something similar been said to me? Such statements are followed by a silent but definite "dummy, question mark!" I strongly dislike being on the receiving end of such questions.

What gets to me even more are broader unjust accusations like: "You *never* do *anything* right!" Or "This is *all* wrong!"--especially when it's really just a matter of opinion. I am immediately goaded to defend myself.

Two days ago I told you how the Lord has been freeing me from the fear of man, using driving the speed limit to show me how that fear was binding me. Now the Lord used that new freedom to bring another break-through with fear of man.

As I've mentioned before, every morning for many years I've meditated/prayed through Ephesians 6:10-18, putting on the armor of God. This past week while doing this, God gave me a new insight from it--which shows the depth and richness of Scripture and the importance of being in it every day! As one author has said, "There is a cumulative value to investing small amounts of time in certain activities [like praying Scripture] over a long period."[10]

Ephesians 6:6 says, "for we do not fight against flesh and blood but against principalities and powers...." While praying that God would help me live this truth, something clicked on both an intellectual and emotional level at the same time. I realized that when I am bothered by accusations, whether implied or direct, I am fighting against people, which is fear of man. I am afraid of what others think and say about me—their opinions matter too much to me—this is fearing man. I'd never made the connection before!

If an accusation isn't true, why do I let it bother me so much? I can let it go, for God knows the truth and that's enough. If it is true, I need to learn from it, ask forgiveness, forgive myself and move on. There is a lot of freedom in fearing God rather than man.

As I have opportunity to apply this lesson, I find myself being more patient, being able to reply with calmness and care instead of rising up in indignant self-defense. What a freedom both for me and those around me! And, guess what--with that new attitude on my part, the other person is often more willing to listen to what I have to say!

Psalm 62:5 again sums up the whole lesson: "Find rest, O my soul, in God alone, for my hope comes from Him."

Prayer: "Lord, help me to see where I am bound by fear of man and give me the courage to reject this and fear you instead, to care deeply what you think rather than what people think. Amen."

October 13

"You are my God, and I will give you thanks; you are my God, and I will exalt you."

Psalm 118:28

Praise be to you, Lord Jesus, for you are the One who has saved us. As we grow in faith, we become more and more aware of the natural depravity of our old nature: "I know that nothing good lives in me, that

---

10 Andy Stanley at
http://www.groupcurriculum.org/questions/questions.jsp?messageID=138

is, in my sinful nature [my flesh]" (Rom. 7:18). And thereby you make us more and more aware of the greatness of the privilege of receiving your grace, of being chosen, called, transformed, adopted and dearly loved—all of this totally undeserved.

We stand before you, not to be condemned, but to be delighted in. We can say with the Psalmist, "Open for me the gates of righteousness; I will enter and give thanks to the LORD" (Ps. 118:19). You opened those gates with your shed blood, Lord Jesus, that we may enter into your holy Presence and live there.

"This is the gate of the LORD through which the righteous may enter" (Ps.118:20). By your grace we have entered this gate because you have made us righteous! We, your evil enemies, your bitter antagonists, your destructive rebels are now your treasured children, your valued partners, your co-heirs!

"I will give you thanks, for you answered me; you have become my salvation" (Ps. 118:21). As I think about this marvelous turnaround of events—from rebel to redeemed, from enemy to embraced, from judged to just—I am ecstatic.

> The condemned becomes the forgiven!
> The criminal becomes the Judge's son!
> The rebel becomes the King's dear child!
> The sinner becomes the Holy One's beloved!
> The spiritually dead one becomes the Creator's living inheritance!
> The evil one becomes an instrument of righteousness!
> The ugly one becomes the beautiful Bride of Christ.

"The LORD has done this, and it is marvelous in our eyes" (Ps. 118:23). It is miraculous, it is majestic, it is monumental, it is marvelous and we praise you for it.

"The LORD is God, and he has made his light shine upon us" (Ps. 118:27). What hope shines out of darkness, what joy comes in the midst of hopelessness, what light shines into utter despair! I give thanks to you, Lord God. I rejoice! I celebrate! I exalt your Name, Lord Jesus, glorify your Grace, honor your Love, magnify your Goodness, revel in your Forgiveness.

"You are my God, and I will give you thanks" (Ps. 118:28). Yes! I will give thanks every day and forever and ever, for you have become MY God! You are worthy of worship, for you are the Great One, the Good One, the Holy One, our Savior, Sustainer, Sanctifier and Transformer. How wonderful to know you, how marvelous to be in your family, how sublime to be your bride.

Prayer: "To you be glory in my motives, thoughts and words today, Lord Jesus. Exalt yourself in and through my life, I pray, for you are worthy. I thank you now for what you will do. Amen."

October 14

"May those who love your salvation ALWAYS say, 'The Lord be exalted.'"

Psalm 40:16b

"God is good," said my friend, and went on to tell how the Lord had answered prayer and worked out a problem. What my friend said is true and right, but God is good not just when He works out the problem; He is also good when things do not turn out well from our perspective. God is good in the midst of an unresolved difficulty, a relational problem, a tragic happening or a disappointment. God is good all the time whether we can sense it, see it or understand it or not.

What made me think more about this was the recent incident of Korean short termers being taken hostage in Afghanistan. At this writing they are still being held after two were shot. The question many are asking is, "Why isn't God answering prayer for their release?"

The answer is that He has a deeper good, a broader plan than just quickly releasing them and relieving everyone's tension. Here is some of the "greater good" that came to mind:

First, in Psalm 40:13-17, while people were trying to kill him, David said: "Let all those who seek you, Lord, rejoice and be glad in YOU." The Lord is teaching all involved to live by faith and to walk in the truth that KNOWING JESUS IS ENOUGH FOR JOY no matter what our circumstances.

Second, He is giving all the captured believers, as well as those praying for them, further opportunity to live the truth of 2 Corinthians 12:9-10, "My grace is sufficient for you, for my power is made perfect in weakness." It's in our weakness that God's power acts and brings Him glory, not in our comfort and security.

Third, God is mobilizing prayer for Afghanistan and the Middle East. He often does this when He's preparing to make advances in an area: He calls us to participate with Him through intercession.

Fourth, He is giving the captured Koreans opportunity to witness to the Taliban as no other short termers get to do! He is giving them grace to live what they believe before their captors as a powerful testimony.

Fifth, He is calling us believers, especially the Korean church, to again count the cost: are we willing to suffer and die for our faith?

Sixth, He is again bringing Isl@m to the world's attention: the fact that there was zero outcry from the Mus.lim world over the capture of these Koreans says something about Isl@m!

And I'm sure there is much more that He is doing. We can trust Him in this because He is the Mighty One—Mighty in wisdom, Mighty in power, Mighty in goodness.

He is moving the world to a conclusion and taking us with Him. Are we going wholeheartedly with praise or reluctantly with complaining? We are called to live in the Truth that God is good, all the time, especially when we can't see it. "May those who love your salvation ALWAYS say, 'The Lord be exalted'" (Ps. 40:16b).

Prayer: "Lord, forgive me for complaining, for in such grumbling I am not believing that you are always good. Help me to live the truth the knowing Jesus is enough for joy, period. Amen."

October 15

"I rejoice in following your statutes as one rejoices in great riches. I meditate on your precepts and consider your ways. I delight in your decrees; I will not neglect your word."

Psalm 119:14-16

Praise you, O Lord God, for your written Word. Without this revelation we could not know you, for you are completely beyond human conception, being Holy, Triune and Eternal.

You are so far above what we see in this fallen world, you are so utterly other, so distinct from all that we are and experience. Without your revealing yourself to us in your acts, appearances and articulation, we would be living in darkness still. Praise be to you, Lord Jesus, that you are Light and that you came into the world to shine on every person (John 1:9), revealing to us the character of the Living, Loving, Literal God.

Your marvelous written Word is a wonder: true and trustable, deep and delightful, revealing and reliable, convicting and convincing, guiding and good, marvelous and mysterious, enlightening and eternal.

Written by forty authors over 1400 years, it is a continual, consistent revelation with no contradictions. You are the center of this story, which shows us your rich, eternal being: your high holiness and deep truths, your righteous wrath and hatred of sin, your pure perfection and great grace, your unquenchable love and wide wisdom in your works.

The Word reflects your character: complex beyond conception, deep beyond divination, trustable beyond time and lavishly loving beyond logic.

Praise be to you that you are a revealing God, that you desire us to see you, that you have opened the way for us to know you first as

Creator, then as King and Lord, then as Savior, then as Father and Brother and finally as our Bridegroom.

Praise you that there is no end to the revelation in you of your work in your Word, of your wonderfully infinite and intricate being. As we read it, study it and memorize it, new truths surface to give us more understanding of your attributes and actions. Praise you that your Word has depth beyond knowing, power beyond comprehension and wisdom beyond words.

Praise you that the whole of our lives we will be learning from your Word with the guidance of the Holy Spirit, seeing new and love-inspiring things about you--the timeless, perfect, unchanging, ever stable God.

May we say and obey with the Psalmist:

"I seek you with all my heart;
    do not let me stray from your commands.
I have hidden your word in my heart
    that I might not sin against you.
Praise be to you, O LORD;
    teach me your decrees.
With my lips I recount
    all the laws that come from your mouth" (Ps.119:10-13).

Prayer: "Lord, forgive me for not cherishing and delighting in your Word more. Help me to be persistent and consistent in reading, memorizing and meditating on your Truth each day so that I may know you better and better and be transformed by the renewing of my mind. Amen."

October 16

"Keep your servant also from willful sins; may they not rule over me. Then will I be blameless, innocent of great transgression."

Psalm 19:13

"Ok," said Jack, "Here's what we will discuss today." He wrote "Confessing Ahead" across the top of the white board.

Dave's eyebrows went up. "What does that mean?"

"When God began answering my prayer for revival, He did it by pointing out sins I needed to deal with more seriously. The initial four or five that the Spirit brought to mind grew to a list of fifty-two!

"The idea came that while praying through and putting on the armor of Ephesians 6, it would be good to confess to God my tendency to sin in these areas. This is 'confessing ahead.' I've begun confessing a few on three or four mornings a week."

"So what's the purpose of doing this?" Dave asked.

"It has proved helpful in three major ways," Jack replied. "First, it reminds me of my weakness in each of these areas, preparing me for being tempted there. Second it is a chance for fresh surrender and strengthening of my resolve to stand against these temptations with the armor of God—it is a kind of 'refocusing' on Truth. And third, it opens the way for further conviction."

Dave looked up from his notebook. "So exactly how do you 'confess ahead?'" he asked.

Jack leaned back in his chair, "In praying Ephesians 6:10, asking God to help me be strong in Him and the power of His might, I pray something like this. 'Lord I confess that I tend to let the fear of man, fear of others' thoughts influence me more than your thoughts. Forgive me and help me to reject fear of man and walk in the knowledge of your presence instead.

"'Lord, I confess to you my tendency to think lustful thoughts: help me to flee from them, remembering how destructive they are. Help me to 'not notice,' to bounce my eyes and thoughts away from sexual stimulation to the light of your beautiful, pure character.

"'I confess my tendency to have critical and negative thoughts and words. Help me to reject them while they are in the forming stage, to neither think them nor speak them....'" Jack paused. "Does that give you the idea?"

Dave nodded.

Jack was quiet for a moment. "I think of this 'confessing ahead' as a kind of rehearsal for the battle of the day which is to come: it is thinking truth and committing myself to applying it before the actual attack occurs. It is practicing the proper and powerful response so it will be more natural to me when temptation comes. I encourage you to begin this practice as part of equipping yourself with the power of God."

–from the book *EQUIPPED!*

Prayer: "Lord, help me to be aware of my areas of weakness, to be consistent in confession, and to learn to confess ahead so I'll be ready for the battle today. Amen."

October 17

"I run in the path of your commands, for you have set my heart free."

Psalm 119:32

Lord Jesus, in your incarnation you showed us how to live a life of weakness and dependency. In your whole life on earth you did only what the Father told you. You had to pray about everything. At times you were hampered by the unbelief of those around you, so were unable to do miracles (Matt. 13:58).

We live in such human weakness within: we are hampered by our own unbelief as well as by our rebellion and pride. Praise you for giving us your Word, which shows the way out of the swamp of pride, selfishness and the desire to gain security by controlling all the events around us.

Praise you for all you did in having this Revelation written down for us, in exactly the words you desired, then preserving it, getting it translated and giving us your Spirit to teach us what it says.

"I run in the path of your commands, for you have set my heart free" (Ps. 119:32). This is echoed in the NT: "You will know the truth and the truth will set you free" (John 8:32). You, Lord Jesus, are the Path Maker, the Freedom Bringer, the Guidance Giver. Your Spirit and Word are the means to bring your freedom to us as we embrace your Way.

Praise you that in your Word you provide us with Truth, giving spiritual sight and being the Way to freedom from self, sin and Satan. Praise you for our weakness that drives us to be strong in you; for the path of your Word to run on; and for the working of your Spirit to keep us on track.

My desire is to live like the Psalmist who wrote, "My soul is consumed with longing for your laws at all times.... Your statutes are my delight; they are my counselors.... I have chosen the way of truth; I have set my heart on your laws.... I hold fast to your statutes, O LORD; do not let me be put to shame" (Ps. 119:20,24,30,31).

I praise you for the opportunity yesterday to live this, as we went to the airport to pick up visitors and couldn't find them. What you have taught in your Word came to mind: that it is good to be weak, and in offering the sacrifice of thanksgiving your salvation comes (Ps 50:23). You led me to praise you for the situation; you brought peace and freedom from anger, fear and frustration. Then I could think clearly and you gave me an idea of where to look, and there they were!

Normally, once things were resolved, out of my frustration and shame at my incompetency, I would have been unkind to the others involved, venting my anger on them. Instead, at the direction of your Spirit to heed your Word and run in the path of freedom, I could let go of my anger, hold on to truth and rise above my natural responses. Then I could be an example, give you glory by resting in you and see again the outworking of your promises. Praise you, Lord God for your goodness and grace poured out upon us through your Word applied in our weakness and failures.

You are the great Transformer, the mighty Corrector, the wise Shepherd, the persistent Counselor, leading us through the swamp of selfishness and pride out into the green pastures of your pleasure. Glory be to you, O Triune God, Honor be to you, Power be to you this day.

Prayer: "Lord, help me to run in the paths of freedom, laying aside my pride, selfishness and independence; help me to live in the light of your Word, to rejoice in my weaknesses knowing they will provide me another opportunity to give you honor and glory in my life. Amen."

October 18

"My flesh and heart may fail, but God is the strength of my heart and my portion forever."

Psalm 73:26

As I look out the window, the morning sun creeps over the horizon. As it emerges, everything is lit with a burst of glory: the sun's first rays shine golden on the maple leaves of fall, their beauty doubled by their reflection in the pond. The still-green grass, clothed in frost, shimmers like a thousand diamonds. Overhead a flock of geese wings towards the south, sent on their way by the barking of our faithful dog, Jack. Such is the beauty of our home in Canterbury.

And from this home we are again called away—it is never easy to leave this beauty and our many friends, especially at this time when we go to a place yet unknown. However, we are called by the One who is trustable. He knows the future and has reminded us that the loveliness we leave behind is only a dim shadow of the beauty He has in store for us, both in service and in Heaven.

Psalm 73:25 speaks of this: "Whom have I in heaven but you, and earth has nothing I desire besides you!"

To live such a truth! That is where I would like to be--so in love with God that all here on earth pales, fading into the background, serving only as a picture frame for the character of Christ.

We can only move towards such an understanding by letting go and moving on when He calls. The pain of separation is there--we will still miss our friends, home, dog and pond as we return to the browns and greys of the dust-covered cities of the Middle East--but thinking Truth brings both perspective and joy: a fierce kind of joy that comes from giving up what we can't keep anyway.

Prayer: "Lord God, more beautiful than any scene on earth, more valuable than all the wealth of the world, more loving than all mothers put together, more powerful than all the energy of every star in the universe--You are the One to love, to worship, to honor, to obey. Help me to nurture my first love for you, to be in your Word every day, to praise you in all things, to live in the light of your love so that I may bring glory to you each day. Amen."

October 19

"My salvation and my honor depend on God; he is my mighty rock, my refuge."

Psalm 62:7

"Trust in him at all times, O people; pour out your hearts to him, for God is our refuge" (Ps. 62:8). You, Lord Jesus, are the only unchanging point/person/aspect of all existence. You are unchanging because you are perfect, as you have always been and you always will be. In you there is no lack, no development, no shifting, no change.

You are our Rock, our Salvation, the High Tower of eternity. Nothing can shake you or your purposes, no one is strong enough to dissuade you, to dislodge you, to dispute you. You are the only Refuge, the only Shelter, the only safe Place in the universe, in existence, in eternity.

Praise you that you are not distant, cold, uncaring or mechanical in your relationship with your creation. You are active, involved, compassionate and gracious. You are always there: real, strong and loving. You are caring, wise, intimate and guiding. You are all knowing, all seeing, all powerful, all forgiving. You are the most high, yet readily stoop down to love your miniscule creatures. You are great, yet involved with every tiny detail. You are mighty yet tender. You are righteous yet forgiving.

Who is like you? Who can comprehend you? Who can escape you? Who is not loved by you? You are a marvel—no, you are *the* marvel of our existence, too good to be true yet absolutely true, too real to be ignored, too great to be resisted, too wonderful to be the product of man's imagination.

What a high and powerful privilege it is to know about you, then to actually know you, then to be honored by being made your child! "My salvation and my honor depend on God...."

Praise you, Lord Jesus, that all we need flows from you, and that you are truly, totally trustable. When we deserve condemnation, you give us pardon. When we deserve punishment, you give us salvation. When we deserve shame, you give us honor. When we deserve failure you give us grace. What a God! What a Savior! What a Lord!

You are, "my mighty rock, my refuge." In the midst of the swamp of this world, filled with the quicksand of selfishness, the bottomless mud of manipulation and the shifting sands of sin, you are my Rock, my Mighty Rock and Fortress: unshakable, unsinkable, unmovable, unchangeable.

And you are my Refuge, a place of protection, provision, personal safety, powerful help. You are the One to be trusted and command us to do so: "Trust in him at all times, O people;"

When things go well, we must trust in you, rejecting the illusion that our success is from our hard work, our intelligence, our training, our resources—it is because you are blessing us. And when things go badly, we must trust in you, for we know that you are good, wise and powerful, that what you are allowing is part of the overall plan to bring an end to evil, as well as part of your personal plan to bring maturity to me and glory to you.

"…pour out your hearts to him, for God is our refuge." (Ps 62:8). What a privilege and wonderful invitation, to pour out our inner being to you, telling you all we are thinking, feeling and wanting.

You, of course, already know these things, but for us to come and tell you is an act of worship, trusting you, being transparent before you, treating you as the true God, with the honesty and obedience that you deserve. And thank you for your Word by which we can measure what is in our hearts, rejecting what is of self, what is neutral and then affirming what is good, of you.

Praise be to you, Lord Jesus, the gracious, good and great God, full of mercy, complete in holiness and overflowing in grace. You are worthy today of trust, of obedience, of praise, of honor, of surrender.

Prayer: "May you be glorified in my thoughts, motives, desires, words and actions today, Lord, by my trust, praise and obedience. Amen."

October 20

"The fear of the LORD is a fountain of life, turning a man from the snares of death."

Proverbs 14:27

The "revival adventure" in my life continues, this time with the fear of man. During a recent unhappy conversation, it came to me that fear of man is essentially giving others power over me. Before I do something, like raising my hands in a church service, I often consider what others will think about my actions or words, and alter my plan so as to avoid their disapproval as much as possible.

When I allow the fear of others and what they think to control me, I have given them permission to use their attitudes, words and actions to beat me into submission.

God confirms this, saying that fear of man is putting people in the place of God. "Listen to Me, you who know righteousness, you people in whose heart is My law: do not fear the reproach of men, nor be afraid of their insults. For the moth will eat them up like a garment.... But My righteousness will be forever..." (Isa. 51:7,8).

We must learn what God thinks (being in His Word regularly) and value it far more than what people think. This is hard because we can see people, but God is invisible. However, when we honor God by believing Him, what others say or imply about us begins to lose its power and great vistas of freedom can open up to us.

In a recent interchange, a friend uttered some words of disapproval for what I'd said, and added a couple of "zingers" about my manhood to emphasize the point. I had three choices: bow my neck to his thoughts and stuff my hurt; reply in kind; or, remembering who I am in Christ, to deal graciously with the issue without attack or anger.

Because the Holy Spirit had been working with me on this, setting me free from the trap of fear of man, I could let go of my anger, hold onto the Truth that I am safe in Him, and rise above the hurt. I calmly asked my friend if the same things could be expressed without resorting to "zingers." The rest of the talk went much better.

We need to take back the power we've granted others over us, and listening more carefully to what God has to say about each thing in our lives. We must measure ourselves by His standards, confessing and repenting where we are living by the standards of others or ourselves, then praising Him and obeying, doing what is right. We can hold up the shield of faith by offering the sacrifice of thanksgiving and ward off the blows that Satan tries to rain down on us through the words and actions of others.

Prayer: "Lord, help me to walk in fear of you, standing in awe of your deep wisdom, giving great weight to what you think and let the negatives of people bounce off the shield of faith. May you ever loom larger and may people be smaller in my evaluation of what I should do or not. May you be glorified as I care deeply about what you think. Amen."

October 21

"Your statutes are my delight; they are my counselors."

Psalm 119:24

I feel somewhat restless, disturbed, unsettled; I am not sure why. But in the midst of this, the rock-solid, unshakable Truth is: Knowing Jesus is Enough for Joy, Period! Praise be to you, Lord Jesus, that you are unchanging, faithful, trustable, reliable, always good and always there. And when things are right with you, they are right, however I may feel. Whatever troubles me will be dealt with in your time and power and can be released to you. You are enough; in you I am complete. Praise you that you are the King and I am your child.

Thank you for your promises, that you will always "preserve my life according to your word." "...strengthen me according to your word." "...be gracious to me through your law" (quotes here and below from Ps. 119:20-32).

Your Word is the clear measure of what you will do. Because you and your Word are good, I can trust you with all my heart, and I can appeal to you according to your Word: "I hold fast to your statutes, O LORD; do not let me be put to shame." You will always come through just as you have promised.

"I have chosen the way of truth; I have set my heart on your laws." Your way is the only way for me. With your strength I can trust and obey.

"I run in the path of your commands, for you have set my heart free." Free to follow, free to obey, free to say "no" to what is contrary to your Word, free to let go of what is temporal and hold on to what is eternal, free to rise above the everyday events of life, to live in the truth of your Sovereignty, of your goodness, of your protection.

As I am, at the moment, trying to buy a ticket to the conference I will attend in November, and keep getting rejected by the system, it is a certainty that you are doing something here, directing me away from what is not good, leading me towards something better.

Perhaps you are making it possible to meet someone; perhaps you are protecting me from lost luggage, a problem, a crash, a delay; perhaps you are going to give me a better seat or connection or place to sleep.

I do not know, but I do know you: that you are absolutely trustable and that I can praise you for the outcome in spite of my natural tendency to complain.

Therefore instead of frustration, there arises a sense of excitement, of adventure as you beckon me to follow you on a trip whose destination is not yet clear. You are the One who will decide, and I can say, "Yes!" to following without knowing the outcome. [You will read about the outcome of my attempt to buy a plane ticket in October 23rd's devotion.]

In the meantime, I praise your holy and trustable Name, I exalt your faithful and fruitful character, I magnify your powerful and productive being, I glorify your wise and knowing heart. Today is in your hand, therefore whatever comes will be good, whatever happens I can praise for, because you are only good, only great, only glorious, only gracious.

Prayer: "Lord, I praise you for what will come today. I trust you to bring what is good. Help me to rest in you when things don't go my way, to remember that you, the Sovereign God, will work what is best for me, whether I can see it or not, understand it or not. To you be glory. Amen."

October 22

"My eyes are ever on the LORD, for only he will release my feet from the snare."

Psalm 25:15

I ran down the street, my hands loaded with heavy shopping bags and a briefcase of truth, desperate to escape the thugs chasing me. Suddenly a shadow crossed my path. Looking up I saw a hot air balloon overhead with a rope dangling down within my reach. I glanced back to see the thugs closing in on me. Looking down at my bags, I realized in a flash how worthless these things were, and dropped all but the briefcase. Then, grabbing the rope, I was lifted to safety by the rising balloon, leaving the thugs behind.

This figuratively happens in my life every day. It is the illustration of following three biblical principles: Let Go, Hold On, Rise Above. As I struggle through life, weighed down by all kinds of nonessentials, I give Satan opportunity to catch me. At the same time God offers a way to rise above Satan's attacks.

As it says in Colossians 3:1 "Since you have been raised with Christ, set your hearts on things above, not on the passing things of earth." To illustrate how this works, let's ask three questions.

Let go of what? All that is temporal. This encompasses almost everything in life. To 'let go' means, to keep things in an open hand, to give them up to God and let Him decide which things to take and which ones are to remain. It means setting our hearts on things above, not on things on the earth. It means denial of self, giving up my impatience, selfishness, pride, "rights" and materialism, recognizing that holding on to them is carrying detrimental baggage that makes me vulnerable to attack. I'm going to lose them anyway (the definition of temporal), so why cling to them?

Hold on to what? To all that is eternal. This means, thinking Truth and acting on it: when I am impatient, I need to think, "Actually God is in control of the timing here; I can trust Him." In order to do this, we need to know the Truth, meaning we need to spend time with God and in His Word every day.

Rise above what? The everyday hassles, hurts and difficulties as well as the big, painful events. As we relax in Him, trust Him to deal with it, join Him in what He is doing, He will raise us above the everyday fight so we can see things from a greater height, to understand His perspective, and make better decisions. Truly, "My soul finds rest in God alone" (Ps. 62:1).

Prayer: "Lord, help me to recognize what I must let go, what I should hold onto, and then help me to do that, so I can rise above with you to live in the atmosphere of truth and praise! Amen."

October 23

"Teach me, O LORD, to follow your decrees; then I will keep them to the end. Give me understanding, and I will keep your law and obey it with all my heart."

Psalm 119:33,34

Praise you, Lord, for the negative feelings I had last night—a combo of not getting a lot done, reading in my book of two negative marriages and having a hurt foot. Thank you for the reminder by your Spirit to think truth: to remember Psalm 62, that my soul finds rest in you alone; that my feelings are not the correct measure of anything; that you are my unchanging Rock, Salvation and high Tower.

"I will walk about in freedom, for I have sought out your precepts" (Ps.119:45). Through your Word, your principles and your precepts, Lord, you give freedom. You provide insight, grace, power and understanding that free us from the hang-ups, baggage, wrong ideas and poor examples we've had in life.

Praise be to you because you continually draw me to yourself, speak intimately with me and are personally, constantly, consistently involved in the happenings in my life. You do these things because you are my loving Lord, the wise One, my gracious King, the great Giver of good, my righteous Redeemer.

Thank you for the practical ways you help me, like your guidance in getting plane tickets yesterday where you prevented me from buying the first possibility, and led me in finding a better schedule and lower price on a different website.

You, Lord, are the great and gracious God, who involves yourself in the tiny details of my small and insignificant existence. You are good through and through. I praise and thank you for your wonderful work in me: undeserved, uncalled for, humanly speaking illogical, but consistent with your Agape Love character.

"I delight in your commands because I love them" (Ps.119:47). Your commands are wonderful, they are radiant, giving light, giving joy, giving grace. To obey them is good, to love them is better. To you be honor and praise today and forever, for you are good.

"...and I meditate on your decrees." To memorize, to personalize, to pray through passages bring change, power, wisdom and grace. Praise you for your greatness, your love, your truth, your light, your joy. Thank you that you are the measure of what is true, what is valuable and what is right. I give you honor and glory, praise and thanksgiving for the deep, rich and undeserved privilege of knowing you.

Prayer: "'Turn my heart toward your statutes and not toward selfish gain. Turn my eyes away from worthless things; preserve my life according to your word' (Ps. 119:36,37). Amen."

October 24

"I will say of the LORD, "He is my refuge and my fortress, my God, in whom I trust. Surely he will save you from the fowler's snare...."

Psalm 91:2,3a

I finished reading the excerpt from my book and looked around at the writers' group for their reaction. Silence was followed by the first trickle of criticism; that opened the gates for a deluge of suggestions. The comments, for the most part, missed the mark of what the book was about.

I felt myself getting more and more defensive. I'd expected some positive comments along with the criticism, and finally supplied those myself! Fortunately I was able to contain my turmoil and not say anything destructive, but inside I was angry, unhappy and disappointed.

The problem was with me, not the critics. We came to the writers' group to share our works for the purpose of getting input. I made the mistake of sharing a portion from the middle of the book; I should have started from the beginning to give them more of a feel for where it was going. My biggest mistake, however, was looking for affirmation from the wrong place.

Psalm 91 came up in my reading the next day, and there, staring me in the face, was the key to my prison cell of turmoil: "He who dwells in the shelter of the Most High will rest in the shadow of the Almighty." The Most High, the Final Authority, the All-Knowing God is the One I must look to for approval, not to men. He has prepared for us a shelter of Truth and Light; if we don't dwell in it, we expose ourselves to attacks of the enemy. God's shelter is His character, His revealed Truth, His salvation, His declaration of who we are in Christ. He is the One who approves of us in Christ. We don't need that from anyone else.

When we dwell in His shelter, we are given the possibility of resting in the protection of the Almighty, the Undefeated One, the Commander of the Hosts of Heaven, the Creator who brought out the stars one by one and knows each by name. No one can attack and defeat us while we rest in His shadow.

Staying in His protection is a privilege we can chose or reject. The only condition is to willfully dwell in His shelter, living in the Truth of all He is and provides, something I failed to do at the writers' group, but could quickly begin to do again as the Spirit pointed out my sins of self-pity and seeking worth in the wrong place.

Praise God for His great patience, His wisdom in exposing our sins and His goodness in providing forgiveness, guidance, grace and restoration.

Prayer: "Lord, help me to dwell in the shelter of Truth you have given. Alert me to when I'm thinking in just human terms, when I am giving credence to my feelings rather than Truth. Lead me to continual rest in your shadow today. Amen."

October 25

"I will run in the path of your commands, for you have set my heart free."

Psalm 119:32

My heart has felt distant from you, Lord. Being out of my schedule can bring a sense of disorientation. However, my stability, peace and sense of rightness should actually come from you alone, O God, not from the structure of my life.

As your Word says, "My God is my rock in whom I take refuge. He is my shield, the horn of my salvation, my stronghold" (Ps. 18:2b). So, whether I am firmly in a protecting schedule, or my life is chaotic, you are there, Lord God: solid, sure, always loving, kind and firm. You are my Light, my Love, my Life.

This unsettledness is actually a positively powerful thing, surfacing my wrong dependence on accomplishment, achievement, action, maintaining control and being good in my own strength. It points me to repentance and setting my eyes and heart on you, Lord Jesus.

So I turn my eyes to you and praise you, Lord God: my Triune, Eternal, Personal and Holy God—utterly other, entirely independent, sincerely sinless and incomprehensibly complex. You created me, chose me, cleansed me, claimed me as your child, commissioned me to special service, and I stand before you dearly loved, delighted in, deeply cared for, doted on and positively dependent on you.

What a wonder! What I actually deserve as a sinner is condemnation, punishment, eternal separation, failure, suffering, death and hell. Your great and marvelous grace—ever flowing, never ending, always giving—pours continually into our lives, bringing undeserved forgiveness, cleansing, transformation, strengthening, guidance, goodness, power and wisdom.

To live in the light of your presence, to walk in the shining paths of your righteousness, to bask in the radiance of your love, to see by the brilliant illumination of your Word—these are the privileges of the children of God and we praise you for them.

We are saved by grace, sealed by grace, sanctified by grace, strengthened by grace. In you, Lord Jesus, we are safe, for you are the Most High, you are the Almighty, you are the undefeated and undefeatable One. In you we can rest. Glory be to your Name!

Prayer: "I praise you for what your power and grace will do in and through me today, in spite of how I may feel and fail. May all be for your glory. Help me to focus on you, draw my stability, wisdom, strength and understanding from you, Lord Jesus. May I honor you in all I do today. Amen."

October 26

"He reached down from on high and took hold of me; he drew me out of deep waters. He rescued me from my powerful enemy, from my foes, who were too strong for me."

Psalm 18:16,17

Life is unpredictable. We never know what will come: an easy, comfortable day, or one with an accident, sickness or disturbing news. The culture we live in teaches us that comfort is the highest value, and that anything that disturbs our comfort is bad.

Not so in Scripture. What is truly bad is what harms us spiritually, not what makes us uncomfortable. What disturbs our comfort may be the most helpful thing in our lives for growth and deepening.

The question each of us must face is: what is my theology of suffering? The following is an example of this, written by a 16-year-old girl, who grew up in the Middle East, struggling to adjust to a new culture (America), to loneliness and to Christian acquaintances who aren't interested in spiritual things.

"I think that God allows difficulty and suffering into our lives to teach us about Him and strengthen our faith and our trust in Him. If we never faced suffering, it would be hard for us to see the depth of His love and appreciate how beautiful He truly is—just like we don't truly appreciate the light until we see darkness.

"It also teaches us that contentment isn't based on circumstances. If I were happy and cheerful all the time because nothing ever went wrong for me, I would never learn the true meaning of being thankful. Nor would my worship and praise be as sincere.

"Going through trials helps us, even forces us to grow. Through my loneliness I have learned more and more what a wonderful friend I have in Jesus.

"And what a patient teacher he is. So often I get stuck in my self-pity box, thinking about all my hardships; but time and time again God convicts me and brings me to a better place. I am so glad He doesn't give up on me because I sure feel like giving up an awful lot!

"Our rest and shelter are in Him. When all else fails, God does not. When all else changes, God stays the same. After a hard day at school and when the tears flow down, He encourages my soul with His truth and His promises.

The biggest and best thing that He provides is Himself. I truly am thankful that I belong to God and am His child because right now it is impossible for me to be joyful without Him but with Him all things are possible!"

She is a great example to follow with her focus on Jesus in the midst of trials.

Prayer: "Lord, when I am frustrated, lonely, unhappy or stressed, help me to flee to you, to pour out my heart to you and fill it again with your Word. Help me to find my sufficiency in you, for you are fully sufficient—all the time! Amen."

October 27

"I run in the path of your commands, for you have set my heart free."

Psalm 119:32

Praise be to you, my Lord and my God, for you have set my heart free, free from the rule of Satan, free from the power of self, free from the chains of sin—as your child I can actually make choices now because you have brought me out of the kingdom of darkness into the Kingdom of Light.

"The way of the wicked is like deep darkness; they do not know over what they stumble" (Pro. 4:19). You have set me free from a life of fumbling and stumbling in the dark, bringing me out into a life of light. You, Lord Jesus, are the light of life and have caused the light of salvation to shine deeply into my heart. You have invited me to walk on the path of the righteous, illuminated by your Word, bringing me ever more into the full light of your day. Now in your grace I can choose the shining way of Truth revealed by your Word and your Spirit.

You are setting my heart free from fear, from bondage to selfishness, from lust, from anger, frustration and negative thinking. You have set my feet free from the shackles of Satan that led me to shuffle down the path of sin, to choose what is destructive, to react with violent, knee jerk negatives.

    Now I can run free in the path of goodness, my feet unbound, my legs strengthened by your Spirit, my eyes opened by the light of your Word, my soul ready to soar.

You are setting me free from the anxiety and fear expressed in my hot anger when things around me are out of my control, when I get lost on a trip, when people fail to follow through, when I feel like a fool.

You are setting me free with the knowledge that in you I am secure, that you are my Shepherd, you are my King, that you are taking me to and through whatever you know is best. In you I am significant and can rest in this no matter how I may act, feel or fail.

You are setting me free from the fear of man, cutting the emotional ties to what others think or value or want. You have established a new connection from your heart to mine. You have given me the knowledge of your presence and a desire to obey you rather than my twisted self-centered doubts and the desires and of those around me.

You are setting me free from impatience helping me to grasp that your plans are unfolding at the right pace; your time table cannot be thwarted; things will come to pass at the optimum time.

You are setting me free from being tied to what I can see. You have opened my eyes to the eternal, to the supernatural, to the working of your hand in all around me. God sightings come often.

You are setting me free from pride, showing me how small, how feeble, how powerless, how sinful I am in myself. You are revealing the depth of the depravity of my natural man and the height of the holiness you have given your children.

You are also showing me your inexorable power and inviting me to join you in your work. You are setting me free from working too hard and are leading me into working smart, away from doing my own thing and into joining you through prayer and seeing you bring all to pass.

    Prayer is your idea and part of bringing freedom. It is your invitation for us to join you in your great work. It is a powerful means of being transformed by you. It is tapping into your strength, your wisdom, your goodness, your desires and having them flow in, through and out of us to those around us.

In providing this broad and beautiful freedom, you are moving me mightily towards living like Asaph who, after repenting of his selfishness and self-pity, could say, "Whom have I in heaven but you and earth has nothing I desire besides you. My flesh and my heart may fail, but God is the strength of my heart and my portion forever" (Ps. 73:25,26).

Eternal praise be to you, O Lord, for you have truly, powerfully, continually, eternally set my heart free!

Prayer: " Help me, Lord, to run freely in the paths of your commandments, in the light of your Truth, in the joy of your presence, that I may give you glory today. Amen"

October 28

"Set your minds on things above, not on earthly things. For you died, and your life is now hidden with Christ in God."

Colossians 3:2,3

The idol was standing there in the trophy case in my heart, right in plain sight, but I didn't see it. Like many sins in my life, I overlooked it until the Lord powerfully and painfully shone His light on it. Each step in the ongoing revival in my life has been like this: God putting His finger on the next area of sin that needs surrender to Him.

Perhaps the reason I didn't notice this next sin is that it didn't look at all like an idol. Of course, anything can become an idol: all I have to do is set my heart on it, to declare, "Without this I can't be happy!" Knowing this makes idol hunting easier: whenever I'm unhappy, all I have to do is look at what disappointed me, and there is an idol to repent of and repudiate.

This one was so obvious, so mundane that I'm embarrassed to even mention it, but I'll give you a clue: it showed up on February 3 when the Patriots football team, after a perfect season, lost their final game, the Super Bowl. I was amazed at how it affected me: I had trouble sleeping that night and every time I thought about it, which was often, sadness came over me.

So what was my idol? It was not being a Patriots fan. Nor was it following the football outcomes. These are acceptable hobbies. My mistake was hanging my happiness on the Patriots having a perfect record. The reality is they had a great season even though they lost the Super Bowl.

It is normal to be a little sad when your team loses. It is not normal to be so down that you have to go through the grief cycle, to be almost depressed about an event that in the grand sum of history has zero importance.

The real significance of this loss has much more to do with what God is doing in the team, the coach and the fans through it. He is exposing the unstable, untrustable, unsound sources of our earthly happiness and contentment. If these are not found in God, we've been making idols and therefore setting ourselves up for unhappiness!

Another factor in this idol is that I like to be linked to a winner, as the Patriots were this season. It gives a sense of significance, of excitement, of glamour. In the end, though, no human being or institution is always a winner; there will always be losses and let downs.

In contrast, as true followers of Christ we are tied to *the* Winner, Jesus, who has defeated death and the devil. He is triumphing each day in helping His children to reject temptation, to live godly lives and in bringing many new believers into His Kingdom; in the end He will complete his triumph over all evil. And He is inviting us to join Him in His great victories and to share in His glory:

"When Christ, who is your life, appears, then you will also appear with Him in glory" (Col. 3:4). And "all kinds of trials…have come so that the proven genuineness of your faith…may result in praise, glory and honor when Jesus Christ is revealed" (1 Pet. 1:6,7).

God is moving history to a conclusion and taking us with Him! Are we following or are we camping out in idol land?

I praise God I was disappointed on February 3rd, for He had far greater things for me (and many others) than a perfect season for my team! This loss took my eyes off the temporal and got them back on the eternal.

Prayer: "Lord, help me to set my heart on things above, to live in the stability of your character, the certainty of your victory, the security of your power. Help me to be quickly aware of idols in my life and confess them immediately. May you be glorified in this. Amen."

October 29

I will walk about in freedom, for I have sought out your precepts.

Psalm 119:45

Praise you, Lord, that I awoke this morning and there you were, waiting to present me with a new day. You are fresh and strong, ready to share this day with me. You will lead me through the maze of events, all of which you already know about, having prepared all in detail. My part is to listen, praise and obey. Guide me in doing this well.

I praise you that you are the Rock, the Shepherd, the High Tower and the Light of my life, shining steadily whether I can sense your presence or not. On you I can depend, for you are wise, you are gracious, you are immutable. In the light of these Truths, may the words of the Psalmist be my attitude:

"You are my portion, O LORD;
    I have promised to obey your words.
    I have sought your face with all my heart;
        be gracious to me according to your promise.

I have considered my ways
    and have turned my steps to your statutes.
I will hasten and not delay
    to obey your commands.
Though the wicked bind me with ropes,
    I will not forget your law.
At midnight I rise to give you thanks
    for your righteous laws.
I am a friend to all who fear you,
    to all who follow your precepts.
The earth is filled with your love, O LORD;
    teach me your decrees" (Ps. 119:57-64).

What a powerful picture of a man's willing response to the revealed Creator and His Word: full, complete, wholehearted, enthusiastic surrender and commitment to obedience. May we do the same.

Prayer: "May my commitment to you, the eternal, living God, be that of the Psalmist today. May you be exalted, glorified, honored and praised in my life throughout the entire day. Amen."

October 30

"But the path of the righteous is like the light of dawn, which shines brighter and brighter until full day."

Proverbs 4:18

We are trying to look ahead to see what our future will be. Should we stay in our Middle Eastern country and get my mother-in-law to move here? Should we move to Germany and take her into our home? Should we get her into assisted living? There are no clear answers; all we can see ahead of us is fog and some indistinct shapes, vague possibilities. We can't move ahead with any plans, so we stay where we are, waiting for direction.

    This is uncomfortable, living in limbo, but it is also a place where we can choose our responses: frustration or faith, distress or discipline, petulance or praise.

    Out front there may be only fog, but if we look up, overhead the sky is clear, the sun (Son) is shining brightly, giving warmth and encouragement. We know that with time the sun will dispel the fog and make our way clear. We just have to wait for guidance which will come in His time, and in the meantime, live in the truth that, "My soul finds rest in God alone" (Ps 62:1).

We need to be concerned not so much with "What will we do in the future?" but with "What are we doing now?" Will we spend our time straining our eyes, trying to make out what lies ahead, or will we gaze at the gracious Son, enjoying the warmth of that relationship, the certainty of His presence and the security of His power, being obedient in the tasks we have here and now? Worry or worship, which will it be?

In worship and trust we are surrendering, giving up to Him our preferences and desires, asking Him to make His way clear. I told the Lord that I am willing to go to Germany at His direction, but He doesn't have to resort to having us expelled from our country to get my attention! We keep reminding ourselves to "Let go, Hold on and Rise Above!" And as we do this, there is a continual flow of joy.

Prayer: "Lord, in the midst of uncertainty, help me to live in, rest in, trust in the Certainty of your Wisdom, Love, Power and Goodness. Help me to praise you in all, to give you glory in all and for all, no matter how I may feel about it. Amen."

October 31

"I love you, O LORD, my strength. The LORD is my rock and my fortress and my deliverer, my God, my rock, in whom I take refuge, my shield, and the horn of my salvation, my stronghold."

Psalm 18:1,2

Thank you, O God, for the opportunity to praise you in and for whatever comes, to trust you to carry me through. I can do this because you are:
- The Lord God,
- Triune Ruler,
- Eternal King,
- Unchanging Sovereign,
- Undefeated Commander,
- Wise Judge,
- All-Powerful Leader,
- Mighty Shepherd,
- Merciful Savior,
- All-knowing Guide,
- Unshakable Rock,
- Safe and High Tower,
- Our Ever-present Salvation.

To you, O Great One, belongs praise and honor, glory and strength. To you belongs awe, amazement, reverence and surrender. To

you belongs fear, denial of self and taking up of our cross daily. We can submit to you because:
- You know what is right,
- You know what is best,
- You know beyond the moment,
- You know all that will be.

Therefore:
- You are the One to be trusted,
- You are the One to be honored,
- You are the One to be obeyed.
-

As I look at today, it is wonderful to know that you are going to work all things out for good, leading me through the maze of events, the succeeding challenges and adventures and the battle against the evil one. In all I can rest in you, in your goodness, in your love and in your power.

Prayer: "Today may you be honored in my life, in my thoughts, in my motives, in my confession, in my transparency before you. May you be glorified by my walking in humility and brokenness, trusting you, not myself. May you be honored in my praise, in my actions, in my relationships, in my eating, in my work.

"Fill me with your Holy Spirit. I bow to you as my Captain and Navigator, surrendering to your wisdom, knowledge and goodness. Help me to hear and obey, to seek your direction and follow it immediately. Glory be to you, Lord God, for you are worthy, deserving of all obedience! Amen."

NOVEMBER

November 1

"You have forsaken your first love. Remember the height from which you have fallen! Repent and do the things you did at first."

Revelation 2:4,5

I've been thinking about how important it is to nurture our first love for Jesus. In Rev. 2:1-7, Christ's letter to the church at Ephesus, He lists out 9 positive qualities of the Ephesian believers and commends them. Reviewing that list, I would say that this was a very healthy congregation.

However, Jesus then adds, "Yet I hold this against you: you have forsaken your first love." Is that so important, a little loss of passion? To God it is *very* important, for Jesus continues with, "Repent!" Forsaking (leaving) our first love for Jesus is a serious sin!

Jesus goes on to say, "If you do not repent, I will come to you and remove your lampstand from its place" (Rev 2:5b). This means the church will go out of existence—and that is what happened in Ephesus. Loss of our first love is so serious that it can cancel out all the other good we do.

For God, our first love for Christ is a critical factor: almost everything else flows from it. It is the spring of good motives, of humility, of obedience, of proper balance, of genuine good works, of growth and spiritual power.

So, what can we do to nurture our first love for Jesus? It has to be an intentional pursuit, for it is not something that happens by itself. Just as un-nurtured love in a marriage withers, so does our love for Jesus when we neglect Him.

There are many things we can do to nurture it; I will mention the three most effective ones in my life.

First is personal worship in our quiet time: praising God for who He is without focusing on how His qualities benefit me. The focus is on Him. The Lord Jesus is infinite in His beauty, greatness, wisdom, power and love. If we take a Psalm each day and exalt Him for the qualities we see there, it will stoke the fire of our first love for Him.

Second is what I call "basking in the love of Jesus:" repeating to myself the wonder of being God's child. The focus here is on what He has done for us. By nature, all I deserve is condemnation, suffering, pain, failure, death, hell and eternal separation from God (Rom. 7:18; Eph. 2:1-4). In spite of this, and against all logic, He chose me, called me, cleansed and transformed me, claimed me as His son, and commissioned me to special service (Eph. 1:1-10; Col. 3:12). Now I stand before Him dearly loved, deeply cared for, doted on and delighted in!

If that doesn't stir your soul, nothing will. I willfully let myself feel both sides of that truth, the despair of what I deserve and the delight of the Creator of the universe being excited to have me as His son! That causes my love for Him to bloom! I find it has also brought a deep, profound emotional stability to my life.

Third is praising Him in and for all things—especially for things that I naturally would be upset about. To do so is a statement of faith: my God is good, He is wise and He has allowed this happening in love and wisdom. In it I can give Him glory. Through it I can demonstrate His grace to those around me. From it I can grow in faith and obedience.

Such praise lifts my eyes and thoughts from natural seeing and thinking to the supernatural, spiritual and supreme Truth of God's beautiful character. My love for my wonderful Lord Jesus is nurtured.

Try these and sense the burgeoning, beautiful growth of your first love for Him. Truly, Knowing Jesus is Enough for Joy, Period—if we choose to live that truth.

Be intentional. Be committed. Be wise. Live like a child of the King, the prince or princess you are.

Prayer: "Lord, help me to worship you each day, to bask in your love and praise you in and for all things. May you be honored and glorified in that, may my love for you be deepened, widened and strengthened. Amen."

An example of the outcome of nurturing our first love for Christ. This past week a friend's elderly acquaintance in South Africa took out his garbage in the early afternoon and was attacked by two masked men. He was forced into his house, robbed and then stabbed to death. His wife was also stabbed and left unconscious. When her pastor visited her in the hospital, he wanted to reach out and comfort her but she showed how God had already filled her with His grace, telling the pastor, "This is a case to believe Romans 8:28. Our God will work this out for good!" Now there is a woman who had nurtured her first love for Jesus, seeing His greatness and learning to trust Him in all!

November 2

"The commands of the LORD are radiant, giving light to the eyes."

Psalm 19:8b

Praise you, Lord, that my failures do not influence your attitude or love for me. You are the great and gracious One who does not change, who cannot change, who is steady, faithful and good. It is a great comfort to know, in the midst of my ups and downs, how consistently, wonderfully loving and reliable you are.

As it says in Psalm 19:7-11, "The law of the LORD is perfect, reviving the soul." It is through your Word that you have brought life to my soul, giving transformation, strength, courage and joy.

"The statutes of the LORD are trustworthy, making wise the simple." When I have no idea what to do or say, your Word gives guidance. It is full of wisdom, overflowing with insight and packed with knowledge. By your Word and the work of the Spirit, we can, to a great degree, understand life, suffering, purpose, our end, and most importantly, you.

"The precepts of the LORD are right, giving joy to the heart." In a world of great uncertainty, shifting values and confusing change, you guide us in knowing what is right, and that gives us joy. Life without boundaries makes us uncertain and sad. Life with the means to determine what is right and wrong gives us security, light and joy. You are the source of all that and this flows to us through your Word.

"The commands of the LORD are radiant, giving light to the eyes." In this world of darkness, confusion and conflict, your Word shines bright and clear, showing us the path, exposing Satan's traps, guiding us in decisions, enlightening us about the future. You, who stand outside of time, know all this and share it with us in your Word.

"The fear of the LORD is pure, enduring forever." To know your Word is not enough. As we obey it out of love, reverence and respect for you, you lead us in doing things that will last forever. You are eternal and what you do is eternal; you bequeath us with the possibility of making decisions that have consequences forever, have significance for eternity. The resulting fear, reverence and awe of you lead us to make decisions according to Truth.

"The ordinances of the LORD are sure and altogether righteous." When all else is uncertain, your Word is trustable and without fault. All you command is right and righteous. We desperately need the wisdom of your Word and the leadership of your Spirit so we can walk in the right way.

"They are more precious than gold, than much pure gold; they are sweeter than honey, than honey from the comb." The things of this world are attractive—the power-giving, comfort-offering, security-promising success and prosperity—but they quickly pass away. In contrast, your Word is forever. In it we can find the true and lasting security, significance, power and comfort every heart desires, for you are the source of all good, everlasting good.

"By them is your servant warned; in keeping them there is great reward." You know every danger, every evil lurking on the path ahead. You warn us, guide us and protect us as we walk in the way of your Word. And when we obey, you reward us, both now and in the future.

As I follow your Word, life is one long series of adventures with you, living in the knowledge that you are at work in every happening, moving things to positive conclusions, leading us through suffering and joy, difficulty and pleasure, evil days and wonderful times.

You, O Lord God, are our Shepherd, our King, the Commander of the Hosts of Heaven and our Savior; to you we bow down in worship, for you are worthy in your goodness and grace to receive all our affection, all our time, all our possessions, all our obedience.

Prayer: "May your name may be lifted on high today before all those we meet. Glorify yourself in our lives today as we live according to your Word! Amen."

November 3

"And this is my prayer: that your love may abound more and more in knowledge and depth of insight, so that you may be able to discern what is best …."

Philippians 1:9,10

Yesterday was a test for me as I set off to do errands, 14 in all. I'd prayed about them and most of them went smoothly except two, the last, and most desired ones. My natural reaction was to focus on these unaccomplished items, to be distressed and upset.

However, as part of the on-going revival in my life, the Holy Spirit reminded me of the habitual sins I had "confessed ahead" just that morning: complaining instead of praising, idol worship ("If this doesn't work out, I can't be happy"), judgmental, negative thinking, and selfishness. So, with His help, I deliberately chose to reject these and instead to praise Him for what couldn't be done and to thank Him for what was accomplished.

With His guidance, I chose to "let go of the temporal, hold on to the eternal and rise above." There is such freedom in this; when I got home, I could be pleasant and positive with my little wife, having no burden of discontent.

What keeps this revival going? There are four principles which open the way to continual refreshment in my life.
1. *Small things repeated often are powerful.*
    Taking vitamins and brushing your teeth regularly bring long term results. Regular quiet times bring bigger results as I follow the disciplines of daily worship, confession, being in the Word and prayer—these are cooperation with the Spirit in being transformed.

    Along with this, asking for revival every day is effective, if we add the next 3 principles.

2. *Deal with the next sin God is pointing out.*

What is God convicting me of? This "next sin" is often something that appears to be small and unimportant, (grouchiness, unnecessary snacks, staying up too late, etc.) but is a key to a significant issue in my life. Deal with it: name it, confess it, forsake it. Adrian Rogers is credited with saying, "What we believe we obey; all the rest is religious talk."

3. *Confess ahead.*

Another small act that adds up. It is powerful to regularly confess my tendency to commit certain sins (at present I have a list of 52! I "confess ahead" 10 or so a day), to ask for help in rejecting these tendencies and commit to obedience. Doing this reminds me of my weaknesses, helps me to be alert to my tendency to react naturally, and to instead choose the supernatural response.

4. *Be aware of how our worldview tends to blind and bind us.*

Ask God to help us discern where our natural thinking and values conflict with His. Ask Him to help us discern what is of the world, the flesh and the devil so we can reject them and do the opposite, obeying Him.

If we practice these principles, our love will "abound more and more in knowledge and depth of insight so that we may be able to discern what is best and may be pure and blameless until the day of Christ, filled with the fruit of righteousness...to the glory and praise of God" (Phil. 1:9-11).

Prayer: "Lord, help me to be consistent in spending time with you in the Word and prayer, in confessing ahead and dealing with the next sin. Help me to see where my natural worldview clashes with yours and to make the necessary shift. Amen."

November 4

"... for Christ's sake, I delight in weaknesses, in insults, in hardships, in persecutions, in difficulties. For when I am weak, then I am strong."

2 Corinthians 12:10

As I think about the situation in our Middle Eastern country at the moment with the new, more restrictive and difficult visa rules, it is sad to see people panicking and leaving out of fear before anything negative actually has happened. Praise you, Lord God, that with you we don't need to panic, for true stability is not found in the laws or situations in a land, but in your Presence, in your Power, in your Person.

Glory be to you for this new opportunity to trust you in the midst of uncertainty, for the chance to praise by faith, to wait for your working and guidance.

It is obvious that you are doing something big—perhaps moving workers who speak this language to other areas where they are needed, perhaps motivating them to get more viable reasons for staying, perhaps to sort out the ones who are afraid from those who trust you, perhaps to make us realize that time may be short and we'd better be doing more training of local leaders, perhaps to spur us on to more outreach, perhaps to stimulate more prayer. You probably are doing all of these! You have allowed and are using this pressure for good; we can trust you.

Everyone would like an immediate solution to such tension, but our eyes must be on you. This is an opportunity to be weak, to praise you by faith, to delight in our difficulties, knowing that in reality being weak is when we are strong in you. With the Psalmist we can say:

"My soul faints with longing for your salvation,
    but I have put my hope in your word...
Though I am like a wineskin in the smoke,
    I do not forget your decrees....
All your commands are trustworthy;
    help me, for men persecute me without cause.
They almost wiped me from the earth,
    but I have not forsaken your precepts."
[And then the great appeal:]
"Preserve my life according to your love,
    and I will obey the statutes of your mouth."
                                  Psalm 119:81,83,85-88

Your love and your Word are the measure of it all, Lord. You will act according to your love, which is wise, gracious, powerful and consistent. What you are allowing is good, for good, out of good. We can trust you in this visa situation and rejoice in what is to come long before we see it, even when all looks the opposite of good.

Prayer: "Lord God, we worship you, we glorify you, we praise you in all, for you are the Wise One, the Kind One, the Powerful One, the Pure One. You are worthy of worship, trust and obedience--and we offer these to you this day. Whatever comes, help me to praise you, to thank you, to trust you, knowing that you will use all to bring glory to your name, mature us and sweep many into your Kingdom. Amen."

Epilogue: *After a week our country changed the visa regulations back to what they had been, eliminating all potential problems for workers. This was a test, a warning, and an opportunity to praise.*

November 5

"Send forth your light and your truth, let them guide me....Then will I go to the altar of God, to God, my joy and my delight."

Psalm 43:3a,4

Dawn comes and I awake to have my time with God. But there is no freshness, He seems far away. What is wrong? Is it sin? (I confess all the Spirit brings to mind.) Work overload? Tiredness? Probably some of each, but mainly it is my feelings. Emotions are definitely the least reliable part of my being. When I allow them to rule, I end up feeling like this fellow here on the left: out of touch and at the mercy of whatever wind might blow.

To combat these negative feelings, I need to keep an ear open to the Spirit's conviction and guidance, and to press on with what is right: worshiping, confessing, reading, praying, trusting that God is near as He promised.

This is a chance to live by faith, to believe God's Word when I have no inner confirmation. It's a chance to be weak, to live by faith, to praise Him for what I don't like (feeling far away) and to go again to Scripture to remind myself of Truth.

Psalm 43:2 expresses my feelings well: "Why must I go about mourning, oppressed by the enemy?" Then verse 3 gives me a good prayer to combat this: "Send forth your light and your truth, let them guide me, let them bring me to your holy mountain, the place where you dwell." God's Word gives light, and I can affirm by faith that I am with Him who is "my joy and my delight, and I praise you, O God, my God."

The advice in the last verse of Psalm 43 speaks strongly to me, "Why are you downcast, O my soul? Why so disturbed within me? Put your hope in God, for I will yet praise Him, my Savior and my God." He is at work and is carrying me along whether I sense it or not! He will work all out, so I can praise Him ahead of time for and in all.

All this brings to mind that beloved saying, "Knowing Jesus is enough for joy." This is a chance for me to live it willfully by faith!

Prayer: "Thank you, Lord, for the opportunity to believe and trust you when my feelings tell me the opposite. Help me to think Truth, to act on Truth, to praise according to Truth today. Amen."

November 6

"I will never forget your precepts, for by them you have preserved my life."

Psalm 119:93

Praise be to you, Lord God: you are the Great I Am, the all-powerful Creator, Sustainer, Director and Ender of history. Your being flows from before time, into history and beyond it into eternity. You are forever, with no beginning and no ending.

Like you, "Your word, O LORD, is eternal; it stands firm in the heavens" (Ps. 119:89). It does not change or shift; it is not altered or abrogated; it is firm and sure, true and right, trustable and good.

"Your faithfulness continues through all generations...." You are the same as when you created Adam and Eve: your wisdom has not diminished, your power is not less, your love has not shifted and your grace has not been depleted. You are forever unaltered: ever trustable, ever faithful, ever present, ever good.

"...you established the earth, and it endures" (Ps. 119:90). Whatever its age, the earth endures, hung on nothing, spinning at the right speed, circling the sun at the needed distance, tilted on the right axis—all this because you are faithful. The enduring earth is the visible evidence that you are the unchanging, unending God whose Word is forever true.

"Your laws endure to this day, for all things serve you" (Ps. 119:91). You created the universe to be dependent on you; you established the laws of physics, the laws of ethics, the laws of morality, and they continue on throughout history. Whatever happens, it serves you. You are able to transform whatever comes into something useful in your Kingdom.

"If your law had not been my delight, I would have perished in my affliction" (Ps. 119:92). This is so true of me: if I had not meditated on your Word, I would not have made it in the Middle East. I would have both exploded and imploded, for the difficult events we lived through would have driven me back home, demolished my emotional life, destroyed my family life and done in my ministry. But you fed and led me through your Scripture.

Your Word brings life, it brings light, it brings truth, it transforms, protects and guides. By it we can understand life to a sufficient degree, enough to make sense. By it we can know you enough to trust you. By it we can see you at work so we can move on with you in life. Your

Word is my light, my lamp, my love. Praise be to you for providing what we need to trust you.

Prayer: "I bow before you, O Lord, Father, Son and Holy Spirit. I give you honor and praise for you have revealed yourself to us in your Word. I rise up from worship to obey you today with all my heart, for all your glory. Amen."

November 7

"God our Savior…wants all men to be saved and to come to a knowledge of the truth."

1 Timothy 2:3b,4

One thing I have been challenged on by some folks is the legitimacy of praying for the lost. Some contend that there is no biblical basis for it, although Jesus prayed for those who would believe and Paul asks for prayer for the gospel to spread.

Others say it essentially makes no difference, God is going to save the elect no matter what, so why bother?

Others present formulas which are "guaranteed" to bring people into the Kingdom, although God says each person must make his own decision.

The foundational truth in this issue is that God commands us to pray about everything all the time (Eph. 6:18). He says that we should be praying according to His will and if we do so, He will answer (1 John 5:14-15). So what is His will?

1 Timothy 2:4 states clearly that God would like all to be saved, so we should pray for that. It also states that some will not be saved because of unbelief, so not all will respond to God's work or our prayers—but many will.

Then we must ask, "What is God doing to bring people to a point of making a clear decision for or against Christ so that I can join Him in this through prayer?" The Word gives us a number of things we can pray for.

1. 2 Corinthians 3:16; 4:4 — God must remove the veil that Satan has put before the eyes of unbelievers.
2. Romans 1:20 — God wants people to see his attributes displayed in nature.
3. 2 Corinthians 4:6 — God must make His light of the gospel shine in the hearts of unbelievers so they can know His salvation.
4. John 16:8-11 — God the Holy Spirit is at work convincing unbelievers of guilt because of their sin of not believing in

Jesus as God and Savior, because of Christ's righteousness and of judgment for the prince of this world is condemned—and with him all who don't believe in Christ.
5. Following examples in Scripture, I also ask that God would speak to them through whatever means He chooses: dreams, visions, tragedy, blessing, fear of death, terrors, questions and statements of truth, etc.
6. 2 Timothy 2:25, Romans 10:17, Ephesians 2:8, Colossians 1:5--Then I ask Him to grant them faith and repentance.
7. And finally I ask Him to pin them down, as He did king Nebuchadnezzar in Daniel, and Paul in the NT, so they have to face the issue of believing or not.

So I ask God to do these things for the unbelievers on my prayer list. This is no magic formula, but it is joining Him, cooperating with God in what He is doing, and asking Him to do what He says He desires--therefore such prayer will be effective. Some I've prayed for have come to Christ after 20 years of prayer, others after more than 50. Perseverance is important!

Prayer: "Lord, help me to join you in your great work of sweeping as many as possible into your Kingdom before they perish. Help me to be, in your power, consistent in prayer, persistent in sharing, insistent in being a living witness for you. Amen."

November 8

We always thank God, the Father of our Lord Jesus Christ, when we pray for you...."

Colossians 1:3

Today I meditated on Colossians 1:9-14. What a powerful passage, and not just because it talks about power! It lays out the marvelous things you have purchased for us, Lord.
Paul writes "...we have not stopped praying for you and asking God to fill you with the knowledge of his will through all spiritual wisdom and understanding."
You, Heavenly Father, have made it possible that we can know you and know your will, not just on a human level, but on a supernatural level, for you have granted us spiritual wisdom and understanding through your Spirit. We can know and understand you far beyond what we could before being born again. How wonderfully you love us, provide for us, reveal yourself to us, and give us understanding of your will!

"And we pray this in order that you may live a life worthy of the Lord and may please him in every way...." Praise you, Lord God, that you make it possible for us to live according to your character, to please you in spite of our being sinful creatures, still having our flesh to fight against. You call us to join you in your great work, then you help us, you guide us and strengthen us.

I praise you for this demonstration of your rich and powerful love wherein you delight in us, you love us dearly, you are pleased when you think of us. You invite us into your presence through prayer and are glad when we come in intercession, for then we give you honor, acknowledging our weakness and your power, our inability and your mighty competence, our ignorance and your deep wisdom, our fickleness and your absolute trustworthiness.

To be your child, to be able to please you, to know your rich, warm, whole-hearted delight in us—not based on our performance, but upon being justified in the shed blood of Jesus—to bask in your love, your acceptance, your delight and pleasure in us because of what you, Lord Jesus, have done—this is one of the great gifts your salvation has brought into our lives.

Colossians 1 tells us what we can do as we live with you:

"bearing fruit in every good work," The Spirit brings the needed fruit as we abide in Christ, denying self, soaking in your Word, thinking your Truth, gazing upon you in worship. Then you lead us to do good to those around us, out of the right motives, for the right reasons, in the right way.

"growing in the knowledge of God...." Your Word, Your Spirit, the life lessons you send, all make it possible to grow in our knowledge of you. And as we grow in knowledge, we are transformed and are better able to obey you.

Praise you that growth in knowledge of you also means growth in the knowledge of ourselves: our sinfulness, our natural untrustworthiness, our rebellion and unbelief, our innate seeking for everything apart from you. When we embrace this revelation and receive your rich, cleansing forgiveness, it highlights again your perfection, beauty, gracefulness and purity. And can lead us to an ongoing revival in our lives.

Along with this is the growing grasp of how we are holy in you: chosen, set apart and equipped for special service. In you we are pure, clean, forgiven, transformed into a new creature. We can see these works of your hand more and more clearly as we walk with you, soak in your Word, bask in your love, deny self, take up our cross daily and follow you by obeying your commands.

Prayer: "Glory be to you, Lord God, Eternal King, Mighty Shepherd. Lead me today in walking in your way, bearing fruit in every good work and growing in the knowledge of your Being. Help me to spend time in your Word because I love you, in worship because you are worthy, in working for you today and every day because you invite me to join you in your great plans. Amen."

November 9

"...that you may live a life worthy of the Lord and may please him in every way...with all power..."

Colossians 1:10a,11a

My meditation on Col. 1:9-11 goes on.
"...being strengthened with all power according to his glorious might so that you may have great endurance and patience...." This is an amazing statement! As we live according to your Word, growing in knowledge of you, pleasing you in our lives, you give us strength. How much? ALL power. According to what measure? Your GLORIOUS MIGHT!

This is the power with which you spoke the stars into existence, formed the earth and created all on it. It is the power with which you raised Christ from the dead and vanquished the devil and death. It is the power with which you will raise up all the dead to judgment or eternal life. And you offer a portion of this power to us so we can walk in your way in this world.

And how is it manifested? In having GREAT endurance and patience. As we look to you, see your power, wisdom, love and faithfulness, we can wait for your timing instead of ours; we can work at your pace, not ours; we can "move through situations with your power" (the meaning of endurance). Therefore we can avoid burnout, melt down, crash and burn, unnecessary depression and disillusionment.

As we get to know you more and more, you grant us a more and more corrected view of life. You give a knowledge of what is important, of what we should be "being" and doing, what we should be avoiding. As we submit to your wisdom and Word, you root out junk stress, eliminate destructive expectations, remove the burdens of possessions, ambition and fear. You guide us to run in the path of your commands, for you have set our hearts free!

We can also be "joyfully giving thanks to the Father," not just grudgingly, not just in teeth-gritting obedience, but in the joy of knowing you, our Heavenly Father, for it is you, our true Father "who has qualified us to share in the inheritance of the saints in the kingdom of light."

Even though we were totally unqualified, totally undeserving, totally outside the line of acceptance, still you granted us, in Jesus, the privilege of being qualified to share in the Kingdom of Light—we, the children of darkness, of rebellion, of twisted desires, of unbelief—you granted us forgiveness, adoption and sainthood.

And the marvelous truth is that "...he has rescued us from the dominion of darkness and brought us into the kingdom of the Son he loves." This is not a future thing, it has happened! We have been rescued, we are out of Satan's dominion, we are in the Kingdom of Christ!

What a great privilege, one to rejoice in! Our God reigns and has taken us to Himself! It all comes down to the same great Truth: He has done this by "the Son he loves in whom we have redemption, the forgiveness of sins."

It is in Christ alone that we have this redemption: being bought out of the grip of Satan, sin and self, and having our sordid and evil record of guilt wiped totally clean. We are rescued, forgiven, cleansed, set free, transformed, adopted and dearly loved.

Prayer: "Praise you, O Triune God, that you, in your great, marvelous and incomprehensible love, would do such a work: great and costly, mighty and painful, marvelous and merciful, eternal and effective! To you be glory and honor in my life today as well as forever and ever. Amen."

November 10

"Oh, how I love your law! I meditate on it all day long."

Psalm 119:97

Praise be to you, Lord, for the goodness of your heart, for you are the God who shares yourself with your enemies. Through your Word you reveal to us what we could never discover with our feeble intellect, will, emotions or experience.

"Oh, how I love your law! I meditate on it all day long" (Ps 119:97). It is only meditation on your Word that has kept me sane, sensible and out of trouble all these years. You have used it to protect me from burnout, broken relationships, failure and suicide.

To memorize, personalize and pray your Word, Lord, makes it possible to think your thoughts, understand your will, surrender my will more deeply and be transformed daily. It is joining the Holy Spirit in what He desires to do, first in our inner being and then through us.

Meditation[11] is the flashlight we can use to discover new doors into greater depths of your Word. Without meditation we pass by these doors, never even noticing them, continually circling around on the

---

[11] see Appendix for a greater explanation of meditation as I mean it.

same level, deprived of riches and sustenance we didn't even know existed.

Without your Word and meditating on it I never would have made it in the Middle East. I praise you for the work that you have done in my life through it and for what you will continue to do.

"Your commands make me wiser than my enemies, for they are ever with me" (Ps. 119:98). Your Word exposes the tactics and wiles of the devil. It shines the light of truth and understanding ever more widely around us, giving us insight and wisdom to navigate the ever shifting sands of society. It draws us from salvation's first light of dawn to the full light of day, to Spirit-given maturity in you.

"I have more insight than all my teachers, for I meditate on your statutes" (Ps. 119:99). Education, good as it is, can never measure up to the insights of meditation on your Word, for it is more than intellectual. Meditation involves the mind, will and emotions, it is cooperation with the Spirit in His great work of transformation, it is grasping things that are beyond the intellect, it is far beyond the merely human act of learning.

"I have more understanding than the elders, for I obey your precepts" (Ps. 119:100). Meditation leads to obedience because it involves praying for what is in the passage to be true in my life. When we personalize and pray, the passage penetrates our life and the Spirit prepares us for application. This goes beyond understanding--which is theoretical--to living it, which is experiential.

Lord Jesus, I praise you freely, lovingly, with great gratitude and thankfulness; I praise you for your character: wonderfully just and good, loving and wise, pure and positive, as revealed in your Word, and discovered through Spirit-led meditation. Praise you that we will spend eternity learning ever more about you!

Prayer: "May you be glorified in my life today, Lord Jesus, as I meditate on your Word; help me to be consistent in meditation and then to live out each moment what I have learned about you. Amen."

November 11

"Consider it pure joy, my brothers, whenever you face trials of many kinds, because you know that the testing of your faith develops perseverance."

James 1:2,3

Wow! So many things changed for the positive following the work of the Spirit at our logistically problem-ridden July conferences, two weeks of non-stop pressures, including the hotel trying to throw us all out on the street, demanding $40,000 more in fees, not having enough rooms available, poor food and failing to provide services promised. Since I was in charge of all the logistics for the three conferences, I had to deal with these difficulties.

The changes He brought through these came on all levels: personal, team, corporate, spiritual, emotional, even physical. Personally, the Lord used the pressures and challenges of these conferences coupled with the good teaching to do several things in me.

First was the challenge to live the truth that "Knowing Jesus is Enough for Joy, Period." There is a definite surrender called for in living that way: denial of self, letting go of idols, rejecting feelings, refusing self-pity. It is the Spirit who worked this new level of surrender in me, using the pressures of the difficulties to help me let go of what is temporal, and hold on to what is eternal (running to the Word for comfort and perspective, especially Psalm 86) so He could enable me to rise above the situation.

In addition, He seems to have lessened my impatience, anxiety, negative/judgmental thinking, my anger, self-centeredness and fear of man, along with my pride and desire for recognition. That means He has also increased the opposite of these: patience, rest, positiveness, Christ-centeredness, desire to see God honored and fear of God.

A third advance is a deeper sensitivity to the Spirit's leading and a desire to trust and obey.

I must hasten to add that all this is God's doing, using the pressures He allowed, so any growth is to His credit. There is much more progress needed in each of these areas in my life, but there was a fundamental step upwards in each to a new level. I look forward to more steps up, to His glory and honor. And I am sure these steps will come through more difficulties, trials and troubles, which are opportunities to offer the sacrifice of thanksgiving, embrace what God allows and move up.

Prayer: "Lord God, help me to rejoice in the difficulties you allow in my life, knowing that you will use them to mature, deepen and guide me. Praise you for your wisdom and love. May you be honored today by my responses to whatever comes. Amen."

November 12

"My soul finds rest in God alone."

Psalm 62:1

The Puritan writer Burroughs says that contentment is not what we have when looking back, able to see what God was doing through a difficult time. It is being at peace in the midst of difficulty and suffering without any visible clue as to what our Shepherd is doing, and in that knowledge vacuum resting in Him.

Knowing the character of God is enough. He whose wisdom created the world, made the human body and gave man dominion over the earth; He who did not give up when Adam sinned and twisted the whole of creation; He who secured salvation at huge personal cost, and loves us to the end, He is trustable when all else is hidden from our understanding.

Knowing You, Lord God, the great Yahweh, holy, glorious, entirely other, hater of sin, lover of the sinner—to know you is enough to give us contentment when everything goes wrong, when we suffer pain, when we are mistreated, when we fail and are, humanly speaking, hopeless.

Contentment is knowing the wisdom of your mind. You, O God, are the One who created the micro world of subatomic particles, who set the laws that govern their states, who combined them into atoms and who holds all the nuclei together. You made the molecules, formed the elements and brought out of them all we see, from microscopic animals to stars a million times bigger than our sun. You who have done this have enough wisdom to bring into my life what is right. I can trust you.

Contentment is knowing the power of your right arm. You, Lord Jesus, spoke and created all that we see, with its incredible variety, beauty and vastness. You hung, spun and run the earth. You ride, guide and hide the winds. You hold, mold and unfold events. You send, bend and end history. Never defeated, never stretched, never inadequate, your power is immeasurable. In you we can trust.

Contentment is knowing the patience of your will. You have a plan, you will reveal it at the pace you know to be best. You will not rush, you will not be late, your timing is perfect. When nothing appears to be happening, you are at work on deep levels, persistently, patiently, powerfully bringing to pass events and conditions that will move history to the conclusion you have determined. We can trust you in your timing.

Contentment is knowing the greatness of your love. You are Agape Love itself: the commitment to act for the good of others, no matter how they may react. The wonder of your rich, deep, powerful, unending, gracious love is an ever-growing joy as we walk with you, learning of you from your Word, from your works, from your way.

Your strong, careful, overwhelming love is revealed in the goodness you give us daily: in being so kind when we give you pain with our sin and selfishness, in the grace you offer us moment by moment when we so often spurn it in pride. We see your love in the kindness you exercise in your correction of our stubborn and self-centered hearts. We can trust your heart of love.

As we climb the golden staircase of your grace, care and love, knowing you more and more each day, we can be content in you and in whatever you bring, whatever we suffer, whatever we lose, for you are good.

Prayer: "When all is meaningless, when all we do seems foolish, when pain obscures our vision, still our hearts to know your heart of love and grace. Help us then to rest in contentment. Glory be to you, the Great God of contentment, worthy of all worship and wonder and trust. Amen."

November 13

"Hear, O LORD, and answer me, for I am poor and needy. Guard my life, for I am devoted to you. You are my God; save your servant who trusts in you."

Psalm 86:1,2

While reading in my journal, I came across notes from a message I heard from the leader of the "Hands of Hur" ministries. He talked about how we can have three reactions to a situation. We can be a victim, a victor or a vector. Joseph in the OT was all three.

When he was thrown into the pit by his brothers, he was a victim, focused on "poor me." Genesis 42:21 says, "…he pleaded with us for his life, but we would not listen". A victim allows his circumstances and suffering to define him. He has a very narrow, self-centered view of life.

A victor has moved beyond that to a trust in God, freeing him to serve more whole-heartedly. When Joseph was working in Potiphar's house, he was a victor: he gave the right responses and triumphed in each situation, even resisting the temptations of Potiphar's wife.

A victor lets his successes define his life. God is there, but He is not the center of the victor's existence. Joseph told Potiphar's wife that everything was in his hands, that he was the greatest in the house and, by the way, that he was obeying God (Gen. 39:8,9). The focus was on himself and his accomplishments, not on God. This continued while he was in prison, as he told the other prisoners how he could interpret dreams rather than giving God credit.

However, when he stood before Pharaoh, Joseph had become a vector, an arrow pointing the way to the True Victor. A vector is one whose life is centered on God, who points others to God, not to success or comfort.

A vector's life is defined not by his suffering, or by his victories, but by God's relationship with him. When asked if he could interpret dreams, Joseph said, "No, but God can" (Gen. 41:16). And when he gave the interpretation he said, "God has chosen to show Pharaoh what he is about to do." Joseph leaves himself entirely out of the picture, pointing all to the Lord of all. He had been truly broken, learning not to trust himself, but to fully trust God.

Paul expounds on this concept in Romans 8:37 in which he tells us we should be MORE than a conqueror, more than a victor, pointing us to the possibility of being a vector, a signpost to God for all those around us.

In each difficulty, disappointment or danger that comes into our lives, we can be a victim, a victor or a vector. A lot of what determines which one we'll be is how we cultivate our first love for Christ in meeting with Him each day in worship, confession, reading the Word and prayer. Are we cooperating with God in doing this?

Prayer: "Lord show me where I am acting like a victim or victor. Bring me to repentance and help me to live as a vector, focused on you and helping others to look to you. Praise you now for the help you will give. Amen."

November 14

"Sacrifice thank offerings to God, fulfill your vows to the Most High, and call upon me in the day of trouble; I will deliver you, and you will honor me."

Psalm 50:14,14

In spite of a heavy downpour, I arrived at the Detroit airport in good time for my flight back to CT. After a week of teaching in Texas and another in Detroit, I was ready to get home.

At the gate it said the plane was on time; in fact it was sitting right there at the end of the ramp. However, at boarding time, an announcement was made that there would be a half hour delay because the crew was late. Then another delay--and another and another.

Each delay was further little adventure with Jesus, a chance to praise and trust. It turned out that the many thunderstorms of the day had stranded our crew on the runway in Columbus, Ohio for four hours.

They finally arrived and we boarded. The pilot then announced that our take off permission had expired and a new one needed to be printed. That took half an hour. Then came another announcement that they couldn't find a machine to push us away from the gate. That took another 20 minutes. Then as we got out on the run way, the pilot stopped and shut off the engines, announcing that we were number 40 in the line to take off, but because of poor weather no planes were being allowed to leave at the moment. Half an hour later the engines started again and we crept to the front of the line and took off.

All this time my cell phone was not working for some reason, so during the last wait I borrowed my seatmate's and called Barbara to tell her of the delays. Unbeknownst to me, she then wisely called the friend who was waiting to pick me up and told him to go home, as it was unclear when or if I would arrive. So when I got to CT more than four hours late, there was no one to meet me.

Well, this was a further adventure with Jesus; I prayed for wisdom and borrowed another passenger's cell phone to call Barbara (there are no more pay phones at the airport!) and she said a neighbor would come to pick me up. Now comes the interesting part.

The fellow whose cell phone I'd borrowed came and sat next to me. His plane to Chicago had been cancelled because of the storms, so he was waiting for a hotel shuttle. In the course of our talk, he told me he had two sons, 6 and 8, both of whom had muscular dystrophy. This meant that by the time they are 10, they will be in wheel chairs, and would have a life expectancy of 25 to 30 years. I asked how he handled that.

"At first I was angry with God, but after a couple of years saw that was not working, so have now turned back to him. I go to church, but don't get much out of it. I'm not sure how to proceed there."

We then had a wonderful talk about God, salvation and reading Scripture. At the end of our talk he eagerly took a brochure on salvation and then made a very insightful comment. "Now I know why my plane home was cancelled and why your plane was late—that made it possible for us to meet and for you to help me!" Pretty amazing that this seeker recognized this significant "Jesus sighting" in both our lives!

The delays and frustrations of our lives are not random and meaningless. God is at work orchestrating events for our protection and growth as well as to provide opportunities to speak into the lives of others. Our praise in the midst of uncertainty prepares our hearts and minds for the chance to be an instrument in God's hands as we offer the sacrifice of thanksgiving (Psalm 50:23), getting up the shield of faith.

Prayer: "Lord, help me to live in the larger reality of your orchestrating power at work within and around me. Help me to offer the sacrifice of thanksgiving for whatever comes, thereby honoring you and opening the way to join you in what you are doing. Amen."

November 15

"My soul finds rest in God alone."

Psalm 62:1

My poor old Bible was worn out, the cover falling off, pages coming loose, so I took it to a bookbinder to have it rebound. When I picked it up, it looked great and I was pleased--until I opened it to the back and found my 5 pages of notes missing. The bookbinder had thrown them away! For years I'd collected sermon outlines and verses on different subjects, resources I'd found very useful. Now all that work was gone! It was like losing an old friend!

But praise God, He immediately brought to mind that phrase, "Knowing Jesus is enough for joy!" Although my emotions weren't lining up with this as I embraced Truth, and exercised volitional faith (giving thanks when I don't feel like it), I was able to thank God for this loss, knowing that He has something good in it.

It seems lately that God is giving us lots of opportunities to put into practice trusting and praising Him when we would rather complain. Here are some things from the last few weeks:

- In getting ready to move to Germany, we got the unexpected news of the need for a stent in my heart.
- We were unable to make an exit to a Greek Island to renew our visas because Greek harbor workers were on strike. This complicates our leaving for Germany, forcing us to go several days earlier, scrambling to complete the end tasks necessary—but God knows what He is doing!
- A fellow worker had his pickup truck stolen from in front of his house, along with his cell phone, plus the registration for another vehicle and equipment. We suspect that this was engineered by the police who would like this particular worker to leave.
- A business started by a local pastor fell into a legal trap and everything in his business was confiscated by the small claims court.
- No word on my stolen car or on a solution to a difficult and expensively unjust situation with a hotel where we held conferences last month.

However, in the midst of all these unresolved difficulties, the truth is: "My grace is sufficient for you, for my power is made perfect in weakness" (2 Cor. 12:9), and "Knowing Jesus is enough for joy." In the midst of unresolved pressure and problems we can find our rest in Him, knowing that He will carry us through in the way He knows is best.

Prayer: "Praise you, Lord God, for your care and protection in my life. Thank you for all you allow to come to me. And thank you for the privilege of offering the sacrifice of thanksgiving to honor you. Help me to do this consistently and fulfill the purpose of my life by bringing honor to your name (Ps. 50:23). Amen."

November 16

"You are my refuge and my shield; I have put my hope in your word."

Psalm 119:114

Praise be to you, O Lord God, Yahweh, the Great and Holy One. You are utterly other than anything in your creation. Here are some ways in which you are so different from us created ones.

You are beyond comprehension—yet you have made yourself known.

You are beyond understanding—yet you clothed yourself in human form.

You are Holy and pure—yet you love sinners.

You are totally just—yet you have made it possible for mercy to triumph over justice.

You are perfect—yet you have great patience with imperfect, twisted, rebellious, stubborn people.

You are complete in yourself—yet you offer relationship to those who don't deserve it.

You are righteous—yet you forgive the unrighteous.

You are eternal—yet you enter time to bring mortals into your forever Kingdom.

I praise you that you have made yourself a refuge for us, an escape from self and sin and Satan. In you we can be freed from the senseless, meaningless, randomness of the unregenerate world—because in you there is meaning and purpose and direction.

You are a refuge from the hopelessness, the powerlessness, the futileness of human life.

You are a refuge from our own anger, frustration, impotence and self-pity.

You are a refuge from the evil of men and devils, from injustice, violence and shame.

You are a refuge from fear, anxiety and anguish.

You are a refuge from idol worship, materialism and the tyranny of the urgent.

You are a refuge from junk stress, wrong values and short-term thinking.

You are a refuge from harmful, self-destructive, caustic behavior.

You are a refuge from lust, lying and laziness.

You are a refuge from failure, factionalism and favoritism.

You are a refuge from all that is negative, sinful and impure. .

You shield us from the daily onslaught of Satan and his forces.

In you we are safe, in you we are accepted, in you we are protected. Praise be to you for your powerful, proven provision. You have given us the armor needed to stand. You have offered us power, endurance, guidance and light—all we need to walk in the valley of this world fallen, to escape the corruption that comes through evil desires and to be more than conquerors.

As we come to you and dwell in the shelter of your Word and the way you have given us, you shield us from wrong thoughts, wrong desires and wrong perspectives. You shield us from what is distracting, destructive and demanding. You shield us from what is caustic, competitive and cynical. You shield us from what is foolish, selfish and unwise.

Truly, Lord God, Triune King, Eternal Ruler, Owner of everything, you are our hope: our only hope; our huge, eternal, almighty, sustaining and entirely adequate hope. And your Word gives us what we need to nurture and sustain this hope.

Praise be you, the God of hope who desires to fill us with all joy and peace, if we will only trust in you, so that our lives may overflow with hope by the power of the Holy Spirit (Rom. 15:13).

Prayer: "Yes, Lord, may the fragrance of your hope flow out of my life throughout the day and edify all those around me! May praise for the Eternal, Great, Good and Glorious God be the keynote of my life, of my day. Glory be to you, the God of Hope, the God of Protection, the God of Refuge, the God who is our shield! Amen."

November 17

"Spread your protection over [those who take refuge in you] so that those who love your name may rejoice in YOU!"

Psalm 5:11b, emphasis added

It was 4 AM, but I was wide-awake, staring up into the darkness. My mind was in turmoil, burdened by the news I'd gotten the previous evening. I'd unwittingly done two negative things to an old friend, hurting him and injuring our relationship. One was a cultural blunder, the other indiscretion in speech (better known as gossip). How could I have been so dumb!? Now here I was 2000 miles away, unable to right these things quickly or easily.

After confessing and receiving God's forgiveness for these sins, I struggled with forgiving myself. This situation was so humiliating—I should have known better than to do these things! But if God says Christ's sacrifice was enough to buy forgiveness, I'd better agree.

As I writhed in emotional pain, the Holy Spirit brought several passages to my mind:

Psalm 62:1, "My soul finds rest in God alone," and its corollary, "Knowing Jesus is enough for joy." Was I going to choose to live this

Truth now, or was I going to unnecessarily continue to rub salt in my wounds, constantly castigating myself?

Psalm 34:1, "I will bless the Lord at all times, his praise shall always be in my mouth...." Will I now, by act of will, praise Him in and for this, accepting His perspective on the situation?

Psalm 86:1, "Bow down and hear, O Lord, for I am poor and needy. Preserve my soul, for I am holy, O Lord my God, save your servant who trusts in you." Will I choose to live in the balance of truth that in my flesh I am sinful, poor and needy while in my new creature status I am holy?

As I meditated on these, peace came, and with it sleep.

But it was not over; for next morning there was still heaviness in my heart, so I opened my journal and began to write. Psalm 23:2 came to mind: "...he makes me to lie down in green pastures." The Spirit helped me see that this failure on my part is a green pasture, both for me and for others—a place where I could feed on His Word and grow spiritually, a profitable place. So I began to list the good things that could come from this.

First is a chance to be humbled, to grasp more deeply how untrustable I am, and how trustable God is. These humiliating failures are, in fact, a clear answer to my own prayer for growth.

It is a chance to be weak so I can be strong in Him.

It is a powerful lesson on the danger of allowing fear of man to dominate, and of indulging in unwisely passing on information (gossip).

It is an opportunity to strike a blow at Satan by praising and by humbling myself in pursuing this injured relationship and asking forgiveness.

It is also an opportunity to demonstrate leadership by handling my failure biblically and to value relationships over pride and appearance.

In short it is a chance to turn failure into a victory that brings glory to God, growth to me and example to others.

Prayer: "Thank you, Lord, for your work of exposing my depravity, so that I will not trust in myself, but in you and your wisdom. Help me to think truth, following the prompting of your Spirit, to offer the sacrifice of thanksgiving and so bring glory to you. Amen."

November 18

"Deal with your servant according to your love and teach me your decrees."

Psalm 119:124

Praise you, Lord Jesus, Heavenly Father, Holy Spirit, the great Triune Revealer and Teacher of Truth. You have given us the written record of your revealed Word, supplying what we need to know so we can believe in you, trust in you, follow and obey you.

It is all there in the Bible, written plainly, yet hidden enough so that we have to dig down into it to see the great Truths you have laid out there. You invite us to the feast of your Word, but we must come, sit down and dig in before we can be nourished and strengthened by it.

Praise be to you for your Holy Spirit and the work He does in opening our eyes to deeper and greater Truths as we spend time in your Word. His activity and involvement in our lives is a great proof of your rich and fine love for us.

I praise you for the partnership you call us to. You supply the Word, then you give us the task and joy of seeking to understand it, searching it, memorizing and meditating on it, internalizing and obeying it. In response to our searching, you teach, give insight, open new understanding, apply truth and bring transformation.

"The unfolding of your words gives light; it gives understanding to the simple" (Ps. 119:130). Such a beautiful phrase, "the unfolding of your words." It is like each chapter is a paper folded over on itself many times; as we lift the first edge, there are hidden gems there, as we go further, there are new layers of truth on each fold beneath. We see these succeeding layers in reading, studying, meditation; each one has a new gem for us, each one revealing an inner shining light that gives further insight, further illumination, further transformation .

The truth is that we are, in comparison to you, Lord, simple, shallow, unknowing and uncaring. But your Word is the means of changing that. With the brightness of your Word, you give understanding to our simple minds so we can begin to see the correct foundation of thought, of life, of truth and philosophy, science and history, politics and religion.

With this foundational grasp of the reality of your existence, of your character, acts and power, we can have some understanding of how you work, what you are doing and how you want us to join in and cooperate with you.

> You are meaning to life, Lord, and bestow through your Word:
> light for living,
> principles for perception,
> wisdom for relationships,
> glimpses of the future,
> a grasp of history,
> a certainty of your presence and
> great guidance and protection.
>
> Your Word is wonderful, Lord Jesus:
> It is living, rich, powerful and deep.
> It is sharp to shape us,

gracious to guide us,
kind to comfort us,
enlightening to empower us,
right to reprimand us,
loving to lead us.

Your Word is what we need.
In it your character is revealed,
your plan explained,
your wisdom displayed,
your grace demonstrated,
your goodness shown,
your power revealed.

In it we can trust,
through it we can believe,
by it we can live.
Praise be to you.

Prayer: "We praise you for your tremendous, transforming, trustable Revelation, Lord. Help us to diligently dig in daily, to learn, apply, live and love it to the end. Amen"

November 19

"The LORD is my rock, my fortress and my deliverer…I call to the LORD, who is worthy of praise, and I am saved from my enemies."

Psalm 18:2a,3

As planned, we arrived at Barbara's mother's (whom we call "Omi"), at 1 pm. The plan, according to Omi, was to help her with garden work. However, when we arrived she was baking cakes, so we sat and talked for an hour waiting for her to finish—this was going to make it hard to get to our next appointment at 4 pm! But the Lord gave grace to praise and rest in Him.

At last, Omi was ready, so we collected the tools and went out. She wanted me to spade the garden for her, but in her eyes I couldn't seem to get it right. She took the spade and did a couple of rows to show me how it is done correctly. After that I managed to get it at least partly right. This was followed by cutting off old flower stems, and then trimming a fir tree, all minutely supervised and critiqued by Omi. Finally there was the cleanup, again directed in detail by Omi, including the final order to wash my hands.

As we walked home, Barbara expressed her amazement at how patient I'd been. Thinking on that, it struck me that it went beyond being patient: there had been NO feelings of impatience at being made to wait; NO frustration or anger at being told repeatedly I couldn't do it right; NO feelings of being a fool when I couldn't get the German commands and Omi was impatient with me; NO resentment at having my intelligence frequently questioned.

For those of you who know me, this is a pretty amazing change. It was not a case of having to restrain my impatience and anger. No, there was none. This is a great work of God, changing me from the inside, with all credit to Him. It is a further step up in the ongoing revival in my life, which is His doing, not mine. It is transformation flowing from His work in me.

My part has been worship, confession, meditation in the Word and prayer, proving the principle that much repetition of small, seemingly unimportant things brings big changes. And it is transformation through brokenness brought on by sin, confession and repentance.

It is also an answer to my consistently praying Colossians 1:9-11, "...that we may live a life worthy of God...being strengthened with all power according to his might that we may have GREAT endurance and patience, joyfully giving thanks to the Father...." God is answering!

This is one of the many gifts He offers us in Christ: the possibility of experiencing on-going transformation as we walk with Him, giving Him ever more glory.

Prayer: "Lord, help me to cooperate with you in the transformation process you want to work in me. Help me to be consistent in reading and meditating on your Word every day, in personal worship, in confession, in intercession. May I live a life worthy of you. Amen."

November 20

"Trouble and distress have come upon me, but your commands are my delight."

Psalm 119:143

I praise you this morning, Heavenly Father, for you are the Sovereign One, controlling all that goes on, all that comes to me. You hold back the tide of evil, allowing Satan only so much rope, and you use the fury of his attacks to advance your Kingdom.

Just yesterday I read of how many thousands in Haiti have come to faith after the great earthquakes of 2010. You used this tragedy to plow the hard and rebellious hearts of people, opening them to hearing Truth and surrendering to you.

Suffering is an unavoidable part of life in this sin-warped world; you are the One who allows what suffering comes to us, regulating it according to what we need to grow and give you glory, as well as what we can bear with your grace. In the suffering that comes, you have reasons, you have goals, you have growth, you have privileges for us. And we have the responsibility to flee to you, to turn to your Word, to take up and use your grace, to praise, to rest in you, to embrace what comes as opportunity to bring you glory.

I praise you:
- for your wisdom, which is far above our understanding;
- for your grace, which is more than enough;
- for your compassion, which provides all we need;
- for your love, which you pour out on us every moment.

Today's reading in EDIFIED! is a very appropriate reminder to us as Barbara goes through this dark valley.

"Trouble and distress have come upon me, but your commands are my delight."
Psalm 119:143

I praise you this morning, Heavenly Father, for you are the Sovereign One, controlling all that goes on, all that comes to me. You hold back the tide of evil, allowing Satan only so much rope, and you use the fury of his attacks to advance your Kingdom.

Just yesterday I read of how many thousands in Haiti have come to faith after the great earthquakes of 2010. You used this tragedy to plow the hard and rebellious hearts of people, opening them to hearing Truth and surrendering to you.

Suffering is an unavoidable part of life in this sin-warped world; you are the One who allows what suffering comes to us, regulating it according to what we need to grow and give you glory, as well as what we can bear with your grace.

In the suffering that comes, you have reasons and purpose, you have goals, you have growth and privileges for us.

And we have the responsibility to flee to you, to turn to your Word, to take up and use your grace, to praise, to rest in you, to embrace what comes as opportunity to bring you glory.

I praise you, Lord Jesus, my good and great Shepherd:
- for your wisdom, which is far above our understanding;
- for your grace, which is more than enough;
- for your compassion, which provides all we need;
- for your love, which you pour out on us every moment.

    The words of Psalm 119:141-144a come to mind, "Though I am lowly and despised, I do not forget your precepts." The negative reactions and hurtful words of people and their rejection of us can easily block out Truth from our thoughts. But our response must be to go immediately to your Word, Lord, to find our comfort, perspective, help and direction. People may not understand us, but you do. We may not understand what's happening and why, but you do and will help us through it.
    "Trouble and distress have come upon me, but your commands are my delight." Not being comfortable or freedom from stress, but your commands are my delight, and in the midst of difficulty your Word is sweeter still.
    "Your righteousness is everlasting and your law is true. Your statutes are forever right…." Praise be to you, O Lord God Almighty, that you are the measure of what is true, right and good.
    We so easily confuse comfort and convenience with good; but you so carefully teach us that weakness, hardships, insults, persecutions and difficulties are also things to delight in—when we have your perspective, think your thoughts and see with your eyes (2 Cor. 12:9,10).

Praise you that with your Word you work to give us the big picture, to help us understand what you are doing. You draw us up above the snares and rebellious thoughts of the world, the flesh and the devil.

Thank you for the shield of faith that we can raise with praise to ward off the fiery darts of self-pity, anger, frustration, impatience, self-centeredness and hurt as well as short-term thinking and feeling.

- Praise raises the barrier of protection.
- Praise heals the wounds.
- Praise opens our eyes.
- Praise produces perspective.
- Praise brings freedom.

All this is true because you, Lord Jesus, are the great Shepherd, intimately concerned with each of us each moment.

- You know us completely.
- You supply all that is necessary.
- You design the next lesson we need.
- You make us lie down in green pastures.
- You give us rest.
- You bring transformation.
- You guide us in the right way.
- You lead us into and through the dark valleys.
- You know exactly what you are doing.
- And we can trust You.

May Your commands be our delight no matter what we may experience.

Prayer: "Praise you for your great wisdom, love, grace and goodness. We bow before you in worship, we lift up your name, we exalt you in your perfection and we surrender our hearts to your love. We rise up now to obey you through the day as part of our worship. May you be glorified in our lives today. Amen."

November 21

"Give unto the Lord the glory due to His name; Worship the Lord in the beauty of holiness."

Psalm 29:2

One desire I have is to be a better worshipper, to exalt God more in my spoken worship, to honor Him more in my living. Here's a poem that I find inspiring help in my worship. Use it to focus on and worship our Great God.

Praise be to You
O Triune One:
Creator of the Sun
Spinner of the earth
Bringer of the dawn.

We glorify Your name
O Holy One,
Sparkling in purity,
Sharing light with every heart,
Shining Truth into every life.

We honor You,
O Mighty One,
Towering far above all creation,
Powerful in every good work,
Filling the universe with Your presence.

We exalt You,
O Good One,
Raining grace upon all,
Planting seeds of good desire,
Watering our souls with love.

We lift up Your name,
O Heavenly One,
 Father, Son and Holy Spirit
Worthy of all honor,
all worship, all glory.

We extol You
O Majestic One,
High and lifted up,
Wrapped in light,
Ruling for Eternity.

We worship You,
The only One deserving full
  Adoration,
    Glorification,
      Exaltation.

To You
It is right we bow down in worship,
In You

It is right we rise up to obedience
For You
It is right we praise forever and ever. Amen.

Prayer: "Yes, Lord God, I bow before you, the great and mighty Lord, worthy of worship, wonderful in your ways, powerful in your purposes. Help me today to live in your ways to bring glory to your name. Convict me of sin, remind me to obey, correct me when I stray, give me your wisdom so that praise will be the keynote of my life. Amen."

November 22

"It is good to give thanks to the LORD, to sing praises to your name, O Most High; to declare your steadfast love in the morning, and your faithfulness by night…."

Psalm 92:1,2

The greatest reason for giving thanks is YOU yourself, Lord: you are full of compassion, you are gracious, "longsuffering and plenteous in mercy and truth" (Ps. 86:15). "You are good and ready to forgive and overflowing with mercy to all who call on you" (Ps. 86:5). "Among the gods there is none like you, neither are there any works like yours. All the nations whom you have made will come before you and worship you, O Lord, and give glory to your name. For you are great and do wonderous things; you are God alone!" (Ps. 86:8-10).

- You are the God of power: speaking the stars into existence, gathering them into galaxies, forming the solar system, making sure the earth was in the proper orbit, tilt and spin. You spoke all the creatures into existence except for man, whom you formed out of dust.
- You are the God of faithfulness, promising a Savior in the garden, selecting Abraham, protecting his line and bringing out the Messiah at exactly the right time.
- You are the God of wisdom, able to weave history together, using even the evil of men and devils to accomplish your purpose.
- You are the God of knowledge, present everywhere, being aware of all that is happening, even before it comes to pass.
- You are the God of goodness, constantly pouring out your gifts on your undeserving and twisted creation: sun, rain, winter, summer, night and day, crops and animals, gems and metals.

- You are the God of wonders, having fashioned us marvelously, giving us our hands and feet, eyes and ears. You have designed the brain and nervous system, the heart and the circulatory system, our lymph and digestive systems. You gave us our ability to think, plan, choose and obey.
- You, Lord are the God of grace, giving all a second, third and many other chances to believe. You give blessing to those who curse you, do good to those who oppose you, offer forgiveness those who hate you.
- You are the God of kindness, working in your enemies to draw them into your family, rescuing them from the dominion of darkness and bringing them into the Kingdom of Light.
- You are the Lord of love, rejoicing in each of your children, looking at what is good and pure and lovely and praiseworthy rather than on our rebellion, selfishness and pride.
- You are the God of patience, working consistently in spite of our resistance and selfishness, working persistently through our pride and unbelief to transform each member of your family into the image of Christ.
- You are the God of eternity with no beginning, no ending, no growing, no diminishing, no change; you are the same total perfection yesterday, today and forever.
- You are the God of both justice and mercy, punishing sin while providing a shelter for the sinner.
- You are the God of righteousness, shining your glory over all your creation, giving light to those in darkness, sight to the blind, joy to the sad and peace to the tormented.
- You are marvelous, magnificent, majestic and mighty. Truly, to you belongs all glory and honor and praise, forever and ever.

Prayer: "May you be glorified in my life today through thanksgiving resulting in trust, faith, praise and obedience to your marvelous Word. Amen."

November 23

"As for God, his way is perfect; the word of the LORD is flawless. He is a shield for all *who take refuge in him.*"

Psalm 18:30

While at a Home Depot store in CT, I found a storm door in the discount rack. I was not sure it was the size I was looking for, but well, it was 75% off, so I thought to take a chance on it. Dragging it to the cash register, I handed the girl the discount tag. She entered the info, then had to reenter her login pin because it was such a big discount. However, the cash register would not accept her pin. Nine times she tried. "This has never happened before!" she exclaimed.

Well, I realized why it was happening at this moment: it was God protecting me from a wrong purchase! So I said, "I'll wait on this," and put the door back. When I got home I found that the door was the wrong size, so it was good I didn't buy it.

This is an example of how our loving Father warns us by giving us red flags or obstacles when we are about to make a wrong decision. He promises to give us direction: "I guide you in the way of wisdom and lead you along straight paths" (Pro. 4:11). But are we listening as He leads? Often I am so focused on the goal or object before me that I am not listening to His inner voice, so He gives me a little tap on the shoulder in the form of an obstacle to get my attention.

The way to "amplify" what God is saying so we can hear Him better is to praise Him for the obstacle. Praise opens our eyes, raises our sight and protects us from our own pushiness, impatience, selfishness and stubbornness. When we praise, we surrender. When we praise, we honor God. When we praise, we open the way for Him to protect, guide and provide (Psalm 50:23).

There have been a number of times in the last six months where God has put up similar red flags for me: an on line order not going through, a sense that I should wait to send a letter, the internet going down just when I wanted to do something. And a day or two later it became clear why God was warning me to wait.

Unfortunately, I didn't heed one of these warnings and now am literally paying for it. While trying to get internet access in Germany, we went to one shop that promised everything we wanted. The girl filled out the contract on the screen for us, but then she could not get it to print out, in spite of working at it for a good 20 minutes. Finally, she said, "Come back in an hour when the manager will be here."

We should have just gone home to pray about it more, but instead we came back and signed the contract. In the end the company couldn't keep their promises and charged us over $200 to end the contract. I failed to accept the light God gave and pressed ahead into trouble.

God wonderfully and lovingly gives us light all the time. Are we accepting it or walking in our own way? "The path of the righteous is like the first gleam of dawn, shining ever brighter till the full light of day. But the way of the wicked is like deep darkness; they do not know what makes them stumble" (Pro. 4:18,19).

Prayer: "Lord I commit myself to walk in your light all the time. Help me to do this, to heed your warnings, to praise you when things don't work out, knowing that you have something better in mind. Amen."

November 24

"Rulers persecute me without cause, but my heart trembles at your word."

Psalm 119:161

This is an astounding statement. When persecuted by powerful rulers, the psalmist is not afraid, he is not shaken—but it is his fear of God, his awe and fear of God's Word that causes him to tremble. This is faith in the unseen, believing and obeying the intangible in the face of very present pressure.

I am not there yet—I am very aware of and responsive to what I can see, and am only developing the life in the unseen, beginning with praise in and for all things.

"I rejoice in your promise like one who finds great spoil" (Ps. 119:162). This is another statement of faith. Think how I would rejoice in getting 100 million dollars. Yet your Word, Lord, is far more valuable than that. I should treasure it thusly, spending time in it, thinking about it, delighting in it, rejoicing in it.

The underlying reason for our trust in you, O Lord God, is your character, revealed in your written record and your living Word. Praise you, Lord Jesus, for the declaration of your perfect, polished, persistent character, each aspect in exact balance, with no evil, no selfishness, no impurity, no darkness.

"Great peace have they who love your law, and nothing can make them stumble" (Ps. 119:165). Praise you, Lord God, that your law clarifies reality for us. You are absolutely sovereign: no wisdom, no insight, no plan can succeed against you (Prov. 21:30). You control and filter all that comes to us; and along with your protection, you give us, who are weak in ourselves, more than enough grace to deal with it.

You have purpose and meaning in what comes. The greatest purposes are our being able to give honor to you, and our spiritual growth along with shining the gospel to all those around us. With these truths as our light, we needn't stumble into the traps of complaining, fear, selfishness and pride.

You are moving all events to a conclusion and are carrying us along at your side in the process. The outcome of our lives is certain (an exit from this world into your arms) and the outcome of history is certain (all evil will be confined to Hell, creation will be "untwisted" and all will be made anew) and our future is secure (we will spend eternity with you).

The confidence that you are at work—deeply, mightily, inexorably—brings growth in faith, rest in you and joy in life. We can know through your law of your great and mighty working, of your powerful, perfect, persistent plan for the universe. We can know of the significant role you have for each of your children, including a personally prepared place in Heaven.

"I wait for your salvation, O LORD, and I follow your commands" (Ps. 119:166). Knowing what is coming, we can patiently wait for what you will bring, and while waiting, confidently follow your commands.

You, Lord God, are Light, you are Love, you are Life. You work for good, you bring about good, you are only good. Your wisdom is right and true, solid and sure, far beyond our comprehension and totally trustable. You are the only One, the only purpose worth living for.

Prayer: "I exalt you, King of Glory, I honor you, God of Love, I praise you, Lord of Justice, I adore you, Ruler of Mercy. To you may there be honor and glory today in my motives, attitudes, thoughts, words and actions before you, before the unseen spirit world, before men, before myself. Amen."

November 25

Trials "have come so that your faith—of greater worth than gold, which perishes even though refined by fire—may be proved genuine and may result in praise, glory and honor when Jesus Christ is revealed."

1 Peter 1:7

"He who persists wins!" This is a saying by which we lived in the Middle East. There were so many obstacles to life and ministry that it would have been easy to give up and go home.

So often we were denied permission or presented with further obstacles when we tried to do the right thing. The government didn't want us there, most locals didn't want us there, some of our supporters didn't even want us there! But we stayed in obedience to God.

Sadly, many, many workers did give up and leave. And this is not unusual, for in Christian circles many believers fail to persist, moving from relationship to relationship, or church to church because things get difficult. I believe that when God specifically calls us to a relationship, or church, or ministry, we should stay there until God specifically calls us away. We should not let Satan drive us away with hardships.

Parenthetically, let me add that when a person is in an abusive relationship or abusive church, the wisest thing often is to leave; that is a different situation. Clear doctrinal reasons can also be a time to leave. And there comes a time when God may call us on to new situations, as

He has now called us to Germany—but never in opposition to His stated will.

Paul had this attitude of sticking to it. In Philippians 3:14 he said, "I press on toward the goal to win the prize for which God has called me heavenward in Christ Jesus." Paul wasn't about to give up because things were difficult (such as getting 39 lashes multiple times, being stoned and imprisoned, ship wrecked, being hungry, cold and sleepless) or because there are no results or he was left alone, as when everyone abandoned him when he was in prison. He went on to say, "All of us who are mature should take such a view of things."

The ultimate example, of course, is Jesus himself, as he wrestled in the garden with the temptation to draw back from the extreme suffering of death on the cross and abandonment by His Father. And He worked it through, sticking to the plan so He could redeem us all.

In the midst of the difficulties into which God has called each of us, He is doing some important things in us. James 1:2-4 is a familiar passage that gives us perspective: "Consider it pure joy, my brothers, whenever you face trials of many kinds, *because you know* that the testing of your faith develops perseverance."

There is the same concept of perseverance again: "He who persists wins." And what does a "persister" win? "… that you may be mature and complete, not lacking anything."

The next time you are tempted to give up on what God has called you to, wanting to move on to something easier and more comfortable, remember these verses in James. He has not called us to comfort but to completeness—and this can only come by persisting in the face of trials. He who persists in obeying God wins.

Prayer: "Lord, I am so weak, so prone to seek comfort rather than your glory. Help me to persist in what you have called me to. Help me to take up your grace, your power, your endurance today and join you in the work you have for me. Amen"

November 26

"May my cry come before you, O LORD; give me understanding according to your Word. May my supplication come before you; deliver me according to your promise."

Psalm 119:169-170

Praise be to you, Lord Jesus, for you are the door to the throne room of Heaven, making it possible for my cry to come before the Father. Praise you that at any moment I can come into the presence of God in your Name and ask for what is right, having confidence that you have opened the way so I will be heard.

You are my Redeemer, my Savior, my Advocate and my Intercessor. You, the Living Word, make sure that I am heard, that I am given grace, that I am delivered.

Lord Jesus, you are the only trustable One. Your record shows this clearly: you were faithful in your entrance into the world as promised in Genesis. You followed through to the end in your sacrifice, saving us to the uttermost, obeying the Father right down to the last detail. So when we ask for help according to your Name, we know that you will respond in your demonstrated faithfulness and deliver as is best.

"May my lips overflow with praise, for you teach me your decrees. May my tongue sing of your word, for all your commands are righteous" (Ps. 119:171-172). How else can we respond to your Revelation but to overflow with praise and sing of your Word. Your Word is filled with Light, it pours out Love, it infuses Life into those who accept it.

Praise and honor, glory and exaltation, surrender and obedience be to you, Lord Jesus, the Living Word. For, you are the Source of all good, the Wellspring of all that is positive, the Author of all that is right. Great goodness, grace and kindness flow out of your Being into our lives each moment. We can and must praise and glorify you whether we are able to see good or not, whether things are going well or not, whether we can understand what is happening or not. In volitional faith we submit to you, to you we sing praise, to you we lift our hearts in worship.

"May your hand be ready to help me, for I have chosen your precepts. I long for your salvation, O LORD, and your law is my delight" (Ps. 119:173-174). Yes, your law is my delight, Lord,—all else in the world pales in comparison. Just as the depths of your Word are endless, so the delight that rises from it goes on and on. The delights of earth—those that come from possessions, power, position and people—all soon fade. But the delight we have from your Word is ever growing, ever deepening, everlasting.

"I have strayed like a lost sheep. Seek your servant, for I have not forgotten your commands" (Ps. 119:176). Truly I tend to stray, failing to check in with you for direction, forging ahead in my own plans, forgetting to ask for wisdom. But you, Lord Jesus, are the patient, kind and persistent King. You work in love to correct, to bring your commands to mind, to guide and to mature us. Praise you for the wonder of your love, the persistence of your grace and the power of your presence.

Prayer: "'Let me live that I may praise you, and may your laws sustain me.' Yes, may the purpose of my life be to praise you, Lord Jesus, may you be exalted in my life every day, every hour, every moment, in every word and every action. Amen."

November 27

"I obey your precepts and your statutes, for all my ways are known to you."

Psalm 119:168

Recently I spent two weeks on a difficult spiritual trek, slogging through a swamp of mists, mud and mind-numbing darkness. I was wrestling with some serious negative issues with no discernible positive outcomes. And the negatives were amplified by my not being well physically.

While in this swamp, the Spirit challenged me to continue to use all that God has taught: praise, journaling, confession, meditation, reading the Word and prayer. Doing these took a lot of effort because I really didn't want to do them. It was like struggling through deep mud, taking one difficult step after another without any seeming progress. Living the truth that "Knowing Jesus is enough for joy, period!" had to be done on faith, without any positive emotions and against plenty of negative ones.

One night I went to sleep meditating on Psalm 31, "I am like a piece of broken pottery, I hear the slander of many, there is terror on every side...<u>but</u>, I will trust in you, Lord. I say, 'You are my God. My times are in your hands....'"

The next morning while still in the last of my dreams, Psalm 62:1-4 welled up in my mind, "My soul finds rest in you alone....From you comes my salvation…you only are my rock...." As I came out of sleep, I noted a difference: I found myself on the edge of the swamp, the Son was shining and there were the first discernable rays of joy in my heart again.

The situations hadn't changed at all; the uncertainty was still there, the hard choices were still going to have to be made. But God's Word proved true again: focusing on Him and obeying what He had taught brought me out of the swamp and into the light once more.

If you are struggling with something, let me encourage you to keep going to Him, processing your thoughts and emotions, offering the sacrifice of thanksgiving, thinking Truth, encouraging yourself in the Word, meditating on Scripture, knowing that He is at work and will bring you out.

"Find rest, O my soul, in God alone."

Prayer: "Praise you, Lord, that your precepts and your statutes guide me in what is right, that they protect me from what is evil and give me light to move forward. Help me to keep on doing what is right no matter what, to keep on thinking and trusting your Word. Forgive me for my unbelief. May I bring you honor by walking in truth and obedience today. Amen."

November 28

"I call on the LORD in my distress, and he answers me."

Psalm 120:1

Praise you, Lord God, my King of Glory, that you are everywhere in the universe all the time and that your Spirit is always in me, with me, by me, for me. At any time, in any place, in any situation when I pray, I am in your presence and you hear me.

Praise you that you are infinite—you can listen to 6 billion people praying all at the same time and give your full attention to each; you can hear and fully comprehend every prayer. You can answer each exactly as is needed in your wisdom, compassion and power. You have no shortage of resources, time, attention or desire to help.

When I call, you promise to answer. "In the day of my trouble I will call to you, for you will answer me" (Ps. 86:7). Your answer will be the right one, delivered at the right time, in the right way, opening the way for me to give you more thanksgiving and praise. Your glory, wisdom, righteousness, goodness, love and power will be displayed in your answer—whether it be a little whispered one, or the great shout of a miraculous one.

"Save me, O LORD, from lying lips and from deceitful tongues" (Ps. 120:2). The passing of history does not change the reality of your answering this prayer. As with David, so we are also surrounded by lying lips: Mus.lims, Hindus, Buddhists, JWs, Mormons, liberals, leftists, communists, fascists, socialists, capitalists, main line churches, Madison Ave, politicians, used car dealers, educators--and ourselves. You, Lord God, are the only One who always speaks the Truth, for you are Truth itself.

In you there is no lie, no deceit, no half-truth, no cover-up, no denial of reality, no deception. You are Light and Truth, Love and Life.

Your written Word is totally trustable. I praise you for the unshakable wonder of your written revelation—40 authors over 1200 years, without contradiction or error. Truth poured out on the page, reality clearly portrayed. In you we have truth to protect us, plus you are active to save us from the attacks of men and devils: "they take delight in lies. With their mouths they bless, but in their hearts they curse" (Ps. 62:4).

Praise you that you deliver us from such lies, starting with reforming our own lips: I so readily lie to myself, declaring such things as, "This is awful, I can't stand it!" when the reality is, "This is uncomfortable, unexpected and I don't like it, but with God's grace I can move through it."

With the media we should learn to ask ourselves, "What's the lie in this ad?" And doing the same with the statements of people, from the merchant to the politician, from the educator to the religious leader, be it Main line, Mus.lim or Mormon.

We must ask you, Lord, for wisdom to discern what is of the world, the flesh and the devil so we can reject it. And we need your wisdom to discern what is true so we can join you in it.

In the flood of lies that flows toward us every day, you give us the comfort of your presence, power and persistence, knowing that you are going to use all this to bring about the end of history while sweeping as many as possible into your Kingdom.

Praise be to you that we can rest in your truth. We can rest in your perfect and beautiful integrity of character, of word and of action. We can rest on your promises, act on your principles and trust in your precepts.

Praise be to you, the Mighty, Trustable, Gracious and Good God who will carry us through the events of today, giving plenty of protection, more than enough grace to deal with whatever comes, sufficient guidance to navigate the obstacles, overflowing love to encourage us and continual insight to make good choices.

Prayer: "Help me to live in the light of your truth today, Lord, discerning the lies within and without, and rejecting them for your reality. May you be glorified in my life. Amen."

November 29

"Through Jesus, therefore, let us continually offer to God a sacrifice of praise—the fruit of lips that confess his name."

Hebrew 13:15

My plane had taken off from Istanbul over an hour late and was now circling Frankfurt for the second time. It was 6:15 and my train left at 7 pm. My train ticket was for this train only and it looked doubtful that I would make it. I could feel the tension of worry building in my body.

God often gives me tests like this, opportunities to trust Him, Will I praise Him in faith, or worry in fear? If I give a response of faith and praise, then God gets great glory, for we are all being watched continually in the battle of life by spiritual beings—angels and demons—as well as people. If I give in to fear, I rob God of glory because I am worshipping the idol of having everything go my way, of being comfortable.

In this case, with His grace, I remembered to praise Him while still struggling with worry. After the plane landed, I quickly made my way to passport control, then to baggage claim where I waited for my bag—and waited and waited—another chance to praise. Finally it came out. Then there was the long dash to the train platform—I got there with 7 minutes to spare. Whew!

Then it began again, for my train was late! Late enough so I would probably miss the next connection. Another chance to praise God! And I did, this time with more enthusiasm, telling Him that if He allowed me to miss my next train, I was sure He had something better for me.

That is a key aspect here: if our plans don't work out, we can be certain that God has a better plan. We can trust Him with that. If we are praising Him in the midst of the changes and challenges, we will be more alert to the opportunities He will give, having us meet someone, be an example, share a word of comfort or witness.

In the end, the other train waited and I made it home. In all this God showed Himself faithful again, while giving me a chance to grow in my faith.

Each such "test" is another chance to put a brick in the wall of faith God is building in our lives, a chance to live by truth, to give Him honor. We just have to recognize what is happening: "He who offers the sacrifice of thanksgiving honors me and opens the way that I may show him the salvation of the Lord" (Ps. 50:23).

Prayer: "Father, help me to praise you when things are not working out, when failure and problems loom. Help me to be a glory giver, praising in faith based on your good character. May you be honored in my life today. Amen."

November 30

"As the Father has loved me, so have I loved you. Now remain in my love. If you obey my commands, you will remain in my love, just as I have obeyed my Father's commands and remain in his love."

John 15:9,10

Praise you, Lord God—Father, Son and Holy Spirit—that you are one God in three Persons. The perfection of your character is not only in qualities but in quantity, and includes relationships. There is nothing lacking in you, you have no need of anyone else, for you have love, communication, interaction, sharing and support amongst the three Persons of your being.

You are complete, perfect, entire, total in yourself. Therefore, the love that flows from you to your creation is fully voluntary—you have no need of anyone to love. On your part there is no emptiness to fill, no lack, no ulterior motive, just the fact that you are love. Therefore, your love is sure, trustable, unquenchable, fully independent of our actions, unrelated to our obedience. It is unending, ever flowing and without limit. Glory be to you, O God, for who you are, what you are, how you are.

I praise you also for the humility exhibited in your Triuneness. You, Father, are, as it were, the architect, while you, Jesus, are the builder, and you Holy Spirit, are the interior decorator.

You, Father, planned the provision of salvation, you, Lord Jesus brought it about, and you, Holy Spirit, work to bring conviction of guilt and opening of eyes resulting in people accepting salvation. You also work to bring sanctification in the lives of those who are born again. You each have your role and are satisfied in it.

In your rich and perfect relationships, you share amongst yourselves the honor and glory you deserve. You, O Father, direct attention to Jesus the Son, exalting Him, sharing your glory with Him. "Therefore God exalted him to the highest place and gave him the name that is above every name, that at the name of Jesus every knee should bow, in heaven and on earth and under the earth, and every tongue confess that Jesus Christ is Lord, to the glory of God the Father" (Phil. 2:9-11).

The Holy Spirit also directs attention to the Son, giving Him honor: "But when he, the Spirit of truth, comes, he will guide you into all truth...He will bring glory to me" (John 16:13, 14).

Jesus brought glory to the Father by His total dependence on Him during His time on earth as He fully, completely obeyed the Father.

I praise you, Lord God, for this perfect unity, this perfect harmony, this willingness to honor each other, to take certain roles, to share glory, to work together in exact and perfect balance.

Your example in the relationship and work of your Triuneness is what we should follow in our relationships: with friends, in marriage, family, church and community. You model this for us in your humility, the joining together, being willing to take specific roles whether primary, secondary, or tertiary, in the giving and sharing of credit (glory), having love and deference for each other—these are qualities we are also to exhibit in our relationships, especially in the believing community.

You, O God, are a wonder, a marvel, a mystery. You are worthy to be glorified and worshiped, obeyed and exalted. So we praise you, O Lord God, for you are triune and complex, triple and one, revealed and mysterious, total and complete, theocratic and compassionate. You are so far beyond our comprehension, and yet have stooped to bring us enough understanding to love you, follow you, worship you and obey you. We praise you for your goodness. You are worthy of all worship, love and obedience.

Prayer: "Today, Lord God, help me to live in the light of your Triuneness, interacting with my fellow believers as you do among Father, Son and Holy Spirit, taking specific roles, esteeming each other, being humble, serving and loving one another. I commit myself to obey you today, for your glory and honor. Amen."

DECEMBER

December 1

"One thing I ask of the LORD, this is what I seek: that I may dwell in the house of the LORD all the days of my life, to gaze upon the beauty of the LORD and to seek him in his temple. "

Psalm 27:4

Life is a battle. Every day. Satan uses my own sin, that of others, events out of my control, sickness, difficulty, persecution and many other things to push me in the wrong direction. There is no end to it. But I want to tell you that in the midst of this battle there is a great hope: life just gets better and better as we walk with Jesus.

Over the last three years there has been a pronounced upward trend in the trajectory of my life. I think I am experiencing a "J" curve; that is, a graph like the one below which for a long time shows just tiny incremental upward progress before there is rapid growth.

Over the years there has been slow progress in my life as God kept me consistent in quiet times, in memorizing and meditating on Scripture, in personal worship, praise, prayer and in persistent obedience. However, when this incremental progress of the J curve reaches a certain point, it turns a corner and begins to go up more quickly, then radically.

This seems to be what is happening in my life in every area: more growth, more patience, more positiveness, more grace, more joy. Barbara says I have definitely become easier to live with! This is more than just a "J curve," it is a "Jesus Curve!"

I must hasten to add two things. First, this is of God, not me! I want to "boast in Him." He is just fulfilling His promises of what He will do if we walk with Him (Psalm 1:1-3).

Second is that as the positives increase, so do the challenges. With more ability comes more responsibility. And with more grace comes more challenge.

One thing that has really stimulated this growth has been seeking to live the truth that "Knowing Jesus is Enough for Joy, Period!" This flows from the truth that: "My soul finds rest in God alone" (Ps. 62:1) —you've heard that one a few times before in this book, haven't you? Repetition of powerful truth is a good thing!

Applying this verse has rooted out a lot of idols, has helped me to "let go" of the temporal, "hold on" to the eternal "and rise above" the everyday hassles as well as bigger challenges.

Today my reading was in Psalm 52 where verses 8 and 9 restate what happens as we faithfully walk with God through the years:

> "But I am like an olive tree
> flourishing in the house of God;
> I trust in God's unfailing love
> forever and ever.
> …in your name I will hope, for your name is good.
> I will praise you in the presence of your saints."

Prayer: "Lord, help me to be faithful in cultivating my relationship with you: daily reading in your Word, daily worshipping you, daily confessing and moving ahead by prayer. Move me along on my Jesus Curve at the right speed and keep my eyes on you, seeking not growth, but you. Amen."

December 2

"I lift up my eyes to the hills—where does my help come from? My help comes from the LORD, the Maker of heaven and earth."

Psalm 121:1,2

This morning, Lord God, I want to lift up your Name and exalt you for who you are. You, O Lord, are the great Creator, spreading out the heavens by your power, speaking the stars into existence, suspending the planets on nothing, setting each in a perfect orbit around the sun, selecting the correct axis for our planet, spinning the earth at just the right rotation, shaping the mountains, rivers and seas and situating your creatures in the proper places.

You made everything well. You are the God of wisdom, of insight, of power and goodness, and these can all be seen in your beautiful creation, even though it is now twisted and warped by sin.

You are the mighty One who keeps this universe moving, literally, as stars, galaxies and larger groups all race outward at incredible speeds toward the edges of space.

You are the Sustainer of all creation, keeping it going until the proper ending time comes. You are the Redeemer of all existence, moving everything towards a conclusion of full cleansing. You are the Transformer, preparing all for the end of every twisted way when you will exclude every evil from eternity in Heaven. You will exalt everyone who believes. You will install an unending age of holiness, purity, celebration and joy.

You are the One to look to, to trust, to believe, to worship, to obey--for you are Truth, Wisdom, Light, Love and Goodness. You are the Most High, the Almighty and the All-righteous Ruler. You are King, Lord and God. You are the exalted One: there is no one like you, no one can approach the perfection of your marvelous character, no one is greater than you.

To you belong all honor, power and glory, O King of my heart, Ruler of my soul, Administrator of my day, Savior of my life. You are my God, my Lord, my Brother, my Bridegroom, Healer of my past, King of my Present, Preparer of my Future.

In you is all I desire, in you is all the world needs, in you is completion, fulfillment, perfection and the embodiment of goodness. What a wonder, joy and privilege to know you, to be your child and live with you each day!

Prayer: "I bow before you, O triune God, I lift up my hands to you, giving you my day, giving you my heart, my mind, my will, my emotions, my whole being. Use me for your glory in all you would have me say and do. Amen."

December 3

"My soul finds rest in God alone."

Psalm 62:1

The time here in the States has been jam packed with work—physical on the farm, mental in preparation, spiritual in teaching and counseling. There has been the temptation to shorten my personal time with God, but with God's help I've resisted this and been consistent, even though at times it is divided into sections throughout the day.

Worship, however, always comes first in the morning, taking time to remember who God is: the great and Triune One, worthy of praise and honor, exaltation and focus. It is in worship that we are sustained and strengthened, transformed and enlightened, giving us the perspective that Knowing Jesus is Enough for Joy! Here's a poem about this that came out of such a worship time, thinking on Psalms 62:1 and 73:25. May it encourage you as it did me.

Whom have I
    in heaven but you?
And Earth has nothing
    I desire besides You.
Knowing Jesus is Enough for Joy!

Elohim—Creator

Adonai—Master
Yahweh—Savior
Nissi—Defender
Knowing Jesus is Enough for Joy!

Stars' Creator
Day's Designer
Life's Sustainer
History's Ender
Knowing Jesus is Enough for Joy!

Creation's Redeemer
Sinners' Savior
Hearts' Transformer
Mansions' Maker
Knowing Jesus is Enough for Joy!

Strong Shepherd
Living Bread
Church's Head
Judge of all dead
Knowing Jesus is Enough for Joy!

Day Giver
Need Provider
Spirit Refresher
Soul Purifier
Knowing Jesus is Enough for Joy!

Heart Pursuer
Spirit Lifter
Soul Lover
Heaven Bringer
Knowing Jesus is Enough for Joy!

Worthy of Praise
You Ancient of Days
Your name we raise
In endless praise.
Knowing Jesus is Enough for Joy!

Whom have I
    in heaven but you?
And Earth has nothing
    I desire besides You.
Knowing Jesus is Enough for Joy, Period!

Prayer: "Lord, help me to live in the light of your glory and to volitionally choose to live in the truth that Knowing Jesus is Enough for Joy. Amen."

December 4

"He will not let your foot slip—he who watches over you will not slumber; indeed, he who watches over Israel will neither slumber nor sleep."

Psalm 121:3-4

I praise you, this morning, Lord Jesus, for when I awoke, you were there, waiting for me; you watched over me in the night; you protected me from harm; you prepared me for this day; and you are ready to carry me through it.

As the Psalm 121:4 says "…he who watches over you will…neither slumber nor sleep." You are the great and eternal God, powerful and present, who never needs to rest: you are ever alert, ever watching, ever protecting. Nothing slips by your notice, nothing happens without your knowledge, nothing comes without your permission. You are all seeing, all knowing, all understanding. You are aware of every danger, every possibility, every pitfall, and you act decisively to protect us from those that will harm us.

"The LORD watches over you—the LORD is your shade at your right hand; the sun will not harm you by day, nor the moon by night. The LORD will keep you from all harm—he will watch over your life…" (Ps. 121:5-7). Praise you for these great promises, reflections of your unshakable character, the basis of praise for you in and for all things.

I praise you that you know what is truly harmful--that which you deem spiritually damaging--and you prevent it from coming. We, from our human view point, confuse harm with being uncomfortable, with the loss of things or abilities, with having pain, illness and suffering.

But your understanding is much deeper, Lord: you see what will be an impetus for growth, a means of maturing, a platform for performing in your power, a demonstration of taking up and using your grace, a living lesson to those around us of what it means to know and walk with God--and therefore you allow these challenging things to come to us.

At the same time you see what will damage us spiritually, and protect us from these. I praise you for your wisdom and understanding, your power and persistence, your protection and love.

"…the LORD will watch over your coming and going" – the King James Version says your "going out and coming in" – "both now and forevermore" (Ps. 121:8). This we experienced in the many, many miles we drove on dangerous roads throughout Europe, the Middle East and Central Asia. On every trip you took us from home and brought us back. Praise be to you for your utter faithfulness, your great and mighty care, your complete involvement, your ever vigilant love in all we do each day. You are most worthy of worship, of trust, of praise, of obedience. I give you glory for who you are and for what you are going to do today out of your faithful and loving heart.

Prayer: "In the midst of today's swirl of activity, help me to remember your presence and protection. Help me to partner with you, playing the part you offer. May you be pleased and honored by my obedience today. Amen"

December 5

"The LORD is my strength and my shield; my heart trusts in him, and I am helped. My heart leaps for joy and I will give thanks to him in song."

Psalm 28:7

This morning I had an epiphany while reading in Paul David Tripp's significant book *Instruments in the Redeemer's Hands* (Phillipsburg, NJ: P&R Publishers, 2002). He writes, "Personal ministry…involves exposing hurt, lost, and confused people to God's glory, so that they give up their pursuit of their own glory and live for His"!!! (p. 184).

That is a massively profound statement, leading to a potential worldview shift. All of our lives we have been taught by our culture that the goal of life is to be independent, fulfilled, successful and comfortable—living for our own glory. And we've unconsciously absorbed this message.

In contrast, as we spend time in personal worship (giving God glory for who He is), our focus can shift away from our own little plans, problems, hurts and fears to the bigger picture of who God is and what He is doing. We can begin to see the major themes of the Scripture that Mr. Tripp points out: the Glory of God, the Greatness of God and the Grace of God.

Mr. Tripp goes on to say that personal ministry is "embedding people's personal stories in the larger story of redemption, so they approach every situation and relationship with a 'God's story' mentality."

In God's plan, He calls us to a partnership with Himself, giving us significant roles and responsibilities: He prepares situations for us, then waits for us to obey His directions, given primarily in His Word. If we willingly choose to obey, our foot can still slip, we can still fall, we can still suffer difficulty, but as we continue walking in obedience, we are lifted up again and again by His love and power.

Joseph in the Old Testament is an example of this. In his later life he understood some of what God had been doing in allowing/sending all the suffering of his early years. He said to his brothers concerning their having sold him into slavery, "You meant it to me for evil, but God meant it for good, to the saving of many people" (Gen. 50:20).

Joseph was thinking about his having saved his extended family, all the Egyptians and people in surrounding countries from starvation. That was true. However, this it was only a small part of what God was actually doing. Through Joseph, God preserved the line of Judah from whence came the Messiah. So Joseph was one of the people prepared by suffering, through whom God brought about the eternal salvation He offers to all. God was doing something immeasurably huge when he sent Joseph to Egypt as a slave! [This insight is from a lecture by Fran Sciacca of Hands of Hur Ministries.]

So what is God doing in our lives with the difficulties He brings to us? Are we, through worship, looking at God's glory daily, and thereby getting glimpses of the great things He's doing? Are we grasping that our disappointments, hurts and sufferings are all being used by Him in the big picture in significant ways we can't understand, and therefore praising Him for these problems?

As an application of this, a doctor comments that getting "over an illness should not be the primary goal" for a Christian. "What glorifies [God] is what is best for all believers; therefore what glorifies Him will be the best for the sick believer. Getting well is not necessarily the best thing…The hope for the believer is victory, not relief. Relief is not inherently wrong, but it becomes wrong when it is the primary goal [an idol]. God promises victory in illnesses and trials, not deliverance from them." (Dr. Robert Smith, *The Christian Counselor's Medical Desk Reference* [Stanley, NC: Timeless Texts, 2004]). The real goal is God's glory!

Prayer: "Lord, I confess that my glory has my goal, not yours. Forgive me for pursuing personal comfort as my goal and idol instead of your glory. Help me today to live instead with the desire to bring you glory and honor through my motives, thoughts, words and actions, trusting you to carry me along in your great plan to end history, eliminate evil and bring in the new Heaven and Earth. Amen."

December 6

"My heart is not proud, O LORD, my eyes are not haughty…."

Psalm 131:1a

This verse is a good exhortation for me today. Unfortunately, my heart and eyes are proud and haughty, certainly in relation to this brother I am struggling with. Thank you for exposing these sins in my heart that I might repent of them.

"I do not concern myself with great matters or things too wonderful for me" (Ps. 131:1b). I often try to concern myself with big things that are actually beyond my power, wisdom, ability and responsibility; help me, Lord to focus on the things you desire to have worked out in my life.

"But I have stilled and quieted my soul; like a weaned child with its mother, like a weaned child is my soul within me" (Ps. 131:2). Being weaned means accepting "NO!" in life. This has to do with being content with what I have, with what you have given, not lusting after more. This has to do with resting in you, rejoicing in you, resolving to focus on you.

Help me to let go of the tinsel and bangles of life, and instead to hold onto the great truths of your Word: your mighty, unwarranted Love, your Holy nature, your Gracious heart, your Gifts of forgiveness, freedom and joy. Help me to delight in your abundant goodness as you grant us an upward walk with you, sufficient security and significance, plenty of patience, protection, provision and power for life. I praise you, Lord, for your wonderful character, your marvelous creativity, your great love of what is right, your endless supply of goodness.

Help me to rise above the petty things I have allowed to ensnare my soul and instead let you rule, let you reign in my thoughts, emotions, will and life.

I praise you for the privilege of lifting my soul to you, of having the Light of your Presence shine down into my mind, will and emotions, exposing sin, bringing me to repentance, cleansing evil, giving love and direction. I praise you, Father, Son and Holy Spirit for your gracious and wise work in my tiny, twisted, self-centered life.

"O Israel, put your hope in the LORD both now and forevermore" (Ps. 131:3). What a great command! I have been subtly and unknowingly putting my hope in my own efforts, in my performing well, looking good, feeling good, being good. Forgive me, Lord, for this. My hope must be only in you, my Lord and God, in your guidance and protection, your provision and presence—then as I partner with you through obedience, you will bring to pass what you desire. You are trustable, for you are wise, loving, patient, persistent, holy, righteous, just, merciful and gracious, ever giving with great abundance all that we need.

Prayer: "You, Lord God, are worthy of my worship in every matter, in every happening, in every thought, word and action. I praise you, I thank you, I lift up your name. May my life be a sweet fragrance of trust and truth before you today. Amen."

December 7

"Let the morning bring me word of your unfailing love, for I have put my trust in you." Psalm 143:8

While in a difficult situation recently, someone asked me how I could be so cheerful. The answer is a Scripture-based phrase that I often use to give myself perspective: "God is moving history to a conclusion and is taking us with Him!" Whatever the present event, it is part of God's plan to finish history and move us into eternity. He is in control; I can trust Him.

This perspective is found throughout Scripture. Colossians 3:2-4 expresses it well: "Set your minds on things above, not on earthly things." This gives us the wider, God-focused perspective.

"For you died, and your life is now hidden with Christ in God." We can leave behind our old culturally-based, performance-oriented, comfort-focused value system. Instead we can choose to rest in the security we have in Christ.

"When Christ, who is your life, appears, then you also will appear with him in glory." He WILL appear, and He WILL bring us with Him, and He WILL give us a place in His glory—we can focus on this long-term truth rather than our short-term accomplishments or failures!

This understanding gives us a wide and long view of what's happening. This view can change our goal from being comfortable and safe, to joining God in what He's doing, to embracing the adventures He's prepared for us.

If, from a human perspective, my whole life collapses around me (illness, accident, loss, poverty, persecution, injustice, war), I can look at it within the bigger picture of God's glory, greatness and grace, knowing that He is doing something significant through it; therefore, I can praise and trust Him in it. My favorite verse sums it up: "My soul finds rest in God alone" (Ps. 62:1).

This is a huge shift from "normal" human thinking. And we can cooperate with God in making this shift by internalizing Scripture, then putting it into practice in little every day events. Disappointments, delays, little hurts and small losses then all become opportunities to offer the sacrifice of thanksgiving (Ps. 50:23) and honor God.

In giving thanks, we affirm that God is good, that God is in control, that God is at work using each irritation to expose my sin, to transform me, to give me opportunity to be a light to those around me, to give Him glory before the unseen hosts. Truly, knowing Jesus is enough for joy, period! Let's join Him today in living in this truth!

Prayer: "Lord Jesus, you are enough. Help me to walk with you through this day in your power, giving you glory in each decision, trusting you rather than myself. Praise be to you for what you will do in me today. Amen."

December 8

"Therefore, as God's chosen people, holy and dearly loved...."

Colossians 3:12a

There is so much to thank and praise you for, Lord, if we open our eyes to see it. Among your gifts to us are: a rich, growing, wonderful relationship with you, eternal life, meaning in life, significant work in living for you, family, good relationships, continual growth spiritually, intellectually and emotionally, a reasonable level of health, a mind that works, hands that function, a small and simple home, good friends, love, life, laugher, light, sight, protection and goodness.

All that is good flows from you, Lord God. You, Heavenly Father, are the giver of every good gift, planning out all for our future and guiding us through each day. You, Lord Jesus, are the supplier of strength, making it possible to work, to achieve, to join you in what you are doing. You, Holy Spirit, are the giver of wisdom, insight and guidance, the One who brings fruit in our lives. You are my Triune Lord, my great Shepherd, my Savior. You are absolutely trustable. I can and must praise you in and for all things.

Praise be to you for your great love that pours out of your heart and into our lives every day. First it flowed to us when we were your enemies: "But God demonstrates his own love for us in this: While we were still sinners, Christ died for us" (Rom. 5:8). Now it flows to us as your children. We are--against all reason, against all hope, against all of what we deserve--dearly loved, determinedly delighted in, definitely doted on and deeply cared for.

Your love is powerful, rich, unquenchable, unstoppable, unending, uninfluenced, unilateral, immeasurable, great and good. Your choosing us to be your children is a call to bask in your forgiveness, love and grace. It is an insistent invitation to delight in your great, wholehearted acceptance of us, in your joy at being our Heavenly Father, in your consistent, almighty, pure, wonderful, goodness-filled, grace-fueled love.

We are yours and you are glad. We come to you in selfish prayer—but you are delighted that we come at all. We obey a bit—it gives you joy. We doubt, disobey, disrespect you—you forgive, chasten, provide guidance and love us again.

This great, wise love, coupled with a growing revelation of how much you have forgiven us, calls us to a deeper, wholehearted obedience, an answering of love to your Love.

I praise you that in you we are chosen, holy and dearly loved; that we are called to abide in you; that we are claimed to be your sons and daughters, commissioned to special service, chosen to bear fruit, to live for your glory, to praise you in all things, to rejoice in your goodness, to obey in your power, to worship in your presence.

Your love is beyond conception, beyond imagination, beyond comprehension, beyond human wisdom. Your love is cleansing, forgiving, transforming, uplifting, edifying, and purifying. Your love is the opposite of selfishness, pride, ambition and control. It is empowering, equipping, embracing, enduring and excellent. It is too good to be true, yet is more than true.

In your love we can bask and be transformed. As we look upon you, shining in your glorious love, we are being transformed into your image (2 Cor. 3:18). And in delighting in you, in being satisfied in you, we give you glory.

Prayer: "Forgive us, Father, for not giving you more glory, honor and praise by basking consistently in your great, glorifying, gracious love. Help me, Lord, to revel in your love all day today, to walk in the light of your goodness, to exalt your name, to rejoice in you, to embrace all that you send, for you are good and worthy of all worship, obedience and love. Amen."

December 9

"My grace is sufficient for you, for my power is made perfect in weakness."

2 Corinthians 12:9

The idea came to write about the concept of processing difficult events for my next prayer letter. To help me with this, the Lord has graciously provided a difficulty in the last couple of days for me to deal with as an example!

I must get a German driver's license. This is not as simple as it is in the States and can be very expensive (well over $1000). At first I was told there was no need for my going to a costly driving school, but this week the verdict came that I must go through a school.

The written test is difficult: there are 927 possible questions, including ones like, "How long does it take for a 1500 kilo car pulling an 800 kilo trailer to stop when it is going 50 kilometers an hour?" And I must know the answers to every question, as the test will consist of 30 random ones. Then when I get my German license, they will take away my US driver's license, which means that the registration of the van in my name in Connecticut may no longer be valid!

My initial response to all this was a natural, "Oh no!" But the Spirit quickly brought Scripture to mind to replace the negative. I lifted my thoughts and feelings to God, writing in my journal: "Lord, I don't like this situation; it has a lot of difficulties, uncertainties and a negative outcome. There's a long, potentially expensive, bureaucratic road ahead of me. I want to complain and gripe, to talk about how "unfair" this is, but your word says, '…for Christ's sake I will delight in weakness, insults, hardships…for when I am weak, then I am strong.' (2Co 12:9,10).

"I am certainly weak in this (I can't change anything or guarantee a good outcome), and getting this license is a hardship (taking time and energy away from the normal tasks you give me of counseling, writing and travel), but it is also a chance to trust you, to praise you when I don't feel like it, to offer the sacrifice of thanksgiving, to honor you (Ps. 50:23).

"I praise you now for what you are going to do in this situation before knowing what you will do; I praise you for how you are going to honor your name, show your power, and work out what is best. Praise and glory be to you, the Most High, the All Powerful, the Holy and Good One."

Writing this out is much more helpful to me than just saying these things. As a result, I was able to let go of what bothered me, hold on to what is eternal, and rise above the coming difficulties. God is good all the time, whether I can see it or not, and I praise Him for it.

Epilogue: *Months after this was written, I am pleased to report that the Lord provided a driving school which made the application for me for the written test and only charged $50! And when I took the test after several months of study, the Lord answered my prayer for one in which I knew all the answers and got 100—a rare happening on these license tests, I am told. God answers in power. And giving up my CT license did not affect my van's registration at home. To Him be the glory.*

Prayer: "Lord, help me to respond to difficulties with praise, prayer and persistence in obeying you. Help me to lift my soul to you, to see things from your perspective and to give you glory before any solution comes. Amen."

December 10

"My help comes from the LORD, the Maker of heaven and earth."

Psalm 121:2

Glory be to you, O Creator God, you who spoke and brought all into being. On this clear morning, as the bright orb of the sun rises over the hills, shooting its first light beams into the fog filling the valley, warming the birds flitting through its new light, we see again your power, your beauty, your grace.

The earth--huge, expansive, not yet fully explored--is your marvelous creation. You made it the ideal size to provide the correct amount of gravity. You gave it specific proportions of sea and land. You made the atmosphere of ideal mixture and size for carbon-based life. You gave it a great variety of climates, of height and contour, with deep valleys, tall mountains and great plains. You provided the minerals for life and work and beauty. You stocked it with interesting, useful and beautiful animals. You demonstrated your wisdom and creativity in the vast variety of species you made with differing modes of movement, sizes and shapes.

Yes, you, the Maker of heaven and earth, are a God of unimaginable power, deep wisdom and great creativity. And the wonder is that, in spite of our smallness and sinfulness, in spite of what we deserve, our help comes from you, a help commensurate to the greatness we see in your creation.

"He will not let your foot slip—he who watches over you will not slumber" (Ps. 121:3). As you know the name of every star, you also know what goes on in every moment of my life, keeping track with full-attention accuracy. In this context you give us your promise, that as we seek to follow you, you will not let our foot slip. Your help is continual, immediate, informed, wise, powerful, constructive and good. You know what should happen and what shouldn't, and will bring the necessary to pass.

"The LORD will keep you from all harm—he will watch over your life" (Ps. 121:7). You, in your deep, rich, complete, unfathomable wisdom know what is harmful to me. My estimation of harm is what disappoints, hurts, makes my life hard or brings loss. In this definition I am focused on me, on a short term, small, self-centered picture.

Your estimation is far different: you look at the great spread of time and history, of the universe and beyond into eternity. You see what will make us grow, shape us spiritually, give us opportunity to glorify you, to act in faith, to play a significant role in the drama of the unwarping of the universe. You want to transform us to be like Christ, to share your glory with us, to give us important work, to move us forward in the Kingdom of light.

These goals sometimes require pain, disappointment, suffering, sickness and loss. But the difficulties which you allow are not harm—they are the means of moving us up the golden staircase towards eternity (as described in the reading for January 1).

What is harmful is what separates us from you, that which hurts us spiritually. Such harm can come from the world, the flesh and the devil—but it has more to do with our inner response than with what comes from the outside.

When I react with complaining, criticalness, negativeness or unforgiveness, I bring harm to myself. I am accepting the harm that the devil offers. This is my choice. But you lead us in the opposite direction, to the freedom of praise, to the sacrifice of thanksgiving, to grace under pressure, to growth in pain, to deepening in difficulty, to joy in all circumstances.

Yes, you keep us from true harm; you protect us from true harm; therefore we can trust you fully and praise you in all.

Prayer: "Praise be to you, our mighty Shepherd, our great God who watches over us in all. We love you, trust you, exalt you, praise you and commit to following you. Help us to obey you today in all that comes so you may receive more and more glory in our lives. Amen."

December 11

"Rescue me and deliver me in your righteousness…."

Psalm 72:1

As I work my way through the Psalms, using them for morning worship, the Spirit has brought to my attention a new emphasis: an appeal to God's character as the basis for prayer. This has two aspects. First is asking God to answer according to His qualities:

"…in your great love, O God, answer me in your sure salvation….Answer me, O Lord, out of the goodness of your love, in your great mercy, turn to me" (Ps. 69:13,16).

This means we can pray like this: "Lord, please answer me out of your love, out of your righteousness, out of your faithfulness, out of your wisdom, out of your goodness, out of your power, out of your grace."

Such praying is in a strong way of submitting ourselves to His standards—His righteousness is much more exacting than my concept of what is righteous! His love may mean saying "no" to my present request in order to give me something better later. It is asking for His will to be done in a way that will reflect His character.

The second aspect has to do with appealing to God on the basis of what the answer to prayer will do for Him:

Help us, O Lord, for when you do, "then men will say, 'Surely the righteous are rewarded; surely there is a God who judges the earth'" (Ps. 58:11).

"Not for our sake, GOD, no, not for our sake, but for your name's sake, show your glory. Do it on account of your merciful love, do it on account of your faithful ways" (Ps. 115:1).

So we can pray, "Answer me for your Name's sake, Lord, that men may know you are God, that men may know there is a God in the church."

Praying this way certainly helps to refine our motives in asking for things: am I asking for my own comfort only, or is this really for God's glory?

In asking God to act according to His character and for His glory, we are in no way "twisting God's arm." Instead we are focusing on the One who will decide how to answer in what is best, we are surrendering to His desire. This is joining Him in what He is doing. It is a step up in prayer.

Prayer: "Lord help me to pray in line with your Word, with your Will, in your Way. Guide me in incorporating these new insights into my prayer life. Answer me according to your wisdom, grace and goodness. Answer me so that those around me may see your glory. Amen."

December 12

"How sweet are your words to my taste, sweeter than honey to my mouth!"

Psalm 119:103

The more I meditate[12] on your Word, Lord, memorizing, personalizing and praying it, the sweeter the Word becomes. I praise you, O Lord, for your great and glorious Revelation; I praise you for the privilege of partnering with your Spirit in understanding, embracing and applying your Word in my life. To you be glory for your powerful plan of redemption, transformation and continual growth.

Your Word shows you to be a consistent giver of goodness to all creatures, whether they be your children or your enemies. You are the God of unbounded grace, pouring out on all peoples the opposite of what we deserve. Your Word helps us to see this, as we so naturally fool ourselves into thinking we are good, comparing ourselves with those we consider worse than us, rather than comparing ourselves to your perfect standard.

You have also revealed your multifaceted and lovely character in how you have created all we can see. Praise you for the beauty of your world, twisted though it may be by sin: a myriad of shades of green, a multitude of types of flowers, a million different colors, a majestic display of your power in forming mountains, plains and seas, a magnificent show of glory in the stars every night.

---

12 see Appendix

You have created the vast variety of animals, the intricacies of the minute world of single celled creatures, the incredible variety of insects, the many means of movement from the flagellum of a virus to the great bodies of elephants, walrus and whales. And the expanse of your creation astounds us: the superb spread of the heavens stretching out and out beyond anything we can comprehend.

Praise you for revealing yourself in both your Word and in your world, giving all people opportunity to know you, to come to you, to enter your shelter, your Kingdom, your Family.

Praise you, too, that you show us more of your beautiful qualities as you take care of us. Every day of our lives you manifest your power in protection, your creativity in custom care, your love in beauty, your sharing in your provision and guidance.

You are also the God to be feared for your justice and holiness, a God to be obeyed for your wisdom and righteousness, a God to be loved for your goodness and grace, a God to be worshiped for your greatness and glory.

In you is more than we could ever imagine; in you is more than we can ever comprehend; in you there is more than enough to keep us learning for all eternity.

You are the God who is too good to be true, while being more than true. Glory be to you, honor be to you, obedience be to you, joy be to you this day in my motives, thoughts, words and actions.

Prayer: "Lord, keep me in awe of you, keep me worshiping you, praising you all day long. Keep my eyes open to the beauty around me that reflects the loveliness of your character. May I delight your heart in my delighting in you. Amen."

December 13

"He who dwells in the shelter of the Most High will rest in the shadow of the Almighty."

Psalm 91:1

It is so good and right to praise God for the gift of His Son, and all that Jesus brought to us. One gift that Jesus gave us is freedom from the oppression of the devil. I've told before of my slavery to irrational fears of the dark with thoughts of "If I open that door, there will be a flaming, ugly face hanging in the air!" or "If I open my eyes, there will be a wolf at the foot of the bed with red, fiery eyes!"

These fears were powerful and palpable even to those around me who did not share them. About 8 years ago, while in Albania, the Lord orchestrated a "show-down" with these fears, and as I wielded the

Sword of the Spirit, using Psalm 23, those fears were vanquished, and I'd not been troubled since--until this fall.

Now here in Germany, Barbara stays with her aged mother about 6 nights a week to help her with going to bed and getting up in the morning, and on those nights, when I am home alone, those irrational, powerful fears began to return. Not as strong as before, but still compelling.

Psalm 23 again was effective against them as I prayed, "'The Lord is my shepherd, I shall not want.' Lord, even if such a face should be there when I open the door, I know that you are with me and would help me."

With the Spirit's help, I was winning, but the fears kept coming—until one night. That night as I got up to go to the bathroom, intentionally not turning on the lights in order to face these fears fully, just as I was opening the bedroom door, a new thought came. "Do you know who's actually on the other side of this door?" I paused and then answered the question: "Jesus!"

Wow, that thought was like a precise atom bomb that blew my fears to smithereens. I was immediately freed, and have had no reoccurrence since! Now every time I open a door in the dark, I think: "On the other side of this door, waiting for me, is the Lord Jesus: my Rock, my Salvation and my high Tower!"

As Psalm 68:6 says, The Lord "leads forth the prisoners with singing, but the rebellious dwell in a sun scorched land." The Lord desires to free us from the corruption of sin and the traps of Satan. May He help you in your struggles as He helped me in mine through meditating on and wielding the sword of the Spirit, obeying the Word.

He always wants to work hand in hand with us in this. When we obey, cooperate, and use the Word, then He moves, just as He did with removing the peoples from the promised land so the Israelites could live there. The Israelites still had to strap on their swords and fight, but God is the One who actually cleared the land for them. And so He fights for us as we obey what we know to be true.

Prayer: "Lord, I praise you that you are the all-powerful One who has defeated Satan, sin and self. Help me to dwell in the shelter of your Word that I may rest securely in the shadow of your Almighty power and protection. Amen."

December 14

"For whom the Lord loves he chastens...."

Hebrews 12:6

You are a wonder, O Lord God, for in your wisdom you always know exactly what you should do. You understand the right role to play in each situation: sometimes our Savior, sometimes our Father, sometimes our Coach, sometimes you are our Rebuker and sometimes our Discipliner.

Your basic invitation to all people is to move from being a child of wrath to being a child of God. You are a judge for all people, for all are sinners, but you want to move from being the Judge of all to being the heavenly Father of all, if they will only believe.

Those who have taken your invitation and have become your children have also been made saints: forgiven, cleansed, transformed into a new creature, adopted into the family of God and are now dearly loved and deeply cared for.

We maybe saints in Christ, but we still continue to sin unintentionally and, sadly, sometimes intentionally. In our rebellion and unbelief, however, you are no longer our judge; you do not condemn us in our sin, for we stand in the forgiveness of Christ. You are now our heavenly Father who convicts us, chastens us, trains us and forgives us (Heb. 12:1-17). I praise you that you are the perfect Father, not too lax, not too strict, but an exact balance of grace and goodness on one side, firmness and force on the other.

You are committed to us, to our growth, to our sanctification. Your love and grace means that you will never reject us. Therefore, we never need to be reticent or reluctant about coming to you to confess.

As it says in Psalm 86:4,5, "Rejoice the soul of your servant, O Lord, for I lift up my soul to you, *for you are good and ready to forgive and plenteous in mercy to all those who call upon you.*" Your goodness, your forgiving heart and your great mercy continually beckon us into your presence.

In our relationship with you there is "no condemnation for those who are in Christ Jesus, because through Christ Jesus the law of the Spirit of life set me free from the law of sin and death" (Rom. 8:1,2). So our motive for obedience is not to earn forgiveness, but to love you.

I praise you that when we sin, we can come humbly in repentance, and with confidence that you will receive us with goodness and grace, with kindness and forgiveness. Your desire is not to punish but to cleanse, heal and transform.

You, the holy God and the perfect Shepherd, are eagerly committed to dealing daily with us, your unruly, unrepentant, unhappy children. Each time we sin, we give you pain, we steal your joy, we rob you of glory. Yet you, as a good Father, patiently, unselfishly, graciously correct us again and again.

We are such slow learners, but you are such a tenacious teacher. Praise you for your patience, for your persistence, for your prompting, for your prodding, for your power at work in our lives each day.

I praise you that you are consistent in your encouragement for us to obey: your Spirit convicts, directs, brings Scripture to mind, has others speak into our lives and sends input for us.

I praise you that when we don't listen, you bring more pressure to bear, letting us suffer some more of the consequences of our rebellion, bringing others to rebuke us, increasing conviction. And if that doesn't work, then you chasten us with more dire conditions to bring realization of sin leading to repentance. You are worthy of worship for your faithful wholehearted work in our lives.

Prayer: "Help us, Lord, to learn faster, to respond immediately to the prompting of your Spirit—so we can bring you glory and honor by praise instead of pouting, obedience instead of obstinacy, service instead of selfishness. You are worthy of worship: may we consistently bow before you in humility, rise up to obey in joy, go with you through the day in submission that you may be exalted before the nations. Amen."

December 15

"See, the Sovereign LORD comes with power, and his arm rules for him. See, his reward is with him, and his recompense accompanies him. He tends his flock like a shepherd: He gathers the lambs in his arms and carries them close to his heart; he gently leads those that have young."

Isaiah 40:10, 11

Honor and glory and thanks be to you, Lord God, our powerful and tender Shepherd, for all you have given. The list of things to praise you for is endless. Starting on the physical level: knees that still function, an eye that sees, glasses to sharpen my vision, hands that can flex and grasp, feet so complex and effective, hair mostly still in place.

On a higher level: brains that still work, thoughts to stimulate, work to do, relationships to enjoy, grace to live, insights for life.

And higher still: being your child, being dearly loved, being chosen and equipped by you for special service, being created in your image, being forgiven, cleansed and transformed, having meaning in life.

Further up: You yourself, Lord God are the ultimate gift to us, in your perfection and glory, your goodness and greatness, your wisdom and righteousness, your discipline and justice, your grace and compassion, your creativity and faithfulness, and most of all, your great, wonderful, powerful and endless love.

You, Lord God, are our Triune King, worthy of worship, for you are awesomely powerful, faithfully holy, persistently just, righteously wrathful, immensely merciful, and eternally right. To bow before you is good, wise and positive; to resist you is utter foolishness, for "no wisdom, no insight, no plan can succeed against the Lord" (Pro. 21:30).

"Splendor and majesty are before you, strength and glory are in your sanctuary" (Ps. 96:6). You are clothed in light, brilliantly shining in your holiness, unapproachable in purity, radiating glory all around you.

You are marvelous in your being: majestic in your might, glorious in your goodness, bountiful in your beauty, astounding in your graces, awesome in your wisdom, almighty in your power. You move with dignity and grace, majestically doing simultaneously and perfectly the next hundred million things in your plan.

You are glorious, you are strong, you are full of wonders, you are pure. We ascribe to you glory and strength, we proclaim your greatness to the nations, we lift up and magnify your marvelous name. You are supreme, you are superb, you are sovereign.

We come before you now with an offering of worship, placing ourselves and all you have given us on the altar of praise, for you are worthy of all honor.

Prayer: "We tremble before you, the Holy God, the great I AM, the righteous Judge, the faithful Father, the resurrected Lamb. You are worthy of our submission; so we bow before you this day in surrender, we rise up to walk in obedience in the light of your presence. Use us today to bring glory to your name. Amen."

December 16

"I lift up my eyes to you, to you whose throne is in heaven."

Psalm 123:1a

Praise you, my Heavenly Father, that you are the sovereign One, reigning over the events of our lives, and at the same time, giving us great latitude in making decisions. Praise you that you can weave all this together to bring about the results you desire.

I think of Jonah, who in his disobedience, was able to tell the sailors on his sinking ship about you, the great Creator God. Then you demonstrated your power to them by calming the storm when they threw Jonah overboard, which resulted in the sailors worshiping you. You can take our sin and use it for good. Amazing!

Praise you for your love in wanting to work with us, inviting us to partnership with you. You share with us the pleasure of action, the satisfaction of achievement, but call us to find joy foundationally in our relationship with you. You are truly a Father, not just an owner.

"Save me, for I am yours..." (Ps. 119:94a). What a wonderful basis for appeal: since I belong to you, since I am your child, since I am your ambassador, since I am you servant, since I am yours, save me! And you will!

What certainty, what confidence we have in coming into your presence, O Lord God, King of the universe. The wonder is that you delight in our coming, you invite us to prayer, you call us to praise, you command us to intercede. We please your heart when we cry out to you in prayer.

Praise you that you are the all-knowing One. You know the deep longings of our hearts, our dreams and desires. You understand our motives, you know how things will work out in the future as a result of our desires, decisions and words. You guide and protect, and you let us go the way of rebellion if we insist. As you said to the people of Israel, "So you think having a king is best? Try Saul for a few years!"

Move in my present situation, Lord: bring healing to this one tense relationship, bring growth and unity, grace and repentance. Only you can do this. I praise you now for what you will do.

Prayer: "Help us to keep our eyes on you, Lord. 'As the eyes of slaves look to the hand of their master, as the eyes of a maid look to the hand of her mistress, [may] our eyes look to the LORD our God, till he shows us his mercy' (Ps. 12:2).

"Help us to live the commands of your Word in our relationships: 'Therefore, as God's chosen people, holy and dearly loved, [help us to] clothe [ourselves] with compassion, kindness, humility, gentleness and patience. [Help us to] Bear with each other and forgive whatever grievances [we] may have against one another. [May we] forgive as [you], Lord, forgave [us]. And over all these virtues [help us to] put on love, which binds them all together in perfect unity' (Col. 3:12-14). Amen."

December 17

"For thus said the Lord GOD, the Holy One of Israel, 'In returning and rest you shall be saved; in quietness and in trust shall be your strength.'"

Isaiah 30:15

God, I think, is like a Haiku. Haiku is a form of Japanese poetry: 17 syllables in four lines usually involving an unexpected twist at the end. For instance:

Spring has come
The snow melts

The village is flooded
With children.

We expected damage from water and end up with happy kids! So it is with God; except that instead of twisting, He untwists things. For instance, to make a Haiku out of my experience,

Unjustly jailed
Put on trial
Prosecutor stood firm
To defend me!

God is the great Transformer, the great Surpriser. He can and does take the most painful and difficult happenings and tenderly turns them into our good and His glory. Think of the death of Lazarus; of the blindness of men Christ healed; and of His own suffering.

Old age is an example of God's transformation powers. Aging is the process of losing things, going from competent, self-sufficient, productive people to helpless, dependent, and in the eyes of some, useless people. However, those who walk with God may be helpless physically or mentally but can still be mighty warriors in prayer and example.

I recently visited a 98-year-old friend. He can no longer walk, but is clear-minded. When I asked him how he is doing he replied, "I have so much to be thankful for! I just can't understand why God is so good to me. I'm such a sinner; I certainly don't deserve it!"

It is clear that, as he has aged, he has grown in his understanding of his depravity, as well as of how much God has forgiven and loves him, and how much God is blessing him.

Old age may be the process of losing things, but maturity is the willingness to let them go. In knowing God we can have the bigger, longer range picture of what He is doing, as well as what He has in store for us in the new heaven and earth. So we can know that it's ok to let go of what we cannot keep anyway.

As a second example of how God untwists things, take a mother whose 15-year-old daughter had a skiing accident with severe head trauma, ending in a coma. Doctors had to remove much of the girl's skull and did not hold much hope for any recovery. What was the mother's response?

> *"We are so reminded to be at peace and not to look forward in fear . . . but to look forward with full hope. . . . Do not fear what may happen tomorrow, the same everlasting Father who cares for you today will take care of you then and every day....*

> *"God . . . You are the Provider of our lives. We are so empty, so grief filled, so tired, so weary of this complicated confusing unwanted journey that has devastated our lives . . . yet we continue forward in hope, watching You show up every day, every moment, providing what we need to care for Jessie, to take the next step, to get up every morning and face the day, to get up every night and care for Jess, to know that this season will change one day, . . . We wait upon You . . . . Thank you for loving and caring for us . . . amen and amen. . . ."*

This woman knows God well; she knows, without seeing any results, that God is at work transforming this tragedy into something for His glory and for the family's good. And she is certainly cooperating, being His "flashlight of praise" in her dark world. She does not know whether God will make Jessie well by healing her or taking her, but she knows God will do what is best.

So, as we face difficulties, let us look to our Haiku, the Lord God Almighty, the Creator, Sustainer and Ender of all. He will carry us through as we come to Him in our weakness and needs, submitting to Him. He always has a sequel, and it will be good.

Prayer: "Lord help me to know you better in the light so that when I walk in the dark, I will trust you fully and give you glory whether I see any answers or not. Help me to live in the truth that you are good, all the time. Amen."

December 18

"Our help is in the name of the LORD, the Maker of heaven and earth."

Psalm 124:8

As I awoke, there was a tightness in my spirit, a worry because of the email I sent on Saturday. I was afraid of what the person would think. This was fear of man, not trusting God, while trying to find my security in others' reactions.

I praise you, Lord God, because in reality, my security is in you. If the person is upset by my letter, then it is an opportunity to demonstrate a positive response on my part, to show how to work through such an issue. It is an opportunity to deepen a relationship, to work more on the issue of motives. It is a chance to lower a burden before you in praise and have it become the next step up in my relationship with you and potentially in my relationship with him.

Psalm 124 speaks of a much more intense and dangerous situation and how you actively involved yourself: "If the LORD had not been on our side," Praise you, LORD, Yahweh, the Holy and faithful One, that you are on our side, that you are intensely, consistently, actively protecting, helping and guiding us.

"…let Israel say— if the LORD had not been on our side when men attacked us, when their anger flared against us, they would have swallowed us alive." Lord, we recognize your holding back the tide of evil. You are always there, you are good, you are active, you are powerfully gracious.

"…the flood would have engulfed us, the torrent would have swept over us, the raging waters would have swept us away." The forces surrounding us are much more powerful than we are; our strength is totally inadequate to deal with them, but you are able and utterly willing to help us stand, commanding us to, "Put on the whole armor of God that you may be able to stand in the evil day, and having done all to stand" (Eph. 6:13).

"Praise be to the LORD, who has not let us be torn by their teeth. We have escaped like a bird out of the fowler's snare; the snare has been broken, and we have escaped." We have gotten away from the power of sin and Satan, not by our own strength or cleverness, but because you, Lord God, our good Shepherd, have broken the trap too strong for us, you made a way out through your own sacrifice, released us, led us to safety.

"Our help is in the name of the LORD, the Maker of heaven and earth." Our eyes are on you, Yahweh, the Holy One whose glory is in His holiness, who hates sin and will punish it, but has made a way out of the trap of sin for sinners.

Your help is astounding, immense, expansive, expensive, wonderful beyond conception and powerful beyond understanding. No person, no angel, no created being would have, could have thought up such a salvation.

Praise be to you, the awesome, exalted, immensely powerful and entirely good God who is at work delivering your quarrelsome, troublesome children from daily harm and eternal condemnation.

Prayer: "May you be exalted in my life today for your goodness, your creativity, your love and your never-ending salvation. Amen."

December 19

"…give thanks in all circumstances for this is God's will for you in Christ Jesus."

1 Thessalonians 5:18

As I went down the ramp to board the first plane on my return trip to Germany from the US, I heard the stewardess announce, "There is no more room in the overhead bins, so the rest of you passengers will have to check your carry-ons."

I was not happy with that news! My carry-on was packed with personal things, many of which I wanted to use on the trip. Fortunately most of these were in my backpack in my carry-on. I took it out, surrendered my carry-on case with wheels, and made my way back to my seat, all the while complaining in my heart about this injustice.

This event and my response to it colored darkly the whole rest of the trip. On my transatlantic flight I was able to have 3 seats across so I could lie down to sleep. Instead of being thankful for this, I complained about not having the fourth seat so I could stretch out fully. I was aware that I was not responding correctly, not "letting go, holding on, rising above," and tried to do so but it was so hard because I was staggering about emotionally, wounded by the fiery darts of the enemy.

Later, in praying about the situation, the Spirit pointed out to me how, at the crucial moment, I had failed to get up the shield of faith: I had chosen to complain instead of praising God for what He was doing in allowing my carry-on to be taken away. In that split second of failing to praise, failing to get up the shield of faith, I got hit with the fiery arrow of self-pity, followed by the arrow of anger.

I was angry at myself for not getting on the plane earlier. I was angry at the stewardess for taking my bag. I was angry at God for allowing this.

Without confession and repentance, I was defenseless. I was down and Satan just kept shooting me with one fiery arrow after another: fear, selfishness, self-pity and more complaining.

It was a painful, joyless time before the Spirit gave insight through my journaling as I lifted my soul to Him and He helped me see where I had committed my initial, tactical sin of choosing to grumble instead of praising. Then I could confess, surrender and be healed. After that I could easily raise the shield of faith and joy could flow again. I had to choose to live the truth that knowing Jesus is enough for joy, period!

How easily I fall, how significant a seemingly small decision can be, how dangerous is the innocuous sin of complaining. It rises from unbelief and rebellion against what God has brought. It comes from pride, from fear, from selfishness, from listening to self rather than the Spirit.

In God's eyes complaining is a serious, destructive and deadly sin: it attacks faith and trust; it questions His goodness and wisdom; it dishonors Him as we reject His gifts. That's why He reacted so strongly to the Israelites' complaining and grumbling: "And the people complained in the hearing of the LORD about their misfortunes, and when the LORD heard it, his anger was kindled, and the fire of the LORD burned among them and consumed some outlying parts of the camp" (Num. 11:1).

It is important also to note that my temptation to complain came after an intense, very full three weeks of successful work and ministry. I was tired and not watchful; I chose to sin without even realizing it. I need to remember that after victory often comes significant temptation.

But praise God that He is faithful, that He brings us back to Himself, into the light so we can be healed, restored, strengthened and again put on the armor He has provided so that we can "take up the shield of faith with which you can quench all the fiery darts of the wicked one" that "you may be able to stand against the wiles of the devil (Eph. 6:11,16).

Prayer: "Lord, help me to keep on the armor of God every day, and especially to raise the shield of faith by giving thanks in every circumstance so that you may have more glory. Amen."

December 20

"Our help is in the name of the LORD, who made heaven and earth."

Psalm 124:8

Praise you, Lord, that as I face a busy week, I can go in your peace, in your strength, in your wisdom and self-control. I give this week over to you and ask that you will help me to be focused, to follow through with my "to do" list, to do first things first in a disciplined, Spirit-led way.

I give over to you the things that burden me, like being out late three nights in a row this week. Help me to pace myself well and to go in your strength. Praise you for your presence, your power and your perspective.

"Those who trust in the LORD are like Mount Zion, which cannot be shaken but endures forever" (Ps. 125:1). I praise you, LORD, Yahweh, the great I AM, that you make us unshakable as we rest in the truth of who you are. You are the unchangeable One, the Almighty One, the Undefeated One, the Eternal One, the All-seeing One, the Righteous One, the Holy One, the Loving One.

You are ever at work, you are aware of all, you are constantly, consistently, compassionately arranging the events that come into my life. You are able to take our mistakes and sins and somehow use them for good: chastening, correcting, counseling, changing us with them.

Praise you for the certainty of your work in my life today, for the certainty of your protection, presence and provision in each step, each moment, each interaction. I praise you for your going before me and preparing each event and relationship. I praise you, LORD, for you are worthy of trust.

"As the mountains surround Jerusalem, so the LORD surrounds his people both now and forevermore" (Ps. 125:2). You, Heavenly Father, are far more stable than any mountain—you are always there, surrounding us with your love, grace and protection. Nothing can move you, remove you or shake you; you are sure, unchangeable, solid, reliable, and trustable. Your faithfulness has no end, your wisdom no bottom, your goodness no top, your power no measure.

You are worthy of praise for your great character: full-orbed, multifaceted, sparkling in purity, shining in goodness, balanced in integrity, perfect in fullness. You are faithful in your love, in your goodness, in your protection, in your wisdom, in your presence, in your power. We can rest in you, on you, by you, with you. To you belongs all praise and honor.

Prayer: "Today help me to exalt you in my responses, glorify you in my motives, lift up your name in my speech, please you in my actions. Help me to remember that no matter what my circumstances, your character is worthy of worship. Amen."

December 21

"Like an earring of gold or an ornament of fine gold is a wise man's rebuke to a listening ear."

Proverbs 25:12

"Rebuke" is not a warm fuzzy word; it has a cold, hard feel of rejection, something we tend to avoid giving or getting. Yet rebukes are very important in our spiritual lives.

Recently I was rebuked well—that is lovingly, constructively, graciously. I had made a comment in a meeting, not a helpful one and I just blurted it out without waiting for permission. The leader, who is responsible to me (that is, I am his "boss") came to me after the meeting and very kindly but directly spoke to me about it. He was right and I asked forgiveness.

How did I feel about this? Along with a sense of shame for acting insensitively, there was a strong sense of being loved and cared for. The leader didn't go and talk with others about my sinful error, he came directly, quietly, carefully to me. He affirmed me as a person while pointing out my wrong action.

It was a good experience, one that we all need to have periodically. To live the truth of Matthew 18 ("If your brother sins, go and talk with him....") is uncomfortable and difficult for both sides, but when done well and received well, it is so good and healing and maturing.

What makes a rebuke good? First of all, it is not done out of anger. If we are angry, we need to go to God and process our anger first. An effective way of doing this is to write out our thoughts, feelings and desires in the situation, telling Him all about it; then to view it in the light of Scripture, and finally forgiving the person as Christ has forgiven us: fully, unconditionally, whole-heartedly.

In this process we need to examine our motives: why am I going to rebuke this person? Personally, I do this by writing down my motives, keeping my heart open to the leading of the Spirit. There will be negative ones ("I'm going to straighten him out!" or "I want to make sure he doesn't hurt me like this again!"). There may be neutral ones ("This is my responsibility"). And there will be positive ones ("He needs to hear this for him to be more useful to God." Or, "I want to help him grow so he can give God more glory." Or, "If he continues in this, he will hurt more people as well as himself."). Then we can reject the negative and neutral ones and affirm the positive motives, acting only out of them.

Before going to the person, prayer is important, asking God to prepare the other person's heart and mine. And asking for wisdom in what to say, thinking it through, making it clear, short and to the point, while also being gracious.

Lastly is giving the rebuke in the proper situation: alone, when tensions are lowered, when you can have his full attention.

I encourage you to be a creative and loving rebuke-giver, as well as a humble and teachable rebuke-receiver. Life gets easier, God is glorified and we all grow, especially in humility, the most important Christian virtue.

Prayer: "Lord, help me to be willing to receive rebuke, whether it is done well or not. Help me to be willing to give rebuke when necessary, that I may give you more glory through obedience and helping a brother or sister to grow in truth and love. Amen."

December 22

"…I am poor and needy; come quickly to me, O God. You are my help and my deliverer; O LORD, do not delay."

Psalm 70:5

Praise you, Lord for your steady presence. As I think on you and your unswerving faithfulness to your Character of love and purity, goodness and forgiveness, faithfulness and grace, I find answering echoes in my own being—a rest in you, a growing trust, a desire to obey you, a lessening of the pendulum swing of my emotions. In you is safety, in you is security, in you is peace.

When I make a mistake, when I sin, you don't jump on me or condemn me or reject me. You put the arm of your Spirit around me, draw me to yourself, tell me of your love, and graciously talk with me about what I have done wrong. You lead me into confession and repentance, reminding me of your purchasing pardon, assuring me of your faithful forgiveness, encouraging me to make right choices from here on. You are a gracious Father, a forgiving Lord, a loving Brother. In my relationship with you I am safe.

I praise you for your Spirit's work of conviction, guidance, teaching and revelation. He shows us what we could never discover with our meager minds, our tiny thoughts, our rebellious research.

Praise you for your positive provision and your continuous care, your fine heart and your gracious intent. With you we have life, with you we have peace, with you we have hope, with you we can choose for joy. These we find nowhere else.

Thank you that you draw me on in this relationship with you, encouraging me to spend time with you, to think your Word, to see as you see. I praise you for your great patience with me, correcting me over and over again, teaching me over and over again, slowly moving me upward on the steps of life while willingly enduring the pain I cause you in my wrong choices.

You are the well-spring of all good; without you life is a desert: dry, hostile, threatening, dangerous and in the end, deadly. With you, life even in the desert of this world is lush, green, growing, refreshing, secure and joyful. You help us get our roots down deep into the water of your Word, you make us fruitful, you keep our life leaves green, you protect us in the midst of danger and make us successful in service to you.

You, O Lord God, are worthy of worship, of following, of obeying, for great is your heart, pure is your mind, eternal is your being, good is your intent.

Prayer: "I love you, Lord Jesus, I praise you, I bow before you, honor you, give you my life, my day, my all. Help me to live worthy of the privilege of being your child. Amen."

December 23

"…take up the shield of faith, with which you can extinguish all the flaming arrows of the evil one."

Ephesians 6:16b

The doorbell rang and there was a crew of movers with a grand piano; the homeowner protested that he hadn't ordered it, but the movers said it was a gift. An hour later the doorbell rang again, and there stood a piano teacher with a big, new music book. He handed the homeowner a letter. "The piano, the books, and the teacher are gifts from me, all paid for. We are going to work together so you can play this piano well and bring joy and beauty to us and to the world. Your job is to practice, practice, practice!" signed, your Heavenly Father.

This is a picture of what happens when we become believers. The piano is our new life, including our new spiritual gifts and abilities. The teacher is the Holy Spirit, the book is the Bible. Our heavenly Father has equipped us with all we need. Now He calls us to work together with Him to learn to use these gifts so we can bring glory to His name, light and music to the world and transformation to our souls. Our job is to practice, practice, practice what He's teaching us.

These last weeks God has been giving me lots of opportunities to practice getting up the shield of faith with praise so I could quench the fiery arrows of the enemy and give Jesus glory before the unseen hosts. Here are a few.

I went on line to buy train tickets to the airport for my flight to Albania—but discovered that my new train discount card was missing. I searched everywhere I could think of, but no card! It had cost me $80! And a replacement cost $25 more! Well, we decided right off to praise God for this loss, thanking Him for what He was doing, giving Him glory for His wisdom when we couldn't see one bit of it yet. Later two things came out:

First, I decided not to buy train tickets but to drive to the airport. This turned out to be good because in the end my flight was cancelled-- a result of a volcanic ash cloud over Europe. If I'd had my card, I would have bought train tickets, which were non-refundable, and lost that money! Then, after a three day test of "trusting God by praise," Barbara found my card! Another chance to praise God, although this time it didn't require faith, for now we had the card in hand.

In a second example, while in a conversation with a friend, he twice said things that normally would have hurt and bothered me. However, at the Spirit's prompting, I chose to get up the shield of faith, thanking God for the chance to think truth. The result was that there was hardly a blip on my emotional radar screen.

Then in a third instance, I failed to communicate some information to a colleague who was not known to be forgiving. After realizing my failure, I was dreading the confrontation about it. But the Spirit pointed out to me that I was letting fear of man control me. I praised Him for this chance to reject my fear and act in faith; this freed me and in the end no confrontation came.

The Lord, to His credit and glory, is bringing deep and lasting change in me as I practice living the truth that knowing Jesus is enough for joy, period!

Prayer: "Father, help me to respond with praise for each unwanted thing that comes in my life, knowing that you have it all in hand. May I give you glory in these small things that I may be ready to do so in the big things, too. Amen."

December 24

"I have told you this so that my joy may be in you and that your joy may be complete."

John 15:11

Praise be to you, Lord Jesus, for you are the Light of the world, the Illumination of my life, the Lamp of my soul and the Sonshine of each day. With you there is warmth, wonder and sparkle in a dark and dismal world. You are the bringer of joy in the midst of a reality that can be hard, cold, severe and painful.

"The LORD has done great things for us, and we are filled with joy" (Ps. 126:3). Because of these great things you have done we can at all times be "…joyfully giving thanks to the Father, who has qualified us to share in the inheritance of the saints in the kingdom of light" (Col. 1:12).

And you, Lord God, have given us a privileged position in your forever family against all logic, against all justice, against all the evidence that we definitely deserved condemnation, punishment, rejection, banishment, suffering, pain and death. Your love is sure and steady, powerful, penetrating and positive.

"For he has rescued us from the dominion of darkness" This is an accomplished fact, a certainty that we are no longer the children of the devil, bound to sin, controlled by the prince of the power of the air, but have been freed by the blood of the Lamb!

"…and brought us into the kingdom of the Son he loves, in whom we have redemption, the forgiveness of sins" (Col. 1:12-14).

What a powerful statement: "…in whom we have redemption,"…not "I hope so" but "I know so!" What a wonder, what a privilege, what an astounding, unbelievable, too-good-to-be-true outcome you have given us, Heavenly Father—we are pardoned, adopted, brought into the Kingdom and made co-heirs with Jesus and with the saints. We live in the light, are dearly loved, delighted in, doted on and deeply cared for. We have a future with you as well as a daily walk with you now. You give total provision, complete protection, loving direction, wise counsel, consistent correction, unswerving goodness and unending grace.

To know the Great Shepherd of souls, the Wise Warrior of prayer, the Powerful Planner of good, the Diligent Director of details, the Lasting Lover of sinners, the Triumphant Transformer of rebels, the Final Forgiver of our sins, the Great Giver of grace—what more could we want?!!! This is far beyond what we could imagine or ask for. This is more than a human being could conceive. You are more than wonderful, more than great, more than good.

To you, Lord God, all creatures must come and bow down in worship and adoration. To you every person must fall on his face and give you glory. To you every believer must surrender and rejoice in your perfection by denying self, taking up his cross and following you.

Prayer: "May this be true today in me, Heavenly Father; may you be pleased with my thoughts and words and actions. May you be glorified in my life today before men, before angels, before the hordes of Satan. May honor and praise flow from my life up to your throne moment by moment. Amen."

December 25

"May the God of hope fill you with all joy and peace as you trust in him so that your lives may overflow with hope by the power of the Holy Spirit."

Romans 15:13

God is an inveterate gift giver. He loves to pour out goodness on His children and Christmas is a good time to remember that.

One of the gifts He's given us through Christ is the privilege of personal worship and the powerful positives that flow from it. Such worship is focusing on our triune God, praising Him for who He is, standing in the light of His presence, looking away from the temporal to the eternal, setting our hearts on things above—these all give Him glory and bring transformation in our souls.

Here's a worship entry from my prayer journal, meditating on Romans 15:13 which lists out other gifts our good God loves to give. "May the God of Hope...." and that is what you are, Lord: the God who is hope, who brings hope, who calls us to hope—a hope which is a rock-solid certainty based on your unchanging, perfect character—you promise and you deliver.

Praise you for your desire to fill your children "with all joy and peace...." This says so much about you, my Lord God. Not just some joy and peace, but *all* joy and peace. You give us a joy that is unquenchable, unalterable by the difficulties, tragedies and suffering in life, because you, the unchanging God are its source.

You give us a peace that is sure and sound, deep and dynamic, restful and responsible. As we confess and receive forgiveness, you give us peace with you, peace with ourselves, peace with others—a vibrant peace, a powerful peace, a renewable peace, one which can be restored each time we sin. You are truly the God of joy and peace, giving us in abundance these deep qualities every person longs for.

Then comes our part: "as [we] trust in him...." Praise you, Lord, for the role you have given us in having this joy and peace. We must trust, believe, live in the truth of who and what you are. As we look away from the problems, aggravations, disappointments and difficulties of life and look up to you, it is clear that we can trust you in all that comes to us. You are the Great Shepherd, the All-Powerful King, the Everlasting Sovereign, the Ruler of the universe, the Lord of Glory, the Spinner of the earth, Bringer of the dawn, the Beginner and Ender of time.

We can trust you by responding with praise, no matter how painful our situation is, because you, in your wisdom, grace and mercy have allowed this for good in our lives and for glory in yours. Forgive us for the many times each day we trust ourselves and not you and therefore complain.

Praise you that trusting is the doorway to more blessing: "trust...so that your lives may overflow with hope by the power of the Holy Spirit." The more we trust you, the more joy and peace you give us and the more Holy Spirit-empowered hope we receive, leading to more praise and positive trust.

And as we trust, we become a cup of hope, a basin of hope, a spring of hope, a river of hope to everyone we meet, for it will flow out in our attitude, in our words, in our actions, in our reactions.

Glory be to you, O Great and Powerful One; you are Wise and Loving, Just and Merciful. You provide so that we may give you ever-increasing glory before the world!

Prayer: "Forgive me for being busy here and there with this and that, and not spending time with you, Lord Jesus. Help me to be in the Word, in personal worship, in prayer and in confession every day, to live in the light of your presence all through the day. Amen."

December 26

"Unless the LORD builds the house, its builders labor in vain."

Psalm 127:1a

What could be more straightforward than building a house? Get a loan, hire a contractor, get it done. What's God got to do with it? Such a question reveals a very near-sighted view of life.

You, O Lord God, are the One who controls the myriad of events layered over and under the act of building a house. You allow or block all kinds of things, ranging from permits to finances to supplies, weather, speed of the work, demonic interference, war, economic collapse, plague, famine or earthquake. We blithely assume that we can plan and do it, but actually the outcome is much more in your hands than in ours.

This verse reveals the truth of your Greatness, O Lord God, Creator of all, Sustainer of all, Ender of all. Without you we can accomplish nothing of note. You are the Source of all good, the

Protector of all creation, the Planner of the overall scheme of what will come to pass: "There is no wisdom, no insight, no plan that can succeed against the Lord" (Pro. 21:30).

In thinking about how many houses do get built, your graciousness and love are very evident in allowing men to succeed so often. Praise you that your love is so great for your enemies that you wish them well, that you pour out kindness and grace on them every day, that you call them to repentance through your goodness.

"Unless the LORD watches over the city, the watchmen stand guard in vain" (Ps. 127:1b). So it is with trying to protect ourselves. We can make all the preparations we want, but unless you, in your great power, actually protect, there is not much that we can do.

Jericho comes to mind: high and thick double walls and a powerful army within, but against the Lord there was no defense as He caused the walls to fall, the army to be defeated and the city to be destroyed. Sodom and Gomorrah, Babylon and Tyre, Samaria and Jerusalem—at the right time your just judgment fell on each and there was nothing that any person could do to prevent the destruction of these cities. Without your care, we are totally vulnerable. With your care, we can live in your security by faith, in trust, with thanksgiving.
You, O Lord God—Triune, Pure and Powerful—are worthy of praise, honor and glory. Your Love, your Wisdom, your Grace are high, mighty, good and everlasting. Your character shines in holiness, gleams in goodness, sparkles in graciousness, illuminates in gloriousness--all exposing your expansiveness. No matter what happens in my life, you, O Lord God, are worthy of worship, honor, praise and obedience.

Prayer: "May you be glorified in my life today, Lord Jesus, as I trust in you with praise and obedience. Amen."

December 27

"Sacrifice thank offerings to God, fulfill your vows to the Most High, and call upon me in the day of trouble; I will deliver you, and you will honor me."

Psalm 50:14,15

The last few days of my time in the States in June brought one disaster after another. The almost new starter in my van went bad and the replacement one I had installed in PA cost twice what one did in CT. I got a sore throat the last night there, the beginning of a cold—and I didn't have time to get sick. My plans to return to CT on the 17th were foiled by the decisions of others, making me wait until the 18th, so I lost one day of work in CT. My computer seized up and wouldn't allow me to send email.

When I finally did leave on Friday for CT, I realized I'd forgotten to give an important item to someone and had to return to do that. On the way home the traffic was the worst I've ever seen, with numerous slowdowns, including going 10 miles an hour for 24 miles.

At the one gas station stop I made, someone was in the single bathroom for a long, long time. Then I locked myself out of the van by accident, with the keys inside. I was late in getting home, losing three hours of good work time. And the materials I'd ordered two weeks ago hadn't been delivered yet! Then when we brought the pickup truck over to unload the roofing I'd brought, it ran out of gas halfway there. Then I realized that I'd forgotten the charger for my computer in PA, and since I was leaving for Germany Monday morning, there probably wouldn't be time to get it.

In each of these happenings, I was weak: things certainly were beyond my power to control. And in each of these happenings the Holy Spirit said to me quietly, "Don't complain; this is an opportunity to praise!" He had to remind me because I'm a slow learner--and with His help in each instance I did praise, for our God is Sovereign and Good, Wise and Strong. Everything that happens comes with His full knowledge as well as His purpose and grace. The chance to be weak, to appear foolish or to have plans foiled, are opportunities to give Him glory and to honor Him through the praise of faith.

As these burdens came one after another, with His help I carefully lowered each one before Him in praise, and was able to stand upright, unencumbered by self-pity, anger, frustration, disappointment, or complaining. Each event then became a step up in my walk with Him, an opportunity to take up His grace, to rest in trust and to rejoice. What a privilege to walk with such a God! What a privilege to go through difficulties so we can honor Him with praise.

And as I praised, He worked all out, true to Psalm 50:23, "He who sacrifices thank offerings honors me, and he prepares the way so that I may show him the salvation of God."

I never really got sick. At the gas station I could get back into the locked van because the back door was not latched but tied shut to accommodate the roofing I was carrying. The building materials arrived early the next day and were exactly enough for the job. God sent people to help. All the work got done. The computer straightened out with a restart. The charger arrived an hour before I left for the airport, and He enabled me to be completely ready for the trip.

What a God we have! Even if things don't work out as we desire, we can still praise Him for His wisdom and for how He will use this. Truly, Knowing Jesus is Enough for Joy.

Prayer: "Lord, help me to always think in terms of Psalm 50:23, praising you in and for all things, knowing that you do what is best and I can trust you. Amen."

December 28

"In vain you rise early and stay up late, toiling for food to eat—for while they sleep he provides for those he loves."

Psalm 127:2

I like this verse, Lord. It is not, of course, a call to laziness, but a call to see where our food actually comes from and to resist putting unnecessary effort into getting more. We are to trust you and work reasonably, knowing that you will provide all that is necessary. That certainly has been my experience.

This concept is repeated often is Scripture; it is a call to cooperation, an invitation to partnership with you. You plan and prepare things and then wait for us to do our part. In each case you promise to act as we cooperate, as the following verses declare.

"The angel of the Lord encamps around **those who fear Him** and he delivers them" (Ps. 34:7).

"Fear the Lord, you his saints, for **those who fear the Lord** lack nothing. The young lions hunger and suffer lack, but **those who seek the Lord** lack no good thing" (Ps. 34:9,10).

"Blessed are all **who fear the LORD, who walk in his ways**. You will eat the fruit of your labor; blessings and prosperity will be yours. Your wife will be like a fruitful vine within your house; your sons will be like olive shoots around your table. Thus is the man blessed **who fears the LORD**" (Ps. 128:1-4).

Our part is to seek and fear the Lord as defined in Psalm 34:13,14 "Keep your tongue from evil and your lips from speaking lies, depart from evil and do good, seek peace and pursue it." Fearing the Lord is doing what we know from His Word to be right; this opens the way for the Lord to give us what He knows we need.

Of course, along with visible blessings, some of what we need for our family to prosper spiritually, may be having difficulty, suffering and lacks on a physical level. It is through such difficulty that we truly grow (Jam. 1:2-4). Jesus our Shepherd is faithful to bring what is right; in every circumstance, we are to be faithful in fearing and obeying Him.

It is astounding that, in spite of his being the Most High, the Lord Jesus chooses to stoop down and work with and through miniscule men, waiting for our cooperation, our obedience, our surrender before proceeding with His mighty works. In great patience He commands us, coaxes us, woos us, chastens us and draws us along. He knows what is best for us as well as for His plans and for eternity.

You are amazing, Lord Jesus: you could do it all yourself much more quickly and with great ease, but instead you choose to involve your rebellious, sinful, selfish and resistant children in the outworking of your astounding plan for the universe.

I praise you, Lord God, for your great heart, your gracious thoughts, your good desires, your grand plans. What more can we do than bow before you in worship, giving you the honor you deserve, then rise up to obey you in what we know to be true so we can bring you more praise and glory by joining you in what you are doing.

Prayer: "Help me, Lord, to cooperate with you in what you plan for this day. May I fear you and play the part you have for me. May I be a channel of praise and glory for you today, Lord, as I seek you, fear you, obey you and honor you. Amen."

December 29

"Jesus said, 'If you hold to my teaching, you are really my disciples. Then you will know the truth, and the truth will set you free.'"

John 8:31b,32

As we watch my mother-in-law struggle with old age, it is painful to see her fight for her significance. All her life she has been strong, talented and successful: a professional cook and seamstress, an avid and productive gardener, a wonderful housekeeper and hostess. These abilities and the resulting achievements made her feel significant and satisfied. But now they are all gone and she has only an inner, undefined emptiness, which she doesn't know how to deal with. She rejects help even though she needs it. She seeks relief by forcing herself to do things that cause her unnecessary physical pain. She is unhappy, sad and angry.

Although she had accepted Christ in her youth, it seems there was no one to teach her how God has given us in Christ all the significance we could ever want: a love and acceptance that nothing on earth can alter, a position of status as a child of God and an invitation to join God in His great work, primarily through prayer. I wish I could effectively share that with Omi, but she will not hear of it; the pain of her losses to old age is creating too much static in her heart to listen.

Recently I heard of one practice that can prevent all of us from falling into this trap of self-pity and living in such frustration: we should stop just listening to ourselves and start talking to ourselves. The difference is huge.

Only listening to ourselves is a trap: "What a terrible day with all this rain" "No one loves me" "Nothing ever goes right" "I can never get ahead" "No luck for me today!"

It is good to recognize these thoughts and then evaluate them according to God's Word. After that we can speak truth to ourselves, which is the way out of this swamp of sadness.

For example, we should say such things as, "Well, I had hoped for a sunny day, but praise God He knows that we need this rain!" "The Lord is my shepherd, I shall not want." "Praise you that you bring to me what I need, Lord, both what is pleasant and what is not!" "Thank you for the lack of progress, as this reminds me that my times are in your hands." "Thank you that you the one who arranges my days."

David practiced this in Psalm 43. First he listened to himself: "Why have you rejected me? Why must I go about mourning, oppressed by the enemy?" (Ps. 43:2). This is how David felt, but his statements were not true: God had not rejected him, and he didn't need to go about mourning. And worse, David was blaming God for this, implying that, "If you are my stronghold, why are you failing to protect me??!"

However, David went on to process his own thoughts by speaking truth to himself. At the end of the Psalm, David said, "Why are you downcast, O my soul? Why so disturbed within me? Put your hope in God, for I will yet praise him, my Savior and my God" (Ps. 43:5). He was moving out of the swamp of despair onto the firm ground of God's Word.

Listen to the inner monologue going on in your heart; break in and speak truth to yourself. This is one step towards the joy that Jesus has for us. Then we can say with Asaph, "Whom have I in heaven but you, and earth has nothing I desire besides you" (Ps. 73:25).

Prayer: "Lord, help me to be aware of what I am saying to myself, to evaluate it according to your Word, and to think Truth, so that you may be glorified and I may walk in the freedom you have bought for your children. Amen."

December 30

"Great are the works of the LORD; they are pondered by all who delight in them. Glorious and majestic are his deeds, and his righteousness endures forever.

Psalm 111:2,3

Praise be to you, O Creator God, Sustainer God, Protecting God, Revealing God, Guiding God, Wise and Loving God. You are the One to be feared, to be revered, to be honored and obeyed.

"The fear of the LORD is the beginning of wisdom..." (Ps.111:10a). One definition of the fear of the Lord is "caring deeply what you think and fearing the consequences of disobeying you."

We can demonstrate our fear of you, Lord God, by asking, "What do you think about this? What do you want here?" and then obeying your desire as revealed in your Word. This is the right way, the beginning of wisdom.

"...all who follow his precepts have good understanding" (Ps.111:10b). Praise you that you have revealed to us in your Word your precepts, your thoughts, your insights and your principles, so we can follow them--if we desire.

I lift up your name and exalt you, Lord Jesus, for you are the great Revelation of the eternal living God. I praise you that you have given us your Spirit to teach, guide and warn us. I praise you that your Word provides direction for all things.

In knowing you, Lord Jesus, we have all we could possibly desire: contra-conditional love, total acceptance and belonging, unconditional worth, ever-upward transformation, unending protection, unalterable significance and absolute security—and these are ours even in the midst of great danger and suffering. You will keep us alive as long as you have work for us to do here.

You also give us the unceasing presence of your Spirit, instant access to your ear, the offer of Wisdom whenever we need it, the hope of help every day and the certainty of eternity with you.

You are wonderful, Lord Jesus, the King of Glory, Bridegroom of Heaven, Shepherd of our souls, Faithful and Powerful Redeemer of all peoples. Truly, "To you belongs eternal praise" (Ps.111:10c), for you are the Eternal High Priest and in you we have rest, we have peace, we have life.

Prayer: "Glory be to you for sharing such riches with your children, in spite of what we are. May you be glorified in my life today! Help me to remember these marvelous truths through the day; help me to make all decisions in the light of your goodness, wisdom and Word. Amen."

December 31

"Do not be like the horse or the mule, which have no understanding but must be controlled by bit and bridle or they will not come to you...the LORD's unfailing love surrounds the man who trusts in him."

Psalm 32:9,10

There it was, the big overhead sign I was looking for: "Exit 19 — 3 kilometers." I was on the way to a friend's house near the Frankfurt airport to leave my car before flying to Albania. I carefully watched the turnoffs that flashed by, but none was labeled "exit 19." Suddenly another big sign appeared, "Exit 21." Oops! Somehow I had missed my exit.

I felt mildly foolish, but I knew the next exit to the South was for the airport, so I could get off there and get back on the Autobahn going North. Now heading back towards my exit the big sign for Exit 19 appeared, and this time a turnoff was clearly labeled and I took it. However, now there was no sign for my friend's town! Nothing looked familiar. I was on another limited access highway, going away from where I should be and I was feeling more foolish.

I stopped at a gas station and asked but the immigrant working there had never heard of the town I was looking for (in the end it turned out I was only about a mile away from it!). I was able to reverse direction again, hoping for a sign for the town on the other side of the highway, but nothing.

Now I was feeling really foolish. I'd been to this friend's house several times! How could I mess up so badly?!!! Then the Autobahn came into sight, so I decided to go North again to the next exit and come back South again, maybe then I could find my exit. It was 20 kilometers before another exit showed up; I reversed direction, carefully checked my Google map printout, and this time found the correct turn off, which had no exit number for some reason, then took the second exit (which went right by the gas station I'd stopped at!), and I felt relieved to be on a familiar road.

I've left out one aspect of this story to help you feel the frustration and embarrassment of making so many wrong choices. With the first error, at the Spirit's nudging, I praised Him for the situation. I thanked Him for what He was doing with my evident incompetence and that helped me forgive myself for being so foolish. I continued to praise for each succeeding failure and to pray for guidance. That helped to keep my mind clear and to think about what to do next.

I got to my friend's place 45 minutes later than planned, gave the keys to his wife and was about to leave to catch a train to the airport when my friend arrived home early from work.

"I'll drive you to the airport," he said, "It'll save you a lot of time and we can talk some." So we had a very good visit and talked about significant things. I think the Lord had me be late so we could meet up and have those talks.

The Lord also had other things to teach me. I had not carefully read through the instructions of my Google map, so missed some important details that could have helped. That reminded me that I hadn't prayed carefully through the details of my trip, so spent time on the plane doing that.

This whole incident brought a picture to mind. When I fall through the open trap door of error or sin into the cellar of humiliation, I can choose how to land. If I think on just a human level, focusing on my foolishness and failure, I will land on the unforgiving stone floor of self-condemnation: hard, cold, painful. Or if I think biblically, praising and focusing on God, thanking Him for what He is doing, I will fall into His swimming pool of grace: warm, embracing, affirming. The choice is mine (and yours)!

Prayer: "Lord, thank you for allowing failure into my life; help me to praise you in and for all, to seize the opportunities to give you glory and honor instead of complaining and allowing feelings of foolishness to control me. I am so thankful to be your child, to have you as my Lord. I praise you for what you will bring today. Amen."

*****

So, you've come to the end of this book. Using it for another year would be profitable—while editing it I've read through it at least 10 times and have profited with each reading. Maybe take a year off and pick it up again in 365 days. Or pass it on to someone else who could profit from it. And certainly recommend it to others who could use it, They can order it from www.edifyingservices.com or from Amazon. May you continue to be edified as you think on what you've read and practice the privileges of worship and praise!

APPENDIX

More on Meditation

In my early twenties, I was able to attend a Bill Gothard seminar[13] and found it very helpful. The first time I went, Bill's teaching impacted me in two ways. First was how he took Scripture as truth, accepting what it had to say at face value. That may seem like a statement of the obvious to believers, but I found that I was picking and choosing what to really believe—that is, to implement in my life. I was convicted specifically that when it came to forgiving and asking forgiveness, I wasn't applying God's directions one bit. When I obeyed Scripture in this area there was release and a new freedom.

The second powerful application was meditation. Bill's

---

[13] For information on Bill Gothard's Institute in Basic Life Principles, see www.iblp.org Check out especially the Embassy Institute where you can easily see the helpful teachings I was able to attend.

presentation of this and the illustrations from his own life impressed me greatly, and I determined to apply it in my own life. Bill gave us a list of ten chapters to begin with and offered us a free book if we completed these. That incentive, however, had no motivating effect on me compared with the desire to cooperate with God in learning His Word.

Meditation is essentially cooperating with God in the transformation of our souls. As we have mentioned, the three major parts of our souls are our mind, our will, and our emotions. Meditation is working with the Holy Spirit to bring change in each of these areas.

Psalm 1 gives some insights into meditation. Interestingly, it begins by telling us three sins to avoid, which correspond basically to the first three parts of the armor of Ephesians 6:10-18. Psalm 1 begins, "Blessed is the man who does not walk in the counsel of the wicked...." Those reject ungodly advice, taking instead the counsel of God who are blessed; their relationship with God is protected by keeping on the *belt of truth*.

"... or stand in the way of sinners . . ." Knowing that the way of sinners would lead to great inner conflict with themselves, they reject it, thus keeping on the *breastplate of righteousness*.

"... or sit in the seat of mockers." Instead of mocking and attacking verbally those the godly don't like or agree with, they forgive them, thereby putting on the *shoes of peace*.

Then the second verse gives us two positive things the godly person does: "But his delight is in the law of the LORD, . . ." God's Word is what this person revels in, rejoices in, delights in. This means that when his or her mind is free, what comes to it is God's Word. It is a great source of joy. We can tell when we delight in something or someone by noticing how we spontaneously think and talk about them. Think sports, think work, think about when you first met your spouse.

"... and on his law he meditates day and night." Second, godly people meditate on God's Word regularly, frequently, continually. It means that they have memorized it so they can think on it at any time, and they refer to it often.

The outcome of avoiding the three sins and implementing the two positives is laid out in verse 3: "He is like a tree planted by streams of water. . . ." The roots of this person have grown deep down into the water of God's Word, drawing refreshment, sustenance, strength, and vitality from it all the time.

"... which yields its fruit in season. . . ." The result of the continual watering is that whatever fruit the godly person needs to bear will come forth. Consider the fruit of the Spirit: if the situation calls for patience, it will
be there; if faith is needed, that will be there.

"... and whose leaf does not wither." No matter what the circumstances around him or her may be, the godly person will remain fresh and vital. I have seen in the Middle East two trees not far apart. One twisted and dried without a single leaf, for it grew fifty yards from the stream; when a drought came, it died. The other tree grew next to the small stream, getting its roots down into the wet soil, deep into the earth. When all else was brown, its leaves were still a rich green, making it stand out from its surroundings.

"Whatever he does prospers." This is the astounding outcome: *whatever* godly persons do will prosper. Not just some things, but whatever they do. This is true, not because they are wise or talented or diligent. It is true because in meditation they have learned to think like God and to trust Him fully and thereby to obey His direction. They have internalized the truths needed for life.

I have witnessed such fruitfulness in the lives of those I know who practice meditation. It is not that meditation is magic, but that meditation is cooperation with God in bringing transformation that allows Him to empower, guide, and protect in a greater way than for those who fail to take the time to meditate. The meditator is then going to make decisions in line with God's will, using the wisdom of God's Word to avoid things that will prevent prospering.

The "How to" of Meditation

Meditation has three parts. The first is to memorize the passage. This is cooperating with the Holy Spirit in the *transformation of our minds*. It is learning to think God's thoughts. This is the mechanical part, but it is necessary to begin the internalization of truth.

Second is to personalize it, putting personal pronouns in where you can. This is cooperating with the Holy Spirit in the *transformation of our emotions*. Personalizing Psalm 1:1 would be to say, "Blessed am I when I don't walk in the counsel of the wicked, when I don't stand in the way of sinners, when I don't sit in the seat of the scornful."

When I read Scripture, it is like looking at a powerful river flowing by. When I personalize the passage, it is like that river flows over me, bringing its power and cleansing into my life.

The third part is to pray through it. This is cooperating with the Holy Spirit in the *transformation of our will*. Praying Psalm 1:1 would be to say, "Blessed am I when I don't walk in the counsel of the wicked. Lord, help me to recognize the counsel of the wicked and then to reject it. Help me to recognize your counsel and to implement it." This is a surrender to God's will, giving Him your will and taking His in its place. Since you are praying for exactly what God wants — praying Scripture, after all, is asking for the clear will of God — He is going to answer that prayer.

Such meditation brings powerful, deep, foundational change in us. I can honestly say that meditation has been the most important source of spiritual, intellectual, and emotional growth in my life. If I hadn't known how to meditate, I never would have made it for thirty years in the Middle East; I would have been chewed up and spit out by the forces of evil. Meditation has resulted in exactly the opposite happening: all that the Lord has put my hand to has prospered—not immediately, but in the long run. This is the Lord being faithful to His Word, not my being successful in my talents and strengths. All glory must go to Him for fulfilling His promises and purposes.

Illustrations.

In an analogy illustrating meditation, think of a piece of tough beef. We can eat it as is, but it is difficult to chew and get it down. This is like reading the Word; there are some difficult things in the Bible and much that we don't know how to implement.

Second, if we dip the meat into a bowl of marinating sauce for five minutes, it will change the taste but not the texture of the meat. This is like study. We still have a lot of questions about how to implement it; we have an intellectual grasp but not necessarily a heart change.

However, if we put the meat into the sauce and leave it there for forty-eight hours, the sauce penetrates to the center of the meat, transforming both its texture and its taste. This is like meditation, which results in transformation of our soul, our relationship with God, our family life, and our work for Him.

Or, to use a second analogy, think about going to the beach. You spread out your towel on the sand, lie on your stomach, and watch the waves. The sunlight sparkles on the water; the waves roll in unceasingly, each one a bit different; some sea gulls fly overhead, puffy white clouds dot the sky — it is an inspiring scene. This is like reading God's Word: uplifting, refreshing, edifying.

Then it gets hot, so you jump up and run into the water, enjoying the coolness. You ride the waves in, and swim out for another try. This is like studying the Word: you are really "into it." It is decidedly different than lying on the beach and watching the water.

After a while you decide to put on your mask and snorkel and go underwater. As you dip below the surface and swim over a ridge, whole new worlds open up to you that could not be seen from the beach or while swimming in the waves: schools of fish, various types of seaweed, brightly colored creatures clinging to the rocks. This is like meditation; it gets you down below the surface into the depths of the Word. It reveals to us things we would probably never see in reading or study. And it provides the application of these truths in our lives through prayer.

Let me give you a simple example of how meditation helps us to see into the depths of Scripture. I memorized Psalm 23 when I was about five years old, and I have used it many times to encourage myself. Once while meditating on it (praying through it while personalizing it), a new point jumped out at me from verse 6: "Surely goodness and mercy shall follow me all the days of my life" (KJV). God promises goodness and mercy, but they *follow* us, so we often cannot see them when walking through difficulties. Later, however, as we look back, we can see how God was pouring mercy on us and working things out for good.

That was a really helpful insight, leading me to greater faith in God when in difficulty and giving more ability to praise when there is no visible reason to praise. I doubt that I ever would have noticed this detail in merely reading or studying.

Helpful hints.

Here are several practical ideas for implementing meditation in your life.

• Have a partner to encourage you. It's easy to begin well, but it's also easy to have your resolve peter out. Memorizing is hard work, and we naturally shy away from it. To make ourselves accountable to someone can help keep us on track, especially if you and your partner are both memorizing the same passage.

• Memorize passages (paragraphs or whole chapters), not just verses. This gives you the context and the flow of what God is saying.

• Memorize a verse or two a day until you have the passage down well. Taking bit-sized chunks makes this a doable task. Doing it at the same time each day also helps—for example, making memorization part of your quiet time, then reviewing what you've memorized in the evening. Also, try to visualize a picture to go with the verse. That's easy with Psalm 1, as it is stated as a series of word pictures.

• After you have the passage memorized, meditate through it (personalizing and praying it) each day for two, three, or four weeks, letting it soak down into your soul.

• Avoid mechanical repetition; connect with the Word, think about it as you meditate, and pray creatively.

• Periodically review passages you have meditated on earlier, not because you should, but because you love God and His Word (that is, you have good motives). I "cycle through" the chapters I've memorized every once in a while to keep them fresh.

• When you experience any difficulty in life, go to a passage that speaks to it and memorize and meditate on it. For instance, I find that in the conflicts I have had with people, Psalm 37:1-10 has been a wonderful refuge, a boost, and a road map of how to respond. Meditating on it always gives me what I need to move ahead.

• When you have a difficulty, it is much easier to memorize a new passage that speaks to your situation than to memorize one that is theoretical at that point in your life.

Here are some passages to start with:

- Psalm 1: God's way to success
- Psalm 23: the all-purpose passage
- Psalm 37: how to respond to conflicts
- Psalm 46: dealing with difficulty
- Psalm 62: God's perspective on life
- Psalm 73: dealing with envy
- Psalm 86: the balance between weakness and God's power
- Matthew 5–7: thinking God's thoughts
- Ephesians 1: the eternal perspective
- Colossians 3: thinking God's values
- Hebrews 12:1-17: difficulties—why they come, what to do with them
- 1 Peter 1 and 4: purposes for suffering

Once you have memorized some of these, you will see other passages in Scripture that you would like to meditate on. As you memorize, give them a title, as that will help you in the process. Once you have memorized and meditated on a passage, you will have a "gift" to give to others who are struggling with something. You can turn to a relevant passage and share from the treasures you have gleaned in your meditation.

So, commit yourself to an adventure with Jesus in mediating on Scripture and see where He takes you!